Advances in Finance & Applied Economics

N. R. Bhanumurthy · K. Shanmugan
Shriram Nerlekar · Sandeep Hegade
Editors

Advances in Finance & Applied Economics

Springer

Editors
N. R. Bhanumurthy
National Institute of Public Finance
and Policy (NIPFP)
New Delhi, India

K. Shanmugan
Maharaja Sayajirao University
of Baroda
Vadodara, India

Shriram Nerlekar
Marathwada Mitra Mandal's Institute
of Management Education
and Research
Pune, India

Sandeep Hegade
Marathwada Mitra Mandal's Institute
of Management Education
and Research
Pune, India

ISBN 978-981-13-4666-8 ISBN 978-981-13-1696-8 (eBook)
https://doi.org/10.1007/978-981-13-1696-8

This Springer imprint is published by the registered company Springer Nature Singapore Pte Ltd.
The registered company address is: 152 Beach Road, #21-01/04 Gateway East, Singapore 189721, Singapore

Contents

About the Editors

N. R. Bhanumurthy is currently Professor at the National Institute of Public Finance and Policy (NIPFP), New Delhi, India. Prior to joining NIPFP, he worked as Assistant and Associate Professor at the Institute of Economic Growth (IEG), New Delhi. He has worked as Macroeconomist at UNESCAP, Bangkok, and the UNDP Regional Centre for the Asia-Pacific region, Colombo. He has been Visiting Fellow at the Maison des Sciences de l'Homme, Paris, France, and at McGill University, Montreal, Canada. He has also been a consultant to ILO, the World Bank and the Asian Development Bank. Currently, he is Secretary of the Indian Econometric Society and Managing Trustee of the Indian Economic Association Trust for Research and Development.

K. Shanmugan is currently working as Associate Professor at the M. S. University of Baroda, India. He is also Treasurer of the Indian Econometric Society (TIES), New Delhi. He has chaired numerous conferences and seminars organized by some of the most prestigious institutions in India and has 27 years of teaching experience.

Shriram Nerlekar is Faculty of Finance at the Savitribai Phule Pune University (SPPU), India. He is currently serving as Director at the Institute of Management Education Research and Training (IMERT), Pune. He has chaired numerous academic and administrative committees formed by SPPU. He is the recipient of the 'Best Professor in Financial Management Award' (awarded in 2010 by Mumbai-based Business School Affaire's Dewang Mehta Business School Awards) and of the 'Young Achiever Award' (awarded in 2012 by Mumbai-based World Education Congress).

Sandeep Hegade is Founder Director of the Centre for Advanced Studies in Policy & Research, Pune. He is Editor-in-Chief of IMERT's journal *Arthkalp: Journal of Finance & Economics*. He is the recipient of the National Research Fellowship—Dr. Babasaheb Ambedkar National Research Fellowship (BANRF) at Dr. Babasaheb Ambedkar Research and Training Institute (BARTI), Pune. He is a researcher, author and blogger on various topics related to finance and economics.

Part I
Development Economics

Federalism in India: An Economic Analysis

Sripriya Srivatsa

Abstract The outcomes of federalism have played out in very different manners in various societies that have chosen to adopt this design of organising themselves. The Indian context is particularly interesting because of how Indian states have formed, evolved or have carved out of one another into existence. In this paper, I explore whether smaller states could perform better on governance outcomes. The measure of governance is legislative activity in Indian state parliaments. The results indicate that as states become smaller units to govern, the legislative in activity in their respective parliaments does increase.

1 Introduction and Literature Review

An important classical argument favouring federalism is laid out by Friedrich Hayek. His thesis is that in a heterogeneous society, apart from for truly national public goods such as defence or energy, the central government does not possess relevant information to frame policies that are suitable for all (Hayek 1948). However, when I observe how federalism has played out in various parts of the world, I see vastly contrasting outcomes.

The United States of America, which is a federal state, is one of the wealthiest and least corrupt nations in the world, while countries such as India, Mexico and Argentina, which are all federal states, have governments plagued with corruption and poor economics (Parikh and Weingast 1997). Comparing federal countries with other non-federal systems may not allow for accounting of several unobservable factors that vary between countries. In this paper, I focus within India's federal structure, hence mitigating this problem of unobservable discrepancies. I am looking at different regions within a country, thus balancing the need for sufficient variation as well as the ability to control for regional idiosyncrasies and time-fixed effects.

S. Srivatsa (✉)
Candidate for Master of Science, Political Economy of Development, School of Oriental and African Studies, University of London, London, UK
e-mail: sripriya.srivatsa@tutanota.com

N. R. Bhanumurthy et al. (eds.), *Advances in Finance & Applied Economics*,
https://doi.org/10.1007/978-981-13-1696-8_1

Over time since independence, Indian states have been splitting into smaller and more homogenous units. The purpose of this paper is to understand whether these splits have resulted in better outcomes for governance. I measure governance using a new data set I collected on the number of bills and amendments passed in each state parliament(s) between 1956 and 2014. In view of state splits, amendments may be seen as the refinement of older existing laws to tailor to the needs of a newer, more homogenous society. Laws may be viewed as fresh legislative activity that actually results in new governance outcomes.

The Indian context is particularly unique because the idea of federalism can be tested in a relatively exogenous sense, i.e. a central government ensuring similar economic climate in all states, but also sufficient diversity among states. Also, there have been numerous state splits over time.

The key contribution of this paper is that so far, nobody has been looked at this issue through an empirical lens. There has been no effort in the Indian context, to test systematically the effect of state splits on economic and governance outcomes. This paper is a first step towards getting a better understanding in this field.

I find that a split causes legislative activity to increase by 12 bills (laws and amendments) approximately. The effect of a split on state domestic product is positive, but not significant. However, when I measure the effect of the split on state domestic product after 1990 (when the liberalisation reforms were implemented at the central level), I find that state domestic product increases by almost 33 lakh rupees. The value added in manufacturing units/factories reduces by 752 crore rupees after a state split.

The vast body of work in the area of fiscal federalism has been segregated into first- and second-generation fiscal federalism. The major difference being in an assumption made about public officials—the former treats them as benevolent, while latter treats them as working for their own good but who are held publicly accountable for their actions.

Second-generation fiscal federalism stresses on the importance of incentivising lower governments with sufficient tax revenues such that they provide 'market-enhancing public goods'. This leads us to examine the concept of an 'ideal' form of federalism which is 'market preserving'. See Weingast (2007) for a survey of literature on first- and second-generation fiscal federalism.

Weingast (2009) embarks on a comparative study across various federal units to understand the necessary elements to result in this ideal form of federalism. His paper discusses the importance of inter-jurisdictional competition to reap the benefits of federalism. Parikh and Weingast (1997) also present arguments for federalism that prevents different ethnic/religious groups from fighting one another over heatedly debated policy concerns. In an ethnically diverse country like India, this feature is beneficial for a functioning democracy. It can thus be seen in the several splits that are caused for reasons such as religion, language, ethnicity, as discussed in the background section below.

Drawing from the axioms of market-preserving federalism which forms a good base for any further comparative studies, I look at the data to see whether state splits are, in fact, resulting in governance improving outcomes and improvements in economic indicators. The main idea I test in this paper is whether the splitting of states into smaller federal units has any impact on governance and whether the outcomes of better governance reflect in economic variables indicators. The exploratory study's findings are elaborated upon in the following sections.

2 Institutional Background

Understanding India's political economy order is a colossal task and can be done through the lenses of various disciplines. In this paper, I wish to understand certain fundamental factors motivating the further fragmentation of India's existing federal units. Before diving further into our research, I will use this section to provide some context on what motivates such a discussion.

Article 3 of the Indian Constitution sets out the right of Parliament of the Union government to create new states and change boundaries if a Parliamentary majority is achieved. As difficult as this may be to achieve, it is quite unique to India's federal system as opposed to other forms of federal governments which allow the states greater protection of their rights in such issues (Singh and Pani 2012).

In the United States of America for example, for a new state to be formed, the consent of the Legislature(s) of the concerned states as well as the Congress is necessary, without which a new state cannot be formed 'within an existing State' or 'by the Junction of two or more States' (Constitution of the United States of America, Section 3).

The current 29 Indian states (as the federal units are called) all have state parliaments that come together for sessions three times a year. Each state parliament amends existing bills or passes new laws in areas that they have jurisdiction over. Upon gaining independence in 1947, state reorganisation was implemented to establish new boundaries of states and alter existing boundaries established in British India.

At the time of independence, the subcontinent was divided into 550 princely states and 14 provinces (Singh and Pani 2012). The Nehru administration set up a State Reorganisation Commission (SRC) whose recommendations were actualised in 1956 through the workings of The State Reorganisation Act, 1956 (Sarangi 2011).

Following Independence, federal organisation occurred on the basis of languages, and the first of such cases was Andhra Pradesh and then part of a larger Madras province. Upon the death of Potti Sriramulu, a well-known Gandhian following a 50-day hunger strike, the central government was forced to concede to the formation of the first linguistic state, Andhra Pradesh, in 1953 (Mawdsley 2002).

This marked the beginning of the development of political experiments, alliances, unrest and insurgency: all outcomes of passing of the Act which recognised fourteen states and six union territories (Sarangi 2011). Post-independence, the major task for the government was to integrate princely states into existing provinces so as to make the country a single geographical unit (Sharma 1967).

In order to be part of the Union of India, states had to sign an 'Instrument of Accession' (Sharma 1967). As Deputy Prime Minister, Sardar Vallabhai Patel managed to accomplish complete territorial integration of the then fourteen states of India into the constitutional set-up as of 1950 (Sharma 1967).

The State Reorganisation Committee (SRC) was later set up by the Congress to further organise the nation into efficient administrative units. This process was propelled by language as a basis of division. Several members of the Congress rejected the notion of 'one language, one state', still traumatised by the aftermath of the Partition. Punjab and Bombay provinces were left as bilingual states, as examples of 'unity in diversity' states. As of 1956, the original lines along which states were divided were linguistic as per the recommendations of the SRC.

Since then, there have been increasing demands for new states that are motivated by several other reasons. For example, some of these groups believe that resources of the state government are not shared equally among all regions within a state (Singh and Pani 2012).

The struggle for Telangana was motivated by such a discussion and resulted in a success in 2014. There are still ongoing struggles for separate states in Coorg, Karnataka and Vidarbha in Maharashtra.[1]

3 Data

The main idea I test through this study is whether smaller states resulting from carving out of larger states are governed better. Governance being a term that can be understood in several ways requires us to impose a restriction on its interpretation for the purpose of this paper.

I measure governance quantitatively by using the number of bills passed/amended in state parliaments. Article 245 of the Indian Constitution lays out the extent of lawmaking power of the Parliament and State legislatures.

Article 246 of the Indian constitution governs subject matter of the laws made by Parliament and State legislatures. When a new state is carved out, the laws of the state it was created from continue to stay in force, unless explicitly repealed/amended.

The reason of choice is as follows: the more active a state legislature is, the more laws it will enact and the state will effectively be better governed. In order to test this, I utilise state-level panel data made publicly available by Timothy Besley and Robin Burgess of the London School of Economics. Below is a table of summary statistics of the variables used:

[1]For a comprehensive account about splits in all states, refer to Appendix

Table of Summary Statistics

	(1) Mean	(2) Std. dev.	(3) Min	(4) Max	(5) Observations
Per capita income	188.4492	199.0094	19	620	N=1062
Factory value added	205.2627	322.243	19	888	N=1062
State population	42643.25	29449.52	3555.474	177869.3	N=572
Laws	41.64501	15.86403	19	62	N=1062
Amendments	67.98495	56.78084	0	393	N=1062
Split	0.1374765	0.3445	0	1	N=1062

This paper makes use of acts and bills data available on two major sources—PRS 'Laws of India' database and Manupatra. The merging of the two data sets was performed on MATLAB by using the unique state IDs to ensure a 100% match of all variables. The fourteen states reorganised as of 1956 have now become twenty-nine through several carving out events. In order to get a clear picture of the effect of state splits, I need a way to capture differential effect across a broad cross section.

Thus, upon importing to stata, combination of states that were initially one at the time of the States Reorganisation Act were assigned a new unique region ID. This acts as an identifier for a 'greater' state region. The data are collapsed into 19 regions within which the splits occur. All state variables are cumulated into the regions. The picture below depicts this:

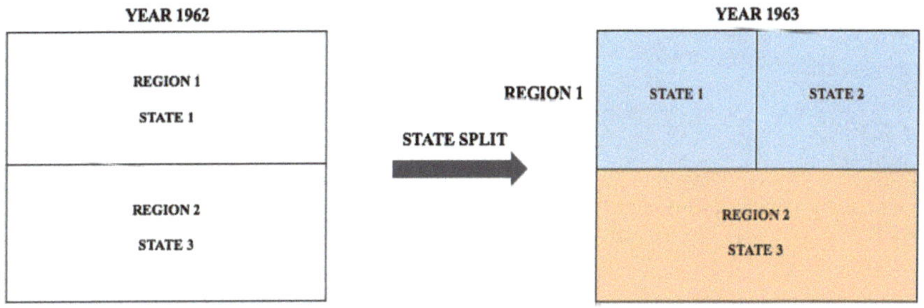

Since the sample period is 1956–2014 (both inclusive), we have 59 * 19, i.e. 1,121 observations or lesser when there are missing data points. The split is accounted for by using a dummy variable which takes value '1' starting from the year that the new state was carved out and otherwise remains '0'. For example, in the image above, Region 1 will take value 1 starting from the year 1963 because State 1 splits in that year.

Laws and amendments have been separated into two separate variables in order to test whether there are any differences: this separation was done by writing a program on MATLAB. Laws are completely fresh legislation representing the policy objectives that are 'new', whereas amendments are simply to modify existing legislation to adjust to changing policy needs rather than changing the direction of policy itself.

Three dummy variables were created to represent the number of times a state was split. The maximum number of times a state has been reorganised in India is three times. Until the year of the respective time(s) of the split, the observations take the value 0 and then take the value 1. States not split always take the value 0. The dummy variable representing the second split is used as a control variable in the regressions.

4 Results

This exploratory activity to understand how governance is affected by state splits can be summed up in the following way:

$$Y_{it} = \alpha_i + \delta_t + \beta_1 \text{split}_{it} + \beta_2 x_{it} + \varepsilon_{it} \quad (1)$$

Equation (1): 'y' represents laws, amendments or a cumulation of both in Tables 1, 2, 3 and 4. 'Split' is the dummy variable which takes the value '0' if a state is never split and the value '1' if a state is split, starting from the year when the split occurred.

'xi_t' represents the vector of control variables, 'δ_t' represents year-fixed effects and 'α_i' represents region-fixed effects. The control variables used are:

Table 1 Baseline results—laws

	(1) Laws	(2) Laws	(3) Laws
Split	−2.812 (1.91)	−6.482* (2.57)	−5.589 (3.24)
Constant	42.03*** (1.91)	44.75*** (1.66)	51.11*** (5.75)
N	1062	572	572
Controls	No	Yes	Yes
Fixed effects	No	No	Yes

Standard errors in parentheses
$^{*}p < 0.05$, $^{**}p<0.01$, $^{***}p <0.001$

Table 2 Baseline results—amendments

	(1) Amends	(2) Amends	(3) Amends
Split	24.90*** (2.770)	17.99*** (3.637)	11.89** (4.163)
Constant	64.63*** (6.128)	72.01*** (9.119)	72.45*** (7.388)
N	1062	572	572
Controls	No	Yes	Yes
Fixed effects	No	No	Yes

Standard errors in parentheses
$^{*}p < 0.05$, $^{**}p < 0.01$, $^{***}p <0.001$

Table 3 Baseline results—total governance activity

	(1) Total	(2) Total	(3) Total
Split	23.25*** (3.718)	12.49** (4.685)	6.302 (5.371)
Constant	106.5*** (6.055)	118.8*** (9.225)	123.6*** (9.533)
N	1062	572	572
Controls	No	Yes	Yes
Fixed effects	No	No	Yes

Standard errors in parentheses
$*p < 0.05$, $**p < 0.01$, $***p < 0.001$

Table 4 Post-reform(s) effect on economic variables

	(1) State GDP	(2) State GDP	(3) State GDP
Split	−2.323 (6.236)	−14.79 (10.74)	6.487 (8.836)
Interaction	79.01*** (8.583)	82.10*** (9.890)	27.74*** (4.650)
Constant	25.26*** (2.092)	21.79*** (3.470)	4.339 (4.292)
N	558	366	366
Controls	No	Yes	Yes
Fixed effects	No	No	Yes

Standard errors in parentheses
$*p < 0.05$, $**p < 0.01$, $***p < 0.001$

1. dummy variable taking the value '1' if a state is split twice and '0' otherwise
2. region's population.

4.1 Governance

The baseline results are presented in Tables 1, 2 and 3. The estimates show that the number of 'fresh' laws decreases by 6 bills when time-fixed effects are not controlled for. But, we see that the number of amendments increases by 18 bills without controlling for time-fixed effects. The overall outcome is that total legislative activity increases by 12 bills with state splits, thus showing that the effect of amendments activity overpowers that of fresh laws (Tables 4, 5 and 6).

These results are in line with the idea of market-preserving federalism which says that a state government has greater incentive to implement policies supporting economic activity when they can reap larger proportions of the rewards. The chances

Table 5 Shift to services economy

	(1) Services GDP	(2) Services GDP	(3) Factory value added	(4) Factory value added
Split	−179076.6* (72202.5)	−155990.6* (67601.2)	887.3*** (118.5)	588.4*** (117.0)
Interaction	225061.4*** (65797.9)	208973.7*** (59525.5)	−1123.3*** (106.0)	−751.8*** (103.1)
Constant	145227.7*** (39094.4)	−4.92e−09 (82993.9)	176.2* (69.84)	−7.76e−12 (143.7)
N	1003	1003	1003	1003
Fixed effects	No	Yes	No	Yes

Standard errors in parentheses
$*p < 0.05$, $**p < 0.01$, $***p < 0.001$

to reap large portions of fiscal rewards are higher when a state is smaller and more homogenous.[2]

4.2 *Economic Outcomes*

This exploratory activity to understand how economic outcomes are affected by state splits can be summed up in the following way:

$$Y_{it} = \alpha_i + \delta_t + \beta_1 \text{split}_{it} + \beta_2 \text{split}_{it} * \text{post}_{1990} + \beta_2 x_{it} + \varepsilon_{it} \tag{2}$$

Equation (2): 'y' in Tables 4 and 5 represents various economic indicators, i.e. net state domestic product per capita, value added in factories, number of man days lost in industrial disputes and proportion of state domestic product coming from service sector activities. The interaction term is between 'split' and a time dummy taking the value 0 before 1990 and 1 after 1990. This was generated because liberalisation reforms in India were implemented after the year 1990.

A potential problem with the results in the previous section is that there could be factors endogenous to each state that has resulted in positive governance outcomes post-split. Therefore, I use the interaction term which accounts for the liberalisation reforms implemented at a country level. I use Eq. (2) for the following reasons. First, I expect the effects of a split to be magnified since states have more opportunities to expand their domestic businesses. Second, this central-level nature of reforms resolves the endogeneity concern.

The reason for using economic indicators as dependent variables is that successful market-preserving federalism results in more tax revenue for governments which therefore promotes business activity in these states (Parikh and Weingast 1997). Drawing from this, I can say that governance matters more when there are market

[2]Given that data is count, I also test this using negative binomial and Poisson results are presented in appendix while being consistent with OLS findings. Refer to Tables 7 and 8 in appendix for output using Poisson and negative binomial methods of estimation.

opportunities. No states face particular disadvantages because of the reforms (enacted at a central level), it can be observed in Tables 4 and 5 that the coefficients confirm this story.

I observe that state domestic product increases by 28 lakh rupees after the reforms are implemented, if a state is split. The interaction term and the per capita state domestic product are thus showing how impact of post-liberalisation reforms magnified the effect of increased governance activity on economic outcomes.

The interaction term provides for exogenous variation. The liberalisation reforms after 1990 were implemented at the central level and were not within the decision-making power of the state governments. I can therefore say that the opportunity for economic development was impartially given to all states.

Interaction term coefficients in columns (1) and (2) of Table 5 indicate that liberalisation does indeed shift economic activity towards the service sector and the benefits of a state split accrue at an increasing rate. There is a positive and significant relationship between the proportion of net domestic product coming from service sectors (banking, insurance, communication, trade, hotels and restaurants), while I observe contrasting results without controlling for reforms. The state domestic product coming from the services sector increases by 2 lakh rupees, post-reform, if the state has been split.

A possible reason could be that the Indian economy shifted away from being manufacturing-oriented to being service-oriented. Seeing that there was a competitive advantage in the services sector, business ventures focused their efforts there.

5 Further Work

The measure of governance that I am currently using is very preliminary. An important concern is that these laws are simply a number which may not be representative of how impactful this activity may be at all. The nature of such laws cannot be determined beyond simply segregating them into fresh laws or amendments. However, this basic study is an important first step towards the direction of in-depth, data-driven study of the Indian federal system. An important caveat to keep in mind is the political structure in India.

The context of these laws depends heavily on the political parties in power in the parliament. Accounting for this will need strong methods to eliminate endogeneity because each state faces its own political challenges. Thus, for the purpose of this paper, I will not focus on political issues that may affect the overall outcome. Taking this study forward would include textual analysis of the content of these laws to determine whether these state splits would result in better governance outcomes.

Finally, as discussed in appendix, the factors leading to demands for statehood are various and idiosyncratic. It is likely that splits are endogenous to economic and governance outcomes. It would be interesting to explore the factors that lead to splits to come to a more comprehensive understanding of both: what causes an increase in federalism and how federalism affects outcomes.

A. **Overview on states**

See Table 6.

Table 6 Summary of state split dates and causes

State name	Year of formation	Cause
Andhra Pradesh	1953	Previously part of Madras province
Arunachal Pradesh	1987	Became a union territory after the North-Eastern reorganisation and then given statehood
Assam	1950	–
Bihar	1950	–
Chhattisgarh	2000	Carved out of Madhya Pradesh
Goa	1987	Got statehood, previously a union territory
Gujarat	1960	Split from the bilingual Bombay province
Haryana	1966	Split from Punjab state
Himachal Pradesh	1971	Split from Punjab state
Jammu and Kashmir	1950	–
Jharkhand	2000	Carved out of Bihar
Karnataka	1956	–
Kerala	1956	–
Madhya Pradesh	1956	–
Manipur	1972	Formed during North-Eastern states reorganisation
Meghalaya	1971	Formed during North-Eastern states reorganisation
Mizoram	1987	Formed during North-Eastern states reorganisation
Maharashtra	1960	Split from the bilingual Bombay province
Nagaland	1963	Formed during North-Eastern states Reorganisation
New Delhi	1992	Got statehood from being a union territory
Orissa	1950	–
Punjab	1966	Split from Punjab state
Rajasthan	1956	–
Sikkim	1975	Became a state in India after giving up autonomous status of kingdom
Tamil Nadu	1950	–
Telangana	2014	Carved out of Andhra Pradesh
Tripura	1972	Formed during North-Eastern states reorganisation
Uttar Pradesh	1950	–
Uttarakhand	2000	Carved out of Uttar Pradesh
West Bengal	1950	–

B. Historical context of state splits—details

At the time of enactment of the Act, because of Nehru's rejection of 'one language, one state' idea, the Marathi- and Gujarati-speaking regions were clubbed into the bilingual Bombay state. The administration, however, had to give into the demands for two separate states following Satyagraha and occasional violent outbursts in Maharashtra. Thus, following the electoral debacle of the Congress, Maharashtra was carved out of Gujarat on 1 May 1960, with Mumbai being included, much to the displeasure of Gujarat (Thakkar and Sanghavi 2011).

Following the partition, the Indian part of Punjab lost most of its agricultural territory to Pakistan, thus rendering majority of Sikh peasants to suffer economically (Kumar 2011a). From here on stemmed the dissatisfaction among the Sikh minority scattered all over a unified Punjab from various factors such as the government's refusal to recognise Sikhism as a separate religion, not a sect under Hinduism (Kumar 2011a).

After prolonged violence and protests in the region led by Akali Dal (a Sikh-dominated political party), the Punjab Reorganisation Act was passed on 18 September 1966: Section 3 resulted in the formation of Haryana, Section 5 transferred Punjabi territory to Himachal Pradesh and Section 4 declared Chandigarh the capital for both Punjab and Haryana. Himachal Pradesh was also carved out of Punjab at this point, although it only attained full State recognition in 1971 Mawdsley (2002).

Nagaland was formed in 1963 by the government of India following armed conflict in the region in the 1950s Baruah (2003). The demands for division of states in the North-Eastern areas were rejected by the SRC because their formations were not based on the linguistic criterion that they promoted Dhar (2011).

The North Eastern Areas Reorganisation Act passed in the Indian Parliament in 1971 led to the reorganisation of the region into Assam, Manipur, Meghalaya and Tripura. Arunachal Pradesh was initially a Union Territory and then become a State in 1987. The North-Eastern people, having been isolated since colonial times, were unsure as to why they had to join the large bloc of Indian states Dhar (2011).

In 2000, the North-central region of India experienced the formation of three new states of Chhattisgarh, Jharkhand and Uttarakhand out of three old states Madhya Pradesh, Bihar and Uttar Pradesh, respectively. Mawdsley (2002) argues that the support for these regional movements comes from BJP's attraction towards electoral pay-offs: BJP won a majority in following elections.

The movement in Chhattisgarh was motivated by demands of local elites who sought privileges through geographical rearrangement Kumar (2011b). They believed that the distance from Bhopal's administrative centre was too large. However, what truly mattered for the carving out of this state were the political numbers. When BJP was contesting for the 2000 elections, A. B. Vajpayee's campaign included a promise to pass the bill allowed by Article 3: BJP won eight seats, and the majority passed in favour of formation of Chhattisgarh (Kumar 2011b).

In Uttarakhand, the majority of the population are upper-caste Brahmins or Rajputs accounting to between 80 and 85% of the population in the region (Singh and Pani 2012). The Government of India allows for reservation of seats in government jobs, universities, etc., based on national statistics of Scheduled Castes (SCs), Scheduled Tribes (STs) and Other Backward Classes (OBCs) (Mawdsley 1997). When the government under V. P. Singh raised the reservation of seats to almost 50%, students in these hilly areas who were of the upper castes began to protest. Eventually, this led to the creation of the State of Uttarakhand in 2000 (Mawdsley 1997).

The formation of the State of Jharkhand in India was the result of due recognition given to tribal identity in the region (Prakash 2011). Jharkhand was separated from Bihar for ethnocultural reasons: the area was predominantly occupied by 'Scheduled Tribes' (Mawdsley 2002). A resource heavy state, Jharkhand, is paradoxically one of the most poverty-stricken areas in India: 85% villages did not have electricity, only 54% were literate and about 56% of the population lived below poverty line (Prakash 2011). Obviously, socio-economic development took centre stage in the establishment of tribal rights to be materialised in the carving out of Jharkhand from Bihar in 2000.

An important case rejecting the linguistic division framework is the struggle for the formation of Telangana in 2014 (Srinivasulu 2011). The Congress hoped that by including Telangana into Andhra Pradesh on linguistic grounds, all the injustices to a backward Telangana would be forgotten. However, the protests went on due to several frustrations such as unemployment of educated youth, privatisation of the Public Sector Enterprises (PSEs), farmers' suicides in Telangana and many other tragic triggers (Srinivasulu 2011). The core of statehood movement in Telangana was inspired by the cultural sphere where people from Telangana felt that their dialect and folk culture were being sidelined by the process of Andhraisation Srinivasulu (2011).

C. Alternate Specifications: Ordinary Least Squares (OLS) and Negative Binomial

See Tables 7 and 8.

Table 7 Baseline with poisson estimation

	(1)	(2)	(3)	(4)	(5)	(6)	(7)	(8)	(9)
Split	−0.08*** (−3.87)	−0.16*** (−0.03)	−0.15*** (−4.45)	0.21*** (15.21)	0.18*** (9.90)	0.13*** (5.96)	0.13*** (10.9)	0.08*** (5.29)	0.05** (3.07)
Constant	−4.58*** (−13.19)	−5.03*** (0.29)	−4.8*** (−11.26)	−1.51*** (−4.68)	−1.46*** (−4.00)	−1 37*** (−3.77)	−2.24*** (−6.81)	−2.27*** (−6.09)	−2.23*** (−5.96)
N	1062	572	572	1062	572	572	1062	572	572
Controls	No	Yes	Yes	No	Yes	Yes	No	Yes	Yes
Fixed effects	No	No	Yes	No	No	Yes	No	No	Yes

Standard errors in parentheses
*$p < 0.05$, **$p < 0.01$, ***$p < 0.001$
Notes
Dependent variable in columns (1)–(3) is the number of fresh laws
Dependent variable in columns (4)–(5) is the number of amendments
Dependent variable in columns (7)–(9) is the total amount of legislative activity
Standard errors in parentheses
*$p < 0.05$, **$p < 0.01$, ***$p < 0.001$

Table 8 Baseline with negative binomial estimation

	(1)	(2)	(3)	(4)	(5)	(6)	(7)	(8)	(9)
Split	−0.0505 (0.046)	−0.125 (0.076)	0.256*** (0.036)	0.226*** (0.044)	0.152** (0.050)	0.169*** (0.033)	0.108** (0.039)	0.0631 (0.043)	0.0630 (0.042)
Constant	2.062*** (0.052)	2.452*** (0.14)	2.741*** (0.057)	2.933*** (0.087)	3.103*** (0.12)	2.931*** (0.053)	3.251*** (0.080)	3.414*** (0.109)	3.41*** (0.108)
N	1062	572	572	1062	572	572	1062	572	572
Controls	No	Yes	Yes	No	Yes	Yes	No	Yes	Yes
Fixed effects	No	No	Yes	No	No	Yes	No	No	Yes

Standard errors in parentheses
$^*p < 0.05$, $^{**}p < 0.01$, $^{***}p < 0.001$
Notes
Dependent variable in columns (1)–{3) is the number of fresh laws
Dependent variable in columns (4)–(6) is the number of amendments
Dependent variable in columns (7)–(9) is the total amount of legislative activity
Standard errors in parentheses
$^*p < 0.05$, $^{**}p < 0.01$, $^{***}p < 0.001$

References

Baruah, S. (2003). Confronting constructionism: Ending India's naga war. *Journal of Peace Research, 40*(3), 321–338.

Dhar, I. (2001). Assam through the prism of reorganisation experience, Chapter 11 (pp. 282–300). Routledge.

Hayek, F. A. (1948). The economic conditions of interstate federalism. *Individualism and economic order* (Vol. 255, pp. 268–269).

Kumar, A. (2011a). Politics of autonomy Punjab and Jammu Kashmir, Chapter 9 (pp. 275–300). Routledge.

Kumar, D. (2011b). A study of Chhattisgarh, Chapter 2 (pp. 76–106). Routledge.

Mawdsley, E. (1997). Nonsecessionist regionalism in India: The Uttarakhand separate state movement. *Environment and Planning A*, 29, 2217–2235.

Mawdsley, E. (2002). Redrawing the body politic: Federalism, regionalism and the creation of new states in India. *Journal of Commonwealth and Comparative Politics*, 40(3), 34–54.

Singh, A., & Pani, N. (2012). Territories beyond geography: An alternative approach to the demands for new states in India. *Common Wealth and Comparative Politics*, 50(1), 121–140.

Parikh, S., & Weingast, B. R. (1997). A comparative theory of federalism: India. *Virginia Law Review*, 83(7), 1593–1615.

Prakash, A. (2011). The case of tribals in Jharkhand, Chapter 1. Routledge.

Sarangi, A. (2011). *Interrogating reorganisation of states*, Chapter 1 (pp. 29–45, pp. 912–915, 2011). Routledge.

Sharma, P. K. (1967). Integration of princely states and the reorganisation of states in India. *The Indian Journal of Political Science*, 28(4), 236–241.

Srinivasulu, K. (2011). *Interrogating reorganisation of states*, Chapter 7 (pp. 164–189, 2011). Routledge.

Thakkar, U., & Sanghavi, N. (2011). *Political currents in Maharashtra: Language beyond*, Chapter 6 (Routledge, 2011).

Weingast, B. R. (2007). Second generation fiscal federalism: Implications for decentralized democratic governance and economic development. Commissioned by ARD, Inc., Sept 2007.

Weingast, B. R. (2009). Second generation fiscal federalism: Implications of fiscal incentives. *Journal of Urban Economics*, 65, 279–294.

Econometric Analysis of Growth Inclusiveness in India: Evidence from Cross-Sectional Data

Paramasivan S. Vellala, Mani K. Madala and Utpal Chattopadhyay

Abstract Development economics witnessed several paradigm shifts, and these shifts happened over a period of time. The current shift from pro-poor growth to inclusive growth is dominating the contemporary economic discourse across the world. Broad-based growth can enhance the accessibility of poor to the newly created economic opportunities sharply different from the concept of pro-poor growth which has transferred the benefits of growth to the poor. Economists called this—"alternate growth strategy"—as inclusive growth. This marked a paradigm shift in development economics in recent times. Though there are few cross-country studies which compared the inclusive growth outcomes across different countries, there is little evidence of detailed investigation within a particular country. Further, the existing literature does not offer ways and means through which the inclusive growth outcome can be measured. It has, thus, remained an unresolved issue. The evolution of inclusive growth debate in the last couple of decades brought new challenges like the inconclusive definition of the term inclusive growth, complexities in the identification of the key drivers of inclusive growth, lack of systematic approach for construction of inclusive growth framework and lack of measurement of inclusive growth. With the above backdrop, this study endeavours to explore the multidimensional aspects of inclusive growth in the Indian context. An empirical verification of growth inclusiveness has been studied using multiple regression analysis with cross-sectional data for the years 2001 and 2011 for 15 major Indian states incorporating 20 socio-economic variables. The result shows that a number of macro-economic variables are the drivers of inclusive growth. These include monthly per capita consumption expenditure, employment, poverty, per capita electricity consumption, life expectancy, infant mortality rate, access to bank, share of women in total employment, share of girls in school education and the share of own tax to state GDP and have empirical significance in explaining growth inclusiveness in the Indian context.

P. S. Vellala (✉)
Institute of Technology, Nirma University, Ahmedabad, Gujarat, India
e-mail: param.vellala@nirmauni.ac.in

M. K. Madala · U. Chattopadhyay
NITIE, Mumbai, India

N. R. Bhanumurthy et al. (eds.), *Advances in Finance & Applied Economics*,
https://doi.org/10.1007/978-981-13-1696-8_2

Keywords Inclusive growth · Productive employment · Poverty · Inequality

JEL Classification D63 · E60 · F43 · 011M · 012M

The world has witnessed several shifts in development economics during the pace of economic growth and economic development which attracted the attention of global researchers to arrive at different growth strategies to guide the development agenda for many underdeveloped and developing economies including India. The current shift from pro-poor growth to inclusive growth is redefining the development agenda and policy responses from different countries which are at different stages of economic growth and development. While pro-poor growth strongly advocated the trickle-down effect of economic growth, inclusive growth mandate not only propagated the creation of new economic opportunities but also making the poor to participate in the growth process. The collapse of Washington Consensus (WC) ended the debate of pro-poor growth and culminated in the drafting of Millennium Development Goals (MDGs) by United Nations (2000) with the promise of reducing poverty to half by 2015. Many countries were given specific targets to achieve the MDGs. However, poverty and inequality continue to plague many countries including the fast-growing economies of India and China. If the poor get benefits but do not participate in the growth process, it will widen the inequality. Therefore, the policy makers should focus on reducing the inequality. This triggered new discourse on the need of broad-based growth, creating economic opportunities which can reduce the poverty and increase the capabilities of the poor and enhance their employability skill resulting in productive employment. Broad-based growth can enhance the accessibility of poor to the newly created economic opportunities sharply different from the concept of pro-poor growth which has transferred the benefits of growth to the poor. Economists called this—"alternate growth strategy"—as inclusive growth. This marked a paradigm shift in development economics in recent times. Though there are few cross-country studies which compared the inclusive growth outcomes across different countries, there is little evidence of detailed investigation within a particular country.

The Problem

The existing literature does not offer ways and means through which the inclusive growth outcome can be measured. It has, thus, remained an unresolved issue. There is adequate literature evidence about the shift in development economics from pro-poor growth to inclusive growth particularly in the developing countries like India, China, Brazil and South Africa, and these countries today are the drivers of global economic growth. However, there is a lack of theory building in the conceptual framework of inclusive growth, which gives enough scope for detailed investigation. The evolution of inclusive growth debate in the last couple of decades brought new challenges like the inconclusive definition of the term inclusive growth, complexities in the identification of the key drivers of inclusive growth, lack of systematic approach for construction of inclusive growth framework and lack of measurement of inclusive growth. With the above backdrop, this paper endeavours to explore the multidimensional aspects of inclusive growth in the Indian context. This paper is organized into four sections. Section 1 deals with the comprehensive review of the existing literature. This is followed by Sect. 2 which deals with the methodology adopted for the study. Section 3 deals with the result and discussion, and finally, Sect. 4 deals with concluding observations.

1 Review of the Literature

1.1 The Pre-Washington Consensus (PWC)

This period refers to the late 1960s and the 1970s when the developing countries considered the Soviet and Chinese model of development as an alternative to modernization. The advocates of this development strategy argued for government intervention through large public investment in the key sectors. Lack of capital was perceived as the biggest impediment to development during this period. Rostow's (1962) five stages of economic growth argued for government coordination through public investment. A big push approach was advocated by Rosenstein-Rodan (1943) to deliver economic growth, employment creation, macro-economic stability and a sustainable balance of payment to reduce poverty through trickle-down process. The main reason why poor continue to remain poor is a lack of capital which includes machinery, infrastructure and money. Under these circumstances, development was considered as a process of systematic transformation through modernization and industrialization (Filho 2010).

1.2 The Washington Consensus (WC)

This period emerged in the late 1970s and early 1980s. This was a period when economists viewed market openness as solutions to the problems created by unnecessary state intervention in the development process. WC strongly believed that the state was inefficient and, therefore, should be replaced by the efficient market. It has laid the foundation for a strong commitment to the free market and the presumption of government intervention as both inefficient and corrupt, not least through rent seeking (Krueger 1974). It has in fact questioned the misguided policies of the state. It strongly advocated globalization in the developing countries and encouraged World Bank and International Monetary Fund to enforce reforms through structural adjustments and conditionalities imposed on poor countries facing balance of payment disequilibrium (Filho 2010). The development process in the 1980s is very often termed as "lost decade" due to the failure of WC.

1.3 Sustainable Development

The idea of sustainable development was introduced by Brundtland Commission (1987) and popularized by World Bank and United Nation Environment Programme. It has brought the environmental dimension in development thinking on international and national strategies for growth and development. Among the multiple definitions, the ideal one was expressed by World Commission (1987)—sustainable development is a development that meets the needs of the present without compromising the ability of future generations to meet their own needs. Sustainable development is "environmentally responsible" and "environmentally friendly", development that takes present and future considerations with short-term and long-term objectives. Those who enjoy the fruits of economic development should not make future generations worse off by excessively degrading the exhaustible resources and polluting the ecology and environment of the earth. Development should not be limited to growth alone. Rather, it should stand for broader goals of social transformation. The valuing environment is a fundamental step in the direction of stopping damages to the environment. The government should devise regulations and incentives that are required to force the recognition of environmental values in decision-making. Environmental impact assessment is indispensable to nullify the adverse implications of negative externalities produced by fast economic growth.

Meadows et al. (1972) outlined the limits to growth in a report for the Club of Rome's projects on the predicament of mankind. Their study viewed that if the present growth trends in world population, industrialization, pollution, food production and resource depletion continue unchanged, the limits to growth on this planet will be reached sooner than expected. It is possible to change the pattern of these growth trends and to establish a condition of ecological and economic stability that is sustainable far into the future needs to be incorporated.

1.4 Human Development

The human cost of structural adjustment programmes in the 1980s undertaken in many developing countries under the directions of World Bank and IMF had been extremely harsh. These programmes prompted questions about the human face of adjustment and about whether alternative policy options were available to balance financial budgets while protecting the interest of weakest and most vulnerable sections of the society. The negative externalities of fast economic growth reminded policy makers about the diseconomies of conventional economic growth models.

At this point of time, Mahbub Ul Haq (1995) presented the idea of preparing an annual human development report to the UNDP. Thus came the first Human Development Report. In the year 1990, UNDP published its first Human Development Report (UNDP 1990) with its newly devised Human Development Index (HDI). The main reason for this paradigm shift to human development can be traced to the wrong picture given by income-based measurement of national progress. Economists, finally, agreed that income cannot be the sole determinant of the progress of the people though it is a dominant one. The first HDR was published on 24 May 1990 in London which addressed some of these issues and explored the relationship between economic growth and human development. Along with per capita income, it also considered health and education in the ranking of countries.

It was a path-breaking moment in development economics since it had challenged the conventional wisdom and reached some important policy conclusions that have redefined development economics subsequently. The human development approach has profoundly influenced the policy makers across the world.

1.5 The Post-Washington Consensus (Post-WC)

Mostly, this period refers to the 1990s. The World Bank scrutinized the WC policies carefully with East Asia's success. The appointment of Joseph Stiglitz as Chief Economist of World Bank promoted the post-WC. Stiglitz et al. (2001) have been the main proponent of new institutional economies. During this period, there was a shift from virtues of the market to institutional settings of economic activity, the significance of market imperfections, the potential outcome of diffusion or changes in institutions, a shift in social inclusion, and distribution of property rights, work pattern, urbanization and family structures. While WC was getting the prices right, the post-WC was getting the institutions right (Filho 2010). There are many factors that contribute to economic stability in the long run such as sound governance, fiscal and debt sustainability, effective institutions, efficient labour market, well-functioning legal system and efficient financial sector (Krueger 2004).

1.6 The Pro-poor Growth (PPG)

The mainstream was compelled to admit that poverty has to be addressed directly through a dedicated set of socio economic policy tools. Thus, there was a definite shift in the discourse of development economics. The focus on policy reform rather than on growth at any cost contributed to downplaying the trade-off and trickle-down views (Kanbur 2000). There were two distinctive definitions of pro-poor growth (PPG) which are commonly found in the literature. For Kakwani and Pernia (2000), pro-poor growth (PPG) is defined by the increase in the income share of poor people which means that the income of the poor should grow faster than that of non-poor which can ultimately reduce the poverty rate faster than if the income of all the people grows at the same rate. Contrary to this view, Ravallion (2004) focused on the absolute improvement of the living standards of the poor, regardless of changes in inequality. Typically, Ravallion (2004) stressed the pro-poor implications of growth. While Kakwani and Pernia rejected Ravallion's definition of pro-poor growth (PPG),

Ravallion criticized Kakwani and Pernia for the inconsistency of their definition of pro-poor growth (PPG). Three potential sources of pro-poor growth (PPG) were identified by Kraay (2004)—a high rate of growth of average income, a high sensitivity of poverty to growth in average income and a poverty-reducing pattern of growth in relative incomes. In such cases, equity remains only as a tool which may be used to enhance the poverty-alleviating impact of a given set of economic policies. However, poverty reduction can be traced to faster economic growth rather than as an outcome of poverty eradication policies (Filho 2010).

1.7 Millennium Development Goals (MDGs)

In September 2000, leaders of 189 countries met at the United Nations in New York and endorsed the most significant policy initiation—Millennium Declaration, a commitment to work together to build a safer, more prosperous and equitable world. The declaration was translated into a roadmap setting out eight time-bound and measurable goals to be reached by the year 2015, known as the Millennium Development Goals (MDGs) (United Nations 2000). This vision has remained as an overarching development framework of world countries for the past 15 years.

1.8 Inclusive Growth

The debates and discourses on inclusive growth gained momentum in the early 2000s with development thinkers like Kakwani and Pernia (2000), Prahlad (2004), Ali (2007), Ali and Son (2007) exploring alternative development strategy to pro-poor growth (PPG) in development economies. They profoundly argued that pro-poor growth is not sufficient to face the challenges posed by the fast growth global economies like continuing poverty, widespread inequalities and unemployment. They argued that the policy maker should not focus only on sharing the growth benefits to the poor but should also make the poor to participate in the growth process and ensure equal access to the economic opportunities to all, particularly to the poor. United Nations Development Programme (UNDP) has set up an exclusive centre—International Policy Centre for Inclusive Growth (IPC-IG). This shift from pro-poor growth to inclusive growth can be traced to the evidences from the existing literature as given below.

According to Ali (2007), the key drivers of inclusive growth are employment and productivity, improvement in human capabilities and fostering social safety nets. He argued for accelerated inclusive economic growth that leads to significant poverty reduction. Ali and Son (2007) argued that inclusive growth should increase the social opportunity function by increasing the average opportunities available to the people in general and to the poor in particular. The concept of productive employment as a fundamental element in inclusive growth was stressed by Bhalla (2007). According to Ali and Zhuang (2007), high and sustainable growth which can cause productive employment opportunities will lead to social inclusion. World Bank (2009) stressed that inclusive growth is about raising the pace of growth and enlarging the size of the economy while levelling the playing field for investment and increasing productive employment. Therefore, its focus is on creating sustainable productive employment rather than income redistribution.

Klasen (2010) pointed out that inclusive growth has become a strategic pillar for guiding the policies of Asian Development Bank in its operational strategy. McKinley (2010) identifies that inclusive growth calls for achieving sustainable growth that will create and expand economic opportunities and ensure broader access to these opportunities to all the members of society who participate in and benefit from growth. In reviewing the ADB literature, Raunier and Kanbur (2010a) point out that while there is no consensus on the common definition of inclusive growth or inclusive development, it is very often accompanied by lower income inequality so that the increment of income accrues disproportionately to those with lower incomes (Raunier and Kanbur 2010b). Inclusiveness of growth is the growth elasticity of poverty in the sense that poverty reduction is the overall objective of any policy debate over a period of time (Hann and Thorat 2013). Both income growth and income distribution are equally important for fostering inclusive growth. We need to address the important determinants of inclusive growth. Macro-economic stability, human capital and structural changes are found to be the key determinants of inclusive growth (Anand et al. 2013). Government can calibrate either their spending programmes or their revenue sources to promote inclusive growth or both. (Asian Development Bank 2014a). It also advocated the Nordic model which features extensive fiscal interventions in labour markets while allowing strong labour unions. This model adopted a high level of spending and a mix of taxes (Asian Development Bank 2014b). Robust economic growth is essential for the rapid revenue growth to expand the fiscal space so that governments can focus on developmental spending in the social sector to foster inclusive growth (Anand et al. 2014).

2 Methodology

2.1 Framework of Analysis

Multiple regression analysis is used to identify the empirical significance of the selected variables. The selected variables are grouped under six dimensions of inclusive growth—economic, amenities, human development, gender equity and financial inclusion (GEFI), sustainability and governance.

2.2 *Estimation Procedure and the Predictive Role of Independent Variables*

Procedure for multiple regression has been followed to arrive at the results with the help of E-Views 8 software. The procedure also checked the econometric tests of heteroskedasticity and normality in all the six dimensions of inclusive growth, both for 2001 and 2011. A brief profile of these variables is given below.

1. **Economic growth**
   High real GDP per capita growth alone cannot trigger inclusive growth. However, researchers very often use the per capita income as the indicator. It must be kept in mind that per capita income will not show the qualitative change in the standard of living of the people. The monthly per capita consumption expenditure can be a better indicator which can show the increase in the people's consumption expenditure with the change in the standard of living of the people (Government of India 2013).
2. **Employment**
   Employment generation is one of the macro-economic objectives, and therefore, the cornerstone of inclusive growth theoretical model is the capacity of the economy to generate productive employment to the people (World Bank 2009).
3. **Poverty reduction**
   The ultimate objective of inclusive economic growth is poverty reduction. The Tendulkar Committee report has a concept of inclusive growth (Government of India 2009).
4. **Inequality reduction**
   Inequality reduction is an important objective of macro-economic management. Therefore, inequality reduction is an integral part of the theoretical model for inclusive growth. Measures are needed to reduce the income inequality which will have a positive bearing on the inclusive economic growth (McKinley 2010).
5. **Human development**
   We need to focus on enhancing the human capabilities of the people which can increase the productivity of the people. Macro-economic stability, human capital and structural changes are found to be the key determinants of inclusive growth in the emerging world (Anand et al. 2013). A positive relationship between human development and economic growth exists on both directions. The two-way causality between economic growth and human development is influenced by several factors.

6. **Gender equity**
   Many governments across the world have initiated various programmes for achieving the gender equity. Gender equity can foster inclusive growth (McKinley 2010).
7. **Basic socio-economic infrastructure**
   Access to safe drinking water, electricity, housing, toilet and transport empowers the capacity of the people to actively participate in the process of economic development.
8. **Financial inclusion**
   Financial inclusion is an integral part of the theoretical model for inclusive growth. Ensuring access to financial services and adequate credit is essential for financial inclusion (Rangarajan 2008). Financial sector contributes significantly to inclusive growth due to its impact on growth and income distribution. Financial outcomes influence economic growth and inequality. Better reforms in the financial sector will foster inclusive growth which has been validated in OECD countries (Boris et al. 2015). Raghuram (2014) stresses the 5Ps required for the financial inclusion: product, place, price, protection and profit.
9. **Sustainability dimension**
   Inclusive growth needs sustainable economic growth in the long run. Therefore, there is an urgent need for policy intervention to protect the environment.
10. **Governance**
    Appropriate policy changes aimed at reforms can remove the negative shock and can act as a positive shock (Patnaik and Pundit 2016). The government, through pro-active policies, has to make it happen, and this is one of the biggest challenges facing the Indian state (Deshpande 2013). In this study, the share of development expenditure to a total expenditure of the state and the share of own tax to the state domestic product are selected as governance variables (Mundle et al. 2016) to make our analytical framework first of its kind in the Indian context which can fuel future studies as well.

2.3 Data Sets and Data Sources:

This study uses cross-sectional data for two time periods of 2001 and 2011 considering the nature of the census data and data obtained from several rounds of NSSO studies and other sources as given in Table 1.

Table 1 Data sources

Indicators	Dimension	2001–02	2011–12
Income—MPCE	Economic	2004–05—NSSO 60th round	NSSO 68th round July 2011 to June 2012
Poverty		Planning Commission 2004–05	Planning Commission 2011–12
Employment		Census 2001	NSSO 68th round
Inequalities (Gini coefficient)		Planning Commission	Planning Commission
Per capita consumption of electricity	Amenities	Central Electricity Authority, Ministry of Power, GoI	Central Electricity Authority, Ministry of Power, GoI
Access to drinking water		Census 2001	Census 2011
Access to toilet		Census 2001	Census 2011
Pucca houses		Census 2001	Census 2011
Transport—road length per 100 sq. km.		Economic Survey of Maharashtra—2005–06	Economic Survey of Maharashtra—2012–13
% of women in LWF	Gender equity and financial inclusion	Census 2001	Census 2011
% of girls in school education		Census 2001	Census 2011
% of HH with banking		Census 2001	Census 2011
Literacy rate	Human development	Census 2001	Census 2011
Life expectancy		Census 2001	Census 2011
Health—IMR		SRS Bulletin 2005–06 Home Ministry, GoI	SRS Bulletin Oct. 2012 Home Ministry, GoI
% of development expenditure to total expenditure	Governance	Finance Accounts of States and CSO	Finance Accounts of States and CSO
% of tax revenue to GSDP		Finance Accounts of States and CSO	Finance Accounts of States and CSO
Crime rate	Sustainability	National Crime Records Bureau, Home Ministry, GoI Report 2001	National Crime Records Bureau, Home Ministry, GoI Report 2011
Air quality		Institute for Financial Management and Research (IFMR)	Institute for Financial Management and Research (IFMR)

2.4 Variables and Their Notations

The different variables, notations and expected sign identified for the analysis are given in Table 2.

Table 2 List of explanatory variables, notations and expected sign

Dimensions	Independent variables	Dependent variable	Notations	Expected sign
Economic	Poverty	Per capita income (PCI)	POV	Negative
	Employment		EMP	Positive
	Gini (rural)		GINIR	Negative
	Gini (urban)		GINIU	Negative
Amenities	Per capita electricity consumption	Per capita income (PCI)	PCEC	Positive
	Access to drinking water		DW	Positive
	Access to pucca houses		PHOU	Positive
	Access to road		ROAD	Positive
Human development	Literacy rate	Per capita income (PCI)	LIT	Positive
	Life expectancy		LE	Positive
Gender equity and financial inclusion	Access to bank	Per capita income (PCI)	Bank	Positive
	Women employment		WE	Positive
	Girl's school education		GSE	Positive
Sustainability	Air quality (environmental dimension)	Environment sustainability index	AQ	Positive
	Crime rate (social dimension)		CR	Negative
Governance	Development expenditure to total expenditure	Governance performance index (GPI)	DE	Positive
	Share of own tax to GSDP		TAX	Positive

2.5 *Model Specifications Six Models Have Been Framed as Given Below, Both for 2001 and 2011*

Table 3 Model specifications

Dimension/indicators	2001	2011
Economics	$Y^* = \alpha + \beta_1$ Emp $+ \beta_2$ Pov $+ \beta_3$ MPCE $+ \beta_4$ GINIR $+ \beta_5$ GINIU $+ u$	$Y = \alpha + \beta_1$ Emp $+ \beta_2$ Pov $+ \beta_3$ MPCE $+ \beta_4$ GINIR $+ \beta_5$ GINIU $+ u$
Amenities	$Y^* = \alpha + \beta_1$ PCEC $+ \beta_2$ DW $+ \beta_3$ PHOU $+ \beta_4$ Road $+ \beta_5$ Toilet $+ u$	$Y^* = \alpha + \beta_1$ PCEC $+ \beta_2$ DW$_+$ β_3 PHOU $+ \beta_4$ Road $+ \beta_5$ Toilet $+ u$
Human development	$Y^* = \alpha + \beta_1$ Lit $+ \beta_2$ EL $+ \beta_3$ IMR $+ u$	$Y^* = \alpha + \beta_1$ Lit $+ \beta_2$ EL $+ \beta_3$ IMR $+ u$
Gender equity and financial inclusion	$Y^* = \alpha + \beta_1$ Bank $+ \beta_2$ WE $+ \beta_3$ GSE $+ u$	$Y^* = \alpha + \beta_1$ Bank $+ \beta_2$ WE $+ \beta_3$ GSE $+ u$
Governance	$Y^{**} = \alpha + \beta_1$ DE $+ \beta_2$ Tax $+ + u$	$Y = \alpha + \beta_1$ DE $+ \beta_2$ Tax $+ + u$
Sustainability	$Y^{***} = \alpha + \beta_1$ CR $+ \beta_2$ AQ $+ u$	$Y^{***} = \alpha + \beta_1$ CR $+ \beta_2$ AQ $+ u$

Y^* is the dependent variable—per capita income which is the proxy variable for inclusive growth.

Y^{**} is the dependent variable—governance performance index score proxy for inclusive growth.

Y^{***} is the dependent variable—environment sustainable index score proxy for inclusive growth.

Note Emp—employment, Pov—poverty, GINIR—Gini rural, GINIU—Gini urban, PCEC—per capita electricity consumption, DW—access to drinking water, PHOU—access to pucca housing, Road—access to road, Bank—access to banking, WE—percentage of women in total labour force, GSE—percentage of girls in school education, DE—percentage of development expenditure on total expenditure, Tax—percentage of own tax to gross state domestic product (GSDP) of the government, CR—crime rate and AQ—air quality.

3 Results and Discussion

3.1 *Evaluating the Regression Models*

The regression models are evaluated with the following criteria.

1. The R^2 value should be greater than 0.60 (60%) to ensure that the whole model is fitted strongly. It means that all the independent variables jointly influence the dependent variable. **R^2 shows joint significance within the sample and, therefore, cannot talk about what happens in real world**.

2. Most of the independent variables (at least 50%) should be significant. T statistics is used for this purpose, and the p value should be less than 0.05 (5%).
3. The independent variables should be jointly significant to explain the dependent variable. For this, F statistics is used and the prob. value should be less than 0.05 (5%). ***F statistics shows joint significance within population and, therefore, can talk about what happens in real world**.
4. Sign of the coefficient. It should follow either the established economic theory or expectation or intuition. Since there is no established theory on inclusive growth, this study evaluates the coefficient values with expected sign.
5. Managing residuals to attain good regression model. The following diagnostic tests have been conducted.

- There should not be serial correlation in the residuals—**Breusch–Godfrey serial correlation LM test is conducted, and the observed probability value should be greater than 0.05 for not rejecting the null hypothesis that **there is no serial correlation**.
- There should not be heteroskedasticity in the residuals—Breusch–Pagan–Godfrey (BPG) is conducted, and the observed probability value should be greater than 0.05 for not rejecting the null hypothesis that **there is no heteroskedasticity in the residuals**.
- Residuals should be normally distributed—Jarque–Bera statistic is used. The observed probability value should be greater than 0.05 for not rejecting the null hypothesis that t**he residuals follow normal distribution**.

*It means that a model can be accepted if F statistics is significant though R^2 value is less.

**Since this study used cross-sectional data, serial correlation LM test is not required. It is required only if the study is based on time series data to check the autocorrelation.

From the above table, it is clear that a number of macro-economic variables are the drivers of inclusive growth. Income (represented by monthly per capita consumption expenditure—MPCE in this study), employment (EMP), poverty (POV), per capita electricity consumption (PCEC), life expectancy (EL), infant mortality rate (IMR), access to bank (BANK), share of women in total employment (WE), share of girls in school education (GSE) and the share of own tax to state GDP have empirical significance in explaining growth inclusiveness in the Indian context. These are separately discussed under different dimensions of inclusive growth as given below.

3.2 Economic Dimension—2001 and 2011

The following observations emerge from Table 4 with respective to "economic dimension".

(1) $\mathbf{R^2}$ value is 0.72 and adjusted R^2 value is 0.61 for the year 2001, which show the significance of the overall fit of the model. For the year 2011, the R^2 value is 0.82 and the adjusted R^2 is 0.73 which show the overall significance of the goodness of the fit of the model.
(2) "**F**" test shows the combined significance of all the variables such as employment, poverty, Gini rural and Gini urban for the year 2002 and employment, poverty, MPCE, Gini rural and Gini urban for the year 2011.
(3) The regression coefficients are given in Table 4—the coefficient of poverty, Gini rural and Gini urban show negative sign as expected. This confirms the general belief that higher inclusive growth reduces poverty and inequality. Poverty is having a negative sign and that of other independent variables are positive as expected.
(4) Among the independent variables, the P value for poverty is significant for the year 2001 and both poverty and MPCE have significant p value for the year 2011 which supports our argument of inclusive growth and should reduce the poverty over a period of time. However, the p value of other independent variable does not show any statistical significance though together they contribute to the changes in the dependent variable.
(5) The variance of residuals is homoscedastic, and the residuals follow normal distribution as the p values are greater than 0.05 in both years for both the tests as given in Table 4. This shows the goodness of fit of the model specified in Table 3 against economic dimension both for the years 2001 and 2011.

3.3 Amenities Dimension—2001 and 2011

(1) $\mathbf{R^2}$ value is 0.81 and adjusted R^2 value is 0.73 for the year 2001, which show the significance of the overall fit of the model. For the year 2011, the R^2 value is 0.76 and the adjusted R^2 is 0.63 which show the overall significance of the goodness of the fit of the model.
(2) "**F**" test shows the combined significance of all the variables together both for 2001 and 2011.
(3) The regression coefficient of per capita consumption of electricity is significant at p value of 0.003 for the year 2001 and 0.019 for the year 2011.
(4) Among the independent variables, the P value for per capita electricity consumption is significant for the years 2001 and 2011 with p values of 0.003 and 0.019, respectively, and there is no statistical significance for other independent variables.
(5) The variance of residuals is homoscedastic, and the residuals follow normal distribution as the p values are greater than 0.05 in both years for both the tests as given in Table 4.

Table 4 Summary of the results in econometric analysis

Dependent variable: per capita income (proxy for inclusive growth)														
	2001							2011						
Ind. vari	Regression coeff	P value	R^2	Ad R^2	F Test	HT/BPGT	NT/JBT	Regression coeff	P value	R^2	Ad R^2	F Test	HT/BPGT	NT/JBT
POV	−496.827	0.0013	0.72	0.61	0.006	0.45	0.48	−27.74	0.9600	0.82	0.73	0.003	0.13	0.78
EMP	212.9137	0.400						1172.45	0.0800					
MPCE	MC	–						26.10	0.0024					
GINIR	−89574.8	0.1196						−1250.36	0.3999					
GINIU	−30458.08	0.2699						−55383.10	0.6051					
PCEC	24.06	0.003	0.81	0.73	0.001	0.67	0.61	35.67	0.0190	0.76	0.63	0.011	0.28	0.95
PHOU	4.558	0.9589						329.27	0.5080					
DW	29.23	0.7074						31.12	0.9400					
ROAD	16.59	0.3067						42.68	0.4990					
TOILET	MC	–				0.61	0.47	220.72	0.5043	0.68	0.60	0.003	0.08	0.77
Lit	57.6	0.71	0.69	0.60	0.003			280.46	0.7800					
EL	2203.78	0.005						570.71	0.3800					
IMR	−283.841	0.058						−7434.08	0.0100					
BANK	426.91	0.003	0.65	0.55	0.007	0.12	0.57	1209.91	0.0440	0.44	0.29	0.080	0.18	0.78
WE	328.07	0.085						249.69	0.4990					
GSE	119.58	0.085						259 86	0.1620					
Dependent variable: environment sustainability index value (proxy for inclusive growth)														
AQ	21.49	0.003	0/53	0.45	0.0105	0.38	0.66	26.45	0.002	0.56	0.48	0.007	0.72	0.56
CR	−0.83	0.531						−0 906	0.564					
Dependent variable: governance performance index value (proxy for inclusive growth)														
DE	−0.0017	0.68	0.51	0.43	0.0130	0.16	0.84	−0.00057	0.884	0.42	0.32	0.037	0.93	0.72
TAX	0.06	0.012						0.0567	0.012					

Note MC: multicollinearity HT/BPGT: heteroskedasticity test/Breusch–Pagan–Godfrey test NT/JBT: normality test/Jarque–Bera test

3.4 Human Development Dimension—2001 and 2011

(1) **R^2** value is 0.69 and adjusted R^2 value is 0.60 for the year 2001, which show the significance of the overall fit of the model. For the year 2011, the R^2 value is 0.68 and the adjusted R^2 is 0.68 which show the overall significance of the goodness of the fit of the model.
(2) "**F**" test shows the combined significance of all the variables together both for 2001 and 2011 with probability value of 0.003 for both the years.
(3) The regression coefficient of the independent variables shows positive sign for literacy rate and expected life and negative sign for infant mortality rate as expected.
(4) Among the independent variables, the P value for expected life is significant for the year 2001 with p value of 0.005 for the year 2001. The P value of infant mortality rate is significant for the year 2011 with the p value of 0.01.
(5) The variance of residuals is homoscedastic, and the residuals follow normal distribution as the p values are greater than 0.05 in both years for both the tests as given in Table 4.

3.5 Gender Equity and Financial Inclusion Dimension—2001 and 2011

(1) **R^2** value is 0.65 and adjusted R^2 value is 0.55 for the year 2001, which show the significance of the overall fit of the model. For the year 2011, the R^2 value is 0.44 and the adjusted R^2 is 0.29 which show the overall significance of the goodness of the fit of the model.
(2) "**F**" test shows the combined significance of all the variables together both for 2001 and 2011 with probability values of 0.007 and 0.008 for the year 2011.
(3) The regression coefficient of the independent variables shows positive sign for all the independent variables as expected.
(4) Among the independent variables, the P value for access to bank is significant for the year 2001 with p values of 0.003 and 0.044 for the year 2011.
(5) The variance of residuals is homoscedastic, and the residuals follow normal distribution as the p values are greater than 0.05 in both years for both the tests as given in Table 4.

3.6 Sustainability Dimension—2001 and 2011

(1) **R^2** value is 0.53 and adjusted R^2 value is 0.45 for the year 2001, which show the significance of the overall fit of the model. For the year 2011, the R^2 value

is 0.56 and the adjusted R^2 is 0.48 which show the overall significance of the goodness of the fit of the model.

(2) "**F**" test shows the combined significance of all the variables together both for 2001 with probability values of 0.01 and 0.007 for the year 2011.

(3) As given in Table 4, the regression coefficient of the independent variable crime rate shows negative sign and air quality shows positive sign as expected. This shows that for inclusive growth the crime rate has to be reduced and the air quality has to be increased so that both social and environmental aspects of inclusive growth can be assured.

(4) Among the independent variables, the P value for air quality is 0.003 which is significant while that for crime rate is not significant.

(5) The variance of residuals is homoscedastic, and the residuals follow normal distribution as the p values are greater than 0.05 in both years for both the tests as given in Table 4.

3.7 Governance Dimension—2001 and 2011

(1) $\mathbf{R^2}$ value is 0.51 and adjusted R^2 value is 0.43 for the year 2001, which show the significance of the overall fit of the model. For the year 2011, the R^2 value is 0.42 and the adjusted R^2 is 0.32 which show the overall significance of the goodness of the fit of the model, though the value has slightly been reduced.

(2) "**F**" test shows the combined significance of all the variables together both for 2001 with probability values of 0.013 and 0.037 for the year 2011.

(3) The regression coefficient of the independent variables shows negative sign for share of development expenditure to total expenditure since the more inclusive growth the less the need for development expenditure. But the regression output shows positive sign for share of own tax to GSDP as expected since more inclusive growth will increase the taxable capacity of the people.

(4) Among the independent variables, the P value for share of own tax to GSDP is 0.012 for both 2001 and 2011 which shows significance level while share of development expenditure to total expenditure does not show any significance level.

(5) The variance of residuals is homoscedastic, and the residuals follow normal distribution as the p values are greater than 0.05 in both years for both the tests as given in Table 4.

4 Concluding Observations

In a nutshell, the following observations emerge from the multiple regression analysis.

(1) Among the independent variables in economic dimension, poverty reduction is an important consideration in determining whether a particular state has achieved growth inclusiveness or not for the year 2001 and it is monthly per capita consumption expenditure which is an important consideration in determining whether a particular state has achieved growth inclusiveness or not for the year 2011. This is because poverty reduction strategy initiated by the successive governments yielded the desired result. Faster economic growth and more per capita income paved the way for more consumption expenditure. Therefore, the monthly per capita consumption expenditure became a significant variable causing growth inclusiveness.
(2) Among the independent variables in amenities dimension, the per capita electricity consumption plays a crucial role in determining whether a particular state has achieved growth inclusiveness or not. It is true both for the years 2001 and 2011.
(3) Among the independent variables in human development, expected life and infant mortality rate play a crucial role in fostering inclusive growth for the year 2001, and in 2011, it is infant mortality rate which plays a crucial role in determining whether a particular state has achieved inclusive growth or not.
(4) Among the independent variables in gender equity and financial inclusion dimension, access to bank is a very significant variable in determining whether a particular state has achieved growth inclusiveness or not. It is true both for the years 2001 and 2011.
(5) In sustainability dimension, it is air quality which determines whether a particular state has achieved growth inclusiveness or not. It is true both for the years 2001 and 2011.
(6) In governance dimension, it is the share of own tax to gross state domestic product (GSDP), which plays a significant role in fostering inclusive growth both for the years 2001 and 2011. There is a rationale here. When a state achieves inclusive growth, the taxable capacity of the people tends to increase which has been established through statistical significance. Development expenditure shows negative coefficient as the more the inclusive growth the less will be the need for development expenditure.
(7) The procedure also checked the econometric tests for heteroskedasticity and normality in all the six dimensions of inclusive growth, both for 2001 and 2011 and the results found satisfactory as given in Table 4.

It would be of great interest in advancing the debate on inclusive growth and devise more effective inclusive growth policies in the world in general and in India in particular. More grounded theories are necessary for further advancing the debate on inclusive growth. There are few issues which remain unresolved like the relationship between fiscal redistribution and inclusive growth, the impact of monetary policies in general and inflation in particular on inclusive growth, the impact of technological advancement on growth inclusiveness, the relationship between structural reforms and inclusive growth and the impact of labour market reforms on inclusive growth. Future research on inclusive growth can accommodate these variables for further strengthening the scope of research in this direction. A detailed study of structural transformation can be useful to understand whether a particular growth episode is inclusive or not. A larger study which can accommodate a broader range of indicators based on state-specific need rather than common indicators, drawn from a wider set of household surveys, would help deepen the understanding and measuring of growth inclusiveness.

References

Ali, I. (2007). Inequality and the imperative for inclusive growth in Asia. *Asian Development Review*, 24(2), 1–16.

Ali, I., & Son, H. (2007). *Defining and measuring inclusive growth: Asian prescriptions*. ERD Policy brief series No. 48, Asian Development Bank.

Ali, I., & Zhuang, J. (2007). *Inclusive growth toward a prosperous Asia: Policy implications*. Asian Development Bank ERD Working Paper No. 97.

Anand, R., Mishra, S., & Peiris, J. S. (2013). *Inclusive growth—Measurement and determinants.* IMF Working Paper 135.

Anand, R., Tulin, V., & Kumar, N. (2014). *India: Defining and explaining inclusive growth and poverty reduction*. IMF WP 14/63.

Asian Development Bank. (2014a). *Asian development outlook, 2014: fiscal policy for inclusive growth*. Cornell University ILR School International Publication.

Asian Development Bank. (2014b). *Fiscal policy and inclusive growth in advanced countries: Their experience and implications for Asia*. Cornell University ILR School International Publication and ADB Working Paper 422.

Bhalla, S. (2007). Inclusive growth? Focus on employment. *Social Scientist, 35*(7/8), 24–43.

Brundtland Commission. (1987). *Our common future—Brundtland Report*. United Nation.

Cournede, B., Denk, O., & Hoeller, P. (2015). *Finance and inclusive growth*. OECD Economic Policy Paper No. 14.

Deshpande, A. (2013). *Exclusion and inclusive growth*. United Nation Development Programme—UNDP.

Government of India. (2009). *Report of the Expert Group to Review the Methodology for; Estimation of Poverty*. Planning Commission, New Delhi.

Government of India. (2013). *Report of the committee for evolving a composite development index of states*. Ministry of Finance, Government of India.

Haan de, A., & Throat, S. (2013). *Inclusive growth: More than safety nets*. DRC/CRDI SIG, International Development Research Centre, Working Paper-2013/1.

Kakwani, N., & Pernia, M. E. (2000). What is pro poor growth. *Asian Development Review*, 18(1).

Kanbur, R. (2000). Income distribution and development. In A. B. Atkinson & F. Bourgingnon (Eds.), *Hand book of income distribution* (Vol. 1). Amsterdam, North Holland.

Klasen, S. (2010). *Measuring and monitoring inclusive growth: Multiple definitions, open questions, and some constructive proposals*. Asian Development Bank, Sustainable Development Working Paper Series No. 12.

Kraay, A. (2004). *When is growth pro-poor? Cross country evidence*. International Monetary Fund—IMF Working Paper No. 04/47.

Krueger, A. (1974). The political economy of the rent seeking society. *American Economic Review, 64*, 291–303.

Krueger, A. (2004). Meant Well, tried little, failed much: Policy reforms in emerging market economies. http://www.imf.org/extend/np/speeches/2004/032304a.htm.

Martin, R. (2004). *Pro poor growth: A Primer.* World Bank Policy Research Working Paper, 3242.

McKinley, T. (2010). *Inclusive growth criteria and indicators: An inclusive growth index for diagnosis of country progress.* ADB Sustainable Development WP Series.
Meadows, H. D., Meadows, L. D., Randers, J., & Behrens, W. W. (1972). *The limits to growth. A report for the club of Rome's project on the predicament of mankind.* New York, USA: Universe Books.
Mundle, S., Choudhury, S., & Sikdar, S. (2016). *Governance performance of Indian states: 2001–02 and 2011–12.* Working Paper No. 164 m, National Institute of Public Finance and Policy (NIPFP), New Delhi, 03 March, 2016.
Patnaik, I., & Pundit, M. (2016). *Where is India's growth Headed?* National Institute of Public Finance and Policy, WP No. 159.
Prahlad, C. K. (2004). *The fortunes at the bottom of the pyramid: Eradicating poverty through profits.* Financial Times/Prentice Hall.
Raghuram, R. G. (2014). *Finance and opportunity in India 20th Lalit Doshi Memorial Lecture.* Mumbai: Lalit Doshi Memorial Foundation.
Rangarajan, C. (2008). *Report of the committee on financial inclusion.* Government of India.
Rauniar, G., & Kanbur, R. (2010). Inclusive Growth and inclusive development: A review and synthesis of Asian development bank literature. *Journal Asian Pacific Economy, 41*(4), 455–469.
Raunier, G., & Kanbur, R. (2010b). *Inclusive development: Two papers on conceptualization: Application and the ADB perspective.* ADB.
Rosentain Rodan, P. N (1943). Problems of industrialization of Eastern and South Eastern Europe. *Economic Journal*, 53(210/211).
Rostow, W. W. (1962). *The stages of economic growth: Non communist manifesto.* Cambridge: Cambridge University Press.
Saad Alfredo, F. (2010). *Growth, poverty and inequality: From Washington consensus to inclusive growth.* Department of Economic and Social Affairs-DESA Working Paper No. 100, United Nations.
Stiglitz, J. E., & Meier, Gerald M. (2001). *Frontiers of development economics: The future in perspective.* Washington D.C: Oxford University Press. ISSN 9780195215922.
Ul Haq, M. (1995). *Reflections on human development.* Oxford University Press.
United Nations. (2000). Resolution adopted by the General Assembly, 55/2, Agenda Item 60(b) United Nations Millennium Declaration, United Nations, New York. http://undocs.org/A/RES/55/2.
United Nations Development Programme-UNDP. (1990). Human Development Report. United Nations Development Programme.
World Bank. (2009). *What is inclusive growth*? World Bank Note prepared by Elena Ianchovichina (PRMED) and Susanna Landstron (PRMED).
World Commission. (1987). *World commission on environment and development merged into Brundtland commission.*

Part II
Environmental Economics

Assessing an Investor's Decision to Invest in Solar Power Across Indian States

Suramya Sharma and Srishti Dixit

Keywords Investment decision · Solar PV · Cost · Solar policy · Corruption

1 Introduction

1.1 Overview of Energy Sector

The global demand for energy is rising at an increasing pace over the years. This surge in energy demand is a result of exponential growth in the world population. "In just one generation, the global population has increased by nearly 2 billion, with a major contribution from developing countries" (Devabhaktuni et al. 2013, p. 556). Secondly, the energy demand of a country increases relative to its economic growth. These possible explanations point toward the fact that the developing nations are one of the major drivers of energy demand. According to the International Energy Agency, "Developing countries will need to double their installed generation capacity in order to meet the growing demand for power by the year 2020" (Devabhaktuni et al. 2013, p. 556). This can be observed in Fig. 1 which clearly shows that the energy demand is increasing in the countries of the Asia Pacific region at the fastest pace.

With the increasing pressure on the environment created by the greenhouse and the high dependence of nations on fossil fuels, there is an urgent need to shift on

S. Sharma (✉)
IIM Udaipur, Udaipur, India
e-mail: suramya.sharma@gmail.com

S. Dixit
Green Sphere Solar Contracting LLC, Mumbai, India
e-mail: srish.dixit@gmail.com

N. R. Bhanumurthy et al. (eds.), *Advances in Finance & Applied Economics*,
https://doi.org/10.1007/978-981-13-1696-8_3

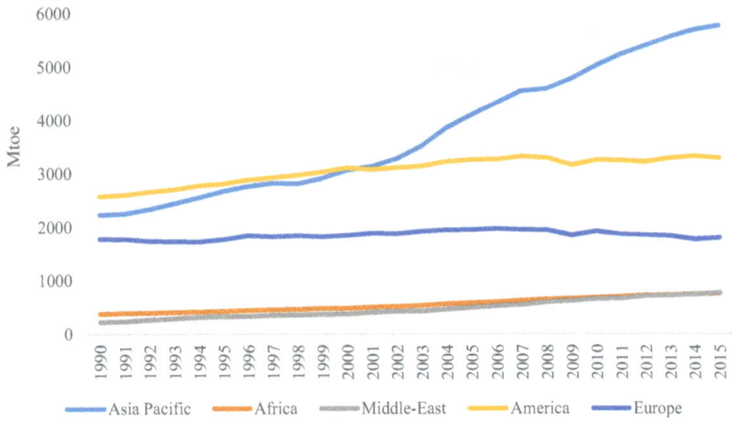

Fig. 1 Global energy consumption from 1990–2015. *Data Source* Enerdata (2016)

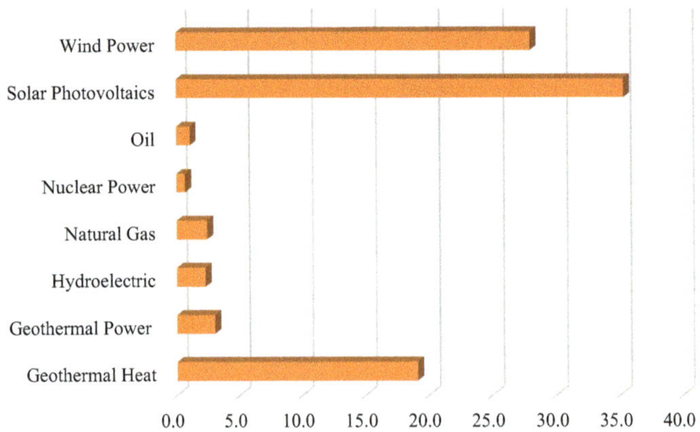

Fig. 2 Average annual growth rates of renewable energy (in percent) for 2000–2010. *Data Source* Earth Policy Institute (2010)

renewable sources of energy owing to their advantages over fossil fuels in the terms of almost non-existent harmful emissions, unlimited supply, low operational and maintenance costs, etc.

The year 2015 witnessed substantial increase in the growth as well as capacity of renewables out of which solar PV has emerged as one of the fastest growing sectors (Fig. 2) worldwide since it has the most "widely adaptable applications and converts sunlight directly into electrical energy with the highest efficiencies" (Pearce 2002, p. 663). According to calculations, Earth receives around 16,000 times more solar energy than needed worldwide. Hence, solar energy encompasses a huge potential to fulfill present and future energy demand.

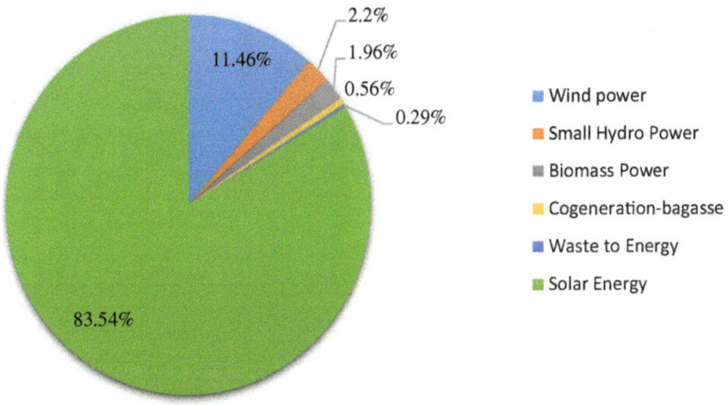

Fig. 3 Total renewable energy potential in India in 2015 (*Note* percentage of total reserves = 896603 MW). *Data Source* MOSPI (2016)

1.2 Indian Perspective

Even though India is a tropical country which receives around 300 days of sunshine, the country has been ranked as the most coal-dependent nation with 74% of electricity generated through coal (Buckley 2015, p. 4). However, it is anticipated that the share of electricity generated through renewables is likely to "increase from 17% in 2014 to 26% by 2040. In fact, if this happens, then by 2030, India will surpass the USA and European Union, in the overall power generation via solar energy" (Iyer 2016).

As depicted in Fig. 3, solar power has huge potentials in the country; however, according to the India Solar Handbook issued by Bridge To India (2016), the total installed capacity of utility-scale power plants, together with small scale rooftop solar plants, is a meager 7350 MW.

Several strategies and commitments undertaken by the government in favor of expanding solar capacity in the country are bringing the Indian solar sector to the forefront at the global level.

It is important to examine the factors that influence the decision of an investor to invest in the installation of utility-scale solar power generation projects in six Indian states, which are Rajasthan, Jammu & Kashmir, Gujarat, Karnataka, Haryana, and Tripura. The paper also attempts to rank these states on the basis of such factors.

2 Literature Review

Solar energy has undoubtingly a promising future. But the shift from conventional sources to renewable sources of energy is taking place rather slowly. The reasons for such a slow-paced transition are high initial cost, imperfect information, lack of infrastructure, lack of legal framework, etc. However, despite such barriers, owing to advancements in technology, a significant cost reduction has been witnessed which has made solar energy one of the fastest growing technologies in the world (Branker

2011, p. 1). It has transformed from "a high-cost, experimental technology to a mature, competitive energy source across the globe over the last five years" (Ryan et al. (2016), p. 507). During these years, the deployment of solar PV has increased by up to 360%; in 2010 alone, approximately 17 GW of new solar PV power was installed globally. While the costs have reduced by more than 50% (Ryan et al. (2016), p. 507), it is estimated that solar PV will reach grid parity by 2020. Hence from an investor's point of view, "financing costs for solar PV have fallen in many countries as experience with solar PV projects has grown and the perceived financial risk reduced" (Ryan et al. (2016), p. 507). With such rapid reduction in the cost of solar PV, areas that earlier were not considered feasible enough to set up solar plants due to geographical or financial constraints have been appealing the investors now. The economic feasibility of a solar power plant can be estimated using various indicators, out of which levelized cost of electricity (LCOE) is widely used and is a convenient summary measure that is used to assess the cost-effectiveness of the energy-generating technology.

Countries like Germany have set an example as to how "a policy has stimulated PV growth even in regions with moderate solar energy resource" (Šúri et al. 2007, p. 1295). Other European countries such as Spain, Italy, Greece have adopted similar policies to utilize the solar resource. The Government of Germany has targeted to reduce 80–95% of greenhouse gas emission by 2050 and end the use of nuclear power by 2022 (Kost et al. 2013, p. 33).

Similarly, it is believed that due to less solar radiation and low electricity prices, solar PV does not have much potential to capture the market in the US Midwest. But as per Jung and Tyner (2014), "current policies can lower the cost of generating electricity with the PV system, measured as the Levelized cost of electricity (LCOE), to the level of mean retail grid price making PV systems cost-competitive" (Sesmero et al. 2016, p. 80). According to Eyraud et al. (2011, p. 21), "Public interventions are necessary to correct market failures stemming from carbon emission externalities." Hence, we can say that the governments play an important role by laying down policies that can promote the prospects of solar PV in their respective countries.

Most of the papers analyze either the cost of solar PV or the policy implications, separately, but the paper by Ryan et al. (2016) combines the analysis of the projected cost of solar PV as well as the impact of the policies for Ireland, a country with very low solar irradiance. The paper finds that for Ireland, it is better to delay the investment decision with continued reduction in costs, since solar PV will become a more lucrative option when it reaches grid parity by 2030. It is expected that benefits from the large-scale deployment of solar PV in larger countries could lead to economies of scale and hence be economically viable for smaller countries like Ireland. Though presently, solar PV is not the best option economically, but policy-wise, "Further study is needed to assess their full value in terms of technical, temporal, and geographic complementarity" (Ryan et al. 2016, p. 516).

The literature has confirmed the importance of the cost and solar policies in determining the investment in solar power. However, there are several other determinants as well that play a leading role in attracting investments such as *Economic growth and income level* (Eyraud et al. 2011), *Population* (Eyraud et al. 2011), *Interest Rates*

(Eyraud et al. 2011), *Cost of conventional sources of energy* (Eyraud et al. 2011), *Geographical condition* (Eyraud et al. 2011; Van Hemmen 2011; Lüthi 2008), *Governance structure* (Lüthi 2008).

As we know the cost and solar policies are the two most significant drivers of investment, nonetheless, to make the study more inclusive, a sociopolitical factor ***"corruption"*** has been included which again influences an investment decision.

According to Transparency International, India, corruption in simple terms is "the abuse of entrusted power for private gain." As per Asiedu and Freeman (2009, p.5), "corruption raises operational cost, creates uncertainty and thereby deters investment." Apart from these explicit costs, corruption leads to a "loss of trust and erodes the credibility of legal enforcement, reduces the transparency of governance, deteriorates the fairness of the judicial system, and increases the likelihood of opportunistic activity" (Lin et al. 2015, p. 3). Empirically, it has been verified that corruption obstructs the growth by driving down private investment and worsening the structure of public expenditure (Mauro 1996, p. 104).

However, these evidences have been proved wrong by the East Asian experience. As stated by Campos et al. (2001, p. 20),

> In many of East Asia's miracle economies, corruption is said to be well organized and systematic so that the degree of predictability is relatively high and despite high levels of corruption, these miracle economies still managed to attract significantly higher levels of investment than other developing countries. The result: compared to many developing countries, these countries have grown faster despite corruption.

The above argument can be verified by the following figure (Fig. 4):

As per the Corruption Index issued by the Transparency International, a high index represents least corruption levels in a country and low index indicates high levels of corruption.

As the figure suggests, the developed nations such as Denmark (one of the least corrupt nations), Finland, Switzerland, USA have extremely low levels of corruption but still economic growth is low. However, a comparison can be drawn with East Asian countries like Thailand, Indonesia, South Korea that are attributed with high levels of corruption, but at the same time, these countries have phenomenal rates of growth of GDP. In fact, according to the Transparency Report, Indonesia has been labeled as the most corrupt nation in 1995. But the "1997 Financial Crisis" challenged the nature of East Asian countries' success. Hence, we can say that the positive relation between corruption and rate of growth in the East Asian countries was altered post financial crisis.

In spite of the above arguments, Campos et al. (2001, p. 21) emphasize that "whatever the degree of predictability, more corruption necessarily means less investment. Hence, to justify corruption on the basis of the East Asian paradox is misleading."

The findings by Lin et al. (2015), Asiedu and Freeman (2009), Ali (2008), Campos et al. (2001, 1999), Mauro (1996), and other authors confirm the negative impact of corruption on growth by reducing investments.

Considering the relationship between corruption and investment, Indian states have also been analyzed on the basis of the extent of corruption in addition to the cost and solar policies.

Fig. 4 Corruption level and Economic growth rate of specific countries in 1995. *Data Source* World Bank Data, Transparency International Corruption Index (1995)

3 Methodology

The methodology involves the following steps: Six Indian states were chosen on the basis of solar potential, followed by the calculation of CUFs. Hence after, the cost of generating solar power (LCOE) is calculated, compared to the bidding results of each state, calculated new LCOE, and ranked the states. Next, state solar policies are analyzed, constructed a binary ranking system, followed by a weighted ranking system. Subsequently, using the ranking of states as given by Transparency International, India, states are ranked on the basis of the extent of corruption. Finally, a combined ranking is attained.

The study has been carried out for six different states of India, namely Rajasthan, Jammu & Kashmir, Gujarat, Karnataka, Haryana, and Tripura. These states have been chosen on the basis of their solar potential given by the solar radiation received by the states. The following table displays state-wise potential of the states provided by MNRE, where four states belong to high potential zones and two belong to low potential zones (Table 1).

Table 1 State-wise estimated solar potential

States	Potential (GWp)
Rajasthan	142.31
Jammu & Kashmir	111.05
Gujarat	35.77
Karnataka	24.70
Haryana	4.56
Tripura	2.08

Source Ministry of New & Renewable Energy, Government of India

3.1 Costs

The next task involves calculating the cost of generating solar power for each state. For this purpose, LCOE is calculated using the following formula:

$$\frac{\sum_{t=1}^{n} \frac{I_t + M_t + L_t}{(1+r)^t}}{\sum_{t=1}^{n} \frac{E_t}{(1+r)^t}}$$

where I_t, M_t, L_t, and E_t represent investment expenditures in year t (including financing), operations, maintenance expenditures in year t, loan repayment, and total electricity generation in year t, respectively. In simpler words, LCOE is the total cost of generation divided by the amount generated. "It is a life-cycle cost concept which seeks to account for all physical assets and resources required to deliver one unit of electricity output" (Reichelstein and Yorston 2013, p. 5). In simpler words, it is a benchmarking or ranking tool that represents the "per-kilowatt hour cost of building and operating a power plant over an assumed financial life" (EIA 2014, p. 1).

Although LCOE is used widely by various authors to compare costs of renewable technology and conventional technology, it suffers from certain limitations such as

- "LCOE is a static measure that looks at price per generated energy, while true markets prices are dynamic" (Branker 2011, p. 4471).
- "Economic and financial systems have a large impact on the price of electricity, although the quality of electricity rarely changes, which is often not reflected by the LCOE" (Branker 2011, p. 4471).
- Comparing LCOE across diverse technologies is not an easy task, and the results can be deceiving.

But weighing the advantages of LCOE over its disadvantages, the concept is used in the study.

The calculations were performed using two LCOE calculation models obtained by Prayas Energy and Indian Power Industry. The results obtained from both the models came out to be identical. The capacity utilization factor (CUF), capital cost, debt–equity ratio, loan repayment period, interest on loan, depreciation, return on equity, discount rate, interest on working capital, O&M expenses escalation (%) p.a. have been used to calculate cost of generating solar power (Tables 9 and 10).

Out of the above parameters, CUF is a technical parameter and the rest are financial parameters. The values of CUF were calculated using commercial PVsyst software performed using 10 MW grid-connected PV power plant.

Incorporating the values of the above parameters from each SERC's tariff order for the year 2015–16 into the LCOE calculation model, tariffs are calculated for each state. These calculated tariffs, based on state specifications, are considered as a ceiling tariff, since in reality, the tariffs that the developers bid for solar projects are much lower. Hence, these bidding results are also considered and an adjusted LCOE which can be termed as a best possible scenario is calculated by integrating the low-cost components of various state tariff orders, interest on loan from Indian Renewable Energy Development Agency (IREDA), accelerated depreciation (AD) benefit for all states, low module price trend for 2015–16.

Finally, combining the LCOE and adjusted LCOE, the states are ranked.

3.2 Solar Policies

Since the initiation of Jawaharlal Nehru National Solar Mission (JNNSM) in 2010, the central government, along with the state governments, has laid out a policy framework that can be implemented effectively. Some of the state governments had announced few initiatives to promote solar power, well before the initiation of the JNNSM. Policies such as mandatory Renewable Purchase Obligation (RPO), introduction of effective mechanisms for Renewable Energy Certification (REC), modernization of technologies and improving manufacturing capabilities by the means of easy loans to firms, promoting the establishment of solar parks have been some of the major highlights of JNNSM.

In this section, these policies and sub-policies of each state government are analyzed and tabulated. To rank the states on the basis of policy strength, binary indices are allotted to each policy. These indices are then summed up and normalized to get a ranking. As the next step, to make the study more profound, weights were fixed to some of the policies and then a final ranking was arrived at.

3.3 Corruption

As already discussed in the second section of the paper that corruption is a sociopolitical factor that adversely affects investment decision, it has been incorporated into the study to make it more inclusive.

Transparency International is an international non-governmental organization with the mission to eradicate corruption and prevent all the activities that stem out of

Table 2 Classification of states on the basis of extent of corruption in the electricity sector

Extent of corruption	Alarming	Very high	High	Moderate
States	Jammu & Kashmir	Rajasthan	Tripura	Gujarat, Karnataka, Haryana

Source CMS (2008, p. 94)

corruption. The organization issues a "Corruption Perceptions Index" that measures the level of public sector corruption globally that is based on the opinion of experts.

The study makes use of the classification of states in terms of corruption in the electricity service domain, a study designed and conducted by CMS and issued by the Transparency International, India, in its India Corruption Study (2008), given in Table 2. The relative positioning of the states has been attained by considering "both the perception of the BPL families regarding corruption as well as the actual payment of bribe in the Electricity service" (CMS 2008, p. 94) which is based on "CRISIL and ICRA performance rating" of states in power sector.

The states are thus ranked on the basis of the extent of corruption as classified by Transparency International, India.

3.4 Final Rankings

Summing up and normalizing all the rankings on the basis of LCOE, policy strength, and extent of corruption, final ranking of states is generated which indicates the most attractive state in terms of investments in solar power and the least attractive.

4 Result and Analysis

4.1 Cost

For the calculation of LCOE, data from various state electricity regulation commissions was obtained for the year 2015–16. The simulation of CUF, performed using PVsyst for the states, was used as an input in calculating LCOE.

For the year 2015–16, the capital cost of the states varied from Rs. 587 Lakhs/MW to Rs. 691 Lakhs/MW. Calculated CUF varied from 17.8 to 22%. Discount rate varied from 10.81% to 14.42%. Moderate variation in the interest on loan, depreciation rate, return on equity, interest on working capital, and O&M expenses has been observed. The calculated LCOE for each state has been summarized in Table 3.

Table 3 State-wise calculated LCOE

State	Calculated tariff (Rs/unit)
Rajasthan	6.07
Jammu & Kashmir	6.53
Gujarat	5.75
Karnataka	6.93
Haryana	7.03
Tripura	6.76

On January 20, 2016, Business Standard reported the result of bidding for a new low solar tariff of Rs 4.34 per unit for a solar project of 420 MW in Rajasthan (Jai, 2016). The quoted tariff, bided by a Finnish solar power company, is the "lowest bid received in solar power projects so far" as per the report.

As can be noticed, the bidding tariff is way lower than the LCOE calculated using the SERC's guidelines. Such divergence between the calculated and bidding tariff has been observed in all the states considered.

The possible justifications for such low bidding tariffs can be:

- AD benefit:

AD benefit is a tax incentive offered to the developers in which case "a company can claim 80% accelerated depreciation in the first year of installation under section 80 IC of the Indian Income Tax Code, leading to savings on income tax" (Bridge To India 2014, p. 16). The AD benefit provides huge relief to the developer by cutting the upfront cost of solar power generation through lowering the overall tax burden.

- Low-interest rates:

The SERC's guidelines mention interest rate on loan within the interval of 12.5% to 13.75%. However, it has been noted that financial institutions such as IREDA, Asian Development Bank lend capital at much lower rates of interest. For instance, IREDA provides loans to developers with high credit ratings at interest rates as low as 10.20% as well. As RBI is cutting down interest rates, the interest rates offered by various financial institutions for solar projects are becoming competitive.

- Dipping PV module prices:

A PV module is an interconnection of several solar cells that absorb solar energy to be converted into electricity. China ranks first among the countries that manufacture solar modules "with 98% of its product shipped overseas" (Center for Study of Science, Technology & Policy, 2015, p. 2). Recent market events have suggested that in China, a situation of oversupply of PV modules is taking place. Moreover, as a result of substantial depreciation of the Chinese Yuan with respect to Indian Rupee, the cost of solar modules has been falling steeply (Bridge To India 2016). The Mercom Capital Group has expected a decline in the module prices from Rs. 353.72 Lakhs/MW in November 2015 to Rs. 240.26 Lakhs/MW in November 2016. Whereas, the cost of PV modules proposed by the Central Electricity Regulatory

Table 4 State-wise ranking on the basis of LCOE

State	Ranking
Rajasthan	2
Jammu & Kashmir	3
Gujarat	1
Karnataka	5
Haryana	6
Tripura	4

Commission (CERC) for the year 2015–16 is Rs 310.19 lakhs/MW. These prices are expected to fall even more. Such a dip in the module prices within a year brings down the cost of generating solar power.

Adjusting for the above-mentioned elements, an adjusted LCOE is calculated and tabulated (Table 11), which was found to be in line with the bidding tariff (except for the state of Karnataka).[1]

As can be interpreted from Table 11, the cost of generating power through solar energy is the lowest in Gujarat, followed by Rajasthan. The two states lead the list in both the cases—when we calculate LCOE based on the parameters decided by SERCs as well as adjusted tariff based on the modifications regarding low bidding tariffs. Summing up and normalizing the cost calculations, we arrive at a raking of the sates shown in Table 4.

4.2 Solar Policies

"JNNSM was launched with two main objectives—To solarise India through addition of 20,000 MW by 2022 under the JNNSM; and to have a thriving solar PV manufacturing industry by having 4000–5000 MW of annual capacity domestically by 2020" (Chaturvedi 2012).

The launch of JNNSM in 2010 has brought the solar sector to the forefront in the list of priorities of the state and central governments. Up till then, India, although being a solar-rich country, could not exploit the source to the fullest due to the lack of proper financial, technological, institutional, and other support systems. Hence for a sustained growth of the solar sector, substantial support was needed which was one of the crucial objectives of JNNSM. Under JNNSM, to harness the solar potential of each state, state-specific solar policies have been launched, out of which RPO targets, facilitation of land allotment, status of industry, tax exemption, sharing of CDM benefit, assistance in clearance of project have been considered for each of the six states (Tables 12 and 13) for analysis in the study.

[1] A likely justification can be low CUF value (17.8%), leading to higher tariff.

Table 5 State-wise RPO targets for 2015–16

States	RPO Target (%)*
Rajasthan	2
Jammu & Kashmir	1.5
Gujarat	1.5
Karnataka	0.25
Haryana	0.38
Tripura	1.1

Source Respective state solar power policy
Note *Percentage of total consumption of electricity

4.2.1 RPO Targets

RPO has been one of the leading forces in India to promote the solar energy sector. RPO is defined as a minimum percentage of electricity generated through renewable sources of energy that has to be purchased by electricity distribution agencies. Such a mechanism enables the existence of a market for renewable source of electricity even when markets are not favorable for renewable power. "While the National Action Plan on Climate Change (NAPCC) has set an ambitious RPO target of 15% by 2020, it is the state electricity regulatory commissions (SERCs) that set year-wise targets in their respective states" (Gambhir et al. 2013). Table 5 represents the RPO targets of the six states chosen.

The RPO targets for Rajasthan are the highest, followed by Jammu & Kashmir and Gujarat. Such high RPO targets indicate the importance these states are assigning to the solar sector.

4.2.2 Facilitation of Land Allotment

Considering that land is scarce and hence it is important to allocate land efficiently, land allotment policies have been put in place by the government. Allotment of government and private land for setting up of solar power projects, conversion of non-agricultural land as well as permitting the purchase of agricultural lands to facilitate the development of solar power projects, preparation of Land Banks by the Nodal Agency, development of solar parks, etc., have been some of the policy initiatives taken by various SERCs.

4.2.3 Status of Industry

A few states have approved to grant the solar power sector, the status of industry in terms of industrial policy of that state, so that the solar sector can avail schemes and incentives available to industrial units. Eligible producers of solar power would be provided infrastructural services such as approach road, supply of water, availability of power during construction period that are offered to industrial units.

4.2.4 Tax Exemption

According to this policy, the solar power producer would be exempted from paying any Central Excise Duty and Custom Duty, entry tax to the government on power generation, royalty in the shape of free power for solar projects, exemption from obtaining clearances of pollution control board, exemption from land use charges, external development charges, scrutiny fee and infrastructure development charges, exemption from electricity duty, sales tax exemption, and other exemptions.

4.2.5 Sharing of Clean Development Mechanism (CDM) Benefit

CDM was introduced by the Kyoto protocol in 1997 which has been "a key part of international emissions reductions agreements, allowing rich countries in the North to invest in emissions-saving projects in the South while they continue to emit CO_2. According to Dr. Hugh Sealy, chairman of the Executive Board of the CDM, it has generated 396 billion dollars in financial flows from developed to developing countries" (Rajalakshmi 2012). The revenues generated from the solar projects are affected by the CDM benefit. Some of the states allow the developer to retain 100% CDM benefit, whereas others allow for a sharing of CDM sharing.

4.2.6 Assistance in Clearance of Project

Setting up solar project involves various clearances and approvals from the state governments. Most of the state solar policies have accorded support to the developers to facilitate the process of setting up of solar power projects. For instance, Rajasthan Solar Policy 2014 allows for "Fast-track process of approval of Mega Solar Power Projects (500 MW or more) by placing them directly before State Level Empowered Committee headed by Chief Secretary."

Analyzing the above six broad policy initiatives by each of the government of the six states considered, a binary ranking system is prepared.

The binary ranking table is a quite basic since it is a mere indication of whether a particular policy exists in the policy document of a state or not. However, two possible critiques of the above framework can be pointed out as follows:

- The strength of policy is difficult to judge since no weights are assigned regarding the intensity of each policy.
- Three out of six states have the same rank; hence, an exact distinction among the states is difficult to carry out.

Table 6 State-wise ranking on the basis of policy strength

State	Ranking
Rajasthan	4
Jammu & Kashmir	3
Gujarat	6
Karnataka	5
Haryana	2
Tripura	1

Keeping in mind the above-stated shortcomings, we develop a weighted binary system which is an improvement over the above ranking system. For this purpose, we attempt to attach weights to the RPO targets of each state (Table 14) and prepare a binary ranking system once again for the land allotment sub-policy (Table 15).

Incorporating weighted RPO targets as well as weighted land allotment policy into the original ranking system, a final ranking framework of the states is obtained, as depicted in Table 16. The final ranks obtained on the basis of policy strength are presented in the following table.

4.3 Corruption

As already discussed, corruption has a significant adverse impact on investments, and hence, inclusion of this sociopolitical factor will help make the study more inclusive. The classification of states on the basis of extent of corruption issued by Transparency International, India, has been given in Table 2. The states are ranked on the basis of the said classification that is presented in Table 7. The states have been ranked on the following basis:

- Alarming—4
- Very High—3
- High—2
- Moderate—1

Summing up and normalizing the rankings from Tables 4, 6, and 7, a final set of rankings for the states is arrived at which is presented in Table 8.

As per the final rankings, Tripura has emerged as the best state for investment in solar power, followed by Gujarat and Rajasthan. Although Tripura is one of the lowest solar potential states, to promote solar energy and to meet its RPO target, the Tripura State Government is offering all kinds of incentives to the producers of solar power. The added benefit of low intensity of corruption and moderate LCOE has benefitted the state. However, such a high ranking for Tripura might be misleading since a separate solar power policy does not exist for the state due to which the policy initiatives used in the study for Tripura are not leading to appropriate results. Secondly, the bidding tariff data is not available for Tripura, and due to geographical

Table 7 State-wise ranking on the basis of extent of corruption

State	Ranking
Rajasthan	3
Jammu & Kashmir	4
Gujarat	1
Karnataka	1
Haryana	1
Tripura	2

Table 8 Final state-wise ranking based on LCOE, policy strength, and extent of corruption

State	Ranking
Tripura	1
Gujarat	2
Rajasthan	3
Haryana	3
Jammu & Kashmir	4
Karnataka	5

and other constraints, considering a best possible scenario (as done for all the states uniformly) might be a flawed assumption.

On the other hand, Gujarat is a high solar potential state with an already developed solar sector. So the state government might have refrained from offering any additional incentive for the producers since Gujarat has been one of the few states that foresaw the potential of solar; hence, it was the only state that came up with a solar-dedicated policy in as early as 2009, and in spite of the high solar prices prevailing during those years, the state witnessed substantial investments. Hence presently, the state government might believe that it will attract huge investments even if the state does not provide the best of policy incentives. Keeping the state of Tripura aside (owing to the limitations discussed), Gujarat and Rajasthan should be considered as the best choice for an investor to invest in solar power among the states examined in the study.

The Government of Jammu & Kashmir, the most solar-rich state in India, has performed poorly. The policies of the government and other political issues such as the ongoing territorial conflicts have been major hindrances. The result obtained from the analysis is consistent with the real situation in the state. As per Verma (2016) and Sharma (2016), in 2014, the state has sanctioned (and received approval from the State Cabinet) two ultra-mega solar projects of 5 GW and 2.5 GW in Leh and Kargil, respectively; however, till now, there has been no progress vis-à-vis the setting up of solar power projects in the cities. Hence, "Despite having the second highest solar power potential in the country, Jammu and Kashmir has drawn a blank in solar power generation, mainly due to lack of seriousness and failure of successive governments to clear administrative bottlenecks" (Sharma 2016).

The states of Haryana and Karnataka have a long way to go to achieve their solar targets since the existing policies have proved to be insufficient in making the solar power sector attractive to the investors.

5 Conclusion, Limitations, and Further Scope

With an ever-expanding population of India and increasing reliance on energy-intensive lifestyle, a switch from conventional to renewable sources of energy is crucial for overall growth of the country. Being a solar-rich country, utilizing the solar energy resource to the fullest is not just required, rather is the need for the hour. A significant step toward reaching the target has been the launch of JNNSM in 2010. The pragmatism of the ambitious target of installing 100 GW of solar power under the mission has been questioned often; however, a positive scaling up of the total installed capacity cannot be overlooked. The remarkable fall of solar tariffs from around "Rs. 17.90 per unit in 2010 to about Rs. 7 per unit in 2015" (Rachit 2016, p. 20) verifies the progress of the solar sector since the launch of JNNSM.

Considering the bright future of solar systems in India, the paper examined three major factors, namely LCOE, state solar policies, and the extent of corruption, that determine the inflow of investments in the solar power sector. Six states have been chosen that represent solar-rich as well as solar-deficient states. After making various adjustments and modifications, the result arrived at can be termed as reasonable as well as coherent.

The result of the analysis, in terms of ranking of states, has been of interest. According to the final ranking, Tripura emerged as the top state for solar investments. However, Gujarat and Rajasthan are not behind since the two states have benefitted from being first movers in the solar sector. Jammu & Kashmir, the state with second largest solar potential, has failed to harness the resource endowment to the optimal level. High corruption level can be a factor responsible for little interest in the investors.

While attempts were made to avoid any systematic error, nonetheless, the study is not free from limitations. First and foremost, data is a major constraint since solar tariff orders by several SERCs for the latest years is not available. Using proxy data for such states might alter the results. Data on solar power project bidding results is not readily available for certain states like Jammu & Kashmir, Tripura for some years. A separate solar policy for the state of Tripura is not available, so solar-specific policies from the policy document titled "Policy for Promoting Generation of Electricity through New and Renewable Energy Sources in Tripura" were used together with few policies intended for renewable energy in general. Second, the CUF values simulated are calculated for a particular city within the state, whereas the CUF can vary within a state as well, especially for a large state such as Rajasthan or Jammu & Kashmir. Finally, the framework designed to rank solar policy strength for the states is somewhat basic. A more precise assessment is needed to be done in depth for each solar policy.

The study undertaken has a huge scope for further research. The first extension to the work is to widen the number of states analyzed. An overall picture of the ranking of all the states of the country would provide a comprehensive analysis. Next, including other determinants of investment such as profitability of developer, population of each state, energy consumed in a state, economic growth, or per capita income levels of each state would make the study broader. A weighted analysis of the work can be performed by attaching weights to each factor to look at the level of impact a factor has on total investments. Finally, the study can be carried out for other sources of renewable sources of energy too that have a scope to grow in the country.

Appendix

See Tables 9, 10, 11, 12, 13, 14, 15 and 16.

Table 9 Tariff determination for solar PV in Rajasthan, Jammu & Kashmir, Gujarat for FY 2015–16

	Rajasthan	Jammu & Kashmir	Gujarat
Tariff period (years)	25		
Capital cost (Lakh Rs./MW)	596.80	691	600
Debt–equity ratio	70:30	70:30	70:30
CUF (%)	20	22	17.8
Loan repayment period (Years)	12	12	12
Interest on loan (% p. a.)	13	13.25	12.5
Depreciation (%)	5.83 (First 12 Yrs) 1.54 (Thereafter)	5.83 1.54 (Thereafter)	5.83 (First 12 Yrs) 1.54 (Thereafter)
Return on equity (% p. a.)	16	18 (for 1st 10 Yrs) 22 (Thereafter)	16
Discount rate (%)	10.89	10.92	13.55
Interest on working capital (% p. a.)	12.50	13.75	13.25
O&M expenses (Lakh Rs/MW)	13	12.29	13
Escalation (% p.a.)	5.85	5.72	5.72
Calculated tariff	6.07	6.53	6.93

Table 10 Tariff determination for solar PV in Karnataka, Haryana, Tripura for FY 2015–16

	Karnataka	Haryana	Tripura
Tariff period (years)	25		
Capital cost (Lakh Rs./MW)	Rs. 600	Rs. 681	Rs. 587.33
Debt–equity ratio	70:30	70:30	70:30
CUF (%)	17.8	19.4	19
Loan repayment period (Years)	12	10	12
Interest on loan (% p. a.)	12.5	13.75	12.30
Depreciation (%)	5.83 (First 12 Yrs) 1.54 (Thereafter)	7 (First 12 Yrs) 1.54 (Thereafter)	5.83 (First 12 Yrs) 1.54 (Thereafter)
Return on equity (% p. a.)	16	16	20 (for 1st 10 Yrs) 24 (Thereafter)
Discount rate (%)	13.55	14.42	10.81
Interest on working capital (%p. a.)	13.25	14	12.80
O&M expenses (Lakh Rs/MW)	13	9	13
Escalation (% p.a.)	5.72	5.72	5.72
Calculated tariff	6.93	7.03	6.76

Table 11 Calculated LCOE, bidding tariff, and adjusted LCOE

State	Calculated tariff (Rs/unit)	Bidding tariff (Rs/unit)	Adjusted tariff (Rs/unit)
Rajasthan	6.07	4.34	4.26
Jammu & Kashmir	6.53	4.43	4.29
Gujarat	5.75	4.43	4.06
Karnataka	6.93	4.43	4.89
Haryana	7.03	4.34	4.28
Tripura	6.76	4.43	4.42

Table 12 Solar policy for Rajasthan and Jammu & Kashmir

Solar policy	Rajasthan	Jammu & Kashmir	Gujarat
Land allotment	• Allotment of land for the development of solar park in the state • Allotment of Government and private land to solar developers • No requirement for land conversion for setting up solar power plant	• Creation of land banks • Provision of Government land to solar developers • In case of non-availability of Government land, the land to be arranged by Science & Tech. department J&KEDA	–

(continued)

Table 12 (continued)

Solar policy	Rajasthan	Jammu & Kashmir	Gujarat
Status of industry	Generation of electricity from solar power plant to be treated as industry and all the incentives provided to industries will be applicable to solar developers	–	–
Tax exemption	–	• Exemption from court fee for registration of documents for lease of land • No entry tax to be levied by the State Government	Exemption from payment of electricity duty for sale of power
CDM benefits	–	–	100% retained by the developer
Assistance in clearance of project	• Government to assist in providing clearances by state government • Fast-track approval of Mega Solar Power Projects	• Government to facilitate obtaining clearances and approvals for solar projects • Assist the developer to get approval of the state transmission utility for interconnection	–

Table 13 Solar policy for Haryana and Tripura

Solar policy	Karnataka	Haryana	Tripura
Land allotment	• Government to facilitate conversion of land for solar projects • Creation of Land banks • The State Government to purchase agricultural land for solar projects	Government to facilitate setting up of solar power projects on panchayat land	Conversion of non-agricultural land to be allowed
Status of industry	–	Generation of electricity from solar power plant to be treated as industry and all the incentives provided to industries will be applicable to solar developers	Generation of electricity from solar power plant to be treated as industry and all the incentives provided to industries will be applicable to solar developers

(continued)

Table 13 (continued)

Solar policy	Karnataka	Haryana	Tripura
Tax exemption	Exemption from obtaining clearances from pollution control board, exemption from custom duties, etc.	Exemption from land use charges, external development charges, etc.	Exemption from electricity duty and sales tax, etc.
CDM benefits	–	Sharing of CDM benefits as per Haryana Government regulations	Sharing of CDM benefits: (a) 100% CDM benefits to be retained by the project developer in the first year (b) In the second year, the share of the beneficiaries shall be 10% which shall be progressively increased by 10% every year till it reaches 50%
Assistance in clearance of project	Government to assist in providing clearances through necessary support	–	Facilitation of clearances and granting of loans to the new and renewable power projects

Table 14 Weighted RPO targets

States	RPO target (%)	Weighted RPO
Rajasthan	2	1
Jammu & Kashmir	1.5	0.8
Gujarat	1.5	0.8
Karnataka	0.25	0.2
Haryana	0.38	0.2
Tripura	1.1	0.6

Table 15 Binary ranking system for land allotment policy

States	Land allotment				Total
	Setting up of solar power plant on private land	Land bank	Conversion of land	Exemption from charges	
Rajasthan	1	0	0	0	0.25
Jammu & Kashmir	1	1	0	1	0.75
Gujarat	0	0	0	0	0
Karnataka	1	1	1	0	0.75
Haryana	1	0	0	1	0.5
Tripura	0	0	1	0	0.25

Table 16 Final state-wise policy strength ranking

States	Solar policies								Ranking
	RPO target	Land allotment	Status of industry	Tax exemption	CDM benefits	Assistance in clearance of project	Total	Normalized values	
Rajasthan	1	0.25	1	0	0	1	3.25	0.54	4
Jammu & Kashmir	0.8	0.75	0	1	0	1	3.55	0.59	3
Gujarat	0.8	0	0	1	1	0	2.8	0.46	6
Karnataka	0.2	0.75	0	1	0	1	2.95	0.49	5
Haryana	0.2	0.5	1	1	1	0	3.7	0.61	2
Tripura	0.6	0.25	1	1	1	1	4.85	0.80	1

References

Ali, N. (2008). Corruption and it's impact on economic growth: Is East Asia special? University of Western Australia Business School.

Asiedu, E., & Freeman, J. (2009). The effect of corruption on investment growth: Evidence from firms in Latin America, Sub-Saharan Africa, and transition countries. *Review of Development Economics, 13*(2), 200–214.

Branker, K., Pathak, M. J. M., & Pearce, J. M. (2011). A review of solar photovoltaic levelized cost of electricity. *Renewable and Sustainable Energy Reviews, 15*(9), 4470–4482.

Bridge To India. (2014). *India solar handbook* (pp. 4–28).

Bridge To India. (2016). Sharp fall in PV module prices to help the Indian solar sector. Retrieved Apr 22, 2017 from http://www.bridgetoindia.com/sharp-fall-in-pv-module-prices-to-help-the-indian-solar-sector/.

Buckley, T. (2015). India's Electricity-Sector Transformation. Retrieved from Institute for Energy Economics and Financial Analysis website. http://ieefa.org/wp-content/uploads/2015/08/IEEFA-Indian-Electricity-Sector-Transformation-11-August-2015.pdf.

Campos, J. E., Lien, D., & Pradhan, S. (2001). Corruption and its implications for investment. *Corruption: The Boom and Bust of East Asia, 1990*, 11.

Campos, J. E., Lien, D., & Pradhan, S. (1999). The impact of corruption on investment: Predictability matters. *World Development, 27*(6), 1059–1067.

Chaturvedi, V. (2012). Give infrastructure status to solar PV industry. Retrieved Apr 25, 2017 from http://www.thehindubusinessline.com/info-tech/give-infrastructure-status-to-solar-pv-industry/article2988438.ece.

Centre for Media Studies. (2008). India Corruption Study. Issued by Transparency International India.

Devabhaktuni, V., Alam, M., Depuru, S. S. S. R., Green, R. C., Nims, D., & Near, C. (2013). Solar energy: Trends and enabling technologies. *Renewable and Sustainable Energy Reviews, 19*, 555–564.

Earth Policy Institute. (2010). World on the Edge—Energy Data—World Energy Profile. Retrieved May 9, 2017 from https://www.google.co.in/url?sa=t&rct=j&q=&esrc=s&source=web&cd=1&ved=0ahUKEwj_hebo6eLTAhXLNY8KHVtNDWkQFgghMAA&url=http%3A%2F%2Fwww.earth-policy.org%2Fdatacenter%2Fxls%2Fbook_wote_energy_world_profile.xls&usg=AFQjCNFvJV9HFXfBE8V7KNrEQ7CWv8idSA&sig2=EXNKQfq39lsKS0W_xinKsg&cad=rja.

EIA, U. (2014) Levelized Cost and Levelized Avoided Cost of New Generation Resources in the Annual Energy Outlook.

Enerdata. (2016). Total World Energy Consumption. Global Energy Statistical Yearbook.

Eyraud, L., Wane, A. A., Zhang, C., & Clements, B. (2011). Who's going green and why? Trends and determinants of green investment. *IMF Working Paper.*

Gambhir, A., Toro, V., & Dixit, S. (2013). Realities of renewable energy in India. Retrieved Apr 24, 2017 from http://www.livemint.com/Opinion/xzO6GshWpFfxPqywqzhNWJ/Realities-of-renewable-energy-in-India.html.

Iyer, R. (2016, November 21). Challenges in India's Path To 100 GW Solar Power By 2022. Retrieved Apr 21, 2017 from http://www.marketexpress.in/2016/11/challenges-in-indias-path-to-100-gw-solar-power-by-2022.html.

Jai, S. (2016). Rajasthan solar bids touch a new low of Rs 4.34 per unit. Retrieved May 11, 2017 from http://www.business-standard.com/article/economy-policy/rajasthan-solar-bids-touch-a-new-low-of-rs-4-34-per-unit-116011900319_1.html.

Jung, J., & Tyner, W. E. (2014). Economic and policy analysis for solar PV systems in Indiana. *Energy Policy, 74*, 123–133.

Kost, C., Mayer, J. N., Thomsen, J., Hartmann, N., Senkpiel, C., Philipps, S., et al. (2013). Levelized cost of electricity renewable energy technologies. *Fraunhofer Institute for Solar Energy Systems ISE*.

Lin, C., Officer, M. S., & Sun, Z. (2015). Does the perception of corruption matter to investors?

Lüthi, S. (2008). *Investment behaviour of solar companies—determinants of foreign direct investment in an emerging clean tech industry*. Gallen: Institute for Economy and the Environment, University of St.

Mauro, P. (1996). The effects of corruption on growth, investment, and government expenditure.

MOSPI. (2016). Energy statistics, Central statistics office, Government of India.

Pearce, J. M. (2002). Photovoltaics—a path to sustainable futures. *Futures, 34*(7), 663–674.

Rachit, S., & Vinod, K. G. (2016). Solar power—current status, challenges and policies in India. *Research & Reviews: Journal of Engineering and Technology, 5*(2), 18–22.

Rajalakshmi. (2012). CDM benefits for Solar Power generation in India, CDM benefit per unit of solar power, how to apply, prospects and challenges of CDM for solar energy generators—EAI Club. Retrieved Apr 25, 2017 from http://www.eai.in/club/users/rajalakshmi/blogs/18501.

Reichelstein, S., & Yorston, M. (2013). The prospects for cost competitive solar PV power. *Energy Policy, 55* 117–127.

Ryan, L., Dillon, J., La Monaca, S., Byrne, J., & O'Malley, M. (2016). Assessing the system and investor value of utility-scale solar PV. *Renewable and Sustainable Energy Reviews, 64,* 506–517.

Sharma, A. (2016). State draws a blank in solar power generation. Retrieved Apr 28, 2017 from http://www.tribuneindia.com/news/jammu-kashmir/state-draws-a-blank-in-solar-power-generation/189023.html.

Sesmero, J., Jung, J., & Tyner, W. (2016). The effect of current and prospective policies on photovoltaic system economics: An application to the US Midwest. *Energy Policy, 93,* 80–95.

Šúri, M., Huld, T. A., Dunlop, E. D., & Ossenbrink, H. A. (2007). Potential of solar electricity generation in the European Union member states and candidate countries. *Solar Energy, 81*(10), 1295–1305.

Transparency International. (1995). 1995 TI Corruption Index. Retrieved from https://www.transparency.org/files/content/tool/1995_CPI_EN.pdf

Van Hemmen, H. (2011). Determinants of international solar panel adoption. *Environmental Science*.

Verma, M. (2016). J&K fails to harness solar power despite having 2nd highest potential in country. Retrieved Apr 28, 2017 from http://www.dailyexcelsior.com/jk-fails-to-harness-solar-power-despite-having-2nd-highest-potential-in-country/.

Urban Sprawl and Transport Sustainability on Highway Corridors Using Stake Holder Analysis

Twinkle Roy and Rahul Budhadev

Abstract The effects of overpopulation in India in the form of an increased pressure on infrastructure and land is well visible in the form of an exponentially increasing population migration in suburb areas and mushrooming of residential townships along highway corridors. The sustainability of this practice calls for an urgent exposition—although its nature is still exploratory, the challenges faced are crucial. This paper proposes a study relating the effect of overpopulation on the acquisition of land in and around the highways and the effect of this practice on the transportation sector. The paper employs a case study of the Mumbai-Pune Expressway to analyse the trickledown effect of overpopulation on the transport sustainability of the corridor. The failure of traffic management system in the corridor has been attributed to multiple reasons ranging from insufficient government funds, to repair and maintenance work, to inefficient traffic management infrastructure, but what has largely remained unspoken of is the explosion of population migration to the suburbs around the corridor, which is also a major potential reason for the unsustainable traffic flow along the corridor, with the corridor now facing a twin burden—that of inter-city trips as well as that of local trips originating from the growing residential blocks along the corridor. This hitherto ignored aspect behind the unsustainable transport flow along the corridor needs a further exploration. The chapter would also discuss strategic measures which could be used to address the challenge faced by commuters and enhance traffic management systems. Stakeholder analysis and financial trends to extrapolate density pressure on roads would be accounted for in the analysis.

Keywords Urban sprawl · Overpopulation · Traffic density

JEL Classification code B26 · C14 · C1

T. Roy (✉)
Strategy Research Unit, Reserve Bank of India, Mumbai, India
e-mail: twinkleroy.roy37@gmail.com

R. Budhadev
Model Risk Management Mumbai, Credit Suisse, Mumbai, India
e-mail: rahul.budhadev10@gmail.com

N. R. Bhanumurthy et al. (eds.), *Advances in Finance & Applied Economics*,
https://doi.org/10.1007/978-981-13-1696-8_4

The Changing Paradigms of Transport Planning

The Transport Paradox - Transport is unique as the only development sector that worsens as incomes rise. While sanitation, health, education and employment tend to improve through economic development, traffic congestion tends to worsen.

~Lloyd Wright, Transport Specialist, Asian

1 Development Bank

Transportation infrastructure is often described as the lifeline of an economy, owing to the major role it plays in economic growth. While this is true, the continuous increase in economic growth, urban population, incomes, and motorization are creating and intensifying new problems for the transportation sector, which were previously either non-existent or were too small to be heeded to. Transportation externalities like congestion, ambient air quality, GHG emissions, urban sprawl, and traffic crashes seem like a 'necessary evil' of an urban life today. There may be improved quality of life with the growing urbanization and economic growth, but along with it, the growth of such transportation externalities severely restricts the quality of life that urban centres offer. If not well managed, transportation externalities can also retard economic growth. New transport policy paradigms focus on building sustainable cities—with improved travel choice (multi-modal transit), efficient land use, and efficient pricing mechanisms that ensure that private motor usage covers full costs of externalities (Asian Development Bank 2009; Litman 1999).

- Is the developing world repeating the mistakes of the developed world?
  Conventional transport planning has largely been supply side. The great motorization era in the now developed world after the World War I, saw policy makers responding to transportation problems of congestion with more and more supply of capacity in the form of roadways and highways. The supply expansion of roadway infrastructure was based on traffic forecasts. It was believed that with the prediction of demand, supply of roadways could be expanded accordingly and that would solve the transportation woes. Peak hour congestion, however, got no better, in fact it grew worse by day, as more capacity meant the encouragement of more automobile ownership. It was in the late 1960s that the debate over supply side transport policies emerged in the Europe and the US. Unfortunately, the developing world today is following the same automobile oriented transit development patterns that the west followed in the past, with a disregard to Travel Demand Management (TDM) strategies, efficient travel choice, and efficient land use.
- A drift away from supply side transport policies
  The position against supply side transport policies was introduced in the 1960s by Downs (1962) and the famous traffic engineer Leeming (1969), through the concept of induced demand, which states that the creation of more roadways does not eliminate congestion, in fact, creates unnecessary trips and in some situations

causes urban sprawl. This is to say that a creation of roadway capacity enables commuters not only to take increased frequency of trips but also trips to farther destinations—something that they would have otherwise avoided. The reasoning behind this is rooted in the basic economic theory of supply and demand. When there is an increase in roadway capacity (supply), it reduces the generalized cost of travelling (price), in terms of reduced commute time (by temporary congestion alleviation) and reduced vehicle operating (fuel) costs. This decrease in price prompts an increased quantity of consumption—reflected in terms of increased travel demand, which is 'induced' in its nature. This induced travel imposes several costs like downstream congestion, accidents, parking costs, pollution, urban fringe development, and other environmental costs.

A lot of transport economists and experts describe the use of roadway expansion to combat congestion, as a 'self defeating' exercise in what is called today as the 'Downs Thompson Paradox'. The basic idea behind this paradox is that road capacity investments as a remedy for congestion can actually make overall congestion even worse. This occurs because when more road capacity is provided, more people get lured towards private motorization and there is a shift away from public transportation. The fact that lesser people would now use public transport, makes the public transit ineffective due to reduced frequency of public transit usage and increased fares by the operators who start suffering losses, which further pushes people towards private motorization, thus exacerbating congestion. A similar voice is also echoed in Downs' Principle of Triple Convergence (1992), which captures the difficulty of eliminating peak hour congestion from highways. According to this principle, if a congested highway is expanded in its capacity, the confluence of three effects, namely, the changes in routes, times and modes of travel will crowd out the congestion reduction benefits that the expansion would offer, making the highway as congested as before. These three effects can be explained as:

i Changes in routes—With an increase in capacity, commuters who were previously using alternative routes will shift to the now convenient highway.
ii Changes in time—The commuters who travelled off the peak hour to avoid peak hour congestion would now be enticed to shift to the peak hour.
iii Changes in modes—With an expanded capacity, some commuters who were hitherto using public transit may now find it convenient (and cheaper) to shift from public transit to private transit modes.

Ultimately, the lethal mix of these three effects would offset the congestion reduction benefits offered by the capacity expansion, thus implying the counter-productive nature of supply side transport policies. It should however be noted that this proposition does not mean that roadway capacity expansion has no benefits. With a capacity expansion, the road can carry more vehicles per hour than before, even if it is congested, so more people can commute it a point of time than before. It also reduces the congestion on other roads (Downs 2004). Thus, roadway expansion is a necessary but not a sufficient condition. Improved travel choice (multi-modal transit), efficient land use, and efficient pricing mechanisms

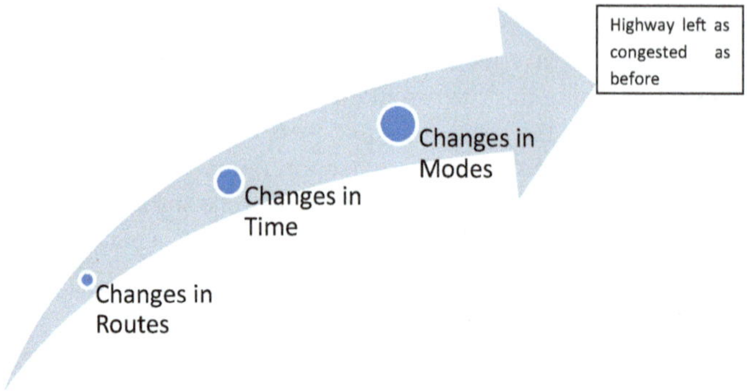

Fig. 1 Downs' principle of triple convergence (1992)

that ensure that private motor usage covers full costs of externalities must be concomitant to a roadway capacity expansion (Fig. 1).

- The New Paradigms
  Post the Brundtland Commission's Our Common Future (1987), the concept of sustainability has also seen itself venturing into transportation. Many definitions for sustainable transport exist and all of them embrace the three pillars of sustainability—social, economic, and environmental. The report "Sustainable Urban Transport in Asia" (2005) by the Partnership for Sustainable Urban Transport in Asia (PSUTA) describes sustainable urban transport as one that eases access and mobility for all groups of the society in a manner that is within the carrying capacity of the environment and is affordable to both the transport providers as well as the transport users. The concept of sustainability requires individual needs to be subordinate to community's long term strategic objectives (Litman 1999). Hence, sustainable transport essentially promotes both inter-generational as well as intra-generational equity across the three pillars of sustainability-social, economic and environmental. Any transport policy decision that transgresses such an equity would not be regarded as sustainable. Thus, whether it is high private motorization levels within the city, that penalizes pedestrians and non motorists, or automobile dependent urban fringe developments that penalize everyone using highways—anything that leaves equity (at an economic, social or environmental level) in jeopardy and does not account fully for the associated external costs generated, is not sustainable.
  One cannot have a highway built and simply assume it would be sustainable by just accounting for the financial costs if the associated congestion, accident, pollution and sprawl costs are ignored. If roadway capacity is implemented without Transport Demand Management (TDM) strategies like commute trip reduction programs, parking management, public transit improvements, rideshare programs, road pricing, congestion pricing, land use management policies, road space rationing etc., the planning cannot be said sustainable, since such a planning would overvalue the economic benefits of capacity increase and undervalue the negative effects.

Sustainable planning also requires that transport models designed for prediction of future traffic take into account the 'diverted traffic' (traffic on the now roadway due to shifts in travel time and route to use the now convenient new roadway) and 'induced traffic' (additional trips generated on the new roadway due to alteration in travel behavior in the form of increased trip frequency and trips to farther destinations, which would have otherwise not been taken), and thus incorporate 'full feedback' in their prediction models (Litman 2001). Omission of diverted and induced traffic (collectively called 'generated traffic') leads to inaccurate predictions and an undervaluation of the costs. Even more accurate are integrated models that take into account interrelationships between transport and land use patterns (Litman 2001). Ignoring all these would tend to skew planning in favour of highways, urban sprawl and automobile dependency.

Land use planning is becoming increasingly recognized as closely linked with sustainable transport planning. The link between land use and transport planning should be such that it reduces the need to travel and increases accessibility by the provision of a multi-modal public transport. Low density urban settlements, which are becoming a quintessential feature of urban life in the form of urban sprawl, are viewed as dangerous to sustainable urban transport. Not only do they make public transit modes ineffective, but also increase travel demand and automobile dependence. The concept of 'smart growth' which is gaining popularity, is based on promoting high density mixed use zoning with a multi-modal transport. The Asian Development Bank (2005) describes the two tools to promote such a smart growth in the form of an essential mix of 'carrots' and 'sticks'. While 'carrots' imply multi-modal public transit, 'sticks' imply the demand management tools.

The new paradigm also prioritizes accessibility over mobility. While mobility oriented approach aims at maximum movement of people, an accessibility oriented approach aims at improving the ability of people to reach the desired services and destinations. Mobility assumes that movement is an end in itself instead of being a means to an end. Accessibility, on the other hand is the ultimate aim of transportation. It promotes not only the interests of the motorists but also the non-motorists and gives consideration to optimal land use with multi-modal transport—both of which, the mobility centred approach ignores.

The following table, borrowed from Litman (1999) crisply brings out the distinction between the old paradigms and the new paradigms of transport planning.

Land Use Patterns & Transport Policies—The Essential Link to Understanding Highway Enabled Urban Sprawl and its Impact

> Sustainability planning is to development what preventive medicine is to health: it anticipates and manages problems rather than waiting for crises to develop. Just as preventive medicine requires individuals to be informed and motivated to maintain healthy habits, sustainable development requires that individuals be involved in community decisions and be rewarded for socially beneficial behaviours
>
> ~Todd Litman (1999), Executive Director, Victoria Transport Policy Insitute

The interaction between land use pattern and transportation is fundamental to sustainable urban transport planning. It is interesting to note how roadway expansions

Basis	Conventional planning	Sustainable planning
1. Transportation	Defines and measures transportation primarily in terms of vehicle travel	Defines and measures transportation in terms of access
2. Objectives	Maximize road and parking capacity to meet predicted traffic demand	Uses economic analysis to determine optimal policies and investments
3. Public involvement	Modest to moderate public involvement. Public is invited to comment at specific points in the planning process	Moderate to high public involvement. Public is involved at many points in the planning process
4. Facility costs	Considers costs to a specific agency or level of government	Considers all facility costs, including costs to other levels of government
5. User costs	Considers user time, vehicle operating costs, and fares or tolls	Considers user time, vehicle operating and ownership costs, fares and tolls
6. External costs	May consider local air pollution costs	Considers local and global air pollution, down-stream congestion, uncompensated accident damages, impacts on other road users, and other identified impacts
7. Equity	Considers a limited range of equity issues. Addresses equity primarily by subsidizing transit	Considers a wide range of equity issues. Favors transportation policies that improve access for non-drivers and disadvantaged populations
8. Travel demand	Defines travel demand based on existing user costs	Defines travel demand as a function, based on various levels of user costs
9. Generated traffic/induced travel	Ignores altogether, or may incorporate limited feedback into modelling	Takes generated traffic into account in modelling and economic evaluation of alternative policies and investments
10. Integration with strategic planning	Considers community land use plans as an input to transportation modelling	Individual transportation decisions are selected to support community's strategic vision. Transportation decisions are recognized as having land use impacts
11. Investment policy	Based on existing funding mechanisms that target money by mode	Least-cost planning allows resources to be used for the most cost-effective solution
12. Pricing	Road and parking facilities are free, or priced for cost recovery	Road and parking facilities are priced for cost recovery and based on marginal costs to encourage economic efficiency
13. Transportation demand management	Uses TDM only where increasing roadway or parking capacity is considered infeasible (i.e., large cities and central business districts)	Implements TDM wherever possible. Capacity expansion only occurs where TDM is not cost effective. Considers a wide range of TDM strategies

Source Litman (1999)

can alter travel behaviour and preferences of commuters, and contribute to sprawl in the long run. Litman (2001) has provided a comprehensive typology of such alteration in the behaviour of commutes with respect to roadway expansion. While diverted trips from off peak hour and alternative routes is known to have short term impact, the induced trips which alter the land use and modal choice have long term impact. With the cost of trips reducing with highway expansion, longer trips may be generated and

Table 1 Litman (2001)'s typology of generated traffic

Type of generated traffic	Category	Time frame	Travel impacts	Cost impacts
Shorter route improved road allows drivers to use more direct route	Diverted trip	Short term	Small reduction	Reduction
Longer route improved road attracts traffic from more direct routes	Diverted trip	Short term	Small increase	Slight increase
Time change reduced peak period congestion reduces the need to defer trips to off-peak periods	Diverted trip	Short term	None	Slight increase
Mode shift; existing travel choices improved traffic flow makes driving relatively more attractive than other modes	Induced vehicle trip	Short term	Increased driving	Moderate to large increase
Mode shift; changes in travel choice less demand leads to reduced rail and bus service, less suitable conditions for walking and cycling, and more automobile ownership	Induced vehicle trip	Long term	Increased driving, reduced alternatives	Large increase, reduced equity
Destination change; existing land use reduced travel costs allow drivers to choose farther destinations. No change in land use patterns	Longer trip	Short term	Increase	Moderate to large increase
Destination change; land use changes improved access allows land use changes, especially urban fringe development	Longer trip	Long term	More driving and auto dependency	Moderate to large increase, equity costs
New trip; no land use changes improved travel time allows driving to substitute for non-travel activities	Induced trip	Short term	Increase	Large increase
Automobile dependency synergetic effects of increased automobile oriented land use and transportation system	Induced trip	Long term	Increased driving, fewer alternatives	Large increase, reduced equity

Source Litman (2001)

people are induced to choose farther destinations, increasing the total Vehicle Miles Travelled (VMT). In the long term, such behaviours alter the land use patterns and automobile dependency as improved access enables people to choose housing and workplaces farther away. Thus, highway expansion stimulates more dispersed, low density, automobile dependent urban fringes (Table 1).

Such automobile dependent urban fringe development transfers the environmental costs to the society at large in the long term, with the society now having to combat more pollution, congestion, and accidents with the increased automobile use. Such low density developments also make public transit and non motorized modes inef-

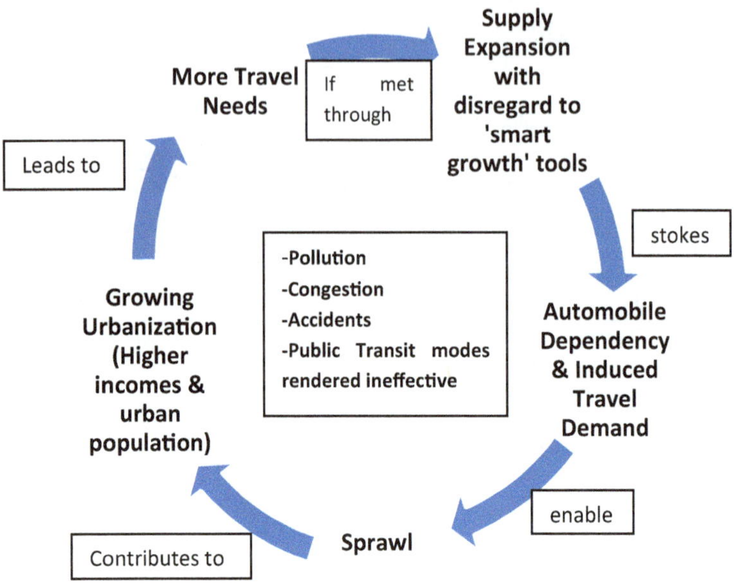

Fig. 2 Vicious circle of unsustainable cities. *Source* Author's own work

fective, and thus creates inequity of access to those who are private vehicle deprived, at the cost of those who are rich and can afford private motorization.

2 Conclusion

How are these transport patterns socially, economically, and environmentally sustainable?
With economic growth and continuous influx in urban population, sprawl keeps growing with more and more people able to buy housing that develops on the urban fringes. This, thus, takes the form of a vicious cycle where more incomes and urban population leads to increased travel needs, which if met by supply expansion and a disregard to the tools of 'smart growth' stokes automobile dependency and induced travel demand, which enables low density sprawling patterns, which further contributes to growing urbanization. As this cycle progresses, the community has to bear the growing negative spill-overs of pollution, congestion, accidents, and ineffectiveness of public transit modes. This brings us to the question of how sustainable are such transport policies after all? (Fig. 2).

It is to be noted that the above vicious cycle does not suggest that highway expansion is a causal force for sprawl. Urban sprawl is a complex phenomenon and is a consequence of a plethora of other factors that might be unrelated to transportation. Since urban sprawl is a difficult concept to quantify, empirical evidence to suggest that highway expansion causes sprawl is mixed, and the relationship between land use and transportation continues to elude empirical researchers. However, most researches while explaining the expansion of metropolitan areas in the United States over the twentieth century recognize highway expansion at least as an enabling force to the increased (and still increasing) suburbanization in the United States.The degree to which additional highway expansion contributes to sprawl by reducing transportation costs and improved accessibilities is, however still debated among empirical researchers (Handy 2005). A great extent of this relationship also varies from region to region with different data sets. Handy (2005) analyses the empirical evidences available and concludes: "Highway building thus appears to contribute to sprawl not by increasing the rate of growth but by influencing where in the region development occurs and by influencing the character of the development that occurs" (Handy 2005). It would also be insightful to quote a 1995 report published by the Transportation Research Board, as cited by Handy (2005): "Major highway capacity additions are likely to have larger effects on travel and to increase emission in the affected transportation corridors in the long run unless some mitigating strategy is implemented in conjunction with the capacity addition".

References

Asian Development Bank. (2009). *Changing Course—A New Paradigm for Sustainable Urban Transport. Philippines: Asian Development Bank*. Retrieved January 11, 2016 from http://www.adb.org/sites/default/files/publication/27552/new-paradigm-transport.pdf.

Definition of Overpopulation. Retrieved from http://stats.oecd.org/glossary/detail.asp?ID=1978.

Downs, A. (1992). In *Stuck in traffic*. Washington, DC: The Brookings Institution.

Downs, A. (2004). Why traffic congestion is here to stay and will get worse. *ACCESS Magazine*, *1*(25). Retrieved January 11, 2016 from http://escholarship.org/uc/item/3sh9003x.

Handy, S. (2005). Smart growth and the transportation-land use connection: What does the research tell us?. *International Regional Science Review*, *28*(2), 146–167. Retrieved January 11, 2016 from http://escholarship.org/uc/item/7j45s8s0.

http://mospi.nic.in/Mospi_New/upload/Infra_stat_2010/1.ch_road.pdf.

Litman, T. (1999). In *Traffic calming: benefits, costs and equity impacts*. Victoria, BC, Canada: Victoria Transport Policy Institute.

Litman, T. (2001). Generated traffic and induced travel—implications for transport planning. *ITE Journal Institute of Transportation Engineers*, *71*(4), 38–47. Retrieved January 11, 2016 from http://www.vtpi.org/gentraf.pdf.

Partnership for Sustainable Urban Transport in Asia (PSUTA). (2005). *Sustainable Urban Transport in Asia—Making Vision a Reality*. Retrieved January 11, 2016 from http://pdf.wri.org/sustainable_urban_transport_asia.pdf.

Policy Interventions for Sustainable Solid Waste Management in Developing Countries

Malladi Sindhuja and Krishnan Narayanan

Abstract Waste collection in developing countries is largely dependant on the informal sector where the waste pickers collect and sort the wastes manually for extremely low wages in unsafe and unhygienic conditions that put them at health risk. It is important to integrate informal workers into the waste management systems through policy intervention. Developing countries which have no or less stringent regulations are the pollution havens for waste disposal for the developed world. The social costs of improper waste management are the negative externalities on public health and the environment. According to the World Bank report on sanitation, improper waste disposal leads to economic losses in the form of death, increased costs on health treatment, loss of productivity time and ecosystem losses. Most of the Asian countries have poor waste management practices due to lack of policy intervention, collection inefficiency, limited financial resources and lack of technology. The major issue in solid waste management (SWM) is the failure to recognise it as an important economic problem. The economist A.C. Pigou's work became the basis for using economic tools such as taxes and subsidies to avoid the problems associated with externalities. In many countries, the costs of waste disposal are zero. When waste disposal is not priced, it creates negative externalities like the NIMBY (not in my backyard) syndrome. In order to reduce externalities, economists have designed several tax and subsidy schemes. History of economic policy in theory and practice show that different combinations of economic and regulatory instruments could lead to a socially optimum quantity of garbage and recycling. The following paper is an attempt to critically evaluate certain policy instruments that lead to cost-effective SWM and other economic benefits. Further, this paper attempts to offer policy suggestions particularly for developing countries that have been languishing poor waste management practices for years.

M. Sindhuja (✉)
IIT Bombay, Mumbai, India
e-mail: sindhusharma93@gmail.com

K. Narayanan
Department of Humanities and Social Sciences, IIT Bombay, Mumbai, India
e-mail: knn@iitb.ac.in; knn.iitb@gmail.com

N. R. Bhanumurthy et al. (eds.), *Advances in Finance & Applied Economics*,
https://doi.org/10.1007/978-981-13-1696-8_5

Keywords Informal sector · Pollution havens · Social costs
Negative externalities · Solid waste management · Taxes · Subsidies
Recycling · Policy instruments

1 Introduction

In March 2010, Mayapuri, a locality famous for its scrap market in Delhi suffered a major public radiation exposure leading to death of a scrap dealer and acute radiation syndrome in seven scrap dealers. This unfortunate incident is attributed to improper and illegal disposal of a 'gamma unit' containing cobalt-60 pencils by a research institute in Delhi (Dey et al. 2012); it is not just a case of violation of national regulations for radiation protection, but also a lesson to be learnt about how waste mismanagement could cost lives.

Economic activities are the backbone of every country, and wastes are an inevitable aspect of production and consumption. The rising consumerism of today does not permit countries to minimise the magnitude of economic activities as a solution to prevent waste generation. There is a need to find sustainable solutions of waste management such that it is a win–win situation for the ecology and the economy. According to the World Bank report on sanitation, improper waste disposal and mistreatment of wastewater and faecal sludge lead to economic losses in the form of death, increased costs on health treatment, loss of productivity time and ecosystem losses.[1] The social costs of improper waste management are what economists call as the 'negative externalities' on public health and the environment. However, proper waste management could turn wastewater and faecal sludge into valuable resources that can provide economic opportunities (e.g. in the energy sector). Developed countries have almost succeeded in achieving this to a large extent through innovative ideas put into practice and advanced technology in the field of solid waste management (SWM). However, in developing countries, more than 50% of wastes are collected by the informal sector. The informal sector purely relies on the revenue generated from selling such wastes. Around 2% of population in Asia and Latin America is dependent on waste picking for livelihood (Wilson et al. 2006). Although the informal waste sector reduces the costs of waste collection and separation for the formal sector in waste management, it is largely ignored by the government in terms of providing job security and financial assistance. The practice of mixed wastes (like the case India, where wastes are not sorted before or after disposal) leads to spread of diseases among humans and animals that are exposed to such unhygienic dumpyards. It is the poor who bear the brunt of such wastes; the harmful and unsorted wastes are disposed in sites close to the slums where people do not wield enough power to fight against the unfairness of such practices. There is a lack of broad understanding of the nature of SWM by public officials—a failure to recognise it as an economic problem. According to the European Union (EU) commission report on waste man-

[1] http://www.worldbank.org/en/topic/sanitation/overview#1.

agement practices (2016), landfill is the worst SWM practice as it leads to loss of potential economic benefits and deteriorates human health and environment. Wastes are still unpriced in most of the developing countries even though landfill capacities are falling and incineration costs are rising. There are various ways in which government intervention can help in tackling the problem of SWM like the command and control regime, which could encourage source reduction and recycling. The socio-economic benefits of solid waste management are oversighted. Sustainable SWM could be the answer to the problem of energy poverty in countries like India. Well-regulated SWM practices are a potential source of direct and indirect employment in the waste sector. Moreover, the health benefits of proper waste management cannot be belittled. Improved human and environmental health is crucial for economic development. The key to efficeint SWM system in developing countries is in the implementation of cost-effective SWM policies. The following paper is an attempt to critically evaluate certain SWM practices and policy instruments used around the world. Although the policy effectiveness varies from one country to another, a fresh assessment of recent trends in SWM policies and practices will offer useful insights for efficient and innovative management of wastes, particularly for developing countries that have been languishing poor waste management practices for years.

2 Categorising Solid Wastes

Wastes are by-products of economic activities. Hoornweg and Thomas (1999) have classified the solid wastes based on the basis of *source of waste generation*:

1. Residential: Food wastes, paper, cardboard, plastics, textiles, leather, yard wastes, wood, glass, metals, ashes, etc.
2. Industrial: Housekeeping wastes, packaging, food wastes, construction and demolition materials, hazardous wastes, ashes, special wastes.
3. Commercial and institutional: Paper, cardboard, plastics, wood, food wastes, glass, metals, special wastes, hazardous wastes.
4. Construction and demolition: Wood, steel, concrete, dirt, etc.
5. Municipal: Street sweepings; landscape and tree trimmings; general wastes from parks, beaches, and other recreational areas; sludge.
6. Process (manufacturing): Industrial process wastes, scrap materials, off-specification products, tailings, etc.
7. Agriculture: Spoiled food wastes, agricultural wastes, hazardous wastes (e.g. pesticides), etc.

The time taken by the earth to decompose wastes varies with the type of waste. Biodegradable wastes like vegetable and fruit wastes, cotton cloth, wood, woollen items take from a week to less than a year to decompose. These wastes are not harmful to the environment. However, non-biodegradable wastes like tin, aluminium and other metal items, plastics, toxic wastes from industries take hundreds to millions of years to degenerate. In most of the Asian countries, waste disposal is merely transportation of the wastes to the nearest available sites for disposal. These countries suffer from problems like lack of policy intervention, collection inefficiency, limited financial resources, lack of technology, etc. (Visvanathan et al. 2007). It is therefore important to follow the 3 R's, namely reduce (the amount of non-biodegradable wastes), reuse (use these in multiple ways before disposal) and recycle (to put them to better use, e.g. as raw materials in industries) when it comes to these wastes.

3 Theories and Concepts Related to Waste Management

3.1 Theories

The problem with improper waste management is that they result in negative externalities. Negative externalities are the costs imposed by the economic activities of individual(s) on the rest of the society for which no payment is made. Although the concept of externality is traced to the economist Alfred Marshall, the concept of negative externality is attributed to A.C. Pigou whose works lead to discussions on pollution as an externality (Karpagam 1999). Pigou's work became the basis for using economic tools such as taxes and subsidies to overcome the problems associated with externalities.

Another seminal work towards addressing the problem of externalities is 'The problem of social cost' by Ronald Coase The essence of Coase's work is that in the presence of externalities between two parties, well-defined property rights and bargaining could lead to economic efficiency if the costs of negotiation are small (Coase 2013).

Kenneth Boulding describes how economists conventionally consider the earth to be a limitless space where there is always new space to move to and wastes can be disposed such that there is unlimited assimilation capacity in the earth; this he calls as perception of a 'cowboy economy'. However, Boulding calls for a shift in perception to a 'spaceship economy' which has limited space and limited waste absorptive capacity; the earth must be considered as a single spaceship with limited resources and capacity, and therefore, there is a need for maintaining an ecological cycle such that what is produced is capable of being returned back to the earth. Boulding suggests that the measure of progress of an economy is not by increasing consumption or production, but by *maintaining the ecological stock and investing in technology that helps reduce the amount of material use in economic activities*. He asserts the importance of pricing, taxation and laws to prevent environmental damage (Boulding 1993).

Ayres and Kneese developed the *material balance model* from Boulding's work. The model explains the interaction between the economy, ecology and the environment through the *first and second law of thermodynamics*. The first law 'matter can neither be created nor destroyed' means that the resources extracted from the environment should be returned in their original form (Ayres and Kneese 1969). However, economic activities transform resources such that they cannot be restored to their original form. The environment can assimilate only some wastes through natural processes; the other wastes can be recycled. However, economic activities lead to environmental degradation in some form or the other. The second law of thermodynamics, also known as the 'entropy law', is a measure of disorderliness and destruction. Economic activities convert resources from a state of low entropy to a state of high entropy—the total amount of energy in resources decline overtime. To bring resources back to the state of low entropy, there is a need to *recycle* resources. Not using environment-friendly methods of production allows wastes to enter the environment's life support system,[2] leading to environmental crisis (Karpagam 1999). There is a need to recognise that economy and ecology are two sides of the same coin.

The contributions by these and several economists have influenced the waste management practices and policy instruments over the years. However, not all the instruments and practices are fully efficient—each one of them has a set of advantages and limitations.

3.2 Concepts and Approaches

3.2.1 Cradle-to-Grave Approach to Waste Management (Life Cycle Assessment)

The growing challenges and concerns in waste management have made it crucial for policy-makers to develop strategies for safe and inexpensive disposal of wastes. Cradle-to-grave approach, also known as the life cycle assessment (LCA), is a holistic approach that quantifies all environmental burdens and all environmental impacts throughout the life cycle of products or processes (Rebitzer et al. 2004). This approach ensures that all waste generators safely manage the wastes from 'cradle' to 'grave', that is from the time wastes are created, transported, recycled, treated and finally disposed. The extent to which regulations are imposed on the waste generators depends on the amount of wastes generated (Fig. 1).

In connection with the cradle-to-grave approach is the '*cradle to cradle*' approach. This phrase was invented by Walter R. Stahel in 1970 and has gained popularity since the 2002 book titled 'Cradle to Cradle: Remaking the way we make things' by Michael Braungart and William McDonough. This framework seeks to use production techniques that are fully waste-free. Products are designed according to the principles of a circular economy. While cradle to grave is concerned with responsible disposal by the producer, cradle to cradle is concerned with putting the

---

[2]Environment provides life support services by maintaining ecological balance and genetic diversity. Life support services convert high entropy to low entropy.

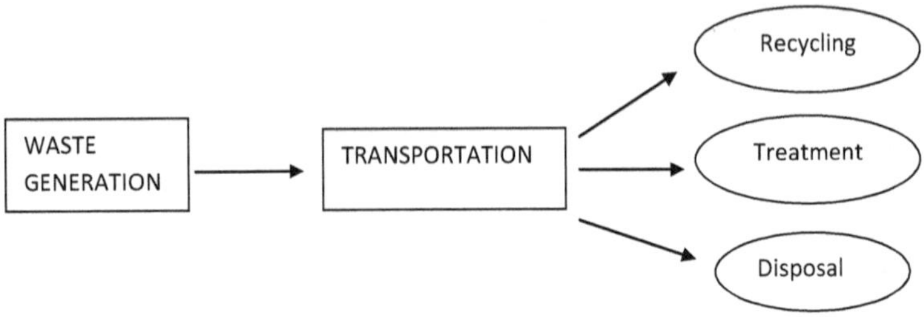

Fig. 1 Cradle-to-grave approach. *Source* https://www.epa.gov/hw/learn-basics-hazardous-waste#cradle

product's inputs back into use.[3] Unlike eco-efficiency and other sustainability tools, cradle-to-cradle approach creates equal social, economic and ecological benefits. There are two cycles in this approach—the 'biological cycle' where materials are returned in the form of nutrients or compost from which new products can be created and 'technical cycle' where materials can be reprocessed and used in a new product. The waste materials of an old product become the food for new products.[4]

3.2.2 The 3 R's of Waste Management

Treating wastes as a valuable resource is a first step towards sustainability. While biodegradable wastes can be managed by the practice of composting and anaerobic digestion, the growing wastes of paper and plastics need to be implemented with the 3 R's of waste management, namely reduce, reuse and recycle. '*Reduce*' refers to decrease the production and consumption wherever possible. '*Reuse*' refers to finding innovative ways to reuse old items like plastic containers, glass jars newspapers instead of disposing them. 'Recycle' refers to the transformation of a product such that it can be used again as a raw material to be reshaped into a new product. Rapid urbanisation, population growth and industrialisation lead to exploitation of natural resources, and the 3 R's concept plays an important role in waste conservation and management. The 3 R's concept has now been extended to 5 R's (reduce, reuse, recycle, recover and responsible disposal) concept in many countries.

3.2.3 Extended Producer Responsibility

Recent environment policies in Canada and several European countries constitute the inclusion of producers in effective post consumption disposal of wastes. The concept of extended producer responsibility essentially means that the producer is responsible

[3]http://www.sustainabilitydictionary.com/cradle-to-cradle/.

[4]http://epea-hamburg.org/en/content/cradle-cradle%C2%AE.

for completing the life cycle of the products that he manufactures.[5] The concept of extended producer responsibility aims at providing incentives to producers to produce products that can be recycled and reduce the quantity of wastes. Regulations on the material used for product packaging, deposit-refund systems and advanced disposal fees come under the umbrella term of extended producer responsibility. These economic instruments are explained in detail in the sections that follow.

3.2.4 Polluter Pays Principle

As the name suggests, this concept simply means that the party that has the major share in polluting the environment must pay the price for complete disposal of the wastes generated. One of the principles for promotion of worldwide sustainable development in the 1992 *Rio declaration* is the polluter pays principle.[6] The interpretation and instruments used for under the polluter pays principle are different from country to country. This principle is a curative approach for solving the damage caused to the environment. Although it could be an effective approach for reducing environmental damage, identification of who caused the damage is always a problem. The environmental damage caused by exploiting common pool resources cannot be valued by this concept.[7]

4 Current Waste Management Practices

While the practice of *landfills* as a source of waste disposal is very popular around the world, many countries like Germany, Austria, Sweden, Denmark, Belgium, the Netherlands, and Switzerland have banned the use of landfills. Landfills are associated with many environmental hazards like air pollution due to the release of green house gases (particularly methane in large quantities); these toxic gases put the people who live close to these dumpsites at health risks like lung and heart diseases and stunting in children. Another hazard associated with landfills is problem to 'leaching' into the groundwater. The liquid that leaches from the garbage dumps to the groundwater releases toxins into fresh waterways that may end up in households as drinking water and also harms animal and plant life.[8] Although the landfills are originally intended to reduce public health expenditure, they are in fact, increasing the social costs. Japan, USA, Ireland and Greece use 'advanced landfill systems' that reduce the negative externalities associated with ordinary landfills to some extent. Advanced landfills are installed with plastic linings at the base, the leachate[9] is col-

[5]http://www.wrfound.org.uk/.

[6]http://www.lse.ac.uk/GranthamInstitute/faqs/what-is-the-polluter-pays-principle/.

[7]http://www.legalserviceindia.com/article/l54-Interpretation-of-Polluter-Pays-Principle.html.

[8]http://www.wegreen-usa.org/landfill-problems.html.

[9]Water that percolates through a solid and leaches out some of its constituents.

lected and treated, the groundwater is continuously monitored, and the garbage is powdered and covered up with layers of sand within hours of disposal. Modern landfill systems also come with a 'gas extraction system' that extracts gas from the landfill pits to prevent bad odour, killing of surface vegetation and greenhouse effects. The expansion of already existing landfills is more economical than construction of new landfills (Kinnaman and Fullterton 1999).

Waste collection in Asia is dependant on the *informal sector*. Although the rag pickers and informal waste collectors play such an important role in getting rid of wastes particularly in urban areas, their services are unheeded and their livelihood issues are overlooked. It is important to integrate these informal workers into the waste management systems through policy-making (Visvanathan and Norbu 2006). A major reason for growing child labour in developing countries is the involvement of children belonging to the poor households in the scrap market as rag pickers. Animals are also equal sufferers of poor health conditions and death because of chewing on the plastics, medical wastes that are disposed in the open dumpsites; humans are at a risk of contracting these diseases from the affected dogs, cattle and other animals.

The disposal of *electronic wastes* is another concern since the advent of technology. Developing countries which have no or less stringent regulations are still the *pollution havens* for e-waste disposal for the developed world. In response to this NIMBY (not in my backyard) syndrome, the 'Basel Convention'[10] was signed in 1989 by 53 countries, including the European Union and the USA. However, e-waste export still continues. In particular, Australia and USA have been exporting large amounts of e-waste to China, India and other Asian countries, violating the Basel convention. To recover many of these metals like copper, the informal sector workers burn the electrical components which release toxic gases that pose industrial and environmental threats. The government, consumers and industries have not taken many steps in countries like India to overcome this problem (Visvanathan and Norbu 2006).

Another common practice of waste disposal in developed as well as developing nations is that of *incineration*. As the name suggests, incineration is the process of burning wastes, however, unlike in developing countries the incinerated wastes are used for energy production through advanced technology in developed countries. During the process of incineration, the waste material that is treated is converted into biomass energy, gases, particles and heat. These products are later used for generation of electricity. The gases are first treated for pollutants to avoid air pollution when released.[11] There are two kinds of problems faced associated with use of incinerators; in developing countries, wastes are burnt without treating them due to the absence of technology to do so. This process releases harmful gases like carbon dioxide, sulphur dioxide, hydrochloric acid and fine particulate matter that are harmful for human

[10]The Basel Convention on the Control of Transboundary Movements of Hazardous Wastes and their Disposal was adopted on 22 March 1989 by the Conference of Plenipotentiaries in Basel, Switzerland, in response to a public outcry following the discovery, in the 1980s, in Africa and other parts of the developing world of deposits of toxic wastes imported from abroad (source: http://www.basel.int/theconvention/overview/tabid/1271/default.aspx).

[11]http://www.wrfound.org.uk/articles/incineration.html.

health. The absence of regulations against burning of wastes is a major problem in developing countries. The second type of problem is that the machines used for incineration in developed countries have a capacity that is in excess of the amount of garbage available (Kinnaman and Fullterton 1999). The absence of enough garbage to make the incinerators function properly and produce energy is a major setback of this system. Also, the initial investment costs of incineration are recovered only after a long period of time.[12] Despite its disadvantages, Japan, USA, Switzerland, Sweden, Denmark and other countries with large population density and less land availability rely on incineration to manage a bulk of their wastes. Advanced incineration systems, however, could be an effective option for solving the problem of energy poverty in largely populous developing countries that have a huge potential of wastes that can be converted to energy.

Curbside recycling is another method of waste management that is gaining popularity. This system calls for a cooperation between the waste generators and the domestic waste management systems administered by the local governments or private waste management companies. This method is popular in Australia, Canada and Europe where *colour-coded bins* are provided by the waste management companies so that households can put the wastes into different coloured bins according to the nature of the wastes (recyclables, organic wastes, etc.). In many countries, it is illegal to dispose recyclable wastes with regular wastes. The 3 R's initiative was introduced in April 2005 by the government of Japan, and by 2006, the concept was implemented with strong commitment at the local, regional and national level. Awareness, public participation and financial resources are essential for the successful implementation of the 3 R's concept in waste management. Japan, Korea, Singapore, Taiwan and Hong Kong have taken significant steps for 3 R's implementation (Visvanathan et al. 2007). Practicing the 3 R's not only benefits the environment but also improves human and animal health by ensuring clean surroundings. Curbside recycling could be an answer to improving the lives of informal workers in the waste sector and a source of employment in largely populated developing countries.

Biological reprocessing is a method for managing food and other organic wastes. When organic wastes are recycled through composting, they become useful for agricultural purposes like fertilisers for plants. Moreover, the gases that are released during this process are used in the generation of electricity. The composting techniques (aerobic and anaerobic techniques) vary depending on the nature of the raw materials—household or industrial wastes. This system requires long-term funding from the government to remain effective; otherwise, landfills are considered the easiest option for disposing organic wastes resulting in wastage of energy potential resources. There is also a lack of public participation and awareness about composting and a common misconception that this method attracts flies and rodents. Studies in Africa, China and Ghana have revealed the importance of education and awareness on target groups in practicing biocomposting. Buy-back arrangements, provision of land, subsidies on price and transport are necessary for reaping long-term benefits of this method (Michaela 2010).

[12]http://www.wrfound.org.uk/articles/incineration.html.

5 Instruments of Waste Management

The major issue in SWM is the failure to recognise *SWM as an important economic problem*. In many countries, the costs of waste disposal are zero; there is no 'pay-as-you throw' system. When waste disposal is not priced, it creates negative externalities like the NIMBY (not in my backyard) syndrome (Goddard 1994). In India, the local municipal corporation employs waste collectors who collect unsorted wastes from door to door. In the absence of government employed waste collectors, communities collectively appoint a private waste collector who collects garbage on a daily basis. In either case, a common monthly or yearly fee is charged irrespective of the amount of garbage disposed. This system is very ineffective as the garbage is unsorted, the waste collectors are paid very low wages, there is no motivation to reduce the amount of wastes, and the wastes ultimately end up in a locally available dumpsite. There is no 3 R's practice at any stage due to the *absence of a pricing policy on every bag of garbage.* Households that generate more garbage pay the same as households that generate less garbage under this system. Instead of this system, a *user fee* (*unit-based pricing*) on every unit of garbage could force households to recycle compost or engage in some sort of source reduction to avoid the marginal cost of an additional bag of garbage. There are again two kinds of user fees like in the USA—the traditional 'bag and tag' programmes where every additional bag of garbage is priced or a system of subscribing to a fixed number of bags each week which has lesser administrative costs. Increased recycling reduces price of recycled materials and encourages producers to use recycled materials even without a recycling subsidy or a tax on virgin materials (Kinnaman and Fullterton 1999). There are no information costs in the system of unit-based pricing.

In order to reduce externalities, economists have designed several tax and subsidy schemes.

One method is to tax the households on every unit of garbage that is disposed or there could be a subsidy provided for practicing recycling. History of economic policy in practice and theory show that different *combinations of economic and regulatory instruments* could lead to a socially optimum quantity of garbage and recycling. *Command and control policies* that mandate recycling and minimal use of recyclables are proven to be effective in theory, however, these policies require lot of information in order to design policies that produce the desired outcomes (Kinnaman and Fullterton 1999).

To encourage recycling, two options are available—*a tax on virgin materials* or a *subsidy on recycled materials*. Economists have mostly favoured a tax on virgin material to be an effective tool for ensuring use of recycled materials; this tax will increase the demand for recycled products and indirectly incentivise the households to recycle their wastes. However, a disadvantage is that only those industries that use the taxed virgin material will find a recycled substitute for it, other industries that do not use the taxed virgin material will not substitute it with recycled material. On the other hand, a subsidy on recycled materials does not mean that the producer will stop the use of virgin materials in production. Subsidies on recycled inputs may lead to excess of production and consumption and wastage of resources unless it is combined with a tax on the final consumption (Kinnaman and Fullterton 1999).

Recycled content standard is another regulation that could produce desirable SWM outcomes. This regulation mandates firms to use a minimum portion of recycled inputs in their products. Use of recycled inputs requires a capital-intensive technology which cannot be afforded by many firms; thus, to enable use of recycled inputs, the capital to buy technology needs to be incentivised by the government (Kinnaman and Fullterton 1999). This regulation also suffers from problems of high administration and information costs. USA, Japan, Canada have laws that mandate the use of at least 50% of recycled content in products such as newspapers, electronic appliances, stationery, furniture (Higashida and Jinji 2006).

Extended producer responsibility (*EPR*) as mentioned in an earlier section is gaining popularity in Canada and many European countries. *Advanced disposal fees* (*ADF*) and *deposit-refund schemes* are the most widely used instruments under this concept for waste reduction and management. A deposit-refund system is a combination of a tax and a subsidy. Under this system, the consumer is first charged a price that increases the cost of purchasing the product (usually a plastic container) and a subsidy is then rewarded to the consumer after the container is returned to an authorised intermediary who in turn returns the product to the manufacturer or a recycling unit and collects the deposit and handling charges. This system is used for reduction and recycling of plastic containers, batteries, automobile parts, pesticide and gas containers, detergent and paint containers, etc. Deposit-refund systems have been implemented in Australia, Canada, France, Germany, Switzerland and the Netherlands. Most of the economic models support the use of deposit-refund systems. The deposit refund is set equal to the social marginal cost of disposing the product wastes; the optimal refund is the difference between the marginal external cost of garbage and the marginal external cost of recycling (Kinnaman and Fullterton 1999).

Advanced disposal fees are additional charges imposed at the point of sale or production. The additional funds are used for waste recycling and reduction process. This method is not popularly used for various reasons. Implementation of advanced disposal fee may encourage source reduction but not recycling. A combination of advanced disposal fee and subsidy on recycling (which is nothing but deposit-refund scheme) produces desired outcomes according to many economists (Kinnaman and Fullterton 1999). Products on which ADF is imposed must be accompanied by regulations that prevent the product from being disposed by other means like landfills in order to be effective. This system also suffers from the problem of huge administration costs. ADF costs can be imposed on the price of the product like in Canada where the ADF is known as 'eco-fee'. ADF can also be applied to imported products. The Province of British Columbia popularly uses ADF system for waste regulation. A challenge for ADF and in general all waste management instruments is in handling of smaller goods like batteries and liquid wastes that can be easily hidden in the trash or poured down the drains; refunds on such small goods could prevent such illegal dumping (Munro 2014). Advanced disposal fee and deposit-refund scheme maximise the utility of the households (Kinnaman and Fullterton 1999).

Another approach to the EPR is the producer 'take-back' requirement—a command and control regulation imposed by the government. The *green dot programme* is an example of this approach of EPR (Munro 2014). The green dot programme was established in Germany during the 1990s. This programme was adopted by the European Union in 1994 with the aim to reduce impact of packaging wastes on the environment. A green dot on the packaging means that the manufacturer of this packaging has paid the licence fees for its collection, sorting and recycling. The packaging wastes that have a green dot are collected for recycling by an industry-funded system. The green dot also symbolises to the consumers that the collection and the sorting of the packing wastes are financed by the producers. Although the green dot programme passes on the costs of disposal to the consumers in the form of high prices, the consumers can dispose the packaging wastes free of cost (Munro 2014). This programme ensures that there are systems in place that enable return and collection of used packaging material and packaging wastes from the consumers and for practicing reuse, recovery and recycling for the packaging wastes (Baughan and Evale 2004). This system ensures that the packaging follows the pattern of 'design for environment'; that is, layers of packaging are cut down and made eco-friendly in order to avoid paying a high licence fee. Austria, the Netherlands, France, Italy, Denmark and Sweden make producers as the major stakeholders in managing their packaging wastes through the green dot programme (Kinnaman and Fullterton 1999).

Producer take-back requirements and precycling insurance programmes are less popular approaches under the EPR. Owing to the increasing menace of product wastes, some countries have made it mandatory for the manufacturers to take back the products at the end of their useful life, the packaging materials and containers of their products from the users. This policy aims at making producers adopt innovative recycling techniques for production and design eco-friendly products. The European Union and USA implemented this regulation for electronic and electrical wastes disposal. *Precycling* refers to the practice of avoiding unnecessary purchase of items that need to be recycled or dealt with as waste in the future. Limiting purchases, buying products in bulk to avoid extra packaging, buying products that will last, etc., are the examples of precycling.[13] Precycling insurance is a premium that is paid by producers on products which may lead to waste generation and harm the environment. This premium is used to insure against the risks associated with industrial activities on natural resources. The European waste electronic directive (WEEE) adopted the precycling insurance to avoid the risks associated with electronic wastes. A general precycling insurance on all products would be a step towards sustainable development. It will make it obligatory for the producers to cut waste risks by producing precycled products with 'cradle-to-cradle' life cycle. This regulation could be a useful tool in making reforms in the energy market by incentivising use of renewable energy sources that produce lesser wastes than that of fossil fuels (Greyson 2007). Producer take-back requirements and precycling insurance have high administrative and transaction costs and are therefore not preferred by policymakers (Munro 2014).

[13]http://whatis.techtarget.com/definition/precycling.

Carbon credits are tradable certificates or permits that allow the emission of green house gases such as carbon dioxide to firms. These credits are awarded to those firms that reduce emissions. The firms that do not exceed their emissions can trade the credits with a firm that cannot do away with increasing emissions. While this scheme is popularly used as a measure to reduce pollution, it can also be used effectively in waste management. Sharma et al. analyse the use of carbon credits in monitoring biological processing of wastes. As pointed out in an earlier section, biological processing can be done using two techniques—aerobic and anaerobic. According to a study in Kerala, aerobic technique results in release of compost and carbon dioxide instead of methane (methane produces 21 times more heat than carbon dioxide which is more harmful to the cnvironment). These reductions in emissions lead to earning of carbon credits that can be sold by the municipality to other regions or countries (Sharma et al. 2012). This scheme is an effective tool to replace anaerobic approach of biological processing with aerobic approach. Carbon credits could be an incentive for better waste management in other areas like recycling content standards for plastics and paper industry.[14]

The success of any of the above-mentioned policies and practices depends on a number of factors such as household willingness and participation in reducing and recycling wastes and the government's involvement in encouraging and mandating waste separation and recycling. While some of the policies have administration, monitoring and information costs, other programmes are easy to implement. Most of the economists favour the use of EPR and in particular the deposit-refund system in international waste management policies to obstruct public from resorting to harmful SWM practices. EPR makes it mandatory for the producers and consumers to share the responsibility of waste disposal at low information, administration and transaction costs; this makes EPR beneficial over other economic tools such as Pigouvian taxes (Munro 2014).

6 Use of Policy Instruments for Solid Waste Management

This section is a brief overview of some policy applications in waste management by countries around the world. These practices are effective policy applications that are slowly gaining popularity.

Europe has been the leader of waste management practices characterised by use of sophisticated and innovative waste management systems. According to the latest *EU commission report on best waste management practices*,[15] Austria, Belgium, Denmark, Germany, the Netherlands and Sweden have landfills that are less than 5% of their waste and also have well-developed recycling systems, sufficient treatment capacity, and proper use of biodegradable wastes. A review of some of the best waste management practices (by private organisations, NGO's or governments) based

[14]http://www.niir.org/information/content.phtml?content=142.

[15]http://europa.eu/rapid/press-release_IP-12-888_en.htm?locale=en.

on the EU commission report 2016 titled 'Waste prevention—Best practices' is as follows:

The Courtauld Commitment, UK:
Initiated in 2005 by a UK-based NGO called Waste and Resources Action Programme (WRAP), the Courtauld Commitment is an attempt towards reducing household waste generation by managing the source that is the cause of such waste—the packaging industries. The objective of this initiative is to achieve reductions in food waste by 2010. Solutions to these emerged in the form of use of *biopolymers and compostable packaging*, providing recycling information on the packaging to the consumers and share information on the best practices with other companies through case studies for collective implementation of the same. Ninety-two per cent of the UK grocery market signed this commitment, and the objective of reduction in packaging was achieved by the year 2007 despite a growth in the UK grocery sector.

Eco-Emballages Packaging Advisory, France: Eco-Emballages Packaging Advisory creates a platform for the interaction between business and other stakeholders to promote recyclable packaging and reduce packaging waste. These objectives are achieved by organising training sessions for engineers and designers on creation of eco-friendly packaging. Members of this organisation maintain *packaging audits* that help to determine the optimum level of packaging with minimum waste. Packaging audit and awareness have long-lasting impact on waste reduction.

Eco-point initiative for bulk goods, Italy: Eco-point project emerged in collaboration of supermarkets with the NGO 'Plant Life economy foundation' in the year 2005. 'Eco-points' are found as a separate section in supermarkets where the customers are allowed to purchase products in bulk as a move towards reductions in packaging wastes. Products like sweets, cereals, pasta, legumes, nuts, coffee, spices are sold in bulk through direct dispensers. This system has the added benefit of increasing the savings of the consumers by 10–70% compared to buying packaged products; there is a visibly low packaging waste. There are about 30 eco-points in Italy and Switzerland that prevent the use of at least a million packages a year.

Love food, hate waste, UK: According to a report by WRAP, about 6.7 million tonnes of food is wasted in a year by the households in UK. The 'Love food, hate waste' campaign began in 2008 with an aim to reduce food wastes by creating awareness among people and inducing a behavioural change in the public. The government and various food organisations came up with practical solutions like a meal planner and portions calculator. Food storage tips and recipes on cooking from leftovers are available on the campaign's website. This campaign has led to 1,137,000 tonnes of food from being thrown a year and thus led to monetary savings as well.

No disposables campaign, South Korea: By organising meetings with all the food joints and restaurants across South Korea, the Korea Zero Waste Movement Network (KZWM) called for a reduction in the use of disposables for serving food and drinks in restaurants as disposable plastics are the main contributors to solid wastes in the economy. Incentives were announced for those who brought their own shopping bag and avoided buying plastic bags in supermarkets, free drinks were served to customers who brought their own cups for a drink at restaurants, and reusable utensils were encouraged across food joints. A levy was charged from restaurants that used disposables to serve food in order to encourage recycling.

7 Summary and Conclusion

Wastes are by-products of economic activities. Improper waste management has harmful repercussions for the ecology and the economy known as negative externalities. The reason for poor waste disposal practices in most developing countries is that waste disposal is free; there is less stringent or complete absence of policies in the waste sector and a total dependence on the informal sector for waste disposal. Landfills and incineration are two popular practices of SWM. However, these systems lead to release of toxic gases, damage to animal and plant life and deterioration of human health. These risks have made some countries to replace them with advanced landfills and incinerators that treat wastes before releasing them into the atmosphere and put wastes to beneficial uses such as converting them to energy. Curbside recycling and biological reprocessing are recent methods of managing recyclable and organic wastes effectively. These two methods have positive implications in the energy and employment sector.

Economists have developed several models of pricing, taxation and subsidies to tackle the problem of negative externalities due to wastes. The economist A.C. Pigou suggested the use of taxes and subsidies to solve the problem of externalities. Unit-based pricing, virgin materials tax, subsidies on recycled materials, recycling content standard are some of the conventional policy instruments of waste management whose success is largely dependent upon the household participation in source reduction and waste separation or producer participation in adopting eco-friendly methods of production. In the recent years, policy instruments such as disposal fees, producer take-back requirement, green dot programme, carbon credit, precycling insurance and deposit-refund scheme are gaining popularity. These instruments which are largely favoured by economists come under the umbrella term of extended producer responsibility (EPR). EPR makes the producers responsible for efficient disposal of the wastes generated during and after the process of product manufacturing. EPR policy does not suffer from the limitation of information cost.

The success of any SWM policy or practice depends on a number of factors such as public participation, government intervention, cooperation between the public and the government, administration costs, information and monitoring costs and industry participation. A review of policy applications in SWM around the world reveals that not all SWM practices are expensive. Participation by non-governmental organisations and private sector in waste management is accelerating in the recent years. Drawing implications particularly for developing countries like India, there are many potential cost-effective waste management practices reviewed in the current paper that are not popular in practice. This paper was an attempt to review and shed light on such instruments and practices which could offer solutions to the problems of rag pickers and informal workers in the waste sector and also to problems of unemployment, disease, ecological damage and political crisis arising out of dumping. To accommodate the rising population and improve the living standards of the people, effective SWM practices such as the 3 R's practice are needed to put resources to multiple uses. For this, awareness and education on sustainable SWM practices and their positive social, economic and environmental benefits needs to be created at the micro level. Improved human and environmental health and therefore economic growth, energy security and direct and indirect employment in the waste sector are some of the many benefits of sustainable SWM. Considering these benefits, there is an immediate need for developing countries like India to implement stringent policies in SWM. Acknowledging the fact that the ecology and the economy are two sides of the same coin is a key to framing policies that help in environmental conservation.

References

Ayres, R. U., & Kneese, A. V. (1969). Production, consumption, and externalities. *The American Economic Review, 59*(3), 282–297.

Baughan & Evale. (2004). *The Green Dot System: Promoting Recycling in the European Union*. World Tarde executive, Inc. Keller and Heckman LLP.

Boulding, K. E. (1993). Spaceship earth revisited. *Valuing the Earth: economics, ecology, and ethics. Massachusetts Institute of Technology, Boston*, (pp. 311–313).

Coase, R. H. (2013). The problem of social cost. *The Journal of Law and Economics, 56*(4), 837–877.

Dey, A. B., et al. (2012) Radiation accident at Mayapuri scrap market, Delhi, 2010. *Radiation protection dosimetry*: ncs162.

Greyson, J. (2007). Systemic economic instruments for energy security and global security. In *NATO Science Programme Advanced Research Workshop on Modelling of Sustainable Consumption of Energy and Environmental Costing*. Naples. Italy. Retrieved from: http://www.blindspot.org.uk/Resources/NATO_Greyson.pdf.

Higashida, K., & Jinji, N. (2006). Strategic use of recycled content standards under international duopoly. *Journal of Environmental Economics and Management, 51*(2), 242–257.

Hoornweg, D., & Thomas, L. (1999). *What a waste: solid waste management in Asia*. The World Bank. http://www.conserve-energy-future.com/reduce-reuse-recycle.php.

Karpagam, M. (1999). *Environmental economics: A textbook*. Sterling Publishers Pvt. Ltd.

Kinnaman, T. C., & Fullterton, D. (1999). *The economics of residential solid waste management* (No. w7326). National Bureau of Economic Research.

Munro, B. (2014). The economics of waste management. In *Extended producer responsibility and its application in British Columbia*. University of Victoria.

Rebitzer, G., Ekvall, T., Frischknecht, R., Hunkeler, D., Norris, G., Rydberg, T., & Pennington, D. W. (2004). Life cycle assessment: Part 1: Framework, goal and scope definition, inventory analysis, and applications. *Environment International, 30*(5), 701–720.

Sharma, R., et al. (2012) Composting of municipal solid waste for carbon credits-A case study from India. *Waste Management, 2*.

Visvanathan & Norbu. (2006). Reduce, reuse and recycle: The 3 Rs in South Asia. Key Note Lecture, In *3 R Waste Management South Asia Expert Workshop*, Katmandu, Nepal.

Visvanathan, C., Adhikari, R., & Ananth, A. P. (2007, November). 3 R practices for municipal solid waste management in Asia. In *Kalmar ECOTECH 07 and Symposium on Environmental Chemistry* (pp. 26–28).

Wilson, D. C., Velis, C., & Cheeseman, C. (2006). Role of informal sector recycling in waste management in developing countries. *Habitat international, 30*(4), 797–808.

Weblinks

http://lisefvestergaard.com/?page_id=16. Accessed on: January 18, 2017.

http://storage.unitedwebnetwork.com/files/26/d35969d83be871a54153b9d08bb8f383.pdf. Accessed on March 1, 2017.

http://cpcb.nic.in/PWM-Website2015.pdf. Accessed on: March 10, 2017.

http://europa.eu/rapid/press-release_IP-12-888_en.htm?locale=en. Accessed on March 20, 2017.

http://www.wrfound.org.uk/. Accessed on March 31, 2017.

Part III
Monetary Economics

MUDRA: The Transformation of Microfinance in India: Review, Experiences and Future Prospect

Manas Roy

Abstract The Government of India has recently launched a range of macroeconomic policy initiatives which are innovative as well as transforming also. Launching of Micro Units Development and Refinance Agency (MUDRA) bank on 8th April, 2015 with an aim to look forward to the development of small entrepreneurs is one of them. The main objective of this initiative is to empower Non-Corporate Small Business Sector (NCSBS), fulfil the financial needs of approximately 5.77 Crore small businesses spreading throughout the country as well as to create as many microfinance institutions (MFIs) as possible. Crossing the main objective of microfinance, the MUDRA BANK is targeting Funding the unfunded as a Last Mile Financiers. In most of the developing countries, financing to the poor through formal financial services failed to meet the requirements. The high risk as well as high transaction costs associated with small loans and savings deposits are the factors which make them vulnerable. It is also estimated that in developing countries, the formal financial system reaches on an average to only top 25% of the economically active population and leaves the bottom 75% without access to financial services. India is not an exception on this front. GOI through this initiative has indicated to lend a loan up to Rupees 10 lakh in three categories, viz, Shishu, Kishor and Tarun through MUDRA Bank. The National Bank for Agriculture and Rural Development (NABARD) will closely monitor the progress of this policy. If implemented in right spirit, this policy initiative has the power to bring revolutionary changes in the Indian economy. This study tries to find out what is new in this initiative and its future prospect after initiation.

Keywords Microfinance · MUDRA · NABARD · PMMY

M. Roy (✉)
Faculty of Arts and Law, Department of Economics, School of Humanities & Social Sciences, Manipal University Jaipur, VPO Dehmi Kalan, Tehsil Sanganer, Off Jaipur - Ajmer Expressway, Jaipur 303007, Rajasthan, India
e-mail: manas.roy138@gmail.com; manas.roy@jaipur.manipal.edu

N. R. Bhanumurthy et al. (eds.), *Advances in Finance & Applied Economics*,
https://doi.org/10.1007/978-981-13-1696-8_6

1 Introduction

Throughout the world, microfinance is reckoned with a means of credit-based poverty alleviation (Pallavi and Bhaskar 2009). India with population of more than 1.2 billion is also facing the greatest challenges of any kind of policy initiative where one-third of its population is poor. Though India is one of the BRICs nations and coined to be an emerging economy, has failed to make a significant improvement in its poverty alleviation as desirable limit with 400 million still is in poverty in spite of starting various poverty alleviation programs. The reasons behind this failure include to reach the proper target group, developing a robust mechanism to control it, drawbacks in the system itself etc. To eradicate poverty like many countries of the world, India also experimented subsidised credit facilities but which has only led to increase in the non-performing assets (NPAs). The microfinance is one of the tool to fill up this gap but its outreach is too small as compared to its requirement as well as potential. With some active role played by NABARD, there is small progress in this. But certain development in recent years initiated by GOI has brought a fresh focus on the problem of regulation in field of microfinance through MUDRA. This study is trying to discuss concept of microfinance as it is understood worldwide, its historical aspect, the growth of microfinance in India and the role played by NABARD and other nationalised banks and the role of government in framing legislation for protection of right of microborrowers through MUDRA. This paper also discusses the need for MUDRA in the paradigm of the factors and theoretical position associated with evolution of microfinance and its role in global scenario.

2 Microfinance

2.1 Concept

Microfinance is a broad and novel approach to provide saving and investment opportunity to the poor around the world. There is no doubt that an improved access and efficient provision of savings and credit can enable the poor to smoothen their consumption, enhance their income and earning capacity, gradually build up their asset base and enjoy an improved quality of life. In other words, it provides poor people the power and means squarely in their hands to come out of poverty. It was observed that this section of society if given guidance, capital and productive assets can emerge as the successful entrepreneur. This can easily be achieved by empowering them with power of microcredit (Akula 2008). It has been estimated that microfinance has reached about approximately 80 million households through about 20,000 micro-finance institutions (MFI's) operating in developing countries of Asia, Africa, Europe and Latin America (Pillai 2011). The distinguishing principles of microfinance is based on small amounts of loan in terms of credit delivery, give emphasis on social collateral, monitoring and focus on women borrowers in particular etc. With these three factors, microfinance is expected to effectively tackle the poor by targeting as well as screening of borrowers and enforcement of the credit contract (Hulme and Paul 1996).

2.2 Requirement

In developing countries, formal financial services for the poor have failed to meet the credit requirements. The main reason behind this failure is absence of any recognised employment and hence absence of assurance, high risk and the high transaction costs of banks etc. (Adams and Graham 1984). Lack of loans facilities from formal institutions leaves the poor to borrow money from money-lenders with high rate of interest (Adams et al. 1984). There have been continuous efforts made by governments of different countries to deliver formal credit to rural areas by setting up special agricultural banks, rural banks or directing commercial banks to provide loans to rural borrowers (Adams and Vogel 1986). However, these programmes have also not worked well due to various reasons like political difficulty for governments to enforce loan repayment, selection of people for bank loans etc. (World Bank 1989). It was estimated that in most developing countries, only 25% people could take the advantage of formal financial system and leaves the bottom 75% out of reach of financial services. So, the emergence of microfinance was based on inability of formal credit institutions to deal with the credit requirements of poor effectively (Women's World banking 1995). This scheme is not only provides a wide range of financial services, build up assets, crises survival, establishment of small business to come out of poverty but also extends small loans to provide various other financial and non-financial services like savings, insurance, guidance, skill development training, capacity building and motivation to start income generating activities as well as enhance the productivity of credit. In many countries of Asia, Africa, Europe and America, this programme has become popular and emerges as a powerful instrument for alleviation of poverty.

2.3 Origin

The concept of microfinance was first originated in Bangladesh with an organisation called Grameen Bank in 1983[1] by Prof. Mohammed Yunus. He experimented to

---

[1]Grameen Bank was originally sponsored by the central bank of Bangladesh and some state owned commercial banks and foreign donor institutions. It was subsequently made into an independent banking organisation through government legislation. For a major part from its inception, Grameen Bank relied on funds from foreign donors. However, since 1995, Grameen Bank claims to have become self-reliant and does not rely on foreign funds.

lend money[2] of his own to the villagers most of whom were unable to obtain credit at reasonable rates to buy materials for various projects (New York Times 1997). The success of this idea encouraged social innovators and organisations all over the world to begin experiments with different microfinance services to the poor. It is now adopted worldwide in the countries of different continents. In fact, many international NGOs[3] are promoting microfinance programme for creating new businesses and combating poverty in a sustainable way. But the concept of providing financial services to low income people is very old.[4] Over the past few decades, microfinance has been experimented in many developing countries (Seibel 2005) some of which is very encouraging also as far as removal of poverty is concerned.[5]

2.4 *Function*

The Asian Development Bank (2000) defines the function of microfinance as the provision of broad range of services[6] to poor and low income households and microenterprises. This definition of microfinance is not only restricted to the below poverty line people but also includes only low income households. The Task Force (Hulme and Paul 1996) terms microfinance as the means of credit and other financial services of small amounts to the poor in rural, semi-urban or urban areas which helps them to raise their income levels and improve standard of living. It also emphasises loans for other credit needs such as housing and shelter (Jayaraman 2001) etc. Microfinance is also termed as the providing financial support to an individual or an eligible client either directly or through a group (not exceeding rupees fifty thousand in aggregate per individual) for small enterprise, agriculture, allied activities (includes consump-

[2]He gave a small loan of 856 Taka ($27) from his pocket to 42 poor bamboo weavers and found that small loans radically changed the lives of these people and they were able to pay back the loans with interest.

[3]Such as Foundation for International Community Assistance (FINCA), Americans for Community Cooperation in Other Nations (ACCION), Freedom from Hunger, Opportunity International, Co-operative for Assistance and Relief Everywhere (CARE), Consultative Group for Assisting the Poor (CGAP), etc.

[4]For example susus in Nigeria and Ghana (15th century), Chit funds, Rotating Savings and Credit Associations (ROSCAs) and Self-Employed Women's Association of India (SEWA) in India, Tontines in West Africa, Pasanaku in Bolivia, Hui in China, Arisan in Indonesia [Bank Rakyat Indonesia, BRI, now one of the largest Microfinance Institutions (MFIs) of the world] (Schwiecker 2004), Paluwagan in Philippines etc. In Europe it has started in Ireland (1720) and Germany (1847) (Seibel 2005).

[5]Some of the examples are Bank Rakyat Indonesia (BRI) in Indonesia, Bancosol in Bolivia, Bank for Agriculture and Agricultural Co-operatives (BAAC) in Thailand, Grameen Bank and Bangladesh Rural Advancement Committee (BRAC) of Bangladesh, NABARD in India, Amannah Ikhtiar Malaysia (AIM) of Malaysia, Agriculture Development Bank of Nepal (ADBN), K-Rep in Kenya and Mibanco in Peru are the few have yielded encouraging results in alleviating poverty and empowering the poor through microfinance (Schwiecker 2004).

[6]Such as savings, deposits, loans, payment services, money transfers, insurance etc.

tion purposes); or for housing or other prescribed purposes per individual (amount not exceeding rupees one lakh fifty thousand) for clients which may be landless labourers, migrant labourers, artisans and micro-entrepreneurs and farmers owning not more than two hectares of agricultural land (Lok Sabha 2007).

2.5 *Growth of Microfinance in India*

The first initiative to introduce microfinance in our country was initiated with establishment of Self-Employed Women's Association (SEWA) initiated by self-employed women workers of the unorganised sector in 1972 in Gujarat.[7] But the financial needs of the rural poor through startup were the first major effort made by NABARD in 1986–1987 with its support and funding of Rupees one million in an action research project on saving and credit management of self-help groups (SHGs) of Mysore Resettlement and Development Authority (MYRADA). In order to meet credit requirements, RBI has issued a circular to the commercial banks to extend credit to the SHGs formed under the pilot project of NABARD in July 1991 and introduction as a pilot project like SHG-Bank Linkage Programme (SHG-BLP) is considered (February 1992) as a landmark development in banking with the poor.[8] To supplement the efforts of microcredit, the Government of India had started a scheme called Integrated Rural Development Programme (IRDP) in 1980. Realising the potential in the field of microfinance, the GOI allowed various private players to provide microfinance in the country (MFI's) which are various NGOs, non-banking financial companies (NBFCs) and other registered companies. Many state governments also amended their state co-operative acts to use co-operative societies for providing microfinance. As a result accompanied by commercial banks (both public and private), regional rural banks, co-operative banks, registered and unregistered NBFCs, societies, trusts etc. are also providing microfinance by using their branch network through different microfinance delivery models.

The model of microfinance in India is different in mainly two respects. First, India provide microfinance by involving its public banks which after bank nationalisation in terms of geographical spread and functional reach is often deemed unparalleled in the world. That is why the microfinance experiment in India has been described as relationship banking rather than parallel banking elsewhere in the world (NABARD 2008). Secondly, credit to SHGs had an extremely small share in total credit and total loan accounts.

Microfinance in India was built up with institutions like NABARD along with Small Industries Development Bank of India (SIDBI) and Rashtriya Mahila Kosh (RMK) in the higher level. At the lower level, it works through Commercial Banks (CBs), cooperatives and Regional Rural Banks (RRBs). The private institutions that

[7]This trade union established their bank known as SEWA Bank in 1974.

[8]In 1996, RBI has instructed to banks to promote this programme further to cover SHG financing as a mainstream activity in their priority sector-lending portfolio.

undertake microfinance services are microfinance institutions (MFIs), NGOs and self-help group (SHGs)[9] (NABARD 2011).

3 Objective

Launching the programme like MUDRA will seem to be hugely beneficial to small manufacturing units and self-employed individuals in rural and urban areas. The prime objective of MUDRA bank is uplifting the small as well as medium enterprises. Its role and prime concern as an apex financer is to provide low-cost finance and thereby hoping to fill the gap in India's microfinance space. There is no cause of confusion that initiation of MUDRA will greatly increase the confidence of young educated and skilled workers of our country, who may be able to become the first-generation enterprises. Not only that, the existing small businesses can also be able to expand their activities through this programme as the MUDRA bank's basic objective is to funding the unfunded. The objective of the paper is to know the background of Pradhan Mantri Mudra Yojana (PMMY), to understand the roles and responsibilities played by the MUDRA bank, offerings of MUDRA bank and to evaluate the loan sanctioned and disbursed under different mudra schemes. Region-wise performance by banks in terms of numbers of accounts and amount disbursed is also being discussed.

4 Methodology and Data Sources

This descriptive study is completely based on secondary data from various reputed sources of government publications like PMMY report, annual publication of National Bank for Agriculture and Rural Development (NABARD), RBI Report etc. Further, it also uses secondary data from survey conducted by National Sample Survey Organisation (NSSO) in several rounds. This study also uses secondary data which has been collected from magazines, newspapers and publications of research articles available in different reputed journals. Various websites including website of MUDRA Yojana has also been consulted during this study. Since the programme was initiated in the year 2015, the time period has taken as 2015–2017 as per availability of the data. The analysis of data is completely based on table and comparative study.

[9]The NGOs that support the SHGs include MYRADA in Bangalore, Self-Help Women's Association (SEWA) in Ahmadabad, PRADAN in Tamil Nadu and Bihar, ADITHI in Patna, SPARC in Mumbai. The NGOs that are directly providing credit to the borrowers include SHARE in Hyderabad, ASA in Trichy, RDO LOYALAM Bank in Manipur etc.

Table 1 Loan sanctioned and disbursed

			Percentage increase[a] (Approx.)
Financial year	2015–2016 (A)	2016–2017 (B)	[(B − A)/A] × 100
Numbers of PMMY loans sanctions	34,880,924	39,701,047	13.82
Amount sanctioned (In Rs. Crore)	137449.27	180528.54	31.34
Amount disbursed (In Rs. Crore)	132954.73	175312.13	31.86

Source Pradhan Mantri Mudra Yojana report, 2015–2016, 2016–2017, PMYY website
[a]Authors own calculation

5 Major Findings

As already mentioned that as the programme was initiated in the year April, 2015 so it is premature to comment on the basis of data for this short period. Still this paper is trying to find out what has already been done on the basis of data mentioned as follows.

5.1 Progress

The total amount of loan sanctioned as well as disbursed by PMYY in the financial year 2015–2016 and 2016–2017 is shown in Table 1. The numbers of loans sanctioned is 34,880,924 and 39,701,047, respectively, in the year 2015–2016 and 2016–2017, respectively. As far as amount of loan sanctioned and disbursement is concerned, it was seen that it was Rs. 137449.27 Crores and Rs. 132954.73 Crores compared to Rs. 180528.54 Crores and Rs. 175312.13 Crores in the year 2015–2016 and 2016–2017, respectively. So it clearly shows that there is an improvement in terms of numbers of loans sanctioned, sanctioned amount and the amount disbursed. In fact, there is a 8.65, 31.34 and 31.86% increment in terms of numbers of loans sanctioned, sanctioned amount and the amount disbursed.

In continuation of the progress of MUDRA, Table 2 shows that amount of loans sanctioned account, sanctioned amount as well as amount disbursed under three different schemes of this programme that is Shishu, Kishore and Tarun in the financial year 2015–2016 and 2016–2017. The maximum amount of loans can be sanctioned under these three schemes is Rs. 50,000, Rs. 50,000 to Rs. 500,000 and Rs. 500,000 to Rs. 1,000,000, respectively. The numbers of sanctioned account under Shishu, Kishore and Tarun in the financial year 2015–2016 and 2016–2017 is 32,401,046, 34,697,814; 2,069,461, 2,663,502; 410,417, 539,732. The percentage increase of number of sanctioned account is 7.08, 28.71 and 31.51. As far as sanctioned amount is

Table 2 Loan sanctioned and disbursed in different schemes

Shishu (loans up to Rs. 50,000)			
Year	Number of sanctions A/C	Sanctioned amount (Rs. Crore)	Disbursed amount (Rs. Crore)
2015–2016	32,401,046	68573.44[a]	62027.69
2016–2017	34,697,813	85100.74	83891.88
Increase (%)[a]	7.08	24.10	35.24
Kishore (Loans from Rs. 50,000 to Rs. 500,000)			
2015–2016	2,069,461	41152.31[a]	41073.28
2016–2017	2,663,502	53545.14	51063.12
Increase (%)[a]	28.71	30.11	24.32
Tarun (Loans from Rs. 500,000 to Rs. 1000,000)			
2015–2016	410,417	27723.52[a]	29853.76
2016–2017	539,732	41882.66	40357.13
Increase (%)[a]	31.51	51.07	35.12

Source Pradhan Mantri Mudra Yojana report, 2015–2016, 2016–2017
[a]Authors own calculation based on the data available up to December 10, 2015

concerned in Shishu, it is Rs. 68573.44 Crore and Rs. 85100.74 Crore in the financial year 2015–2016 and 2016–2017 which shows an increase of 24.10%; under Kishore it is Rs. 41152.31 Crore and Rs. 53545.14 Crore in the financial year 2015–2016 and 2016–2017 which shows an increase of 30.11%; under Tarun it is Rs. 27723.52 Crore and Rs. 41882.66 Crore in the financial year 2015–2016 and 2016–2017 which shows an increase of 51.07%. If we compare amount disbursed in these three schemes, then in Shishu it is Rs. 62027.69 Crore and Rs. 83891.88 Crore in the financial year 2015–2016 and 2016–2017 which shows an increase of 35.24%; under Kishore it is Rs. 41073.28 Crore and Rs. 51063.12 Crore in the financial year 2015–2016 and 2016–2017 which shows an increase of 24.32%; under Tarun it is Rs. 29853.76 Crore and Rs. 40357.13 Crore in the financial year 2015–2016 and 2016–2017 which shows an increase of 35.12%.

5.2 *Region-Wise Performance by Banks (Number of Accounts)*

The Region-wise performance by banks is discussed on the basis of number of accounts and amount disbursed in four regions of the country like north, west, east and southern part of the country in the financial year 2015–2016 (Data of other years is not available). The division of these regions with respect to states is given in the table itself (Table 3). Based on the data, it is seen that as per sanctioning of account is concerned the percentage share of south is highest with 32% and lowest in west

Table 3 Region-wise performance by banks (Number of accounts) (2015–2016)

Category	North	West	East	South	Total
Shishu	2,382,453	1,864,905	1,893,789	2,563,432	8,704,579
Kishore	414,020	331,002	375,376	852,109	1,972,507
Tarun	120,636	95,641	60,320	132,814	409,411
Total	2,917,109	229,148	2,329,485	3,548,355	11,086,497
Share (percentage)	26	21	21	32	100

Source Review of performance in Pradhan Mantri Mudra Yojana report, 2015–2016 (North: Chandigarh, Haryana, HP, J&K, Delhi, UP, Uttarakhand, Punjab and Rajasthan; West: Dadra and Nagar Haveli, D&Diu, Gujarat, Lakshadweep, MP, Maharashtra; East: NE States, Odisha, WB, Sikkim, Bihar and Jharkhand; South: Karnataka, Kerala, Pudicherry, TN, Telangana, AP, and Andaman and Nicobar)

and east having 21% each. The North has percentage share of 26%. The numbers of accounts is highest in case of Shishu in all the four regions followed by Kishore and Tarun (Table 3). So it is obvious that the total sanctioning account is also highest in Shishu as compared to the other two schemes.

5.3 Region-Wise Performance by Banks (Amount Disbursed)

The region-wise performance in terms of amount disbursed by the banks in the all four regions as discussed above (north, west, east and south) is shown in Table 4. This table shows that again the amount disbursed in south is highest with 36% follows by north, west and east with 26, 21 and 17%, respectively, in the financial year 2016–2016. One interesting finding is that unlike sanctioning of account, the amount disbursed as well as total amount disbursed in Kishore is more than the other two schemes in all these four regions (Rs. 40291.59 Crore as compared with Rs. 16983.82 Crore in Shishu and Rs. 29774.90 in Tarun).

6 Conclusion

From the above discussion, this study may conclude that the idea of MUDRA Bank is based on providing credit and financial needs of small enterprises. In the same time, it also based on the approach under which access to credit will be combined with various enterprises development and welfare related services. The basic objective of MUDRA Bank is to provide much needed financial access to promote growth of small businesses, create job in the coming times and in turn help boost the country's GDP.

Table 4 Region-wise performance by banks (Amount disbursed) (2015–2016)

Category	North	West	East	South	Total
Shishu	4090.28	3478	3746.97	5668.02	16983.82
Kishore	9436.71	7312.71	7116.48	16426.35	40291.59
Tarun	9022.46	7143.29	4219.29	9389.86	29774.90
Total	22549.45	17933.89	15082.74	31484.23	87050.3
Share (percentage)	26	21	17	36	100

Source Review of performance in Pradhan Mantri Mudra Yojana report, 2015–2016 (North: Chandigarh, Haryana, HP, J&K, Delhi, UP, Uttarakhand, Punjab and Rajasthan; West: Dadra and Nagar Haveli, D&Diu, Gujarat, Lakshadweep, MP, Maharashtra; East: NE States, Odisha, WB, Sikkim, Bihar and Jharkhand; South: Karnataka, Kerala, Pudicherry, TN, Telangana, AP, and Andaman and Nicobar)

In our country since 1990s, when poverty reduction has taken priority at both national and international development levels, it was found that economic development of any country is severely influenced by the availability of financial services as a well-developed financial system that promotes investment opportunities in an economy. Therefore, it was necessary that the Government of India have to focus on extending financial services to both rural and urban people to ensure growth which is sustainable. The initiatives of Government for poverty alleviation in various plan period[10] could not succeed to the desired level. In fact, Government tries to help the poor by way of subsidies, but these initiatives hardly reduce poverty levels of the country due to the fact that they do not make them realise their own potential to deal with their own problems and hence unable to provide a long term solution.

The mid-term appraisal of the ninth plan had took a serious note about functioning of multiple programmes without desired linkages and also suffering from lack of bank credit, lack of market linkages and over-crowding as well. Moreover, these programmes were basically subsidy driven and ignored about follow up action and lack of a continuing relationship between borrowers and lenders for success of self-employment programmes (Thirumaran and Selladurai 2013). So, the planning commission recommended the merger of all these self-employment programmes.

In this regard, the importance of microfinance has caught the attention as an effective tool for poverty reduction and socio-economic development programme in India. Small business units generally face lot of challenges to get loans from banks and they end up taking high-cost loans from private financiers. It is believed that creating a bank like MUDRA will hugely benefit self-employed individuals and

[10]For example IRDP (Integrated Rural Development Programme), TRYSEM (Training of Rural Youth for Self-Employment), DWCRA (Development of Women and Children in Rural Areas), SITRA (Supply of Improved Toolkits to Rural Artisans), GKY (Ganga Kalyan Yojana) and MWS (Million Wells Schemes) etc.

small business units[11] in rural as well as urban areas with financing requirements and thus will greatly increase the confidence of young skilled workers as well as existing small businesses.

In a nutshell, this paper concludes that there is no doubt that small businesses need to be strengthened and supported for economic development of the country like India. MUDRA Yojana as a most recent scheme helps to boost up the small- and microbusiness units in India. Though it is too early to comment on either the success or failure of this programme, there is no doubt that there is an impact of the programme which seems to be positive. This type of scheme will add to the well-being of the individuals engaged in small-scale industries which will positively shape the progress of the economy as a whole. This will definitely make a dramatic change and will help in making a developed India and would be the first step towards reaching the goal of bank credit as a human right as advocated by Nobel laureate Professor Mohammed Yunus (Reddy 2007). Moreover, this is one of the modes of financial inclusion as ensuring bank account to all families that want it (RBI 2007).

References

Adams, D. W., Graham, D. H. & Von, Pischke. J. D. (1984). *Undermining rural development with cheap credit*. Boulder, Colorado, USA: Westview Press.

Adams, D. W., & Vogel, R. C. (1986). Rural financial markets in low-income countries: Recent controversies and lessons. *World Development, 14,* 477–488.

Asian Development Bank. (2000). *Finance for the poor: Microfinance development strategy*, Manila.

Akula, V. (2008). *A fistful of rice*. Boston: Harvard Business Review Press.

Chavan, P., Birajdar, B. (2009). Micro finance and financial inclusion of women: An evaluation. RBI occasional papers, Vol. 30, No. 2.

Hulme, D., Paul, M.(1996). *Finance against poverty*. (Vol. I). London: Routledge Publications.

Jayaraman, B. (2001). Micro finance: Retrospect and prospects. Occasional Paper, No. 20, NABARD.

Micro financial sector development and regulation bill. (2007). Bill No. −41, introduced by the Union finance minister in Lok Sabha on March, 20.

NABARD. (2008). State of micro finance in India, 2006–07, Mumbai.

NABARD. (2011). Progress of SHG-Bank linkage in India, Chapter IV.

NSSO. (2009). *Report on Employment and Unemployment among the Social Groups, 66th Round*. GOI: Ministry of Statistics and Programme Implementation.

Pillai, A. (2011). Status of microfinance in India. *International Journal of Marketing, Financial Services and Management Research 1.*

RBI speeches. (2007). What RBI means to the common person. Lecture delivered by Dr. Y. V. Reddy, Governor, Reserve Bank of India at Karamchedu Village, Ongole District, Andhra Pradesh, February 18.

Schwiecker, S. (2004). *The impact and outreach of microfinance institutions: The effect of interest rates*. Master's Degree Thesis, University of Tubingen, Germany.

[11]There are 5.77 Crores of small business units that are mostly individual proprietorships, running small manufacturing and training business, out of that 66% of these are owned by Scheduled Caste, Scheduled Tribes and Other Backward Castes (NSSO 2009).

Seibel, H.D. (2005). Does history matter? The old and the new world of microfinance in Europe and Asia. From moneylenders to microfinance—Southeast Asia's credit revolution in institutional, economic and cultural perspective. In *An Interdisciplinary Workshop*, Asia Research Institute, Department of Economics and Department of Sociology, National University of Singapore, October, 7–8.

The New York Times. (1997). Micro loans for the very poor. Editorial, February 16.

Thirumaran, S., & Selladurai, M. (2013). An analysis of poverty eradication measure in India. *Indian Journal of Applied Research*, *3*(2).

World Bank. (1989). *World development report*. New York: Oxford University Press.

Women's World Banking. (1995). *The missing links: Financial systems that work for the majority*. New York.

Impact of Fiscal Policy Initiatives on Inflation in India

Amrendra Pandey and Jagdish Shettigar

Abstract This paper examines the impact of fiscal policy initiatives on wholesale price index (WPI) based inflation in India. Total central government expenditure has been taken as the proxy for fiscal policy initiatives. The models used are VECM and ARDL-bound testing for estimating long run relationship. The results show that there is long run relationship between total central government expenditure and inflation in India. The IRF shows that if fiscal expenditure is given a positive shock of 100.0%, its cumulative impact on WPI in 5 years will be 14.0%.

1 Introduction

The relationship between fiscal policy and inflation is one of the widely debated topic among economists and policy makers around the world. The Reserve Bank of India (RBI) and the central government signed the ways and means advances (WMA) agreement in March 1997, which put the issuance of ad hoc T-bills to an end. At the same time the Government of India and state governments since 2004, after signing the Fiscal Responsibility and Budget Management Act, 2003 (FRBMA) have been adhering to consolidation norms though there have been instances of lapse in between. Even after these measures the RBI has not been able to consistently achieve its inflation target range. One of the causes could have been relaxation in terms of fiscal policy of the government due to lack of coordination with the monetary policy which resulted in neutralizing monetary policy initiatives. Keeping this hypothesis in mind *the following research questions would be tested empirically in this research paper: (i) what has been the impact of the fiscal policy on inflation in India since the beginning of the liberalization period? And (ii) if there is such relationship then how much fluctuation in inflation can be explained by fiscal policy variable?* This paper attempts to find answer of these questions.

A. Pandey (✉) · J. Shettigar
Birla Institute of Management Technology, Greater Noida, India
e-mail: amrendra.pandey@bimtech.ac.in

J. Shettigar
e-mail: j.shettigar@bimtech.ac.in

N. R. Bhanumurthy et al. (eds.), *Advances in Finance & Applied Economics*,
https://doi.org/10.1007/978-981-13-1696-8_7

India's fiscal position since 1980s has been one of concern, then hope and then confusion. Over the years the combined central and state government fiscal deficit kept increasing which hit 9.57% of the gross domestic product (GDP) in 2001–02, which was a record since 1980. But from this peak the centre and states brought down their combined fiscal deficit to 4.57% by 2007–08, mainly due to the FRBM Act, introduced by the then finance minister Yashwant Sinha in 2003. The act required the government to live within its means. But, a pause button was pressed on this fiscal consolidation in 2008 in the wake of the global financial crisis mainly due to expanding fiscal expenses and increasing global oil price. This caused doubling of fiscal deficit of central and state government combined to 8.4% of GDP. Fiscal deterioration continued well till 2013 and only when the 'taper tantrum' of the Federal Reserve Board of the U.S. threaten India's external account the central government put in place a solid fiscal consolidation plan by phasing out different subsidies on petroleum and fertilizer products.

Fiscal policy and its relationship with inflation is an issue of contention between central banks and governments. Many researchers have studied this relationship, out of which some important studies are discussed below:

Friedman (1968) had pointed out that fiscal deficit was inflationary to the extent of its monetization. Bond financed fiscal deficit would be inflationary only if monetary authorities followed interest rate stabilization strategy, because this would require increasing money supply in cases where government debt demand driven up interest rate. But, Sargent and Wallace (1981) said that fiscal deficit was always inflationary because the central bank would monetize the deficit either now or in the long run.

Hamburger and Zwick (1981) and Darrat (1985) suggested that inflationary surge of the U.S. in 1970s was caused mainly by expansionary fiscal and monetary policy.

Dwyer (1982) using the U.S. data from 1952 to 1978 and a vector autoregression (VAR) found no evidence of the relationship between government deficit, inflation and money supply.

Miller (1983) on the other hand argued that even if the deficit was not financed by monetization, deficit was inflationary as it would crowd out the private investment, which would reduce the real growth of the economy. At the same time higher interest rate would force the financial market to innovate the payment system so that government bonds could be used as a substitute for money.

Krishnamurty et al. (1984) had noted that inflation was the result of conflicts between different economic agents of an economy in their attempt to garner to itself a larger share of resources available at any time. The authors using the data of the Indian economy for the sample period, 1961–80, showed that government's effort in its developmental endeavor of the economy had resulted in it taking the larger share of economic resources than the society was willing to give it. This according to the authors, resulted in budgetary deficit and monetary expansion on one hand, and the expansion of parallel economy on the other. Both of these phenomenon fed inflation. The authors concluded that rapid inflation was always a fiscal phenomenon.

Scarth (1987) and Langdana (2002) had shown that if time path of fiscal expenditure and taxes were exogenous, fiscal deficit even if bond financed would not be sustainable since increasing interest rate would force the central bank to increase money supply which in turn would fuel inflation.

Rangarajan and Arif (1990) after analyzing the pre-reform macroeconomic conditions concluded that the inflationary impact of fiscal deficit had been worse in the cases when larger share of the deficit was met by the RBI borrowing. And, their model summarized that inflation impacted the increase in reserve money base which increased to accommodate fiscal deficit.

Fischer and Easterly (1990) argued that the extent of inflationary tendency of fiscal deficit depended upon the size and growth of the economy. If the growth rate was high, government could obtain more revenue by printing money. The authors also pointed out that this logic explained the high deficit, but single digit inflation in countries like India, Malaysia, Pakistan and Thailand, where the growth was at or above 5.0% over 1980–86, whereas Argentina and Brazil with negligible growth but with comparable inflation-adjusted deficits had quadruple-digit inflation during the period.

Easterly and Schmidt-Hebbel (1993) using the data of ten diverse countries from 1978–88, pointed out that for the countries with moderate inflation, like India, to generate an additional percentage of the long-run seigniorage revenue to meet government deficit, it would require 15.0–20.0% of inflation. It meant that inflation and the long run fiscal deficit had strong relationship. Similarly, Dogas (1992) and Darrat (2000) had found that fiscal deficit impacted inflation in Greece.

Shabbir et al. (1994) using the data of Pakistan from 1971–72 to 1987–88 had found, that 1.0% increase in budget deficit led to 6.0% increase in inflation, which they attributed to the fact, that budget deficit led to the formation of inflation expectations.

Similarly, Ansari (1997) using a VAR model and annual data from 1963 to 1993 for government expenditure, M_1, GDP deflator and GDP of India had shown that fiscal deficit contributed positively in price rise. From the variance decomposition the author had shown, that after 6 month, government expenditure explained 44.0% of variation in prices.

Özatay (1997) using the data from 1977 to 1995 had found that before the 1994 turkish financial crisis, the fiscal policy was unsustainable which made the inflation targets unachievable.

Similarly, Metin (1998) using the annual data of Turkey from 1950 to 1987 and Johansen cointegration test had shown that increased in budget deficit immediately increase inflation and the effect was significant.

Mohanty et al. (2000) noted that due to high fiscal deficit during 1993–96, where the central government gross fiscal deficits were 5.7%, 7.4% and 6.1% in 1992–93, 1993–94 and 1994–95 respectively, WPI inflation remained close to double digit reflecting the effect of fiscal deficit on inflation.

Mohanty et al. (2001) observed that a sustainable decline in inflation required long-term improvement in the fiscal balance and monetary growth, so that actual output was matched closer to the potential. The authors recommended better coordination between monetary and fiscal policies.

Neyapti (2003) using panel data of 54 developed and less developed countries had found that budget deficits exerted significant positive influence on inflation.

Alavirad and Athawale (2005) using a autoregressive distributed lag model (ARDL) and data of Iranian government deficit and inflation from 1963–99, had shown that the budget deficit and inflation shared a long run relation and the relationship was positive, i.e., in the long run government budget deficit had positive impact on inflation.

Catao and Terrones (2005) using the data of 107 countries from 1960–2001 and ARDL model had shown that budget deficit had strong positive impact on inflation in most of the countries except low inflation countries and advanced economies. The authors had pointed out that for the countries having more than 15.5% average ratio of M_1/GDP, 1.0% reduction in budget deficit lowered inflation by 9.25%.

Kia (2006) using the data of Iran from the period 1970:Q_1 to 2002:Q_4 had empirically found that fiscal policy was positively related to inflation in Iran, but if there was unanticipated change in fiscal policy it would cause negative impact.

Mohan (2008) noted that the growing fiscal deficit of the Indian government from the 1970s, 1980s and 1991–1997 were responsible for inflationary pressure in the economy which reached 9.0%, 8.0% and 10.0% respectively in these three decades from 6.4% in 1960s and 1.2% in 1950s.

Khundrakpam and Pattanaik (2010) using the data for the period of 1953–2009 of India showed that 1.0% increase in the level of fiscal deficit caused 0.25% increase in the wholesale price index (WPI). They also found significant short run relationship, but the error correction term was small.

Patra and Ray (2010) found that the role of fiscal policy in shaping inflation expectation in India was marginal and negative, i.e., an increase in real government expenditure lowered inflation expectations. The authors attributed this to the strong fiscal responsibility legislation in 2004, after which it was expected that any increase in fiscal expenditure would be offset by increase in taxes and other revenues, so lowering inflation expectation.

Lin and Chu (2013) using the data of 91 countries from 1960 to 2006, showed that the effect of fiscal deficit on inflation was higher during the high-inflation period because of faster money creation during the inflationary period. Hence, they postulated that the fiscal deficit-inflation relationship varied across countries with varying level of inflation.

2 Impact of Government Expenditure on Inflation

Growth in the central government's total expenditure and growth in WPI based inflation index is summarized in Table 1 and Fig. 1. From the figure it becomes clear that the central government expenditure generally follows political cycle rather than economic cycle. Just preceding the election years the expenditure growth followed positive path but in subsequent years it showed negative growth. After external payment crisis and subsequent deal with International Monetary Fund (IMF) the government expenditure management mainly concerned with reducing subsidies leak and non capital expenditure in the economy. But, a component of the expenditure was on

Table 1 Trend in government expenditure growth and WPI inflation rate, April 1991–92 to March 2014–15)

Year	Total gov. exp. (growth) (%)	Inflation rate (%)
1991–92	5.8	16.0
1992–93	10.1	10.1
1993–94	15.7	8.4
1994-95	13.3	12.4
1995–96	10.9	8.0
1996–97	12.8	4.6
1997–98	15.5	4.4
1998–99	20.4	5.9
1999–2000	6.7	3.3
2000–01	9.2	7.2
2001–02	11.3	3.6
2002–03	14.1	3.4
2003–04	14.0	5.5
2004–05	5.7	6.5
2005–06	1.5	4.4
2006–07	15.4	6.6
2007–08	22.1	4.7
2008–09	24.0	8.1
2009–10	15.9	3.8
2010–11	16.9	9.6
2011–12	8.9	8.9
2012 13	8.1	7.4
2013–14	10.6	6.0
2014–15	14.0	2.0

(Compiled by the researcher from the Reports of the RBI and World Bank databse. Data Retrieved from www.rbi.org.in/Scripts/AnnualReportMainDisplay.aspx. and http://data.worldbank.org/country/india)

account of interest payment which constituted 36.0% of the central government's revenue expenditure in 1995–96 which remained at the same level until 2000–01. While, at the same time subsidies expenditure increased from 9.0% in 1995–96 to 10.0% in 2000–01. This shows how difficult it is to change the composition of government expenditure. Subsidies further increased to 11.0% in 2005–06, while expenditure on account of interest payments decreased to 30.0%. The Fiscal Responsibility and Budget Management (FRBM) Act which was adopted in 2003 after 3 years of deliberation set medium term target of phased reduction of the gross fiscal deficit (GFD) to 3.0% of GDP. This brought the fiscal discipline in the government expenditure. This fact can also be observed from Table 1 which shows, that growth in total fiscal expenditure followed negative path successively for 3 years from 2003–04 to 2005–06. This helped in containing GFD to 3.2% of GDP in 2006–07.

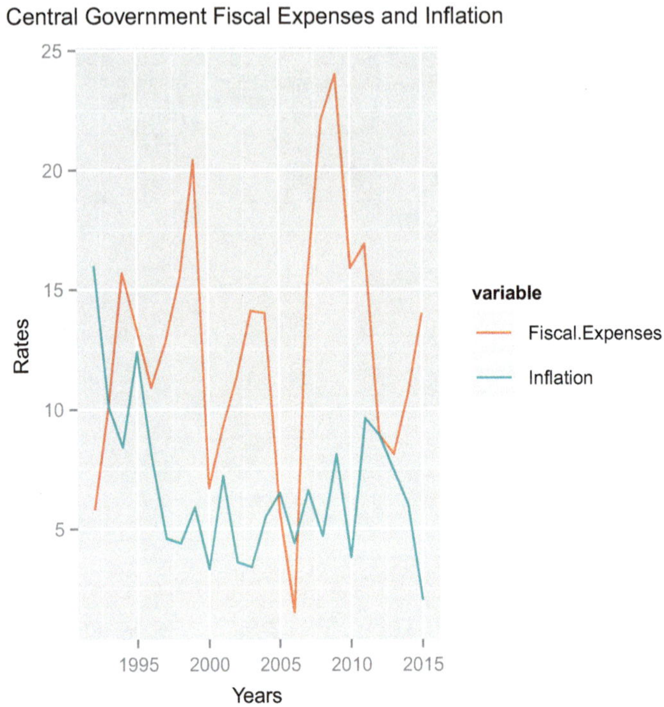

Fig. 1 Fiscal policy and inflation (WPI), 1991–92 to 2014–15 (Drawn by the researcher from the Table 1)

Just before the mortgage crisis hit the global economy in 2008 the government expenditure was already on expansionary mode with rural farm loan waiving scheme, expansion of the National Rural Employment Guarantee Act (NAREGA), 2005 and implementation of Sixth Pay Commission recommendations. This led to increase in the total central government expenditure by 24.0% in 2008–09. In 2008–09 WPI based inflation too increased to 8.1% from 4.7% in the previous year. To boost the domestic demand under the bearish global demand conditions the central government announced many stimulus packages, like, reduction in excise duty, increasing planned expenditure, reduction in service tax and interest subsidies for export. All these led to increase in the fiscal deficit to 6.5% of GDP in 2009–10. Similarly, WPI also increased by 9.6% in 2010–11.

Emphasizing the need to return to fiscal prudence the Thirteenth Finance Commission report reiterated strict adherence to the fiscal deficit targets. The fiscal policy adopted exit approach from the fiscal stimulus and the result was evident from negative path in total expenditure growth which grew by only 8.9% in 2011–12 as compared to 16.9% growth in 2010–11. The downward growth trend continued even in 2012–13 when the expenditure grew by only 8.1%. During these 2 years the inflation also followed downward growth path and it decreased from 9.6% in 2010–11 to

8.9 and 7.4% in 2011–12 and 2012–13 respectively. In the financial year 2013–14 the government's budgeted increase in planned expenditure was 6.6%. The focus of the policy during that year was to help the economy in revival as well as to decrease the GDF to GDP ratio 4.8%. The actual total expenditure of the government grew by 10.6% during that year and inflation decelerated to 6.0%. Similarly, in the financial year 2014–15 the government expenditure grew by 14.0% while inflation measured as growth in WPI index increased by merely 2.0%.

From Table 1 and Fig. 1, it becomes clear that generally whenever there is shock in the government expenditure, WPI has responded either immediately or with a lag, e.g, 1993–94, 1998–99, 2005–06 and 2007–08. Analysis of the total government expenditure during the 24 years showed positive path in 14 years, while it has shown negative path in the remaining 10 years. Similarly, WPI has followed positive path in 9 years and negative path in 15 years. When we look at the same path followed by both the fiscal expenditure and WPI, both have followed same path in 11 years while they have followed opposite path in 13 years. So, when we look at the shock to the fiscal policy there seems to be strong relationship between fiscal policy and inflation but when we look at the same path followed by both the variables the relationship seems to be weak.

3 Models and Data

It is possible that the time series data being considered in the study will not be stationary individually, but when one or more of the time series data will be regressed on another time series data, the combination may be stationary, i.e., their linear combination will cancel out stochastic trend. This econometric phenomenon is called *cointegration* and in economic terms it implies that the time series variables have a long run, or equilibrium relation between them.

Before doing further analysis with the time series, stationarity of the time series variables will be tested for which two tests, namely, Augmented Dickey Fuller (ADF) test and Kwiatkowski-Phillips Schmidt Shin Test (KPSS) will be used. After testing the stationarity if the data set is found to be non stationary then cointegration relationships among the time series variables will be checked. If there has been cointegration then Impulse Responsive Function (IRF) and Forecast Error Variance Decomposition (FEVD) has been used to analyze the results.

Vector Error Correction Model (VECM)

Johansen (1988), Johansen and Juselius (1990) and Johansen (1991) developed maximum likelihood estimators of cointegrating vectors for an autoregressive process. This approach uses canonical correlation analysis. In the VECM the variables adjust to their existing long run relationship. It also explains how long run error correction term explains the movement in the short run. The general structure of the VECM model used for the analysis is as follows:

$$\Delta y_t = \mu + \alpha\beta' y_{t-1} + A_1 \Delta y_{t-1} + \cdots + A_{p-1} \Delta y_{t-p+1} + \epsilon_t \quad (3.1)$$

where

$$y_t = \begin{bmatrix} WPI_t \\ FE_t \end{bmatrix} \quad (3.2)$$

y_t denotes the variables under consideration. Where WPI_t denote inflation rate and FE denotes fiscal expenses.

Also α denote the vector of adjustment parameter and β is the cointegrating vector and A_i,$i = 1, \ldots, p-1$ are the short run impact parameters.

Autoregressive Distributed Lag Model (ARDL)—Bound test

Pesaran et al. (1999) and Pesaran et al. (2001) developed ARDL—bound testing to test the cointegration in a set of time series variables. It has certain advantages over VECM. The advantages are as follows;

- If some of the variables are I(0) whereas others are I(1) ARDL can be applied.
- There is only single—equation to solve, which makes it simple to interpret.
- One of the biggest advantages over other cointegrating tests is that different variables can enter in the equation with different lags.

The steps of the analysis are as follows:

1. This step will involve testing the stationarity of the variables. The variables must not be I(2).
2. Then if the variables are either I(1) or a mix of I(0) and I(1), an unrestricted ECM (UECM) will be estimated. The generic UECM is as follows:

$$\begin{aligned}\Delta y_t = B_0 + \sum_{i=1}^{p} B_i \Delta y_{t-i} + \sum_{i=0}^{q} Y_j \Delta x_{1t-j} + \sum_{i=0}^{r} \delta_k \Delta x_{2t-k} + \\ \phi_0 y_{t-1} + \phi_1 x_{1t-1} + \phi_2 x_{2t-1} + \varepsilon_t\end{aligned} \quad (3.3)$$

3. In the next level appropriate lag length of the of p, q and r in the Eq. 4.4.20 will be selected using Akaike Information Criteria (AIC) and Schwarz Criterion (SC).
4. After selecting the lag lengths the Eq. 4.4.20 will be estimated and then the residuals of the model will be tested for the serial correlation independence. The test used for this purpose will be Breusch-Godfrey (B-G) test.
5. After ascertaining that the residuals of Eq. 4.4.20 are serially not correlated, 'bound testing' is performed. For this Wald testing is used. The null hypothesis in the test is, H_0: $\phi_0 = \phi_1 = \phi_2 = 0$ (where ϕ_0, ϕ_1 and ϕ_2 are from Eq. 4.4.20). The critical F values for this test is taken from Pesaran et al. (2001).
   As a cross check 'bound t-test' of $H_0 : \phi_0 = 0$ is also performed. Critical t-values are again taken from Pesaran et al. (2001).

6. In step 5 if the null hypothesis is rejected then it will be concluded that there is cointegrating relationship between Y, X_1 and X_2. In this case long run relationship can be meaningfully estimated between the variables:

$$y_t = a_0 + a_1 x_{1t} + a_2 x_{2t} + v_t \tag{3.4}$$

7. Now usual ECM will be estimated:

$$\Delta y_t = B_0 + \sum_{i=1}^{p} B_i \Delta y_{t-i} + \sum_{i=0}^{q} Y_j \Delta x_{1t-j} + \sum_{i=0}^{r} \delta_k \Delta x_{2t-k} + \varphi v_{t-1} + \varepsilon \tag{3.5}$$

where v_{t-1} are the lagged residuals of OSL regression 4.4.21

To answer the research questions raised above the monthly fiscal expenses of the central government has been taken as the fiscal policy variable. Similarly, inflation indicator is the wholesale price index (WPI). WPI series have been converted to the base year of 1981–82 using conversion rate at 2.478 for 1993–94 base year and 1.875 for 2004–05 base year index as provided by the office of Economic Adviser, Govt. of India, Ministry of Commerce and Industry, Department of Industrial Policy and Promotion (DIPP).

The sample period for the study is from April 1997 to June 2015, since monthly data of the total fiscal expenses is available from this period on the World Bank database website. The total fiscal expenditure of the central government has been taken because it is the direct result of fiscal policy decisions. At the same time in all the years analyzed the government has always run in fiscal deficit, i.e., it has borrowed from the market to finance its expenditure need, so the total government expenses can be taken as a proxy for fiscal policy.

4 Empirical Analysis

For estimating the impact of fiscal policy on inflation in India, the present model has included monthly fiscal expenditure and WPI. Before testing the stationarity of the time series variables, logs of monthly central government's total fiscal expenditure and WPI have been taken. The stationarity of the time series variables have been tested using ADF and KPSS tests. Both of these tests indicate that both the series variables are non-stationary in level form, but stationary in first difference, i.e., they all are $I(1)$ (Table 2).

First, the cointegration relation has been tested using the Johansen cointegration test, for which lag length has been selected using the diagnostics of residuals of the VAR model. Then if the vector error correction model (VECM) suggested cointegration relation, the autoregressive distributed lag model (ARDL) bound test has been used to recheck the cointegration relation and to find out the best fitted regression model.

Table 2 Stationarity and integration of total government expenditure and WPI: ADF and KPSS test, April 1997–98 to June 2015–16

Variable	In level form		Stationarity	First difference		Stationarity
	ADF	KPSS	Result	ADF	KPSS	Result
WPI	−1.79	5.518	Non stationary	−4.00	0.08	Stationary
Gov. exp.	−1.16	5.80	Non stationary	−8.82	0.02	Stationary

Where ADF and KPSS critical values at 95% are −3.42 and 0.46 respectively

Table 3 Cointegration rank (Johansen cointegration test-eigenvalue statistics, with linear trend in cointegration)-total expenditure and WPI, April 1997–98 to June 2015–16

Cointegration rank

Cointegration rank	Test statistics	10%	5%	1%
$r \leq 1$	0.0	6.50	8.18	11.65
$r \leq 0$	138.85	12.91	14.90	19.19

Diagnostics of VAR model have suggested using lag length of 11 (B-G LM test p-value = 0.18). After selecting the lag, the cointegration rank has been estimated, the result of which has been shown in Table 3. The table suggests the cointegration rank of 1 at 5.0% level of significance.

The results of the restricted VECM is reported in Table 4. The table presents the pass through of government expenditure on inflation in India. *It shows that in the long run elasticity of relationship between the total central government expenditure and wholesale price index (WPI) is 0.43, means if government expenditure increases by 1.0%, WPI increases by 43 basis points. Any deviation from the long run relationship tends to correct itself by 5% points in the next month, i.e., once the system is disturbed it comes back again to equilibrium at the rate of 5% every subsequent months.*

Orthogonal Impulse response function (IRF) has been used to explore the impulse response on a variable because of shock on another variable, by taking into account the impact on other variables simultaneously. The result has been depicted in Fig. 2. 100.0% shock in fiscal expenses (denoted as t), increases inflation by 17 basis points in the very next month (t + 1) with the peak impact being seen at the end of 8th month (t + 8). Five year cumulative impact of 100.0% shock in fiscal expenses at time t,

Table 4 Long run and short run dynamic relationship-WPI and total central government expenditure, April 1997–98 to June 2015–16

Long run and short run dynamic relationship

Variables	Long-run relation	Error correction term
lnWPI		−0.05
Gov. exp.	0.43	

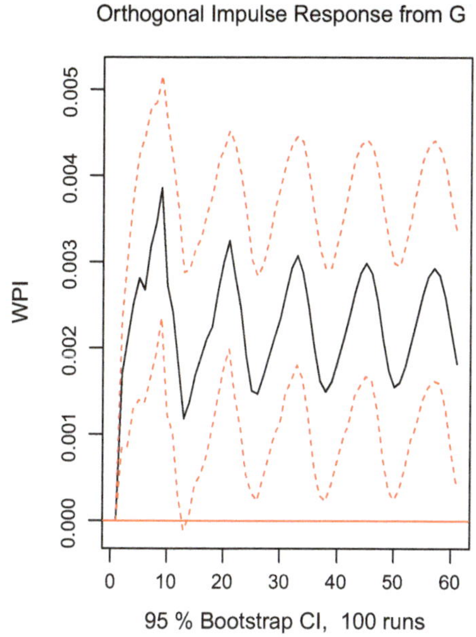

Fig. 2 Impulse response of WPI to a unit shock in fiscal expenditure, April 1997–98 to June 2015–16

Table 5 Forecast error variance decomposition—WPI and fiscal expenditure, April 1997–98 to June 2015–16

FEVD-WPI

Variable	Variance error in WPI explained-6 months ahead (%)	Variance error in WPI explained-12 months ahead (%)	Variance error in WPI explained-18 months ahead (%)	Variance error in WPI explained-24 months ahead (%)
WPI	92.0	91.0	91.0	91.0
Gov. exp.	8.0	9.0	9.0	9.0

on inflation will be 14.0%. The result also shows that once the fiscal expenditure is given a shock it will have impact on inflation even after 5 years.

The variance decomposition analysis is shown in Table 5. It shows that fiscal expenditure explains 8.0% of the variation in WPI 6 months ahead, while it explains 9.0% of the variation after 2 years.

To check the validity of VECM results, ARDL bound test has been applied, the results of which has been shown in the Table 6. From the table it becomes clear that there is cointegrating relationship between WPI and total fiscal expenditure. From the B-G serial correlation test it is clear that the errors of unrestricted error correction model (UECM) is serially not correlated. The error correction term (ECT) is −0.0043. The long run multiplier between WPI and total central government expenditure is 0.43, which means that in the long run 1.0% increase in M_3 will lead to 0.47 increase in IIP-manufacturing. This result is same as given by the VECM model. The model has been depicted in Eq. 3.1.

Table 6 ARDL bound test for WPI and total fiscal expenditure, April 1997–98 to June 2015–16

Bound test and restricted ECM results for ARDL (2, 7)

Variables	Result value	Other relevant value
Bound test (Wald F statistic)	25.85	Pesaran and Shin critical values at 95% confidence level 4.94 for $I(0)$ and 5.73 for $I(1)$
$lnWPI_{t-1}$ bound t statistic	−6.91	Pesaran and Shin critical t-values at 95% confidence level −2.86 for $I(0)$ and −3.22 for $I(1)$
B-G serial correlation unrestricted ECM	p value = 0.60	
Error correction term	−0.0043	p value = 0.04
Long run effect	0.43	
B-G serial correlation restricted ECM	p value = 0.21	

$$\begin{aligned} \Delta lnWPI = 0.0024 + 0.43\Delta lnWPI_{t-1} + 0.03\Delta lnWPI_{t-2} - \\ 0.00026\Delta lnG_{t-1} - 0.00147\Delta lnG_{(t-2)} - \\ 0.00137\Delta lnG_{(t-3)} - 0.00106\Delta lnG_{(t-4)} - \\ 0.0015\Delta lnG_{(t-5)} - 0.000015\Delta lnG_{(t-6)} + \\ 0.000065\Delta lnG_{(t-7)} - 0.0043(lnWPI_{t-1} - 0.47lnG_{(t-1)}) \end{aligned} \tag{4.1}$$

5 Conclusion

In this chapter empirical examination of the impact of fiscal policy on inflation since the onset of liberalization has been carried out. The study has used monthly data from April 1997–98 to June 2015–16 to analyze.

The study has found that there is the long run relationship between the total central government expenditure and WPI based inflation in post liberalization period of India. This relationship is strong and any deviation from it is corrected by 5.0% in the subsequent months.

The IRF shows that if fiscal expenditure is given a positive shock of 100.0% its cumulative impact on WPI in 5 years will be 14.0%. At the same time total fiscal expenditure explains around 9% variance error in WPI 24 months after the initial shock.

Based on the empirical analysis in this chapter it is argued that fiscal policy is important in explaining inflation in India. So, there should be coordination between monetary and fiscal policy, for monetary policy to succeed in containing inflation within targeted range.

References

Alavirad, A., & Athawale, S. (2005). The impact of the budget deficit on inflation in the islamic republic of iran. *OPEC Review*, *29*(1), 37–49.

Ansari, M. I. (1997). Monetary vs. fiscal policy: Some evidence from vector autoregression for india. *Journal of Asian Economics*, *7*(4), 677–698.

Catao, L. A., & Terrones, M. E. (2005). Fiscal deficits and inflation. *Journal of Monetary Economics*, *52*(3), 529–554.

Darrat, A. F. (1985). Inflation and federal budget deficits: some empirical results. *Public Finance Review*, *13*(2), 206–215.

Darrat, A. F. (2000). Are budget deficits inflationary? A reconsideration of the evidence. *Applied Economics Letters*, *7*(10), 633–636.

Dogas, D. (1992). Market power in a non-monetarist inflation model for greece. *Applied Economics*, *24*(3), 367–378.

Dwyer, G. P. (1982). Inflation and government deficits. *Economic Inquiry*, *20*(3), 315–329.

Easterly, W., & Schmidt-Hebbel, K. (1993). Fiscal deficits and macroeconomic performance in developing countries. *The World Bank Research Observer*, *8*(2), 211–237.

Fischer, S., & Easterly, W. (1990). The economics of the government budget constraint. *The World Bank Research Observer*, *5*(2), 127–142.

Friedman, M. (1968). The role of monetary policy. *American Economic Review*, *22*(2), 165–172.

Hamburger, M. J., & Zwick, B. (1981). Deficits, money and inflation. *Journal of Monetary Economics*, *7*(1), 141–150.

Johansen, S. (1988). Statistical analysis of cointegration vectors. *Journal of Economic Dynamics and Control*, *12*(2), 231–254.

Johansen, S. (1991). Estimation and hypothesis testing of cointegration vectors in gaussian vector autoregressive models. *Econometrica: Journal of the Econometric Society* 1551–1580.

Johansen, S., & Juselius, K. (1990). Maximum likelihood estimation and inference on cointegration with applications to the demand for money. *Oxford Bulletin of Economics and Statistics*, *52*(2), 169–210.

Khundrakpam, J. K. & Pattanaik, S. (2010). Fiscal stimulus and potential inflationary risks: An empirical assessment of fiscal deficit and inflation relationship in India. *Journal of Economic Integration* 703–721.

Kia, A. (2006). Deficits, debt financing, monetary policy and inflation in developing countries: Internal or external factors?: Evidence from iran. *Journal of Asian Economics*, *17*(5), 879–903.

Krishnamurty, K., Saibaba, P. & Kazmi, N. (1984). Inflation and growth: a model for India. *Indian Economic Review*, 16–111.

Langdana, F. (2002). *Sustaining domestic budget deficits in open economies*, Routledge.

Lin, H.-Y., & Chu, H.-P. (2013). Are fiscal deficits inflationary? *Journal of International Money and Finance*, *32*, 214–233.

Metin, K. (1998). The relationship between inflation and the budget deficit in turkey. *Journal of Business & Economic Statistics*, *16*(4), 412–422.

Miller, P. J. (1983). Higher deficit policies lead to higher inflation. *Quarterly Review* (Win).

Mohan, R. (2008). Growth record of the indian economy, 1950-2008: A story of sustained savings and investment. *Economic and Political Weekly* 61–71.

Mohanty, D., Rath, D. P. & Ramaiah, M. (2000). Measures of core inflation for India. *Economic and Political Weekly* pp. 273–282.

Mohanty, M., Klau, M., et al. (2001). What determines inflation in emerging market economies? *BIS Papers*, *8*, 1–38.

Neyapti, B. (2003). Budget deficits and inflation: the roles of central bank independence and financial market development. *Contemporary Economic Policy*, *21*(4), 458–475.

Özatay, F. (1997). Sustainability of fiscal deficits, monetary policy, and inflation stabilization: The case of turkey. *Journal of Policy Modeling*, *19*(6), 661–681.

Patra, M. D., & Ray, P. (2010). *Inflation expectations and monetary policy in india*. International Monetary Fund: Technical report.

Pesaran, M. H., Shin, Y., & Smith, R. J. (2001). Bounds testing approaches to the analysis of level relationships. *Journal of Applied Econometrics*, *16*(3), 289–326.

Pesaran, M. H., Shin, Y., & Smith, R. P. (1999). Pooled mean group estimation of dynamic heterogeneous panels. *Journal of the American Statistical Association*, *94*(446), 621–634.

Rangarajan, C. & Arif, R. (1990). Money, output and prices: A macro econometric model. *Economic and Political Weekly* 837–852.

Sargent, T. J., & Wallace, N. (1981). Some unpleasant monetarist arithmetic. *Federal Reserve Bank of Minneapolis Quarterly Review*, *5*(3), 1–17.

Scarth, W. M. (1987). Can economic growth make monetarist arithmetic pleasant? *Southern Economic Journal* 1028–1036.

Shabbir, T., Ahmed, A. & Ali, M. S. (1994), Are government budget deficits inflationary? evidence from pakistan [with comments]. *The Pakistan Development Review* 955–967.

Monetary Policy and Private Investment in India: The MIDAS Experience

Debasis Rooj and Reshmi Sengupta

Abstract Recent evidence shows that Indian economy is experiencing a slowdown in private investment. Even after a significant decline in interest rates over the last two years, credit growth, particularly industrial credit growth, and private investment have remained sluggish. We examine the link between monetary policy and private investment in India by applying mixed-frequency vector autoregressive (MIDAS-VAR) method to monthly yield on 91-day T-bill, a proxy for monetary policy tool on quarterly bank loans, private investment, and gross domestic product. Mixed-frequency regression analysis includes variables of different frequencies into the analysis without the need for aggregating the higher frequency variables into lower-frequency ones. Converting higher-frequency variables into lower-frequency variables often referred to as temporal aggregation is known to have an adverse impact on statistical inferences. MIDAS performs better in recovering the causal relationships between variables released at different frequencies when compared to the conventional common low-frequency approach by allowing having heterogeneous impacts on a low-frequency variable within each low-frequency time period. The mixed-frequency analysis reveals an interesting mix of results linking the monetary policy to the private investment in India. A comparative analysis with single-frequency (quarterly) analysis underestimates the influence of monetary policy. The mixed-frequency approach, therefore, yields richer economic insights into India's sluggish investment than the classical single-frequency approach.

Keywords Monetary policy · Mixed-frequency data analysis · Private investment · Indian economy

---

D. Rooj (✉) · R. Sengupta
FLAME University, Pune, India
e-mail: debasis.rooj@flame.edu.in

N. R. Bhanumurthy et al. (eds.), *Advances in Finance & Applied Economics*,
https://doi.org/10.1007/978-981-13-1696-8_8

1 Introduction

Private investment is considered to be an essential driver of economic growth. It is a reflection of expectations about the future economic activity. Private investment generally contributes significantly toward the business cycle. Schembri (2017) argues that private investment contributes to the productive capacity which is essential for the sustainable increases in living standards of a nation. Hence, it is crucial that countries focus on continuously improving their private investment scenario to promote higher economic growth.

India is one of the fastest economies in the world. However, if we carefully look at the Indian growth story, one strange aspect that comes out is that India's sluggish private investment. Even though India is growing at close to 7%, private investment growth has remained muted in India. The share of private investment with respect to GDP has mostly remained at the level of 30% of the GDP and has not shown significant improvement. In fact, after reaching a high of 38% in the first quarter of 2013, it has shown only downward movement. Therefore, it is crucial to examine the causes behind such sluggishness in the private investment. Over the last two years, the Reserve Bank of India (RBI) has significantly decreased the benchmark interest rate. However, that has not helped the private investment scenario in India. The primary question remains what caused such investment slum. The problem could be due to firm-specific factors or bank-specific factors, or it could be related to some other macroeconomic factors affecting both firms and banks. Firms may be discouraged to invest whether their current or expected future profit decreases. On the other hand, banks facing credit crunch may take a stricter lending attitude which might further prohibit private investment. Overall economic environment and aggregate demand may also influence investment decisions.

This paper re-examines the factors driving the private fixed investment in India over the last decade. Understanding the underlining causes of the investment slowdown is essential for formulating policy responses that would promote private investment in India.

A large body of the literature has attributed the post-2008 economic crisis sluggishness in private investment in advanced economies to uncertainty (e.g., Barkbu et al. 2015; Lewis et al. 2014; Bussière et al. 2015). International Monetary Fund (IMF 2015) fond that subdued aggregate demand was responsible for the weakness in investment. Leboeuf and Fay (2016) examined some of the advanced economies and found that the primary driver behind the post-crisis weakness in investment is pessimism on the part of firms about foreign demand prospects. Heightened uncertainty, tight credit conditions, and weak corporate profits also attribute toward the slowdown in investment.

Empirically, Saarenheimo (1995) using vector autoregression (VAR) shown that credit supply played a statistically significant and economically important role in determining investment in Finland. On the other hand, Sadahiro (2005) using VAR found that the investment slump post-1990 in Japan was Granger-caused by a decrease in firm profit and not by bank credit. Hence, empirical evidence suggests toward mixed evidence of factors contributing toward private investment sluggishness. In the Indian context, Anand and Tulin (2014) argued that compared to standard macro-financial variables, economic policy uncertainty better explained the recent investment slowdown. In a recent paper, Das and Tulin (2017) used firm-level data and found that the debt burdens of Indian firms are the primary reason behind India's sluggish private investment. They observed that firms with higher financial leverage and firms with lower earnings relative to their interest expenses prefer to invest less.

The key variables used in the previous studies include private investment, banking lending for investment, and firm profit. These variables are generally sampled at a quarterly frequency. On the hand, other variables, such as stock prices and interest rates, are available at monthly and even higher frequencies. Most of the previous studies used some form of temporal aggregation method to convert high-frequency variables into low-frequency variables. For instance, Motonishi and Yoshikawa (1999) and Sadahiro (2005) used quarterly data of Japan for their analysis. However, temporal aggregation may cause an adverse impact on statistical inference (Silvestrini and Veredas 2008).

In this paper, we use the newly developed mixed-frequency data analysis approach of Ghysels et al. (2004), Ghysels et al. (2016), and Andreou et al. (2010). The analysis of mixed frequency is often referred as the mixed data sampling (MIDAS) regression. MIDAS regression leads to more efficient estimation compared to the classical approach of aggregating all the time series into a single frequency (Ghysels et al. 2004).

The multivariate mixed-frequency models have since been independently introduced by McCracken et al. (2015), Anderson et al. (2016), and Ghysels (2016). In this paper, we follow Ghysels' (2016) mixed frequency VAR (henceforth MF-VAR). This methodology is straightforward and easy to implement and does not rely on any filtering procedure.

The remainder of the paper is structured as follows. In Sect. 2, we describe the MF-VAR methodology. In Sect. 3, we explain our data and provide some descriptive analysis. In Sect. 4, we present our empirical results. Section 5 concludes the paper.

2 Methodology

In this section, we first present the single-frequency VAR model and then mixed-frequency VAR model (Motegi and Sadahiro 2018) to show that the choice of sampling frequency can change empirical results considerably.

2.1 Quarterly VAR Model

Let t ∈ {1, …, n} indicate each quarter. Let SR_t^Q be the short-term interest rate. Superscript 'Q' is used to distinguish a quarterly level from a monthly level. Let C_t be the growth rate of the outstanding stock of bank credits; let π_t be the growth rate of firm profit. Finally, let I_t be the growth rate of private investment. For each series, the growth rate implies 100 times log difference of original series from the previous year. The year-to-year difference is taken to remove stochastic trends and seasonality.

As a benchmark, we formulate a quarterly VAR (4) model:

$$\begin{bmatrix} SR_t^Q \\ C_t \\ \pi_t \\ I_t \end{bmatrix} = \sum_{k=1}^{4} \begin{bmatrix} a11,k\ a12,k\ a13,k\ a14,k \\ a21,k\ a22,k\ a23,k\ a24,k \\ a31,k\ a32,k\ a33,k\ a34,k \\ a41,k\ a42,k\ a43,k\ a44,k \end{bmatrix} \begin{bmatrix} SR_{t-k}^Q \\ C_{t-k} \\ \pi_{t-k} \\ I_{t-k} \end{bmatrix} + \begin{bmatrix} \epsilon_{1t} \\ \epsilon_{2t} \\ \epsilon_{3t} \\ \epsilon_{4t} \end{bmatrix} \tag{1}$$

Lag length is set to be 4 so that we can capture potential seasonality left after the year-to-year differencing. A constant term is omitted to save the number of parameters. We demean each series before fitting the model.

2.2 Mixed-Frequency VAR

We now present the MF-VAR of Ghysels (2016). Our model consists of monthly interest rate and quarterly C, π and I. Hence, the quarterly interest rate is presented as

$$SR_t^Q = \frac{1}{3}\sum_{j=1}^{3} SR_{jt} \tag{2}$$

Thus, $\{SR_{1t}, SR_{2t}, SR_{3t}\}$ represent the monthly interest rates, and SR_t^Q represents the quarterly interest rate.

The MF-VAR model is as follows:

$$\begin{bmatrix} SR_{1t} \\ SR_{2t} \\ SR_{3t} \\ C_t \\ \pi_t \\ I_t \end{bmatrix} = \sum_{k=1}^{4} \begin{bmatrix} a11,k\ a12,k\ a13,k\ a14,k\ a15,k\ a16,k \\ a21,k\ a22,k\ a23,k\ a24,k\ a25,k\ a26,k \\ a31,k\ a32,k\ a33,k\ a34,k\ a35,k\ a36,k \\ a41,k\ a42,k\ a43,k\ a44,k\ a45,k\ a46,k \\ a51,k\ a52,k\ a53,k\ a54,k\ a55,k\ a56,k \\ a61,k\ a62,k\ a63,k\ a64,k\ a65,k\ a66,k \end{bmatrix} \begin{bmatrix} SR_{1t-k} \\ SR_{2t-k} \\ SR_{3t-k} \\ C_{t-k} \\ \pi_{t-k} \\ I_{t-k} \end{bmatrix} + \begin{bmatrix} \epsilon_{1t} \\ \epsilon_{2t} \\ \epsilon_{3t} \\ \epsilon_{4t} \\ \epsilon_{5t} \\ \epsilon_{6t} \end{bmatrix} \tag{3}$$

or in a compact form, the above equation can be written as follows

$$Y_t = \sum_{k=1}^{4} A_k Y_{t-k} + \epsilon_t \tag{4}$$

Lag length is set to be 4 for a fair comparison with the quarterly model.

A key feature of (3) is that SR_{1t}, SR_{2t}, and SR_{3t} are stacked in a vector. To see an advantage of this approach, pick the last row of (3).

$$I_t = \sum_{k=1}^{4} \left[\sum_{j=1}^{3} a_{6j,k} SR_{j,t-k} + a_{64,k} C_{t-k} + a_{65,k} \pi_{t-k} + a_{66,k} I_{t-k} \right] + \epsilon_{6,t}$$

Since $a_{61,k}$, $a_{62,}$ and $a_{63,k}$ can take different values from each other, $SR_{1,t-k}$, $SR_{2,t-k}$ and $SR_{3,t-k}$, are allowed to have heterogeneous impacts on I_t

Recall from (1) and (2) that the quarterly VAR(4) model implies that

$$I_t = \sum_{k=1}^{4} \left[a_{41,k} \left(\frac{1}{3} \sum_{j-1}^{3} SR_{j,t-k} \right) + a_{42,k} C_{t-k} + a_{43,k} \pi_{t-k} + a_{44,k} I_{t-k} \right] + \epsilon_{4,t} \tag{5}$$

Equation (5) assumes implicitly that $SR_{1,t-k}$, $SR_{2,t-k}$ and $SR_{3,t-k}$ have a homogeneous impact of $a_{41,k}/3$ on I_t. This classification rules out the possibility of seasonal effects and lagged information transmission within each quarter. Hence, the MF-VAR is more flexible than the quarterly VAR. In terms of asymptotic theory, MF-VAR can be treated in the same way as classical VAR—note that MF-VAR model (4) has an identical appearance with a standard VAR with six variables. Standard regularity conditions, therefore, all carry over to MF-VAR. First, we assume that all roots of the polynomial $det\left(I_6 - \sum_{k=1}^{4} A_k Z^k\right) = 0$ lie outside the unit circle, where det(·) means the determinant. Second, $\{\epsilon_t\}$ is a strictly stationary martingale difference sequence with a finite second moment. Third, $\{X_t, \epsilon_t\}$ obeys α-mixing. These assumptions ensure the consistency and asymptotic normality of least squares estimator $\widehat{A_k}$.

We perform impulse response analysis and forecast error variance decomposition for both the quarterly model and mixed-frequency model. We follow the standard Cholesky order. We set SR → C → π → I for the quarterly model and SR1 → SR2 → S R3 → C → π → I for the mixed-frequency model. These orders are in line with actual data announcement schedules in India.

3 Data

In India, the Reserve Bank of India (RBI) conducts the monetary policy. RBI uses repo rate as the primary policy instrument. Before 1997, the monetary policy used to be reviewed twice in a financial year. Then, the review process moved to quarterly frequency. At present, RBI follows a bimonthly system of announcing its policy statement from April 2014. For our analysis, we consider the yield on the 91-day Treasury bill (T-bill) from the RBI database as a monetary policy tool, where the yield is reported in monthly frequency. This will help in capturing the heterogeneous impact of the monetary policy on investment in India, which is our primary goal.

The second variable is the bank loan (C), and we use the market value of the credit for all the sectors for the private non-financial firms in India. This series is available from the Bank of International Settlements (BIS) Web site under the category credit to the non-financial sector.

Private investment (I), the primary variables of concern in our analysis, is the gross fixed capital formation (GFCF). This variable is available in quarterly frequency. The variable is obtained from OECD database (the base year is 2010). For firm profit data (π), we rely on the data on profit of the private corporate sector from Oxford Economics. This variable is available in quarterly frequency. Our analysis covers the period from 2005 Q1 to 2016 Q4 having 47 quarterly observations.

3.1 Descriptive Data Analysis

Figure 1 plots the monthly interest rates corresponding to each quarter, year-to-year growth rates of quarterly bank loans, firm profit, and private investment from 2005 Q2 to 2016 Q4. From Fig. 1, it is observed that apart from some intervals; there is no apparent correlation between interest rate and bank lending. A similar pattern is observed for firm profit and private investment. However, firm profit and investment seem somewhat correlated. Interestingly, post-2013, even after a significant decline in the interest rate, the growth of the bank lending, firm profit, and private investment has remained stagnant questioning the role of monetary policy in spurring India's investment growth.

Table 1 reports sample statistics of SR1, SR2, SR3, SRQ, C, π, and I. We find that SR1, SR2, and SR3 have some exciting differences. First, the mean is 6.944, 7.115, and 7.073%. The minimum of SR3 is higher than that of SR1 and SR2. On the other hand, maximum of SR2 is higher than that of SR1 and SR3. Second, their skewness is −0.414, −0.277, and −0.778, respectively. SR2 thus has weaker asymmetry than

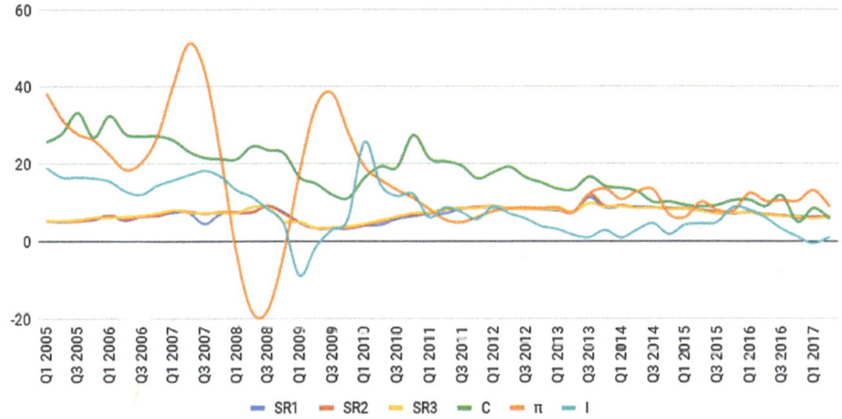

Fig. 1 Monthly interest rates, quarterly bank loans, firm profit, and private investment. *Source* Authors' own calculation. *Note* SR1, SR2 and SR3 represent the short-term interest rate (yield from 91-day T-bill) stacked monthly, while SRQ represents the average quarterly interest rate. C is growth in bank credit, π is growth in corporate profit, and I represents growth in private fixed investment. C, π, and I are quarterly percentage change (annualized)

Table 1 Descriptive statistics

	SR1	SR2	SR3	SRQ	C	π	I
Mean	6.944	7.115	7.073	7.044	7.211	5.649	3.684
Median	7.269	7.352	7.269	7.311	7.080	4.564	3.096
Min	3.235	3.275	3.316	3.316	1.814	−8.745	−4.516
Max	11.257	12.022	9.695	10.991	12.782	17.948	10.796
Std. Dev	1.727	1.715	1.534	1.626	2.757	5.179	3.015
Skewness	−0.414	−0.277	−0.778	−0.504	0.160	−0.230	−0.150
Kurtosis	3.053	3.725	2.970	3.236	2.045	4.387	3.097

Source Authors' own calculation
Note SR1, SR2 and SR3 represent the short-term interest rate (yield from 91-day T-bill) stacked monthly, while SRQ represents the average quarterly interest rate. C is growth in bank credit, π is growth in corporate profit, and I represents growth in private fixed investment. C, π, and I are quarterly percentage change (annualized)

SR1 and SR3. The heterogeneous characteristics of SR1, SR2, and SR suggest a potential benefit of the MF-VAR.

Table 2 reports contemporaneous and lagged correlation coefficients between each pair of variables, where lags are taken up to k = 4. Results from Table 2 are consistent with the lead/lag relationships observed in Fig. 1. We find that the contemporaneous correlation between bank credit and interest rate (SRQ_t) is positive and small. Similar correlations are observed for $SR1_t$, $SR2_t$, and $SR3_t$. Moreover, we also find that the

Table 2 Contemporaneous and lagged correlation coefficients

	$SR1_t$	$SR2_t$	$SR3_t$	SRQ_t	C_t	π_t	I_t
$SR1_t$	1.000						
$SR2_t$	0.962	1.000					
$SR3_t$	0.908	0.945	1.000				
SRQ_t	0.979	0.990	0.969	1.000			
C_t	0.030	0.121	0.137	0.096	1.000		
π_t	−0.495	−0.403	−0.414	−0.448	−0.058	1.000	
I_t	−0.052	0.080	0.163	0.061	0.473	0.080	1.000

Source Authors' own calculation
Note SR1, SR2 and SR3 represent the short-term interest rate (yield from 91-day T-bill) stacked monthly, while SRQ represents the average quarterly interest rate. C is growth in bank credit, π is growth in corporate profit, and I represents growth in private fixed investment. C, π, and I are quarterly percentage change (annualized)

contemporaneous correlation between short-term interest rate and investment is also insignificant. Interestingly, we find that the contemporaneous correlation between $SR1_t$ and I_t is −0.052, but for $SR3_t$ and I_t, it is 0.163. Next, the correlations between I_t and SRQ_{t-k} are −0.195, −0.450, −0.488, and −0.546 for k = 1, …, 4. There is a large impact of SRQ on I with four-quarter lags. If we replace SRQ_{t-k} with $SR1_{t-k}$, $SR2_{t-k}$, or $SR3_{t-k}$, we find similar evidence. We also find that the correlations between I_t and π_{t-k} are 0.331, 0.575, 0.657, and 0.524 for k = 1, 2, 3, 4. There is a large impact of π on I with three quarter lags. As seen from Table 2, each variable (especially C) has high autocorrelations. An autocorrelation coefficient at lag 1 is 0.822 for SPQ, 0.889 for C, 0.802 for π, and 0.546 for I.

	$SR1_{t-1}$	$SR2_{t-1}$	$SR3_{t-1}$	SRQ_{t-1}	C_{t-1}	π_{t-1}	I_{t-1}
$SR1_t$	0.770	0.788	0.873	0.825	−0.003	−0.481	0.103
$SR2_t$	0.744	0.774	0.861	0.807	0.065	−0.355	0.198
$SR3_t$	0.714	0.753	0.841	0.783	0.078	−0.283	0.247
SRQ_t	0.759	0.788	0.877	0.822	0.046	−0.384	0.184
C_t	−0.108	−0.030	0.040	−0.037	0.889	−0.041	0.576
π_t	−0.370	−0.359	−0.412	−0.387	0.046	0.802	−0.116
I_t	−0.282	−0.208	−0.071	−0.195	0.300	0.331	0.546

	$SR1_{t-2}$	$SR2_{t-2}$	$SR3_{t-2}$	SRQ_{t-2}	C_{t-2}	π_{t-2}	I_{t-2}
$SR1_t$	0.616	0.661	0.746	0.685	−0.070	−0.265	0.236
$SR2_t$	0.578	0.633	0.728	0.656	0.005	−0.148	0.320
$SR3_t$	0.547	0.608	0.683	0.622	0.017	−0.031	0.310
SRQ_t	0.594	0.648	0.736	0.669	−0.018	−0.156	0.293
Ct	−0.304	−0.218	−0.127	−0.225	0.796	0.122	0.618
π_t	−0.197	−0.279	−0.322	−0.269	0.187	0.331	−0.196
I_t	−0.509	−0.462	−0.338	−0.450	0.321	0.575	0.359

	$SR1_{t-3}$	$SR2_{t-3}$	$SR3_{t-3}$	SRQ_{t-3}	C_{t-3}	π_{t-3}	I_{t-3}
$SR1_t$	0.451	0.517	0.576	0.523	−0.126	0.019	0.220
$SR2_t$	0.378	0.438	0.516	0.450	−0.068	0.107	0.276
$SR3_t$	0.303	0.400	0.485	0.400	−0.051	0.218	0.322
SRQ_t	0.388	0.464	0.538	0.470	−0.085	0.113	0.276
C_t	−0.480	−0.390	−0.328	−0.411	0.681	0.355	0.704
π_t	−0.039	−0.180	−0.211	−0.143	0.302	−0.166	−0.193
I_t	−0.510	−0.451	−0.470	−0.488	0.292	0.657	0.205

	$SR1_{t-4}$	$SR2_{t-4}$	$SR3_{t-4}$	SRQ_{t-4}	C_{t-4}	π_{t-4}	I_{t-4}
$SR1_t$	0.273	0.367	0.415	0.356	−0.173	0.241	0.181
$SR2_t$	0.192	0.281	0.336	0.272	−0.102	0.303	0.184
$SR3_t$	0.156	0.236	0.280	0.226	−0.097	0.367	0.211
SRQ_t	0.213	0.303	0.353	0.293	−0.128	0.307	0.195
C_t	−0.639	−0.557	−0.489	−0.577	0.577	0.581	0.563
π_t	−0.016	−0.155	−0.152	−0.107	0.337	−0.452	−0.140
I_t	−0.546	0.539	−0.517	−0.546	0.284	0.524	−0.052

Source Authors' own calculation

Note SR1, SR2, and SR3 represent the short-term interest rate (yield from 91-day T-bill) stacked monthly, while SRQ represents the average quarterly interest rate. C is growth in bank credit, π is growth in corporate profit, and I represents growth in private fixed investment. C, π, and I are quarterly percentage change (annualized)

4 Empirical Results

This section reports our empirical findings for the quarterly and mixed-frequency VAR models.

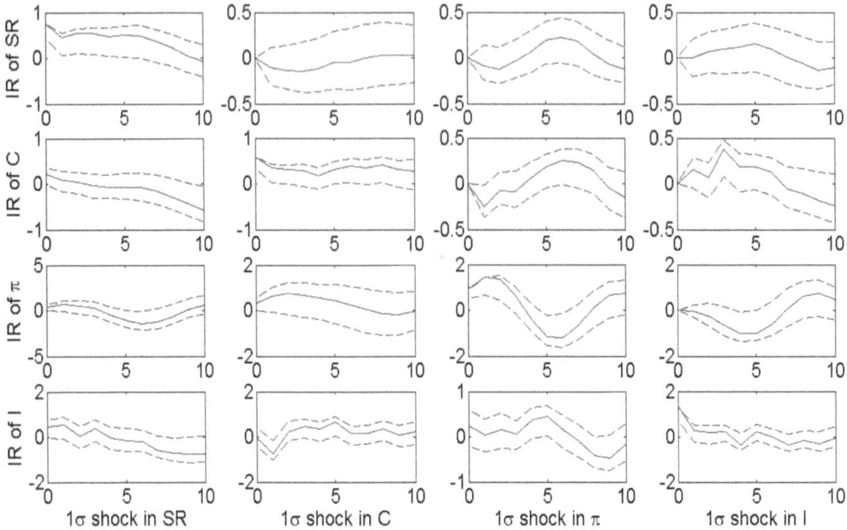

Fig. 2 Impulse response functions based on quarterly VAR(4). *Source* Authors' own calculation. *Note* SR1, SR2 and SR3 represent the short-term interest rate (yield from 91-day T-bill) stacked monthly, while SRQ represents the average quarterly interest rate. C is growth in bank credit, π is growth in corporate profit, and I represents growth in private fixed investment. C, π, and I are quarterly percentage change (annualized)

4.1 Quarterly VAR

We first present the results from the quarterly VAR model. Figure 2 plots the impulse response functions (IRFs) with 95% confidence intervals. The confidence intervals are constructed by parametric bootstrap for each horizon h = 0, 1, …, 10, using the least squares estimator $\widehat{A_k}$, error covariance estimator $\widehat{\Omega} = \left(\frac{1}{n}\right)\sum_{t=1}^{n}\widehat{\epsilon}_t\widehat{\epsilon}_t'$, and normal random numbers. The number of bootstrap samples is 10,000.

It is clear from the impulse responses that the effect of the short-term interest rate on investment is insignificant. Interestingly, on the quarterly VAR model, the interest rate has no significant effect on either corporate profit or bank lending. This finding leads to question the importance of monetary policy in the real economy for India. We also find that bank credit has a negative effect on investment, but it becomes significant only at lag 1.

4.2 Mixed-Frequency VAR

We now focus on the MF-VAR(4) model. Figure 3 plots the impulse response from the mixed-frequency regression analysis. Here again, we find that firm profit has a positive but insignificant impact on the investment for India. Hence, we find no

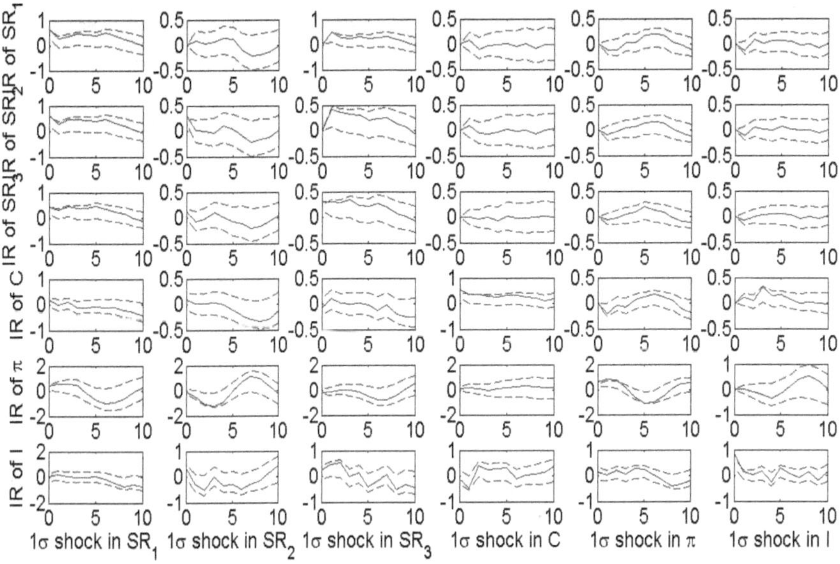

Fig. 3 Impulse response functions based on mixed-frequency VAR(4). *Source* Authors' own calculation. *Note* SR1, SR2 and SR3 represent the short-term interest rate (yield from 91-day T-bill) stacked monthly, while SRQ represents the average quarterly interest rate. C is growth in bank credit, π is growth in corporate profit, and I represents growth in private fixed investment. C, π, and I are quarterly percentage change (annualized)

evidence of the relevance of the firm-specific factor in driving the private investment in India. Also, we find that although SR1, SR2, and SR3 impact private investment differently, overall the effect remains insignificant. Moreover, the impact of bank credit impacting private investment is also insignificant suggesting strong evidence against the bank-specific factor. These results are consistent with the quarterly model.

To summarize the impulse response analysis, the MF-VAR provides an interesting picture on how investment and other variables interacted to each other. However, our analysis fails to find any evidence of either firm-specific factor, bank-specific factor, or monetary policy impacting the private investment decision in India.

5 Conclusion

This paper examines the causes behind the sluggish private investment in India by taking advantage of the mixed-frequency VAR model. Our MF-VAR model consists of monthly short-term interest rate (SR), quarterly bank loans BL, firm profit π, and investment I. The classical VAR aggregates the monthly variables into a quarterly frequency which may lead to a loss of a certain degree of information. MF-VAR can combine variables of different frequencies. Mixed-frequency methodology thus allows us to examine the heterogeneous impact of monetary policy on investment. However, we find no substantial evidence of any impact of monetary policy on investment from both the classical and the MF-VAR analyses. We also fail to find any significant evidence of either the firm-specific variable or bank-specific variable impacting private investment in India. However, the mixed-frequency approach yields richer economic insights compared to the single-frequency approach. In future, we plan to further this investigation by incorporating variables such as economic policy uncertainty and stock prices to examine their heterogeneous impact on private investment in India.

References

Anand, R., & Tulin, V. (2014). Disentangling India's Investment Slowdown. Working Paper 14/47, International Monetary Fund, Washington, DC.

Anderson, B. D. O., Deistler, M., Felsenstein, E., Funovits, B., Koelbl, L., & Zamani, M. (2016). Multivariate AR systems and mixed frequency data: G-identifiability and estimation. *Econometric Theory, 32,* 793–826.

Andreou, E., Ghysels, E., & Kourtellos, A. (2010). Regression models with mixed sampling frequencies. *Journal of Econometrics, 158,* 246–261.

Barkbu, B., Berkmen, S. P., Lukyantsau, P., Saksonovs, S., & Schoelermann, H. (2015). Investment in the Euro Area: Why Has It Been Weak? International Monetary Fund Working Paper No. 15/32.

Bussière, M., Ferrara, L., & Milovich, J. (2015). Explaining the Recent Slump in Investment: The Role of Expected Demand and Uncertainty. Banque de France Working Paper No. 571.

Das, S., & Tulin, V. (2017). *Financial Frictions, Underinvestment, and Investment Composition: Evidence from Indian Corporates* (No. 17/134). International Monetary Fund.

Ghysels, E. (2016). Macroeconomics and the reality of mixed frequency data. *Journal of Econometrics, 193,* 294–314.

Ghysels, E., Hill, J. B., & Motegi, K. (2016). Testing for Granger causality with mixed frequency data. *Journal of Econometrics, 192,* 207–230.

Ghysels, E., Santa-Clara, P., & Valkanov, R. (2004). The MIDAS Touch: Mixed Data Sampling Regression Models, Working Paper, UCLA and UNC.

International Monetary Fund (IMF). (2015, April). Private Investment: What's the Holdup? World Economic Outlook (pp. 111–143).

Lewis, C., Pain, N., Strásky, J., & Menkyna, F. (2014). Investment Gaps after the Crisis. OECD Economics Department Working Paper No. 1168.

Leboeuf, M., & Fay, R. (2016). What Is Behind the Weakness in Global Investment? Bank of Canada Staff Discussion Paper No. 2016-5.

McCracken, M. W., Owyang, M., & Sekhposyan, T. (2015). Real-Time Forecasting with a Large, Mixed Frequency, Bayesian VAR, No. 2015-030, FRB St Louis Paper.

Motegi, K., & Sadahiro, A. (2018). Sluggish private investment in Japan's Lost Decade: Mixed frequency vector autoregression approach. *The North American Journal of Economics and Finance, 43,* 118–128.

Motonishi, T., & Yoshikawa, H. (1999). Causes of the long stagnation of Japan during the 1990s: Financial or real? *Journal of the Japanese and International Economies, 13,* 181–200.
Saarenheimo, T. (1995). Credit crunch caused investment slump? An empirical analysis using Finnish data.
Sadahiro, A. (2005). *Sengo Nihon no Makuro Keizai Bunseki*. Tokyo: Toyo Keizai Inc.
Schembri, L. (2017, March 21). Getting Down to Business: Investment and the Economic Outlook. Remarks to the Greater Vancouver Board of Trade, Vancouver.
Silvestrini, A., & Veredas, D. (2008). Temporal aggregation of univariate and multivariate time series models: A survey. *Journal of Economic Surveys, 22,* 458–497.

Part IV
Public Economics

Incidence of Specific or Employment Tax in Non-Walrasian Fixed Price Model with Efficiency Wage

Sucharita Roy and Arpita Ghose

Abstract The present study formulates a generalized model which integrates standard efficiency wage model (henceforth *SEWM*) and standard non-Walrasian macromodel (henceforth *SNWMM*) allowing the firm to set efficiency real wage by introducing the possibility of commodity demand constraint where price is assumed to be exogenously fixed. In this integrated model, unemployment is the result of both demand and efficiency effect and is higher as compared to both *SEWM* (where demand effect is absent) and *SNWMM* (where efficiency effect is absent) This model also reveals that, under the constrained commodity demand situation, imposition of pay - roll specific tax generates employment when elasticity of effort with respect to specific tax equals or exceeds unity; this result strongly contrasts *SEWM* (signifying unconstrained commodity demand situation with flexible price) where imposition of such tax always lowers employment. Again, impact of such taxation is missing in *SNWMM* in the absence of efficiency wage consideration.

Keywords Efficiency wage · Non-Walrasian model · Payroll tax · Specific tax Employment · Effort elasticity

1 Introduction

Standard efficiency wage models (henceforth *SEWMs*)[1] explain real wage rigidity and give rise to involuntary unemployment. These models rule out *the possibility of deficient commodity demand by the assumption of price flexibility*. Thus, prevailing commodity demand has no impact on optimum solution and also on the policy

[1] Solow (1979), Salop (1979), Weiss (1980), Akerlof (1982), Shapiro and Stiglitz (1984), etc.

S. Roy (✉)
Department of Economics, Banwarilal Bhalotia College, Asansol, West Bengal, India
e-mail: sucharitasaraswati@yahoo.co.in

A. Ghose
Department of Economics, Jadavpur University, Kolkata, West Bengal, India
e-mail: arpitaju@gmail.com

N. R. Bhanumurthy et al. (eds.), *Advances in Finance & Applied Economics*,
https://doi.org/10.1007/978-981-13-1696-8_9

impacts[2] in *SEWM* structure. However, if one drops the assumption of price flexibility and considers price to be exogenously fixed, there can be a possibility that the firm may face commodity demand constraint. The role of such perceived demand constraint in the commodity market is analysed extensively in the standard non-Walrasian macro-models (henceforth *SNWMMs*).[3] Wage in these types of *SNWMM* is either set exogenously or linked to price (Benassy 1986), but is not determined by the firm on the basis of worker's efficiency consideration.

This paper formulates a generalized model which integrates standard efficiency wage model (which assumes price flexibility) and standard non-Walrasian macro-model (where wage is exogenously fixed) by introducing the possibility of commodity demand constraint assuming fixed exogenous price and allowing the firm to set efficiency real wage. It also observes that the impact of payroll labour taxation such as specific tax (employment tax) on optimum solutions in the present set-up differs from that of *SEWM* (specifically of Yellen 1984 having similar properties of the effort function as that of the present model).

The novelties of the finding of the present generalized model and the contribution to the literature are to show that in the face of commodity demand constraint, (i) resulting unemployment is combined effect of lack of demand (demand effect) and high-efficiency wage (efficiency effect) and may be higher as compared to both the *SEWM* (where demand effect is absent) and *SNWMM* (where efficiency effect is absent), and more interestingly here specific tax acts as an instrument for employment generation if elasticity of effort with respect to specific tax equals or exceeds unity, which is a strong contrast to *SEWM*[4] where rise in specific tax always lowers employment. Again if effort elasticity with respect to specific tax is less than unity, impact of rise in specific tax on optimum output is ambiguous and depends on (a) the magnitudes of the specific tax imposed, (b) effort elasticity with respect to specific tax, (c) effort elasticity with respect to real wage.

The paper is furnished as follows: Sect. 2 presents the basic model. Section 3 discusses regime classification of the present generalized non-Walrasian structure. In Sect. 4, regime with commodity demand constraint is explained. Section 4.1 highlights the incidence of payroll specific tax in the present framework. Finally, Sect. 5 draws the conclusion of the present study.

---

[2]Yellen's (1984), Johnson and Layard (1986), Shapiro and Stiglitz (1984), Pisauro (1991), etc., considered the impact of both ad valorem and specific tax on optimum wage and employment, with efficiency wage relationship.

[3]Don Patinkin (1956), Clower (1965), Barro and Grossman (1971), Malinvaud (1977) and Benassy (1975, 1982, 1986).

[4]With the incidence of specific tax, employment falls in Yellen (1984), Shapiro and Stiglitz (1984), Pisauro (1991) and remains unchanged in Johnson and Layard (1986).

2 The Basic Model

The model assumes an aggregate monetary economy with three representative agents: a firm, a household and also the government. Since in the present generalized model the firm sets real wage and hence employment, in order to trace out the impact of efficiency wage on wage income and hence on aggregate demand, we assume two classes in the household: wage and profit earner having different marginal propensities to consume (unlike Benassy 1986) as supported by Kaldor (1955).[5] The wage earner sells labour and earns wage, and the profit earner earns profit. There are three types of goods, consumption good; labour and money; and two markets, goods and labour.

Price is assumed to be exogenously fixed. Equilibrium supply and demand can be generated through ***quantity signals*** as in non-Walrasian model by Benassy (1986). Transaction settles at the minimum level of total supply and demand (short side of the market rule) and determines aggregate effective demand and supply. The model allows determination of the levels of optimum real wage, employment and output.

The behaviour of each of the agent is explained in the following subsections.

2.1 The Firm

As in *SEWM* of Solow (1979), firm's output depends on both the number of workers it employs and on their efforts; hence, the short-run production function is

$$Y = F(eL), \quad F'(eL) > 0 \quad F''(eL) < 0 \tag{1}$$

where Y is the output produced and L and e denote the amount of labour hired and worker's effort, respectively.

Effort function takes the form

$$\begin{aligned} &e = e((W/P), \theta), \quad e' > 0 \quad e'' < 0, \quad e_\theta > 0 \\ &e' = de/d(W/P) > 0 \quad \text{and} \quad e'' = d^2e/d(W/P)^2 < 0 \end{aligned} \tag{2}$$

As in Solow (1979), e depends on real wage (W/P)[6] implying the fact that productivity depends on workers wage. Here, commodity price 'P' is assumed to be exogenously fixed.

---

[5] *Kaldor* made a distinction between wage earners and profit earners, noticing that the propensity to save of the first group can be assumed to be smaller than that of the second group (see Kaldor 1955, pp. 95).

[6] There are literature justifying inclusion of unemployment rate as an argument of effort function (Shapiro and Stiglitz 1984; Summers 1988, etc.), which can easily be incorporated in the extended version of the present study.

Further, in the present framework we assume that effort of the workers also gets affected due to change in parameter θ, which signifies the change in exogenous factors like access to and quality of health care, the quality and affordability of education and training, investment on infrastructure, quality of job environment.[7] Exogenous policy measures that improve one (or more than one) of these above factors would increase the value of the parameter θ leading to upward shift in effort function in (2).

At the exogenously fixed price, the firm may or may not face constraint in the commodity market. In the next two broad subsections, behaviour of constrained and unconstrained firm is explained.

2.1.1 Unconstrained Firm

If at the given price,P, the firm can realize its profit-maximizing supply of output, then it is unconstrained in the commodity market.

Optimum real wage $(W/P)^*$ and employment L^* are the solutions of the following problem where π is the real profit of the firm,

$$\begin{aligned} &\text{Maximize}\,\pi = Y - [(W/P)L] \\ &\text{s.t}\quad Y \leq F(eL) \end{aligned} \tag{3}$$

The optimum real wage and employment are determined by solving the first-order conditions with respect to (W/P) and L that is by setting $d\pi/d((W/P)) = 0$ and $d\pi/\delta L = 0$.[8]

$$e'((W/P), \theta) = 1/F'(e((W/P), \theta)L)) \tag{4}$$

$$F'(e((W/P), \theta)L) = (W/P)/[e((W/P), \theta)] \tag{5}$$

The above two equations yield elasticity of effort function with respect to real wage,

$$\mu_W = \frac{e'((W/P), \theta)(W/P)}{e((W/P), \theta)} = 1 \quad \text{(Solow condition)} \tag{6}$$

Here, optimum real wage, $(W/P)^*$, is determined on the basis of the effort function alone satisfying the above Solow condition.[9]

Following (5), employment in efficiency unit is

[7] Impact of these factors on efficiency of the workers is explained in the studies by Stringer (2014) in *NBRI*, http://www.nbrii.com, http://www.tutor2u.net, etc.

[8] Second-order conditions are assumed to be satisfied.

[9] Akerlof and Yellen (1986) termed this condition as Solow Condition.

$$\left[e\left((W/P)^{*},\theta\right)L\right]^{M} = [F'^{-1}((W/P)^{*}]/[e\left((W/P)^{*},\theta\right)]) \quad (7)$$

Therefore, optimum employment is

$$L^{M} = [[F'^{-1}((W/P)^{*}]/\left[e\left((W/P)^{*},\theta\right)\right])]/\left[e\left((W/P)^{*},\theta\right)\right] \quad (8)$$

Optimum output is

$$Y^{M} = [F(F'^{-1}((W/P)^{*}]/[e\left((W/P)^{*},\theta\right)]) \quad (9)$$

Condition (6) implies that optimum real wage, $(W/P)^{*}$, is determined at the point where effort elasticity with respect to real wage equals unity, $(\mu_W = 1)$. This corresponds to the point where the slope of effort function signifies maximum effort–real wage ratio, $e/(W/P)$, or minimum wage cost per efficiency unit, $(W/P)/e$, which is also the minimum marginal cost, MC.

Further, employment in efficiency unit, $[e((W/P)^{*},\theta)L]^{M}$, is determined where corresponding marginal productivity of employment in efficiency unit, MP_{eL}, is equal to minimum MC (following (5)). Once $(W/P)^{*}$ and hence effort, $e((W/P)^{*},\theta)$, are known, actual employment, L^{M}, is solved from optimum employment in efficiency unit, $[e((W/P)^{*},\theta)L]^{M}$ (as in (8)).

The above equilibrium signifies the standard efficiency wage model ($SEWM$) by Solow (1979) where commodity market is always in equilibrium due to price flexibility and the firm faces no commodity demand constraint. However, for the unconstrained firm of the present model, though commodity price is exogenously fixed unlike Solow (1979), the assumption is that the price is fixed in such a way that there exists either excess demand or equilibrium in the commodity market and thus the firm faces no commodity demand constraint and realizes the profit-maximizing level of supply. Hence, the system of equations in the present optimization problem of the unconstrained firm is similar to that of Solow (1979).

The above optimization solution can be described with the help of a four-panelled diagram[10] as shown in Fig. 1. In panel (1), e represents effort curve showing the relationship between effort of the workers and real wage. Higher the real wage, greater is the effort of the workers. Initially, increase in real wage entails more than proportionate increase in effort of the workers. Effort per unit of real wage, $e/(W/P)$ is maximum at point 'M' where slope of the effort curve, ON is tangential to the effort function. This point corresponds to $\mu_W = 1$ (as in (6) where $(W/P)^{*}$ implies optimum real wage that results in maximum $e/(W/P)$ in panel (1)). Since wage cost per efficiency unit, $(W/P)/e$, is inverse of $e/(W/P)$; as $e/(W/P)$ increases, $(W/P)/e$ falls and vice versa. In panel (2), relationship between $(W/P)/e$ and (W/P) is shown. Since $(e/(W/P))$ is maximum at point 'M' with efficiency wage, $(W/P)^{*}$,

[10]While explaining the working of standard efficiency wage model of Solow (1979), Snowdon and Vane (2005) used the diagrammatic representations of wage cost per unit of effort, $[(W/P)/(e(W/P))]$, curve that is marginal cost curve and the corresponding effort curve. However, they have not considered this four-quadrant diagrammatic representation as developed in the present paper.

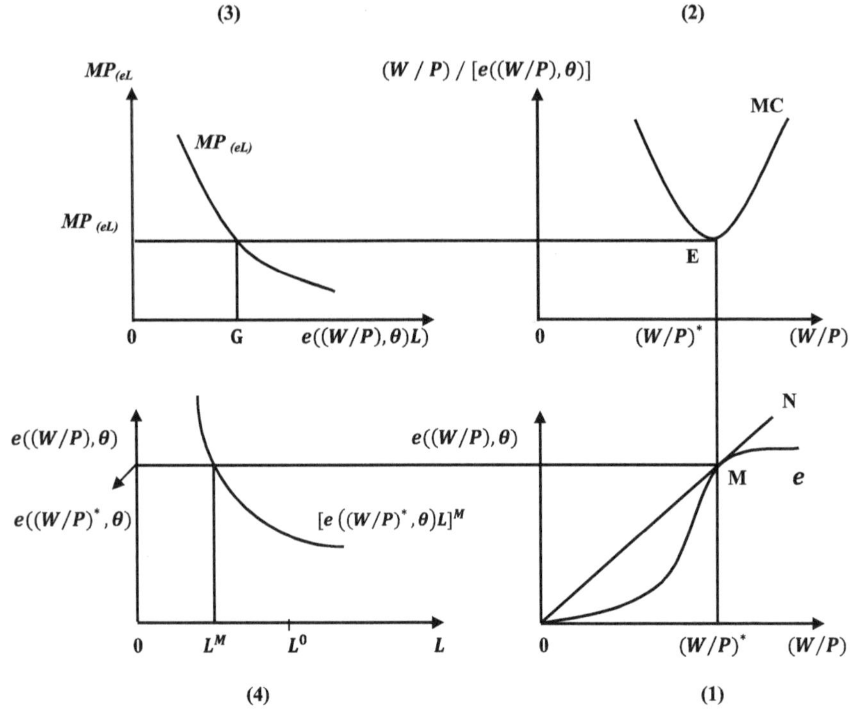

Fig. 1 Determination of optimum efficiency wage and employment in the unconstrained case

$((W/P)/e)$ is minimum at point 'E' in panel (2). Panel (3) depicts marginal productivity of employment in efficiency unit, $MP_{(eL)}$. Level of optimum employment in efficiency unit, $[e((W/P)^*, \theta)L]^M$, is determined at point 'G' in panel (3) where the corresponding marginal productivity equals the minimum MC in panel (2) (depicting equilibrium condition in (5)).

Panel (4) represents employment in efficiency unit (eL) curve, which is a rectangular hyperbolic curve in effort e and employment L plane. Different combinations of e and L provide fixed level of $[eL]$. As optimum effort $e((W/P)^*, \theta)$ corresponding to optimum real wage, $(W/P)^*$, and optimum employment in efficiency unit, $[e((W/P)^*, \theta)L]^M$, are already known, the resulting optimum actual employment can easily be determined and is set at L^M in panel (4). If the profit-maximizing level of optimum employment, L^M, is less than the Walrasian full employment L^0 corresponding to output, Y^0 that is $L^M < L^0$, there is involuntary unemployment. In that case, profit maximizing level of output, $Y^M <$ Walrasian level of output, Y^0.

If $(W/P)^0$ is the real wage corresponding to Walrasian full employment, L^0, then involuntary unemployment persists when $(W/P)^*$ as set on the basis of the given effort function is greater than $(W/P)^0$, that is $(W/P)^* > (W/P)^0$. If, $(W/P)^* = (W/P)^0$, optimum employment will be the full employment one, there will be no involuntary unemployment. However, if $(W/P)^* < (W/P)^0$, the firm will be forced to pay

$(W/P)^0$ till labour demand equals labour supply.[11] Thus, the scope of excess demand for labour is absent in the present structure.

Following *SEWM* (Solow 1979), optimum efficiency real wage, $(W/P)^*$, is assumed to be set above the market clearing level, $(W/P)^0$, and thus involuntary unemployment. $(L^0 - L^M)$ is being created in panel (4) of Fig. 1.

Following (6), (8) and (9).

Optimum real wage, actual employment and output are functions of θ only.[12]

$$\text{Real wage, } (W/P)^* = \omega(\theta), \quad \omega_\theta < 0 \tag{10}$$

$$\text{Optimum actual employment, } L^M = \alpha(\theta), \quad \alpha_\theta \gtreqless 0 \tag{11}$$

$$\text{Optimum output, } Y^M = S(\theta), \quad S_\theta > 0 \tag{12}$$

$$\text{Wage cost per efficiency unit, } (W/P)^*/\left[e\big((W/P)^*, \theta\big)\right] = g(\theta), g_\theta < 0 \tag{13}$$

At the given price when the firm is unconstrained in the commodity market, exogenous positive shift in effort of the workers or increase in θ would lower optimum real wage and increase output supply, but the impact on employment is ambiguous.

2.1.2 Constrained Firm

If the exogenously given price, P, is such that there exists excess supply situation in the commodity market, the firm faces demand constraint and fails to sell the profit-maximizing level of supply due to deficient demand.

Demand for commodity, Y^d <Profit maximizing level of supply, Y^M and Walrasian output Y^0.

As there is no inventory, due to short-side rule based on quantity signal (as in *SNWMM* (Benassy 1986), the output production, Y, is equal to demand for output Y^d,

$$Y = Y^d \tag{14}$$

Thus,

$$Y^d = F(e((W/P), \theta)L) \quad \text{(following (1) and (2))} \tag{15}$$

---

[11] See Abel and Bernanke (2001).

[12] Impact of exogenous shift in effort function on optimum values is explained in Appendix.

The optimum solution of real wage and employment of the constrained firm are determined by the following programme

$$\text{Maximize} \quad \pi = Y - [(W/P)L] \tag{16}$$

$$\text{s.t} \quad Y = F(e((W/P), \theta)L), Y = Y^d$$

The above problem can be solved by maximizing the following Lagrangian

$$\Lambda((W/P), L, \lambda) \equiv F(e((W/P), \theta)L) - [(W/P)L] + \lambda\left[F(e((W/P), \theta)L) - Y^d\right] \tag{17}$$

First-order condition with respect to (W/P), L and λ of the above problem implies[13]

$$\begin{aligned} d\Lambda/d(W/P) = {} & F'(e((W/P), \theta)L)e'((W/P), \theta)L - L \\ & + \lambda\left[F'(e((W/P), \theta)L)e'((W/P), \theta)L\right] = 0 \end{aligned} \tag{18}$$

$$\begin{aligned} d\Lambda/dL = {} & F'(e((W/P), \theta)L)[e((W/P), \theta)] - (W/P) \\ & + \lambda[F'(e((W/P), \theta)L)e((W/P), \theta)] = 0 \end{aligned} \tag{19}$$

$$d\Lambda/d\lambda = F(e((W/P), \theta)L) - Y^d = 0 \tag{20}$$

Solving Eqs. (18) and (19), we get

$$\mu_W = \frac{e'((W/P), \theta)(W/P)}{e((W/P), \theta)} = 1 \quad \text{(Solow Condition satisfies)}$$

Optimum real wage, $(W/P)^*$, is still determined at the point where $\mu_W = 1$, as in the unconstrained case (in Eq. (6)). Thus, at the given P and θ optimum real wage in the constrained case is exactly equal to the optimum real wage corresponding to the unconstrained one and depends only on parameter θ.

Here again, $(W/P)^* = \omega(\theta)$, $\omega_\theta < 0$

From commodity demand constraint in (20)

$$F(e((W/P), \theta)L) = Y^d \tag{21}$$

Optimum employment in efficiency unit is

$$[e((W/P)^*, \theta)L]^d = F^{-1}(Y^d) \tag{22}$$

Actual value of optimum employment is

[13]Second-order conditions are assumed to be satisfied.

$$\bar{L} = [F^{-1}(Y^d)]/[e((W/P)^*, \theta)] = \alpha(\theta, Y^d) \tag{23}$$

Here, actual optimum employment depends both on shift parameter θ and on prevailing commodity demand, Y^d. Since, $Y^d < Y^M$, corresponding employment in efficiency unit, $[e((W/P)^*, \theta)L]^d$, is less than the profit-maximizing level, $[e((W/P)^*, \theta)L]^M$. Again as optimum real wag, $(W/P)^*$, remains unchanged, effort, $e((W/P)^*, \theta)$, does not get altered. Here, lower level of employment in efficiency unit as compared to the profit-maximizing one is possible only by lowering the actual employment. This follows that the optimum actual employment L in the constrained situation (in (23)) is less than profit-maximizing level L^M, that is $\bar{L} < L^M$.

The above optimization problem is explained with the help of Fig. 2. In Fig. 2, the relationship in panel (1), panel (2), panel (3) and panel (4) resembles that of Fig. 1. As is clear from the above optimization problem, optimum real wage is still determined at the point where $\mu_W = 1$; hence in panel (1), effort–real wage ratio, $e/(W/P)$, is maximum at $(W/P)^*$ similar to the unconstrained case and the corresponding wage cost per efficiency unit, $(W/P)^*/e$, that is MC is also minimum at point 'E' in panel (2).

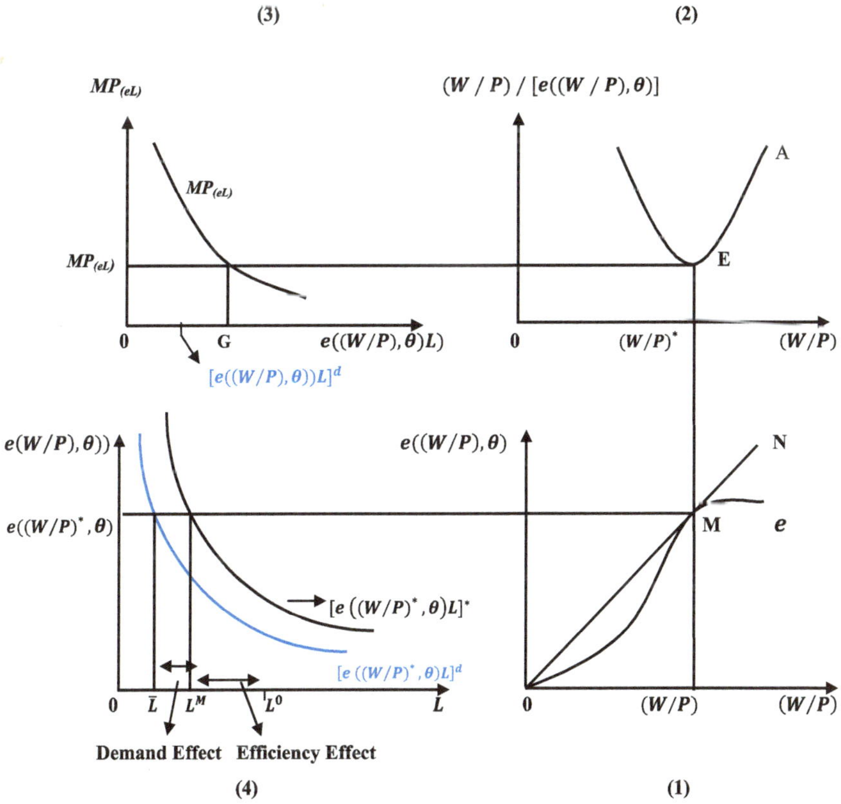

Fig. 2 Determination of optimum efficiency wage and employment in constrained case

As explained earlier in Sect. 2.1.1, when the firm is unconstrained in the commodity market, the profit-maximizing level of employment in efficiency unit, $[e((W/P)^*, \theta)L]^M$, is determined at point 'G' in panel (3) (where $MP_{(eL)}$ equals the minimum MC). But in the present case as the firm faces constraint in the commodity market, supply of output is demand determined. Hence, employment in efficiency unit, $[e((W/P)^*, \theta)L]^d$, is also set on the basis of prevailing demand and is less than the profit-maximizing level, $[e((W/P)^*, \theta)L]^M$ (shown in panel (3) of Fig. 2).

Actual optimum employment, $\bar{L}$, in the constrained situation is thus determined in panel (4), at the given level of employment in efficiency unit, $[e((W/P)^*, \theta)L]^d$, and optimum effort level, $e((W/P)^*, \theta)$ (corresponding to optimum real wage, $(W/P)^*$ in panel (1)).

As is clear from panel (4) of Fig. 2, $\left(L^0 - \bar{L}\right)$ is the net unemployment in the present case of which $(L^M - \bar{L})$ is due to demand effect and $(L^0 - L^M)$ is due to *efficiency effect*. $(L^0 - L^M)$ is the level of unemployment in the unconstrained case which is only due to high-efficiency real wage, whereas the extra unemployment $(L^M - \bar{L})$ is created due to deficient commodity demand. Thus, in the present situation unemployment is due to both demand and efficiency effect and is larger as compared to unconstrained situation (i.e. *SEWM* (Solow (1979)) where unemployment arises only due to efficiency effect. However, unemployment here is also higher than that in *SNWMM* (Benassy 1986) where only *demand effect* is prevalent but efficiency effect is absent.

Proposition 1 *(i) At the given price, if the firm faces constraint in the commodity market, optimum efficiency real wage remains unchanged and is set at the same level as in the unconstrained case (where Solow Condition holds similar to SEWM); (ii) resulting unemployment is higher in the constrained situation (which arises due to demand and efficiency effect) as compared to both SEWM (Solow 1979) where only efficiency effect works and SNWMM (Benassy 1986) where only demand effect is prevalent.*

2.2 *The Household*

The consumption demand of the representative household is generated by both ***wage and profit earners*** having positive marginal propensity to consume c_w and c_π, respectively.

2.2.1 Consumption Demand of the Wage Earner

The representative wage earner sells L of labour, at real wage, (W/P), which is assumed not to exceed the constant level, L^0. He has an initial money holding, $\bar{m}_w/P$, earns real wage income, $[(W/P)L]$, creates consumption demand, $\breve{C}_w$ and has a final money holding, m_w/P. τ_w is the total real tax on wage income.

The budget constraint of the wage earner is

$$C_w + m_w/P = \bar{m}_w/P + [(W/P)L] - \tau_w$$

and has a utility function, $U_w(C_w, [m_w/P])$. The wage earner has no utility for leisure so that his labour supply is constant, that is L^0.

Effective consumption demand of wage earner in the household is determined in the *constrained and unconstrained case.*

The Unconstrained Case

When the firm is unconstrained in commodity market, it determines optimum real wage, $(W/P)^*$, and profit-maximizing level of employment, L^M. Therefore total wage income earned by the wage earner is $[(W/P)^* L^M]$. The representative wage earner creates consumption demand by solving the following programme

$$\begin{gathered}\text{Maximize} \quad U_w(C_w, [m_w/P]) \quad \text{s.t.} \\ C_w + m_w/P = \bar{m}_w/P + \left[(W/P)^* L^M\right] - \tau_w\end{gathered}$$

The effective consumption demand of the wage earner in the unconstrained case is

$$\breve{C}_w = C(\left[(W/P)^* L^M\right], [\bar{m}_w/P], \tau_w) \tag{24}$$

The Constrained Case

If the firm faces constraint in the commodity market, it employs optimum employment, $\bar{L}$, which is less than unconstraint profit-maximizing level of employment, L^M, at the same level of real wage, $(W/P)^*$.

The wage earner is constrained in the labour market as $\bar{L} < L^M$; that is, the resulting wage income in the constrained case is lower than that of the same in unconstrained case, $[(W/P)^* \bar{L}] < [(W/P)^* L^M]$. The representative *wage earner* creates consumption demand by solving the following programme

$$\begin{gathered}\text{Maximize} \quad U_w(C_w, [m_w/P]) \, \text{s.t.} \\ C_w + m_w/P = \bar{m}_w/P + \left[(W/P)^* \bar{L}\right] - \tau_w \\ [(W/P)^* \bar{L}] < [(W/P)^* L^M]\end{gathered}$$

The general form for effective consumption demand in the constrained case is

$$\breve{C}_w = \text{Min}[C([(W/P)^* L^M], [\bar{m}_w/P], \tau_w), C([(W/P)^* \bar{L}], [\bar{m}_w/P], \tau_w)$$
$$= C([\bar{m}_w/P], \tau_w, (W/P)^* \min(L^M, \bar{L}))$$

$$\breve{C}_w = C([(W/P)^* \bar{L}], [\bar{m}_w/P], \tau_w) \tag{25}$$

2.2.2 Consumption Demand of the Profit Earner

A representative profit earner in the household has an initial money holding, $\bar{m}_\pi/P$, and earns nominal profit, Π, which is being totally distributed by the firm. C_π and m_π/P are the consumption and final holding of the profit earners, respectively, where τ_π is the real tax on profit income collected by the government.

The budget constraint of the profit earner in the household is

$$C_\pi + \bar{m}_\pi/P = \bar{m}_\pi/P + \Pi/P - \tau_\pi$$

And his utility function is $U_\pi(C_\pi, [m_\pi/P])$.

The profit earner will not always be able to realize his notional profit at the exogenously given price. Thus, he may or may not face constraint in the commodity market.

In the unconstrained case, the representative consumption demand of the profit earner is determined by solving the following programme

$$\text{Maximize} \quad U_\pi(C_\pi, [m_\pi/P]) \text{ s.t.}$$
$$C_\pi + (m_\pi/P) = \bar{m}_\pi/P + \bar{\Pi}^M/P - \tau_\pi$$

The consumption demand of the profit earner of the household in the unconstrained case is

$$\breve{C}_\pi = C([\Pi^M/P], [\bar{m}_\pi/P], \tau_\pi) \tag{26}$$

where $\Pi/P = \Pi^M/P = F(e((W/P)^*, \theta)L^M) - (W/P)^* L^M$

In the constrained case, the representative consumption demand of the profit earner is determined by solving the following programme

$$\text{Maximize} \quad U_\pi(C_\pi, [m_\pi/P]) \text{ s.t.}$$
$$C_\pi + [m_\pi/P] = \bar{m}_\pi/P + \bar{\Pi}/P - \tau_\pi$$

The consumption demand of the profit earner in the household in the constrained case is

$$\breve{C}_\pi = C([\bar{\Pi}/P], [\bar{m}_\pi/P], \tau_\pi) \tag{27}$$

where $\bar{\Pi}/P = Y^d - (W/P)^*[F^{-1}(Y^d)/[e((W/P), \theta)]$

In the constrained case, the firm produces the prevailing commodity demand, Y^d, and employ labour, $\bar{L} = F^{-1}(Y^d)/[e((W/P), \theta)]$.

2.2.3 Aggregate Consumption Demand

The aggregate consumption demand, $\breve{C}$, is generated by both wage and profit earner in the household. As already discussed, different marginal propensities to consume for the wage earner and profit earner in the household following Kaldor (1955) are being assumed in the present model. Hence, the aggregate consumption demand can be determined my combining (24), (25), (26) and (27) and is expressed as

In the unconstrained case, $\breve{C} = C((W/P)^*, L^M, \Pi^M/P, \bar{m}_w/P, \bar{m}_\pi/P, \tau_w, \tau_\pi)$

In the constrained case, $\breve{C} = C((W/P)^*, \bar{L}, \bar{\Pi}/P, \bar{m}_w/P, \bar{m}_\pi/P, \tau_w, \tau_\pi)$

Here, we consider a specific form of consumption function with different marginal propensities to consume for the wage and profit earner following Kaldor (1955).

$$\breve{C} = \breve{C}_w + \breve{C}_\pi = c_w[(W/P)L] - \tau_w] + c_\pi[\pi - \tau_\pi] + \beta[\bar{m}/P] \quad (28)$$

where c_w and c_π are the marginal propensities to consume for the wage earner and profit earner, respectively, and π is the real profit. $\bar{m} = \bar{m}_w + \bar{m}_\pi$. $c_w > 0$, $c_\pi > 0$, $\beta > 0$ and $c_w > c_\pi$.

2.3 *The Government*

The government collects income tax, τ_w and τ_π, and has an expenditure demand, $\hat{g}$. Apart from income tax, the government also has the scope of collecting payroll taxes in the form of specific tax or employment tax (the incidence of which is discussed later).

The aggregate demand (Y^d) function in the economy is

$$Y^d = c_w[(W/P)L] - \tau_w] + c_\pi[\pi - \tau_\pi] + \beta[m/P] + \hat{g} \quad (29)$$

3 Regime Classification

In the present model, real wage as determined on the basis of efficiency wage relationship is set above the Walrasian level both with and without commodity demand constraint. Thus, excess demand or equilibrium in the labour market is absent and excess supply in the labour market is persistent in the present framework. Here, only two regimes are found to be relevant that is (i) equilibrium or excess demand in the commodity market with excess supply in labour market (*RWODC*) and (ii) excess supply of commodity and labour (*RWDC*).

It is clear from Sect. (2.1.1) that in case of unconstrained situation (*RWODC*) optimum solution of real wage using profit maximization problem is similar to *SEWM* (Solow (1979)) and hence the impact of imposition of specific tax too is identical to the rudimentary efficiency wage model of Yellen (1984). This paper thus concentrates only on the working of *RWDC* and examines the incidence of specific tax in the same regime. The results are then compared with unconstrained case (i.e. *SEWM* of Yellen 1984, where the property of the effort function is same as assumed in the present study).

4 Regime with Commodity Demand Constraint (*RWDC*)

At the exogenously given commodity price, P, this case corresponds to the situation of excess supply on the markets of both labour and output. Here, the firm fails to sell the profit-maximizing level of output, hence while determining optimum real wage and employment faces constraint in the commodity market.

As explained earlier (in Sect. (2.1.2)) in the presence of the demand constraint, the firm still maintains the same level of efficiency real wage $(W/P)^*$ (at $\mu_W = 1$). But optimum employment, $\bar{L}$, in the constraint case is lower than that of the profit-maximizing level, L^M, in the unconstraint case. This is because the level of output supplied, Y, is equivalent to commodity demand, Y^d, prevailing in the economy (short side of the market rule), and since Y^d is less than Y^M the profit-maximizing level of output, employment in efficiency unit corresponding to Y^d, $[e((W/P)^*, \theta)L]^d$ is less than the profit-maximizing level, $[e((W/P)^*, \theta)L]^M$. Thus, actual employment has to fall as real wage, $(W/P)^*$, and associated effort level, $e((W/P)^*, \theta)$, remains unchanged. Hence, employment in the constrained case $\bar{L}$ < profit-maximizing level of employment, L^M, in unconstrained case.

Total effective demand, E, can be derived from (29) in *RWDC* by substituting the expressions for π and $\bar{L}$ and also by denoting $(W/P)^*/[e((W/P)^*, \theta)] = g(\theta)$,

$$\begin{aligned} E &= [c_w - c_\pi]g(\theta)F^{-1}(Y) + c_\pi Y - c_w\tau_w - c_\pi\tau_\pi + \beta[\bar{m}/P] + \hat{g} \\ &= Z(Y, \theta, P, \tau_w, \tau_\pi) + \hat{g} \end{aligned} \tag{30}$$

Here, wage income is $(W/P)^*[F^{-1}(Y)/(e((W/P)^*, \theta)] = g(\theta)F^{-1}(Y)$

The solution of Y can be determined, where aggregate demand (E) curve crosses the 45° line in $Y - Y$ plane.

$$dE/dY = [c_w - c_\pi]g(\theta)F'^{-1}(Y) + c_\pi > 0 \tag{31}$$

$$d^2E/dY^2 = -[c_w - c_\pi]g(\theta)F''^{-1}(Y) < 0 \tag{32}$$

where $F''^{-1}(Y) < 0$, due to diminishing marginal productivity.

From (31) and (32), it is clear that the aggregate demand function is concave in nature. In *SNWMM* with equal marginal propensities to consume for wage and profit earners, aggregate demand function is always linear, but in the present study in the presence of efficiency wage with different marginal propensities to consume between the wage earner and profit earner aggregate demand function is nonlinear and concave in nature.

In Fig. 3, optimum equilibrium output, Y^k, is determined at the point where aggregate demand curve, E, intersects the 45° line.

Solution of equilibrium output in this regime is

$$Y^* = Y^k = [[c_w - c_\pi]g(\theta)F^{-1}(Y^*) - c_w\tau_w - c_\pi\tau_\pi + \beta[\bar{m}/P] + \hat{g}]/[1 - c_\pi] \\ = K(\theta, \tau_w, \tau_\pi, \hat{g}, P) \quad (33)$$

In this regime, $K(\theta, \tau_w, \tau_\pi, \hat{g}, P) \leq \min[S(\theta), Y^0]$

In the presence of commodity demand constraint, the firm still maintains the same level of efficiency real wage $(W/P)^*$ (at $\mu_W = 1$).

Following (23), optimum employment is

$$L^* = \frac{F^{-1}(Y^*)}{[e((W/P)^*, \theta)]} \quad (34)$$

In this regime, $(W/P)^* > (W/P)^0$ and output $Y^* < Y^M < Y^0$.

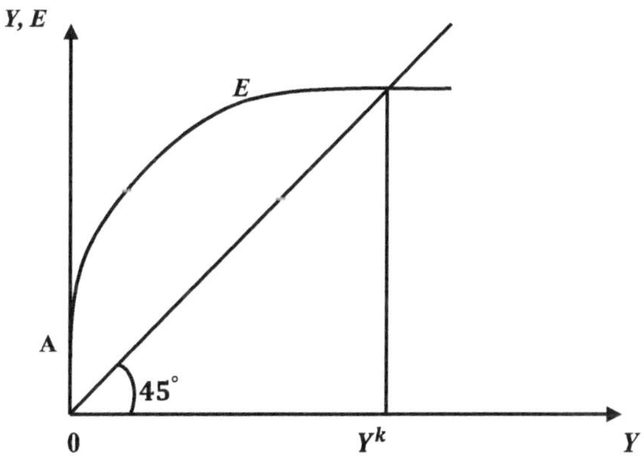

Fig. 3 Determination of equilibrium output in *RWDC*

4.1 Incidence of Specific Tax in RWDC

In *RWDC*, the firm produces the level of output, Y^d, just necessary to produce the prevailing effective demand in this regime.

Here, level of output produced is $Y = \min[K(\theta, \tau_W, \tau_\pi, \hat{g}, P), S(\theta, P, t_s,), Y^0]$.

where $S(\theta, P, t_s,)$ is the post-tax profit-maximizing level of supply in the unconstrained situation.

In *RWDC*, the firm fails to supply $S(\theta, P, t_s)$ in the presence of specific tax. It produces the level of output, Y, just necessary to produce the prevailing effective demand in this regime, $Y^d = K(\theta, \tau_W, \tau_\pi, \hat{g}, P)$.

Optimum solution of real wage and employment in the presence of specific tax are determined by maximizing the post—tax profit, π_s.

$$\text{Maximize} \quad \pi_s = Y - [(W/P) + t_s]L$$
$$\text{s.t} \quad Y = F(e((W/P), \theta)L), Y = Y^d \tag{35}$$

The above problem can be solved by maximizing the following Lagrangian

$$\Lambda((W/P), L, \lambda) \equiv F(e((W/P), \theta)L) - [(W/P) + t_s]L + \lambda\left[F(e((W/P), \theta)L) - Y^d\right]$$

First-order condition of the above problem implies[14]

$$d\Lambda/d(W/P) = F'(e((W/P), \theta)L)e'((W/P), \theta)L - L + \lambda\left[F'(e((W/P), \theta)L)e'((W/P), \theta)L\right] = 0 \tag{36}$$

$$d\Lambda/dL = F'(e((W/P), \theta))L)e((W/P), \theta) - (W/P)t_s + \lambda\left[F'(e((W/P), \theta)L)e((W/P), \theta)\right] = 0 \tag{37}$$

$$d\Lambda/d\lambda = \left[F(e((W/P), \theta)L) - Y^d\right] = 0 \tag{38}$$

From Eqs. (36) and (37), we have

$$\mu_W = (W/P)/[(W/P) + t_s] < 1 \tag{39}$$

As specific tax t_s is fixed cost of employing an extra unit of labour, the firm no longer operates at the minimum *MC* (where $\mu_W = 1$). The firm increases optimum real wage to increase efficiency of the workers to meet the fixed cost at the new optimum where $\mu_W < 1$; that is, Solow Condition does not satisfy. $(W/P)_s^*$ is actually similar to the post-tax real wage in unconstrained case and the corresponding effort being $e((W/P)_s^*, \theta)$.

Thus, optimum real wage is $(W/P)_s^* = \omega(\theta, P, t_s)$

From (38), optimum employment in efficiency unit is

$$[e((W/P)_s^*, \theta)L]^d = F^{-1}(Y^d) \tag{40}$$

[14] Second-order condition is assumed to be satisfied.

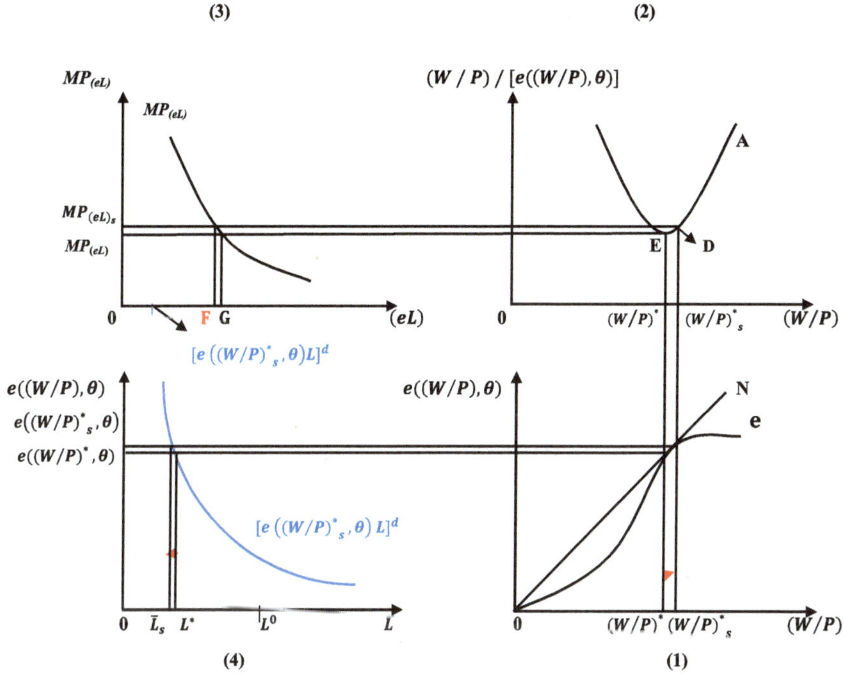

Fig. 4 Determination of optimum efficiency wage and employment in the presence of specific tax in *RWDC*

Optimum post-tax actual employment is

$$\bar{L}_s = F^{-1}(Y)/\left[\left(e((W/P)^*_s),\theta\right)\right] \tag{41}$$

As the firm faces commodity demand constraint, employment in efficiency unit, $[e((W/P)^*,\theta)L]^d$, is set on the basis of Y^d (as in (40) similar to (22) in the pre-tax situation). Since $(W/P)^*_s$ is set at a higher level in the presence of specific tax as compared to pre-tax situation, the corresponding effort level, $e((W/P)^*_s,\theta)$, is also higher. $[e((W/P)^*,\theta)L]^d$ being unchanged at the given commodity demand level, as effort, $e((W/P)^*,\theta)$ increases, actual employment, L, will fall in the post-tax situation.

The above optimization problem can be described with the help of Fig. 4. Optimum real wage increases to $(W/P)^*_s$ with the imposition of the specific tax, and consequently the wage cost per efficiency unit (*MC*) increases to point 'D' as compared to point 'E' in the pre-tax situation in panel (2) of Fig. 4. However, optimum employment in efficiency unit, $\left[e\left((W/P)^*_s,\theta\right)L\right]^d$, is determined on the basis of prevailing effective demand in panel (3). With unchanged $\left[e\left((W/P)^*_s,\theta\right)L\right]^d$ in panel (3), as effort increases to $e\left((W/P)^*_s,\theta\right)$ with rise in real wage to $(W/P)^*_s$ in panel (1), employment falls to $\bar{L}_s$. But this rise in real wage and fall in employment affect wage income and will have spillover effect on effective demand '*E*'.

4.1.1 Impact on Wage Income and Profit Income

As $(W/P)^*$ increases with the imposition of specific tax, corresponding effort, $e((W/P)^*, \theta)$, increases; but at the given Y^d, since employment in efficiency unit, $[e((W/P)^*, \theta)L]^d$, is fixed, rise in effort is equivalent to fall in employment. Moreover, at the optimum, $\mu_W < 1$, implying rise in effort is less than the rise in real wage; hence, rise in real wage is larger than fall in employment. ***Post-tax wage income thus increases***.

Again corresponding post-tax profit income is $\pi_s = \Pi_s/P = Y-(W/P)_s^*\bar{L}_s-\bar{L}_s t_s$.

On the one hand, as post-tax wage income increases, profit income falls, but on the other as employment falls expenditure on employment tax falls leading to rise in profit. ***Change in post-tax profit income is thus ambiguous***.

4.1.2 Post-tax Aggregate Demand

The pre-tax effective demand, Y^d, thus gets affected with new consumption demand, and let E_s be the new level of post-tax effective demand,

$$E_s = c_w[(W/P)_s^*\bar{L}_s]-\tau_w] + c_\pi[\pi_s - \tau_\pi] + \beta[\bar{m}/P] + \hat{g}$$

Substituting the expression for $\bar{L}_s$ and π_s in the above equation and denoting $(W/P)_s^*/[\big(e(W/P)_s^*, \theta\big)] = j(\theta, P, t_s)$, we can rewrite E_s as

$$\begin{aligned} E_s &= [c_W - c_\pi]j(\theta, P, t_s)F^{-1}(Y) + c_\pi Y \\ &\quad - c_\pi[F^{-1}(Y)/\big[e((W/P)_s^*, \theta)\big]]t_s - c_W\tau_W - c_\pi\tau_\pi + \beta[\bar{m}/P] + \hat{g} \end{aligned} \tag{42}$$

The solution of Y_s^k can be determined, where aggregate demand (E_s) curve touches the 45^0 line in $Y - Y$ plane in Fig. 5. Thus,

$$dE_s/dY = [c_W - c_\pi]j(\theta, P, t_s)F'^{-1}(Y) + c_\pi\big[1 - [F'^{-1}(Y)/\big[e((W/P)_s^*, \theta)\big]]t_s\big] > 0$$

$$d^2E_s/dY^2 = -[c_W - c_\pi]j(\theta, P, t_s)\big[F''^{-1}(Y)\big] + c_\pi\big[F''^{-1}(Y)\big]/\big[e((W/P)_s^*, \theta)\big]]t_s$$

Here, $\boldsymbol{d^2E_s/dY^2 \gtreqless 0}$ depending on $\boldsymbol{t_s} \gtreqless \frac{[c_w - c_\pi](W/P)_s^*}{c_\pi}$, since $F''^{-1}(Y) < 0$.

The shape of aggregate demand functions and hence the equilibrium post-tax output Y_s^k differs depending on magnitude of specific tax based on above condition.

It may be linear similar to *SNWMM* (Benassy 1986) when the value of specific tax imposed is $t_s = [[c_W - c_\pi](W/P)_s^*]/c_\pi$. However, aggregate demand curve may have concave shape similar to the pre-tax situation of *RWDC* of the present model (explained in Sect. 4) when $t_s < [[c_W - c_\pi](W/P)_s^*]/c_\pi$. In both these cases, there is a unique solution for equilibrium output. The aggregate demand curve may also be convex in nature when $t_s > [[c_W - c_\pi](W/P)_s^*]/c_\pi$, where one may or may not have

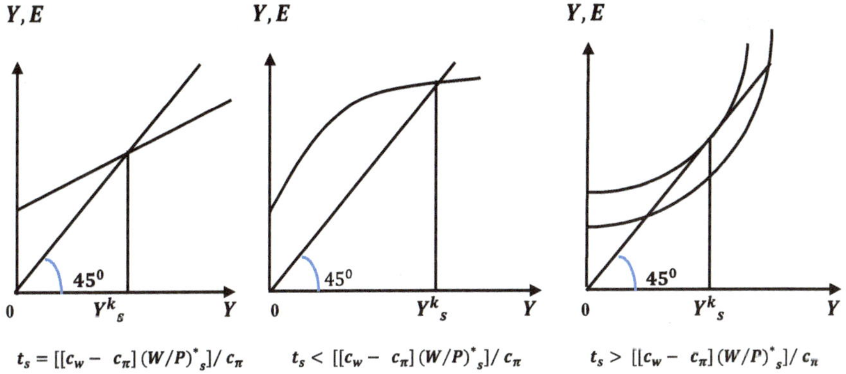

Fig. 5 Different shapes of aggregate demand curves and corresponding equilibrium output in the presence of specific tax in *RWDC*

any unique solution for the equilibrium output. However, to keep the analysis simple, in the present case we are disregarding the probability of non-unique solutions; that is, we are not considering those values of the parameters like t_a, c_w and c_π which generate non-unique solutions.

Thus, the equilibrium output is

$$\begin{aligned}\boldsymbol{Y_s^*} &= \boldsymbol{Y_s^{k*}} = \boldsymbol{E_s} = [[c_w - c_\pi]/[1 - c_\pi]]j(\theta, P, t_s)F^{-1}\left(Y_s^{k*}\right)\\ &- [c_\pi/[1 - c_\pi]]F^{-1}\left(Y_s^{k*}\right)/\left[\left(e(W/P)_s^*, \theta\right)\right]t_s - c_{\tau_w}\tau_w/[1 - c_\pi] - c_{\tau_\pi}\tau_\pi/[1 - c_\pi]\\ &+ [\beta(\bar{m}/P)]/[1 - c_\pi] + \hat{g}/[1 - c_\pi] = \boldsymbol{K_s}\left(\boldsymbol{\theta}, \boldsymbol{\tau_w}, \boldsymbol{\tau_\pi}, \hat{\boldsymbol{g}}, \boldsymbol{P}, \boldsymbol{t_s}\right) \end{aligned} \quad (43)$$

where post-tax wage cost per efficiency unit is $(W/P)_s^*/\left[\left(e(W/P)_s^*, \theta\right)\right] = j(\theta, P, t_s)$

$$(W/P)_s^* = \omega(\theta, P, t_s)$$

Here, $K_s(\theta, \tau_w, \tau_\pi, \hat{g}, P, t_s) \leq \min[S(\theta), S(\theta, t_s), Y^0]$

Optimum post-tax actual employment is $L_s^* = \frac{F^{-1}(Y_s^*)}{[e((W/P)_s^*, \theta)]}$.

4.1.3 Specific Tax Multiplier

Specific tax multiplier can be derived from (43),

$$dY_s^*/dt_s = \frac{[F^{-1}(Y_s^*)/[(e(W/P)_s^*, \theta)][[c_w - c_\pi]d(W/P)_s^*/dt_s][1 - \mu_{(W/P)}] - c_\pi[1 - \mu_{(W/P)}\omega_t]]}{1 - [c_w - c_\pi]j(\theta, P, t_s)F'^{-1}(Y_s^*) - c_\pi\left[1 - t_s[F'^{-1}(Y_s^*)/e((W/P)_s^*, \theta)]\right]} \gtreqless 0 \quad (44)$$

Here, $\omega_t = \left[d(W/P)_s^k/dt_s\right] \cdot [(W/P)_s^k/t_s]$, that is, elasticity of real wage with respect to specific tax.

The denominator of (44) is positive as responsiveness of net savings of the household with respect to income is positive. Hence,

$$1 - [c_w - c_\pi]j(\theta, P, t_s)F'^{-1}(Y_s^*) - c_\pi\big[1 - t_s\big[F'^{-1}(Y_s^*)/[e((W/P)_s^*, \theta)\big]\big] > 0 \tag{45}$$

(i) In the numerator of (44),

$$[c_w - c_\pi][F^{-1}(Y_s^*)/\big[e((W/P)_s^*, \theta\big]\big][d(W/P)_s^*/dt_s]\big[1 - \mu_{(W/P)}\big] > 0 \tag{46}$$

where $d(W/P)_s^*/dt_s > 0$ and $\mu_{(W/P)} < 1$.

As wage income increases with increase in specific tax, that is $[F^{-1}(Y_s^*)/\big[e((W/P)_s^*, \theta)\big]][d(W/P)_s^*/dt_s]\big[1 - \mu_{(W/P)}\big] > 0$, net consumption demand out of it increases as $[c_w - c_\pi] > 0$, that is

$$[c_w - c_\pi][F^{-1}(Y_s^*)/\big[e((W/P)_s^*, \theta)\big]][d(W/P)_s^*/dt_s]\big[1 - \mu_{(W/P)}\big] > 0$$

(ii) But again in the numerator of (44)

$$-c_\pi[F^{-1}(Y_s^*)/\big[e((W/P)_s^*, \theta)\big]]\big[1 - \mu_{(W/P)\omega_t}\big] \gtreqless 0, \quad \text{as} \quad \big[1 - \mu_{(W/P)\omega_t}\big] \gtreqless 0 \tag{47}$$

Since change in profit income with rise in specific tax is ambiguous, that is $[F^{-1}(Y_s^*)/\big[e((W/P)_s^*, \theta)\big]]\big[1 - \mu_{(W/P)\omega_t}\big] \gtreqless 0$, change in demand from profit income too becomes ambiguous. Change in profit income thus depends on the factor $[1 - \mu_{(W/P)\omega_t}]$, where $\mu_{(W/P)\omega_t} = \mu_t$,[15] implying elasticity of effort with respect to specific tax. If $\boldsymbol{\mu_t} \geq 1$, elasticity of effort with respect to specific tax is equal or larger than unity, which implies rise in effort is larger or equal to the rise in specific tax, that is $[1 - \mu_{(W/P)\omega_t}] \leq 0$.

At the given level of output, employment falls as effort increases with specific tax, t_s; thus, when $\mu_t \geq 1$, employment falls more than or at the same amount of rise in t_s. Fall in tax expenditure due to fall in employment is larger or equal to the rise in cost due to rise in t_s.

Thus, profit income would increase and so as the demand out of it in (47) that is

$$c_\pi[F^{-1}(Y_s^*)/e((W/P)_s^*, \theta)][1 - \mu_{(W/P)\omega_t}] \geq 0 \tag{48}$$

15
$$\mu_{(W/P)\omega_t} = \frac{de((W/P)_s^*, \theta)}{d(W/P)_s^*} \frac{(W/P)_s^*}{[e((W/P)_s^*, \theta)]} \cdot \frac{d(W/P)_s^*}{dt_s} \frac{t_s}{(W/P)_s^*}$$
$$= \frac{de((W/P)_s^*, \theta)}{dt_s} \frac{t_s}{[e((W/P)_s^*, \theta)]} = \mu_t,$$ effort elasticity with respect to specific tax.

Thus, net demand out of wage income increases (in (46)) and demand from profit income too increases or remains unchanged in (48) with the rise in specific tax, that is the numerator in (44),

$$[F^{-1}(Y_s^*)/[(e(W/P)_s^*,\theta)]][[c_w - c_\pi][d(W/P)_s^*/dt_s][1-\mu_{(W/P)}] - c_\pi[1-\mu_{(W/P)}\omega_t]] > 0$$

And hence, aggregate demand or output increases with the rise in specific tax, $\boldsymbol{dY_s^*/dt_s} > 0$

If $\mu_t < 1$, effort increases less than the rise in t_s, that is $[1-\mu_{(W/P)}\omega_t] > 0$

Fall in expenditure due to fall in employment is less than the rise in cost due to rise in t_s. Thus, profit income and the corresponding demand out of it in (47) falls.

$$-c_\pi[F^{-1}(Y_s^*)/e((W/P)_s^*,\theta)][1-\mu_{(W/P)}\omega_t] < 0 \tag{49}$$

As net demand out of wage income increases in (46), but demand from profit income falls in (49). The numerator in (44) is

$$[F^{-1}(Y_s^*)/[(e(W/P)_s^*,\theta)]][[c_w - c_\pi][d(W/P)_s^*/dt_s][1-\mu_{(W/P)}] - c_\pi[1-\mu_{(W/P)}\omega_t]] \gtreqless 0$$

Hence, $\boldsymbol{dY_s^*/dt_s} \gtreqless 0$ depending on

$$\frac{[c_w - c_\pi][d(W/P)_s^k/dt_s]}{c_\pi} \gtreqless \frac{[1-\mu_{(W/P)}\omega_t]}{[1-\mu_{(W/P)}]} \tag{50}$$

Aggregate demand and thus optimum output increases/falls or remains unchanged based on the above condition.

Proposition 4 *(i) Aggregate output increases with per unit rise in specific tax when effort elasticity with respect to specific tax is greater or equal to unity; (ii) increase in specific tax thus has an employment-generating role in RWDC which is a strong contrast to RWODC of the present model and existing studies in SEWM where imposition of specific tax always lowers employment; (iii) however, if effort elasticity with respect to specific tax is less than unity, impact of rise in specific tax on optimum output is ambiguous and depends on: (a) the magnitudes of the specific tax imposed, (b) effort elasticity with respect to specific tax, (c) effort elasticity with respect to real wage and (d) also on marginal propensities to consume for both wage and profit earners; (v) imposition of specific tax in RWDC has positive impact on wage income, while impact on profit income is ambiguous.*

5 Conclusion

In this paper, a non-Walrasian fixed price model is formulated where optimum real wage is determined on the basis of efficiency wage consideration unlike *SNWMM* of Benassy (1986) (where both nominal wage and price are exogenously fixed).

By assuming exogenously fixed commodity price, this model also revisits *SEWM* (Solow 1979) where price is considered to be flexible. Further, the present paper examines the impact of payroll tax like specific or employment tax in the present non-Walrasian structure with efficiency wage. Though study on impact of specific tax is prevalent in *SEWM* (Yellen 1984; Shapiro and Stiglitz 1984; Johnson and Layard 1986; Pisauro 1991, etc.), analysis related to impact of such payroll tax is missing in standard non-Walrasian structure.

Two regimes are found to be relevant in the present model, that is (i) equilibrium or excess demand in the commodity market with excess supply in labour market signifying the regime without commodity demand constraint (*RWODC*) and (ii) excess supply of commodity and labour signifying regime with commodity demand constraint (*RWDC*). It has been observed that in both the cases the firm sets optimum real wage at the point where effort elasticity with respect to real wage is equal to unity (i.e. Solow Condition holds). Though in *RWODC* employment solely depends on effort function, in *RWDC* optimum employment is determined on the basis of both the effort function and the prevailing level of effective demand in the economy. It is clear that level of unemployment in *RWDC* is higher than that of both *SNWMM* (Benassy 1986) where only demand effect is prevalent and *SEWM* (Solow 1979) where only efficiency effect works.

Moreover with the incidence of specific taxing in *RWODC*, optimum post-tax real wage increases and employment falls (similar to *SEWM* of Yellen 1984), However in *RWDC*, (i) aggregate demand for output increases with the rise in specific tax if effort elasticity with respect to specific tax is greater or equal to unity; in this particular case, increase in specific tax may have an employment-generating role which is a strong contrast to the existing studies in *SEWM* (Yellen 1984 in particular) or in *RWODC* of the present model, where imposition of specific tax always lowers employment, and (ii) if effort elasticity with respect to specific tax is less than unity, impact of rise in specific tax on aggregate demand for output is ambiguous and depends on the magnitudes of (a) the specific tax imposed, (b) effort elasticity with respect to specific tax, (c) effort elasticity with respect to real wage and (d) marginal propensities to consume for both wage and profit earners.

Appendix

Impact of Exogenous Shift in Effort Function

The impact of exogenous upward shift in effort function is explained in Fig. 6. As the parameter θ increases with the improvement of the exogenous factors like access to and quality of health care, the quality and affordability of education and training, investment on infrastructure, etc., the effort curve in panel (1) shifts upward to e_1. In panel (1), the maximum effort–real wage ratio $e/(W/P)$ corresponding to new level of effort e_1 increases as compared to initial level e. This implies the fact that the worker can now exert more effort at the lower level of real wage. The point associated with maximum effort–real wage ratio (where $\mu_W = 1$) shifts leftward,

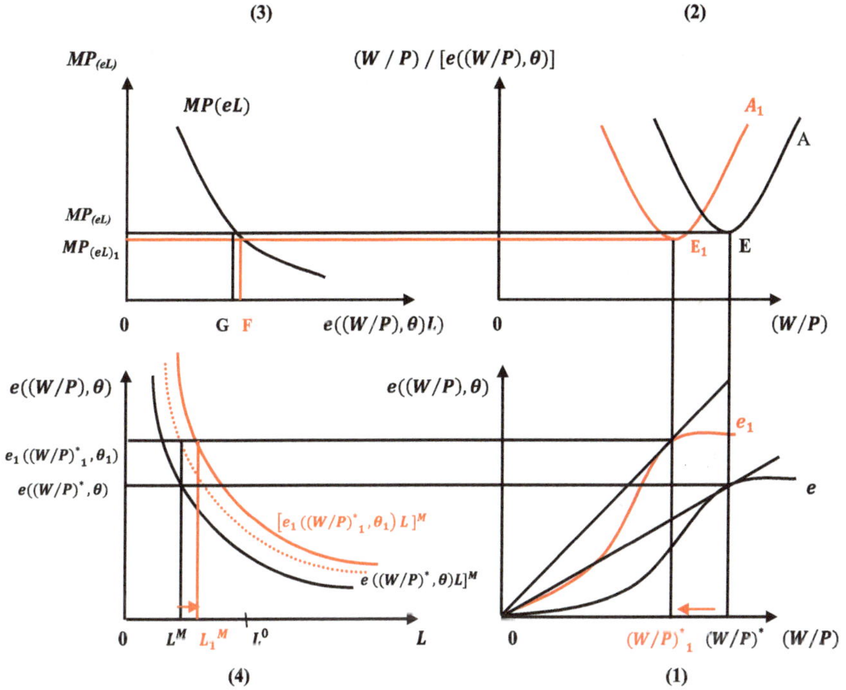

Fig. 6 Impact of exogenous shift in effort on real wage and employment in the unconstrained case

and optimum real wage, $(W/P)^*$, falls to $(W/P)_1^*$ which corresponds to the maximum $e/(W/P)$ with respect to new effort function, e_1.[16] Accordingly, minimum wage cost per efficiency unit, $((W/P)/e)$, falls as depicted in panel (2), where the minimum point of new MC curve (A_1) is now at 'E_1'. At the optimum, corresponding $MP_{(eL)}$ falls and employment in efficiency unit, $[e((W/P), \theta)L]$, increases to point 'F' as shown in panel (3). With the rise in $[e((W/P), \theta)L]$, profit-maximizing level of output increases (say from Y^M to Y_1^M).

Finally, the impact on actual employment is shown in panel (4). As optimum employment in efficiency unit, $[e((W/P)^*, \theta)L]^M$, curve shifts upward to $\left[e\left((W/P)_1^*, \theta_1\right)L\right]^M$ in panel (4) and at the same time since effort, $e((W/P)^*, \theta)$, increases to $e\left((W/P)_1^*, \theta_1\right)$, change in employment L depends on the magnitude of the shift in employment in efficiency unit $[e((W/P), \theta)L]$,[17] as compared to increase in effort. If the magnitude of the shift in $[e((W/P), \theta)L]$ is higher/lower or equal to increase in $e((W/P), \theta)$, employment, L, increases/falls or remains unchanged. In

[16] Upward shift in effort function is shown in Snowdon and Vane (2005) where unemployment rate is the exogenous factor that affects effort of the worker and rise in which shifts effort function upward.

[17] Increase in employment in efficiency unit, $[e((W/P), \theta)L)]$, depends on the shape of the marginal productivity curve in panel (3).

panel (4), profit-maximizing level of actual employment, L^M, rises to L_1^M when shift in $[e((W/P), \theta)L)]$ is higher than the rise in $e((W/P), \theta)$ but remains unchanged when both the shifts are equal (dotted employment in efficiency unit curve).

Here, $(W/P)^*$ is determined only on the basis of the given effort function. However, since effort function shifts upward with the rise in parameter, θ, $(W/P)^*$ falls to $(W/P)_1^*$. Thus, $(W/P)^*$ is sensitive to θ. Again, minimum wage cost per efficiency unit, $(W/P)^*/[e((W/P)^*, \theta)]$, falls with the rise in θ, but profit-maximizing level of employment, L^M, may rise/fall or remain unchanged. Hence, optimum real wage, actual employment and output are functions of θ only.

References

Abel, A. B., & Bernanke, B. S. (2001). *Macroeconomics*. New York: Addison-Wesley.

Akerlof, G. A. (1982). Labour contracts as partial gift exchange. *Quarterly Journal of Economics, 97,* 543–569.

Akerlof, G. A., & Yellen, J. L. (1986). *Efficiency wage models of the labor market*. Cambridge: Cambridge University Press.

Barro, R. J., & Grossman, H. (1971). A general disequilibrium model of income and employment. *American Economic Review, 61,* 82–93.

Benassy, J. P. (1975). Neo-Keynesian disequilibrium theory in monetary economy. *Review of Economic Studies, 42,* 503–523.

Benassy, J. P. (1982). *The economics of market disequilibrium*. New York: Academic Press.

Benassy, J. P. (1986). *Macroeconomics: an introduction to the non-Walrasian approach*. London: Academic Press.

Clower, R. W. (1965). The Keynesian counter revolution: a theoretical appraisal. In F. H. Hahn & F. P. R. Brechling (Eds.), *The theory of rates*. London: Macmillan.

Johnson, G. E., & Layard, R. (1986). The natural rate of unemployment: Explanation and policy. In O. Ashenfelter & R. Layard (Eds.), *Handbook of labour economics* (pp. 921–999). Amsterdam: Elsevier Science Publishers.

Kaldor, N. (1955–56). Alternative theories of distribution. *Review of Economic Studies, 23,* 83–100.

Malinvaud, E. (1977). *The theory of unemployment reconsidered*. Oxford: Blackwell.

Patinkin, D. (1956). *Money interest and prices: An integration of monetary and value theory*. Evanston, IL: Row Peterson.

Pisauro, G. (1991). The effect of taxes on labour in efficiency wage models. *Journal of Public Economics, 46,* 329–345.

Salop, S. C. (1979). A model of natural rate of unemployment. *American Economic Review, 69,* 117–125.

Shapiro, C., & Stiglitz, J. E. (1984). Equilibrium unemployment as a worker discipline device. *American Economic Review, 74,* 433–444.

Snowdon, B., & Howard, R. V. (2005). *Modern macroeconomics, its origins, development and current state*. UK, USA: Edward Elgar.

Solow, R. M. (1979). Another possible source of wage stickiness. *Journal of Macroeconomics, 1,* 79–82.

Stringer, J. (2014). 5 Factors That Affect Your Employee's Productivity. NBRI. http://www.nbrii.com.

Summers, L. H. (1988). Relative wages, efficiency wages, and Keynesian unemployment. *American Economic Review Papers and Proceedings, 78,* 383–388.

Weiss, A. (1980). Job queues and layoffs in labour markets with flexible wages. *Journal of Political Economy, 88,* 526–538.

Web site. http://www.tutor2u.net.
Yellen, J. L. (1984). Efficiency wage models of unemployment. *American Economic Review, 74,* 200–205.

Married Women's Education Levels and Agency Outside the Home: Evidence from Rural India

Nisha Vernekar and Karan Singhal

Abstract The importance of women's agency towards the nation and its children's well-being has been well established in the literature. While the role of education of a woman has been linked to her agency, there is limited rigorous evidence studying the relationship of her agency freedoms across different public spheres. Using a nationally representative data set, we investigate the association of education levels of women and her family members, with distinct agency freedoms outside the household which represent her overall agency—whether allowed to work, membership in a social group (e.g. Self Help Groups), and mobility within the village, in rural India. While we find a positive association between agency and education levels of women, this is not consistent across all agency variables. Some of these effects diminish when we look at heterogeneous specifications which require further exploration.

Keywords Women · Agency freedom · Education. Post-marital household

JEL Codes B23 · I24 · J16

1 Introduction

Women are found to enjoy less agency freedom across different stages of their lives, relative to their male counterparts. Girls are less likely to be enrolled in schools and complete fewer years of education than boys, and women are less likely to be enrolled in institutions of education or employment outside of their natal villages and less likely to be gainfully employed. These trends have been attributed to the idea that women, once married, no longer contribute to the natal family, making male children the primary breadwinners for their families, thus incentivizing their educa-

N. Vernekar (✉) · K. Singhal
Indian Institute of Management Ahmedabad, Ahmedabad, India
e-mail: nisha03100@gmail.com

K. Singhal
e-mail: karansinghal1993@gmail.com

N. R. Bhanumurthy et al. (eds.), *Advances in Finance & Applied Economics*,
https://doi.org/10.1007/978-981-13-1696-8_10

tion and employment. At the same time, the importance of women's independence and freedoms that might contribute to the well-being of her children, her community, and herself has been well documented in the literature. (Quisumbing and Maluccio 2000; Haddad et al. 1997).

With reference to freedoms of women outside the household, many have studied agency freedom, a concept that we wish to use for our study. A component of Sen's capability approach, agency freedom refers to '*...a person's role as a member of society, with the ability to participate in economic, social, and political actions*', whether or not it contributes to one's personal well-being (A. Sen 1985). Similar to the positive impact that a woman's independence might have on the well-being of her family, studies suggest that households where women are empowered to participate in activities outside the households tend to have fewer children and lower child mortality rates (Rosenzweig and Schultz 1982; Kanbur and Haddad 1994), better education for their children (Thomas 1990; Llyod and Blanc 1996; Aslam 2007), and particularly better education for the girl child (Smith and Bryon 2005). An increase in women's incomes, which might represent them having financial independence, is shown to be associated with increased expenditure on health of their children (Phillips and Burton 1998; Lundberg and Pollak 1996). Haddad (1995) shows a positive association between women's income and expenditure on food for the household. Similarly, empowerment of the woman was found to positively affect her family's social status (Quisumbing and de la Bri'ere 2000).

In the context of rural India, the variations in agency freedom amongst women are largely determined by the socio-economic background of households they belong to. The literature suggests that upper caste women in India often do not work as being outside the household is discouraged to protect the dignity of the woman, while those who do choose to work might only work certain kinds of jobs (such as government jobs) (Kodoth 2005). Amongst historically backward/lower castes however, economic deprivation necessitating that the woman also works has disassociated the stigma of women participating in activities outside the households.

In trying to better understand this link between education and agency in the post-marital household of a woman in rural India, this paper gauges the influence that being educated and having educated family members might have on her agency across public spheres. Using IHDS (2011–12), a nationally representative data set we assess whether a woman's education is associated with her overall agency as is suggested in the literature. We control socio-economic characteristics of her household and cultural factors that might impact her agency including social customs such as wearing burkah or purdah,[1] acceptance of domestic violence, and incidence of harassment that are associated with women empowerment.

We consider a woman's participation in three distinct activities in the public sphere as representations of her overall agency—whether she is allowed to work conditional

[1]The b*urkah/purdah* system is a religious and social practice in South Asia, wherein Hindu and Muslim women cover their faces with part of the garments they wear when in public and even when amongst certain male relatives in their family. This practice has been found to be adversely associated with freedom of women outside the household (Dyson and Moore 1983).

on her wanting to, whether she is allowed to be mobile within her own village, and whether she is a member of any social group such as a self-help group (SHG), *Mahila Samakhya*,[2] or credit/savings (*bachat*) group. We work under the assumption that the agency variables we have selected factor into the interests of women and might be valued in the absence of deprivation or from the eyes of a neutral observer (Sen 1985). Each of the three public spheres, due to their nature and historical association with gender stereotyped roles in society, might be associated with the education and agency of women in different ways.

Economic participation or employment is largely considered a male-dominated sphere, except for women belonging to households of historically disadvantaged castes for whom women working are an economic necessity. With respect to education, while employment would be expected to be closely associated with education levels, this might not be the case for relatively unskilled labour.

Mobility within a village is a relatively gender neutral sphere, where both men and women might require to be mobile on a day-to-day basis. However, both the variables selected as representing mobility are not functional tasks. It is also well documented that more often than men women treat public spaces as operational rather than for leisure. We would further not expect education to have a definitive impact on this.

Social groups considered here are female-oriented spaces, often designed by external intervention with the purpose of encouraging female participation, making it distinctively different from the two other agency variables.

Our results reflect that more educated women enjoy greater agency in being allowed to work and being members of social groups; however, these effects are disproportionately higher for women belonging to richer households and women belonging to Scheduled Caste (SC) or Scheduled Tribe (ST) households.

The structure of our paper is as follows. In the following section, we discuss the concept of agency freedom and its definition, and the discourse surrounding the association between education and agency freedoms. Section 3 details the data and variables used in our study. Section 4 discusses the method and analysis used. Section 5 presents the descriptive statistics tables and results from the regression analysis, and we conclude in Sect. 6.

2 Agency and Education

Our paper refers to agency freedoms—certain capabilities associated with the ability to partake in activity in the public sphere. This is closely related to the concept of empowerment—overcoming feelings of voicelessness or disempowerment by increasing control over their own lives, such as through institutional participation,

[2] A nationwide programme launched in 1988 that aims to increase self-esteem enables women to make informed choices, provides skills for economic independence, and increases access to literacy for women.

or in such activities that might be directed towards the benefit of society (Subaiya and Vanneman 2016; Alkire 2005).

Relevant to an individual's well-being and often a part of policy discussion as a route to accessing gainful employment or participation in society are education and schooling. Education is considered to be an indicator of development in itself (Stiglitz et al. 2009), having an instrumental value whereby it might enhance other capabilities of a person (Sen 1999; Nussbaum 2003). The capabilities approach specifically discusses, albeit not in detail, the role of education as a 'capability enhancer' that may increase other freedoms of a person (Sen 1999). Finally, education is said to enhance one's ability to reason, where practical reason is identified as important for recognizing what one chooses to value and pursues, thereby enhancing those capabilities (Unterhalter 2003; Nussbaum 2000). Jejeebhoy (1995) presents evidence that access to education provides women the ability to reflect on and question their circumstances by introducing them to new ideas. Education is thus identified as having intrinsic value and being a capability that should be valued.

Many studies have associated better education, especially of mothers, with greater agency freedom. The better-educated tend to have lower unemployment, more social connection, and higher engagement in civic and political life (Stiglitz et al. 2009). Better-educated women have greater bargaining power and influence over household decisions and resources (Rahman and Rao 2004; Acharya et al. 2010; Mahmud, Shah and Becker 2012). At the same time, there are certain studies that refute the claim that education might lead to greater agency for women. Kuenning and Amin (2001) in reference to Bangladesh argue that education as is cannot change or challenge circumstances of limited freedom. Kabeer (2005) furthers this claim on grounds that content taught in schools is often gendered, which might perpetuate inequalities.

3 Data and Variables

Our study uses data from the Indian Human Development Survey (IHDS) jointly conducted by National Council of Applied Economic Research, New Delhi, India, and the University of Maryland, published in 2011–12. The nationally representative survey was administered on over two lakh individuals.

We primarily consider only one component of the survey—the Women's Questionnaire—which interviewed approximately 39,800 women between the ages of 15–49 years (as of 2005), residing in rural India, and captured women's perspectives about their decision-making power, agency freedom, and social customs such as acceptability of domestic violence, within their household and community, amongst other questions.

3.1 *Outcome Variables*

The three categories of agency freedoms considered in our study are economic participation, social group participation, and mobility within a village/neighbourhood. The three activities represent varied public spheres within which women might participate.

Economic participation is measured using a binary variable, which captures if a woman is allowed to or not allowed to take up a job conditional on their willingness to work and on finding a suitable job. Given this conditionality, this sample of women is already selective.

Social group participation considers whether a woman is a member of any one of the three social group organizations that were mentioned in the questionnaire—*Mahila Samakhya*, credit/savings group, or self-help group. We consider that a woman is a member of these social groups if she has responded that she participates in at least one of the three groups. As access to these social groups varies across villages and states, we find membership to any one of the three social groups as a sufficient condition.

Variables we use that represent mobility are—whether the women must take permission to be mobile within the village, i.e. for visiting the local *kirana*[3] shop, or for visiting the homes of a friend/relative within the village. This variable is also treated as a binary variable where a woman is said to have agency if she need not ask for permission for either of the mobility activities.

3.2 *Explanatory Variables*

3.2.1 Education Controls

The primary variable of interest is the education level of the woman. We further control education of the woman's mother, her husband, and the difference in education between a woman and her husband.

A variable capturing difference between woman and her husband's education level is treated as a categorical variable for when the education levels of a woman and her husband are equal, when the woman is more educated than her husband, and when her husband is more educated than her.

Education levels of a woman's mother and husband are categorical variables. Categorized as number of years of schooling, these variables are constituted of three categories—(1) below 5th (primary education), (2) 6th–10th (upper primary and secondary education), and (3) 11th and above (including bachelor's, postgraduate studies). Categorization was done on the basis of variation provided across groups and to maintain observations in each category allowing for comparison. Preliminary analysis prior to this categorization does not show any change in the analysis.

[3]Local supermarket, grocery, or 'general' store.

3.2.2 Age

We control age of the woman as there is empirical evidence suggesting agency of women increases with age. This is treated as a continuous variable. We control the difference of age between the woman and her husband, which is also treated as a continuous variable moving from women being older than their husbands to their husband being older.

3.2.3 Economic Characteristics

We control monthly per capita expenditure of the household (normalized using natural log) and the house type (*pucca/kutcha*).

3.2.4 Social Group and State Dummies

We control caste and religion, and geographical distribution of households across the states. Caste and religion are important controls as Scheduled Castes and Tribes tend to have more agency freedoms to pursue economic pursuits because their economic status is usually comparatively lower than other caste groups, while Muslim women tend to enjoy least freedom in most domains. As a result, education levels also systematically differ across these groups.

3.2.5 Cultural Factors

Regression results are presented with and without cultural factors that might influence agency of women. They are associated with various degrees of deprivation of women in the households—whether the woman wears burkah/purdah, whether it is acceptable in the village for a husband to beat his wife, and how frequently incidences of harassment take place in the village. All three variables are binary.

4 Empirical Strategy

We run a linear regression model.[4] To measure the association of the dependent variables with the explanatory variables, we assume the following function:

$$Yi = \beta 0 + \beta 1(\text{Educational characteristics}) + \beta 2(\text{Controls}) + \beta 3(\text{State dummies}) + \varepsilon$$

[4]Results do not change using probit regression model.

Y indicates the dependent variables allowed to work, allowed to visit a relative, friend, or kirana shop, and whether a member of any social group for every woman *i* in the sample. $\beta 1$ is woman's education level and the coefficient of interest, while $\beta 2$ is a vector of all controls. $\beta 3$ is a vector of all state dummies, and ε is the error term for every woman/household *i*. Standard errors are clustered at the district level.

We further run regressions using the same specification as above, within subgroups of social group and class. For social group subgroups, we run specifications for households falling within forward castes (Hindu Brahmin, and forward caste) and backward castes (Scheduled Tribes, Scheduled Castes).[5] For class subgroups, we create four expenditure quintiles and run the specification for households falling within the first (richest) and fourth (poorest) quintiles separately.

A limitation in the functional form and data we have opted to use is that it does not permit us to determine causality between education of women and their agency. However, our aim is to find associations of educational characteristics with various agency freedoms and hence causality is outside the scope of our analytical framework.

5 Results

5.1 Descriptive Statistics

Of the total sample of rural women under study, approximately 66% women reported they were allowed to work, conditional on wanting to and finding a suitable job, and almost 75% women reported they did not need to take permission to be mobile within the village. Only 21% women, however, were members of any social group. This is surprising as the workforce of the country is considered a male-dominated sphere, as are public spaces used primarily for leisure, while the social groups we use in our study are spaces created specifically to incentivize participation of women in the public sphere. Thus, we would expect greater participation in social groups compared to employment, which is not the case as per our descriptive analysis. (Table 1).

Table 1 Proportions of women allowed/enjoying different agency activities

Agency variables	Rural	Urban
Allowed to work	65.89	45.16
Member of social group	20.95	15.77
Allowed to be mobile within village	74.7	73.52

[5]Specification is not run for Other Backward Classes (OBCs) given the difficulty in interpreting results for this due to varied economic backgrounds they belong to.

Table 2 Household characteristics (associated with woman) across agency variables

Socio-economic background variables	Overall	Allowed to work	Member of social group	Allowed to be mobile within village
Caste/religion groups				
Brahmin and forward castes	18.41	19.92	17.94	19.77
OBC	34.94	34.14	38.09	35.35
Dalit (SC)	22.48	23.35	25.62	22.77
Adivasi (ST)	11.04	9.12	10.59	9.85
Muslim	10.89	11.08	5.98	9.75
Christian, Sikh, Jain	2.24	2.4	1.78	2.5
No. of obs	135,085	11286	5,456	19,305
Age of woman (mean)	29.31031	33.59453	37.76145	35.10902
Marital status: married	93.69	96.29	92.78	96.54
No. of obs	26,078	11,288	5,457	19,305
Marital household type				
None	16.82	17.18	17.35	15.82
Patrilocal	7.22	5.79	10.47	6.62
Matrilocal	73.56	74.55	69.52	75.05
Both	2.4	2.48	2.66	2.52
No. of obs	13660	6699	2,484	10808
Per capita monthly consumptions expenditure (quintiles)				
First		18.67	13.27	16.53
Second		20.25	16.94	19
Third		20.7	21.41	20.32
Fourth		20.07	22.62	21.39
Fifth		20.32	25.77	22.76
No. of obs		11286	5456	19301
House wall type				
Pucca	62.97	63.8	61.68	64.6
No. of obs	133,690	11,245	5,430	19,220

In Tables 2, 3, and 4, we present socio-economic background characteristics of women across the three agency (outcome) variables.

In Table 2, we find that more women belonging to backward caste groups (OBC, Adivasi, and Dalits) were members of social institutions, compared to Muslim and Hindu or forward caste women. More women who were older than the sample average had agency in all three outcome variables.

In Table 3, we look at variables representing cultural factors and societal behaviour that might impact a woman's agency, across the three outcome variables. We find that fewer women who practiced *purdah/gunghat were members of social groups*. Of the women who were allowed to work, more practiced *purdah/gunghat*, and reported acceptance of domestic abuse in the community.

Table 3 Cultural and social behaviour

Cultural and social behaviour	Overall	Allowed to work	Member of social group	Allowed to be mobile within village
Follow purdah/gunghat	62.68	73.16	40.31	62.48
No. of obs	*26,059*	*11,285*	*5,455*	*19,300*
Reported wife-beating is accepted in their community	90.43	92.6	90.72	91.53
No. of obs	*26,018*	*11,275*	*5,441*	*19,283*
Girls in village are harassed sometimes or often	25.92	22.26	29.15	26.36
No. of obs	*25614*	*11132*	*5289*	*18984*

Table 4 Household educational background across agency variables

Educational background variables	Overall	Allowed to work	Member of social group	Allowed to be mobile within village
Woman's education				
Below 5th	64.1	60.21	60.04	62.75
6th–10th	28	30.07	32.23	28.91
Above 10th	7.95	9.72	7.73	8.34
No. of obs	*26,079*	*11,287*	*5,458*	*19,306*
Husband				
Below 5th	57.94	40.95	48.42	44.64
6th–10th	31.36	41.42	38.16	39.65
Above 10th	10.71	17.63	13.42	15.71
No. of obs	*61,360*	*9734*	*4172*	*17250*
Mother				
Below 5th	93.39	92.19	92.76	93.49
6th–10th	6	7.1	6.95	5.98
Above 10th	0.52	0.71	0.29	0.53
No. of obs	*25,993*	*11,271*	*5,427*	*19,243*

In Table 4, we find that more women who were allowed to work were educated up to 6 years or more, and women who had agency in all three outcome variables had more educated husbands.

Table 5 Regression results

	Allowed to work		Require permission for mobility within village		Member of social group	
	(a)	(b)	(a)	(b)	(a)	(b)
Woman's education level						
Ref: 5th or below						
6th to 10th	0.0111	0.0103	0.0134	0.0171[a]	0.0293[c]	0.0266[c]
	(0.0127)	(0.0129)	(0.0103)	(0.0102)	(0.00884)	(0.00890)
Above 11th	0.0964[c]	0.0975[c]	0.0141	0.0209	−0.00600	−0.0117
	(0.0215)	(0.0217)	(0.0154)	(0.0154)	(0.0152)	(0.0152)
Cultural factors	No	Yes	No	Yes	No	Yes
Age of woman and age difference between husband and wife	Yes	Yes	Yes	Yes	Yes	Yes
Education controls (woman's mother, her husband, and educational difference between husband and wife)	Yes	Yes	Yes	Yes	Yes	Yes
Economic characteristics (expenditure and pucca wall)	Yes	Yes	Yes	Yes	Yes	Yes
Social group	Yes	Yes	Yes	Yes	Yes	Yes
State dummies	Yes	Yes	Yes	Yes	Yes	Yes
Constant	1.614[c]	1.533[c]	1.074[c]	0.980[c]	−0.334[c]	−0.331[c]
	(0.101)	(0.108)	(0.0859)	(0.0913)	(0.0627)	(0.0686)
N	16219	15963	23948	23539	24098	23682

Note Standard errors have been clustered at the district level. Significance levels: [a]at 10%; [b]at 5%; [c]at 1%

5.2 Regression Results

In Table 5, we present regression results for all outcome variables.[6]

In our first specification, we find that a woman's education level is positively associated with her being allowed to work and with her being a member of a social group. Women with education above 11th grade are almost 10% more likely to be allowed to work than women with education levels of 5th grade and below. Women with education levels between 6th and 10th grade are almost 3% more likely to be members of social groups compared to women with education levels of 5th grade and below; however, there is no significant association at higher education levels. In the case of both these variables, controlling societal factors or customs does not change results.

[6]Results are shown using a linear regression model. Due to paucity of space and time, results for marginal effects have not been reported and thus only the direction and significance of the coefficient are reported. A probit regression model yields similar results. Results for both the probit model and marginal effect regressions are available on request.

We further explore these findings using subgroup effects within caste and per capita expenditure.[7]

Within backward caste groups (SC and ST), we find higher education of women is associated with being allowed to work, but is not significantly associated with the other agency variables, whereas for upper caste households (including Brahmin and forward caste households) and for Muslims there is no significant association between education levels of women and their agency freedoms.

Within the richest households (first quintile), we find results are similar to findings in Table 5 (regression on overall sample), where education levels of women are associated positively with being allowed to work and being a member of a social group. However, there is no significant association amongst poorest households. This suggests that economic advantage drives the relationship between education and agency.

5.3 Discussion

Our results on the association between the education of a woman and her overall agency are consistent with the literature where more educated women enjoy greater agency; however, we find that mobility has a weak negative association with education levels. Thus, education of women is not positively associated with her overall agency freedom in the public sphere.

The subgroup effects further suggest that the significant positive association of education levels of women with being allowed to work is being driven by richer households and by SC and ST households over forward caste and Muslim households, while the significant positive association between education levels and the likelihood of a woman being a member of a social group is being driven by relative economic advantage.

6 Conclusion

The association of education levels of women to the agency freedoms she enjoys outside the households has not been explored rigorously in the context of rural India. Once controlling socio-economic backgrounds and educational background of households, we still find a statistically significant association of education levels with agency. The three agency variables we choose—whether a woman is allowed to work, requires permission to be mobile, and is a member of a social group (e.g. SHG)—represent distinct public spheres, specifically in relation to gender. Thus, if education levels were found to be positively associated with all three agency vari-

[7]Regressions estimating subgroup effects are not presented in this version of the paper, but are available on request.

ables, we might be able to say that it is associated with 'overall agency freedoms' of women outside her household, which is not the case in our findings.

References

Acharya, D. R., Jacqueline S. B., Simkhada, P., van Teijlingen, E. R., & Regmi, P. R. (2010). Women's autonomy in household decision-making: A demographic study in Nepal. *Reproductive Health*, *7*(15), 1–12.

Adato, M., De la Briere, B., Mindek, D., & Quisumbing, A. (2000). *The impact of PROGRESA on women's status and intrahousehold relations*. Washington, DC: International Food Policy Research Institute.

Alderman, H., Haddad, L., & Hoddinott, J. (1997). 17 policy issues and intrahousehold resource allocation: Conclusions. *Intrahousehold Resource Allocation in Developing Countries*, 275.

Alkire, S. (2005). Subjective quantitative studies of human agency. *Social Indicators Research, 74*(1), 217–260.

Arends-Kuenning, M., & Amin, S. (2001). Women's capabilities and the right to education in Bangladesh. *International Journal of Politics, Culture, and Society, 15*(1), 125–142.

Aslam, M. (2007). Rates of return to education by gender in Pakistan.

Desai, S., Vanneman, R. & National Council of Applied Economic Research, New Delhi. India Human Development Survey-II (IHDS-II), 2011–12. ICPSR36151-v2. Ann Arbor, MI: Inter-university Consortium for Political and Social Research [distributor], 2015-07-31. http://doi.org/10.3886/ICPSR36151.v2.

Dyson, T., & Moore, M. (1983). On kinship structure, female autonomy, and demographic behavior in India. *Population and Development Review, 9*(1), 35–60.

Hoddinott, J., & Haddad, L. (1995). Does female income share influence household expenditures? Evidence from Cote D'Ivoire. *Oxford Bulletin of Economics and Statistics, 57*(1), 77–96.

Jejeebhoy, S. (1995). *Women's education, autonomy, and reproductive behaviour: Experience from developing countries*. Oxford: Clarendon Press.

Kabeer, N. (2005). Gender equality and women's empowerment: A critical analysis of the third millennium development goal 1. *Gender & Development*.

Kanbur, R., & Haddad, L. (1994). Are better off households more equal or less equal? *Oxford Economic Papers, 46*(3), 445–458.

Kodoth, P. (2005). Fostering insecure livelihoods: Dowry and female seclusion in left developmental contexts in West Bengal and Kerala. *Economic and Political Weekly*, 2543–2554.

Lloyd, C. B., & Blanc, A. K. (1996). Children's schooling in sub-Saharan Africa: The role of fathers, mothers, and others. *Population and Development Review*, 265–298.

Lundberg, S., & Pollak, R. A. (1996). Bargaining and distribution in marriage. *The Journal of Economic Perspectives, 10*(4), 139–158.

Mahmud, Simeen, Shah, Nirali M., & Becker, Stan. (2012). Measurement of women's empowerment in rural bangladesh. *World Development, 40*(3), 610–619.

Nussbaum, M. (2000). Women's capabilities and social justice. *Journal of Human Development, 1*(2), 219–247.

Nussbaum, M. (2003). Capabilities as fundamental entitlements: Sen and social justice. *Feminist economics, 9*(2–3), 33–59.

Phillips, S. A., & Burton, P. S. (1998). What's mine is yours? The influence of male and female incomeson patterns of household expenditure. *Economica, 65*(260), 593–613.

Quisumbing, A., & Maluccio, J. (2000). Intrahousehold allocation and gender relations: New empirical evidence from four developing countries. International Food Policy Research Institute (FCND) Discussion Paper 84.

Rahman, L., & Rao, V. (2004). The determinants of gender equity in India: examining Dyson and Moore's thesis with new data. *Population and Development Review, 30*(2), 239–268.

Rosenzweig, M., & Schultz, T. P. (1982). Market opportunities, genetic endowments, and intrafamily resource distribution: Child survival in rural India. *The American Economic Review, 72*(4), 803–815.

Sen, A. (1985). Well-being, agency and freedom: The Dewey lectures 1984. *The Journal of Philosophy, 82*(4), 169–221.

Sen, A. (1999). Commodities and capabilities. *OUP Catalogue*.

Singh, A., Gaurav, S., & Das, U. (2013). Household headship and academic skills of Indian children: A special focus on gender disparities. *European Journal of Population/Revue européenne de Démographie, 29*(4), 445–466.

Smith, L. C., & Byron, E. M. (2005). *Is greater decisionmaking power of women associated with reducedgender discrimination in South Asia?*. Washington, DC: International Food Policy Research Institute.

Stiglitz, J., Sen, A., & Fitoussi, J. P. (2009). The measurement of economic performance and social progress revisited. In *Reflections and overview. Commission on the measurement of economic performance and social progress, Paris*.

Subaiya, L., & Vanneman, R. (2016). The Multi-dimensionality of Development and Gender Empowerment: Women's Decision-Making and Mobility in India.

Thomas, D. (1990). Intra-household resource allocation: an inferential approach. *The Journal of Human Resources, 25*(4), 635–664.

Unterhalter, E. (2003). The capabilities approach and gendered education: An examination of South African complexities. *School Field, 1*(1), 7–22.

Part V
Behavioral Economics

Mental Accounting—Saving with Virtual Shoeboxes

Chinmayi Srikanth, Ketan Reddy and S. Raja Sethu Durai

Abstract People find themselves falling prey to excessive spending tendencies despite their continued efforts to prevent the same from happening. The paper analyzes the viability of applying the concept of 'mental accounting' in the operation of bank accounts so as to enable people to monitor their expenditure with greater accuracy.

Keywords Mental accounting · Nudge · Decision points · Savings · Sub-accounts

1 Introduction

People find themselves falling prey to excessive spending tendencies despite their continued efforts to prevent the same from happening. The paper analyzes the viability of applying the concept of 'mental accounting' in the operation of bank accounts so as to enable people to monitor their expenditure with greater accuracy.

The study is predominantly based on three fundamental concepts of behavioral economics, namely mental accounting, nudge and the theory of decision points.

Mental accounting is a concept in behavioral economics that was developed by Richard Thaler. It refers to the notion of seeing money differently depending on how it is earned, how it is spent and where it is kept. This concept disproves the universally accepted notion that money is a fungible commodity.

C. Srikanth (✉)
Indian Institute of Management, Kozhikode, India
e-mail: srikanthc12fpm@iimk.ac.in

K. Reddy
Department of Humanities and Social Sciences, IIT Madras, Chennai, India
e-mail: ketankreddy94@gmail.com

S. R. Sethu Durai
School of Economics, University of Hyderabad, Hyderabad, India
e-mail: rdurai@uohyd.ac.in

N. R. Bhanumurthy et al. (eds.), *Advances in Finance & Applied Economics*,
https://doi.org/10.1007/978-981-13-1696-8_11

Under the theory of decision points, a decision point is defined as any intervention that is designed to get an individual to pause and think about the consumption they are engaging in (Cheema et al. 2010).

Thaler and Sunstein (2008) define a nudge as any aspect of the choice architecture that alters people's behavior in a predictable way without forbidding any options or significantly changing their economic incentives.

The paper explores the prospects of visualizing bank accounts to be segregated in the form of separate mental accounts for rent, food, entertainment, etc., which is similar to how people generally carry out mental accounting. The practice of earmarking money in this way is still common in many households; anything from jars to shoeboxes serves this purpose. Although the age of digitization is underway, many basic services that can have a major impact on how people plan their expenditure continue to be ignored. This paper stresses on the need for banks to intervene and redesign their bank accounts by proving that the segregation of each bank account into sub-accounts can have a significant impact on increasing the rate of savings of people, thereby narrowing the gap between how people wish to spend vis-à-vis how they actually spend.

One of the most pressing issues with regard to money management is that a major proportion of the people are unable to save enough money for future contingencies. The impact of a simple intervention or a 'nudge' in ensuring a favorable outcome—increase in savings is what the paper is primarily about. For this, an experiment was conducted.

2 The Experiment

Due to the difficulties associated with direct involvement of a bank for this purpose and because of the technical problems pertaining to implementation of segregation of actual bank accounts, an experiment was considered to be ideal to test the idea. The experiment was undertaken to study how individuals' decisions on spending are influenced by the manner in which their account is presented to them.

75% of the respondents chosen were students, and the remaining consisted of income-earning individuals. They were given situations where they had to make decisions as to how much they wanted to spend. Some of the situations represented cases where the respondents incur expenditures that are inevitable such as medical emergencies and mobile recharge among others. The participants in the experiment were divided according to the money balances that they were endowed with. There were ten participants each for income or endowment groups of 5000, 10,000, 15,000 and 20,000 rupees, respectively, which they had at their disposal for carrying out a month's worth of expenditure. The group with 20,000 as endowment were all income-earning individuals.

Each respondent was subject to two cases where the situations given were the same. The first case is one where the respondents have a regular savings account from which transactions were made without the use of cash. This is to enable the bank to record each transaction with regard to the purpose for which a given expenditure is incurred. Before the situations were given, the respondents were asked how much they wished to save. This was done in order to compare their expected savings with actual savings at the end of the first case. In the second case, the bank accounts of each of the respondents were such that each individual account was segregated into several sub-accounts under the following heads:-

1. Shopping/personal care
2. Entertainment
3. Food
4. Transport
5. Education
6. Miscellaneous
7. Savings
8. Rent
9. Investment

The group with 5000, 10,000 and half of the respondents under 15,000 had their accounts split into the first seven sub-accounts mentioned above, and the rest of the participants had additional sub-accounts—rent and investment—because the latter group belonged to the working class.

Participants were then asked to divide their endowment and decide on the balance they wished to hold under each sub-account. The amount they wished to save in this case was transferred to the savings sub-account. The segregation of accounts is to be offered by the bank as a service to its customers. The balances in each of the sub-accounts were to be determined by the participant before the situations were given. Since the transactions were identical to those of the first case, they had a fair idea as to how much they needed to put in each sub-account. In addition to this, many of the participants also based the segregation on the level of importance they gave to the different types of transactions and expenditure decisions they came across on a daily basis. Some of the situations were such that participants could decide on the amount they wished to pay. Whenever there was an inadequacy of balance in a sub-account, the participants had an option to transfer from any other sub-account; but a transfer from the savings account entailed an implicit cost in terms of effort. The participant had to fill a form stating that (s)he authorizes the bank to transfer a given sum of money from the savings sub-account to any given sub-account.

3 Findings

The experiment was undertaken with a total of forty respondents which gave the following results.

In Case 1 where the experiment was conducted in the absence of sub-accounts, across all the income groups combined, only 13 out of 40 respondents had their actual savings greater than the expected savings, whereas in Case 2 with sub-accounts being

Table 1 Comparison of actual savings to expected savings between the two cases

Income group	Actual savings > Expected savings	
	Case 1	Case 2
5000	5	10
10,000	2	8
15,000	5	9
20,000	1	9
Total	13	36

Table 2 Comparison of actual savings between the 2 cases

Income group	Actual savings in Case 2 > Actual savings in Case 1
5000	9
10,000	10
15,000	8
20,000	6
Total	33

offered to the participants, it was observed that 36 out of 40 respondents ended up saving more than they expected (Table 1).

Upon comparing the actual and expected savings under the two cases, it can be said that segregation of accounts enables people to save more. In addition to this, it was also observed that in Case 2 participants invariably set a more realistic proportion of their endowment as expected savings because presentation of accounts in a more organized form enabled them to earmark money under the various heads or sub-accounts in a more pragmatic way (Table 2).

Apart from the outcome mentioned, the experiment itself was designed so as to create decision points for the participants so that they think about the necessity of the transactions they come across. Inadequacy of money in a given sub-account created decision points for participants to rank the expenditures and forgo those that are not absolutely necessary; in the same way the complexity associated with transferring money from the savings sub-account served as a nudge which in majority of the cases ensured that the savings sub-accounts largely remain untouched. The idea behind making savings sub-account transfer cumbersome was to take advantage of the inherent lethargy of people and nudge them toward thrift (Figs. 1, 2, 3 and 4).

Under the 5000 group, a major decline in personal care/shopping expenditure was noticed when accounts were segregated. This means that many of the respondents tried to forgo shopping expenditure to save more or to a least reduce their efforts in making frequent transfers from one sub-account to another. Expenditure on entertainment remained more or less stable over the two cases, miscellaneous expenditure also saw a few changes but not a major one, and the expenditure on food remained relatively constant, but Fig. 5 shows otherwise because two respondents out of ten

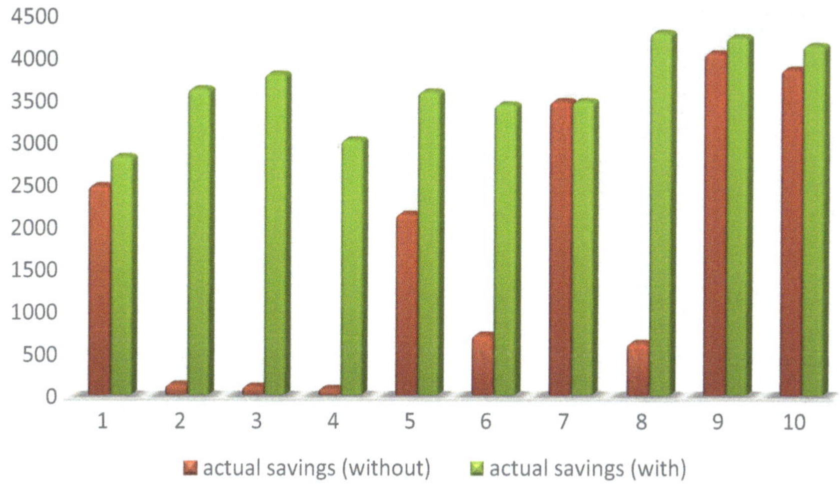

Fig. 1 Comparison of actual savings between 2 cases for income group of 5000

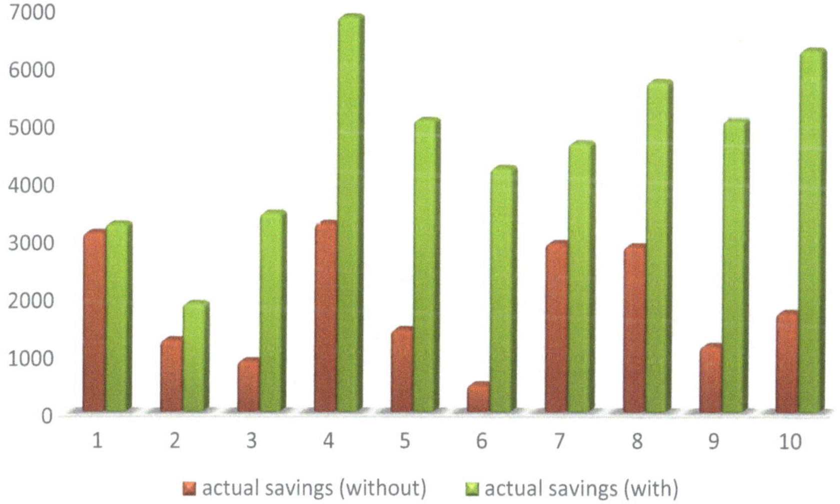

Fig. 2 Comparison of actual savings between 2 cases for income group of 10,000

had a considerably high consumption expenditure (about 2500) on food as compared to the other eight whose expenditures were constant in both the periods. The two respondents were the ones who benefitted most from the introduction of segregation, and they could save much more in Case 2 than in Case 1. Therefore, in order to reduce expenditure, participants in this group tended to cut down on shopping expenses with food and entertainment staying more or less unchanged.

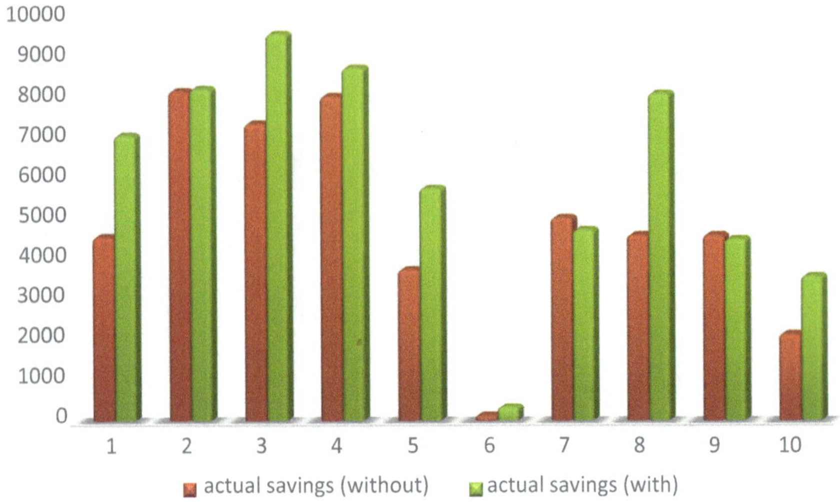

Fig. 3 Comparison of actual savings between 2 cases for income group of 15,000

Fig. 4 Comparison of actual savings between 2 cases for income group of 20,000

Under the 10,000 group, major reduction in spending took place in the form of food consumption pattern despite their holding a large amount as balance in the sub-account for food. Personal care/shopping expenses were highly compromised by the participants in this group. There was, however, no significant decline in expenditures under other heads which largely remained constant.

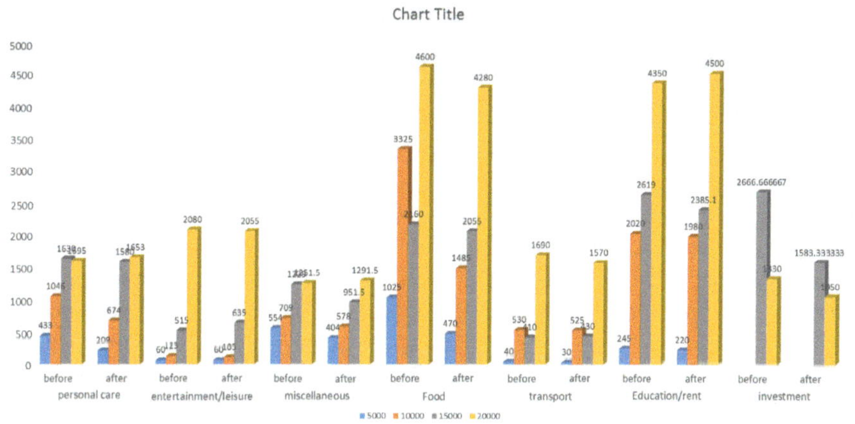

Fig. 5 Comparison of average expenditures before and after segregation under various heads

The group with 15,000 as endowment saw significant changes in their expenditure coming from a reduction in the education segment which reflects a fall in expenditure on stationary and books.

For the participants under the 20,000 income group, fall in expenditure in Case 2 as compared to Case 1 was largely attributed to food and investment.

4 Limitations

The experiment was mostly conducted with students as respondents. However, 20% of the dataset included income-earning individuals. The respondents chosen were from different places in the country; the price variations and standard of living across various cities were ignored. The situations were such that it represented a month in which a respondent incurred maximum expenses.

5 Conclusion

The study highlights the role played by nudges such as account segregation, in initiating a thought process that leads to evaluation of the expenditure and its importance, thereby reducing expenditure on consumption of those goods and services which do not carry immense importance.

The experiment also points toward individual behavior where one is relatively comfortable with transferring extra balances from other sub-accounts as opposed to that of savings. During the experiment, it was observed that individuals would make use of savings sub-account for meeting their expenses only in the absence of any other alternatives. This led to a substantial increase in overall savings which was in stark contrast to the level of savings observed in the case where there were no sub-accounts.

Although the banks have little incentive to implement such an idea, an intervention of this kind can reduce the number of non-performing assets—when sub-accounts are provided for each account, banks can easily ascertain their creditworthiness simply by looking at the sub-account for 'savings.' This would enable banks to assess creditworthiness in a much better way than with the help of customers' income. Banks' intervention in this way will also help them to increase provision of loans to deserving customers. It is also true that the overhead costs associated with its implementation are high and from the banks' point of view it makes sense for them to provide such a facility only to high-income earners. But from the welfare point of view, it is better that banks allow segregation of accounts of low-income groups because we such groups have small savings not because their income is meager but because of some factors that can be favorably changed through nudges. One such nudge is what the paper proposes; the process of transferring money from one sub-account to another no matter how easy it may be creates 'decision points' which allows the customer the opportunity to think about his spending. As theory of decision points suggests, this will have a favorable impact on their spending patterns. The benefits of a higher level of savings for a developing economy like India are immense and as for the banks, the amount of loans they can provide is greater. The advent of demonetization has led to a greater stress being laid on the need to stimulate a cashless economy; the experiment makes the assumption that all transactions are cashless so that banks can trace every rupee being spent by is customers. If implemented, it would work on the lines of a cashless economy and boost digital transactions.

India as a country faces several challenges, and one major challenge is the decline in savings rate among people. When the country relies heavily on savings from abroad, there is great deal of pressure on the current account. Domestic savings are essential to boost investment in the country, and excessive reliance on foreign capital will only aggravate the issue. The government has been trying to address the issue but with little success. This is primarily because most interventions only provide incentives for households to save more and does nothing to solve the real problem—bridging the gap between people's desire to save and their inability to do so which can be solved using a nudge such as segregation of their bank accounts.

References

Soman, D., Xu, J., and Cheema, A. (2010). Decision Points: A Theory Emerges. *Rotman Magaine Winter*.

Thaler, R. H. (1999). Mental accounting matters. *Journal Of Behavioral Decision Making, 12,* 183–206.

Thaler, R. H., Sunstein, C. R. (2008). *Nudge improving decisions about health, wealth, and happiness*. Yale University Press.

Trading Behaviour of Investor Categories and Its Impact on Indian Equity Market

Saji George and P. Srinivasa Suresh

Abstract The study is carried out in the Indian equity market based on the data drawn from both BSE and NSE for a period spanning from 2004–2016 to examine the trading behaviour of investor categories and its association with major indices in Indian equity market. Three common characteristics in the trading behaviour of FIIs, banks, NRIs, proprietary traders, insurance companies, and DIIs (including bank and insurance) were analysed based on principal component analysis. The study observed disconnection of trading activity by investor categories with the performance of the economy. Further, it is also observed that the characteristic that is heavily influenced positively by the commonality in client trading, FIIs, banks, insurance and DIIs and negatively influenced by proprietary trading was found to be significantly associated with irrational sentiment in the market. The component which is significantly positively related to the irrational sentiment in the market and negatively associated with economic indicators though not significant showed a negative association with all the major indices in the market. It is concluded from the analysis that FIIs, DIIs and client trading activities are much similar to those of noise traders in the market, but following contrarian trading strategies while proprietary trading taking opposite position in the market by trading against these groups indirectly increase the errors in the market in the guise of market making. Insurance companies are the group which trade in line with economic fundamentals and positively influence the movements in Indian equity market.

Keywords Trading behaviour · Investor categories · Irrational sentiment Economic fundamentals · Principal component analysis

JEL Classification G1 · G12 · G14 · G40

S. George (✉) · P. Srinivasa Suresh
Department of Economics, North Eastern Hill University,
Shillong 793022, Meghalaya, India
e-mail: sjtjohn2008@yahoo.co.in

P. Srinivasa Suresh
e-mail: sureshps03@yahoo.co.in

N. R. Bhanumurthy et al. (eds.), *Advances in Finance & Applied Economics*,
https://doi.org/10.1007/978-981-13-1696-8_12

1 Introduction

The enactment of SEBI Act of 1992 and setting up of SEBI (Securities and Exchange Board of India) as a regulatory authority together with the structural reforms that the economy underwent in the post 1990s have vitalized the activities in the Indian stock market. Technological upgradation in trading mechanisms and practices, reforms in the disclosure standards, introduction of rolling settlements, regulation of merchant banks, portfolio manager, brokers and sub-brokers, capital adequacy reforms and corporate registration of intermediaries, entry of FIIs, mutual funds and funds, promotion of retail trading, reforms in clearing and settlements, measures of investor protection, opening of derivative trading and other various measures taken up during this period have brought in the higher level of transparency and have raised Indian securities market to comparable standards in both the developed and emerging market economies. The total market capitalization of the Indian market which was Rs. 507272 in March 1996 has surged to Rs. 18785799 by March 2016. The market has witnessed an increase in the listings, coverage of sectors and in types of investment instruments traded as well.

The participation of different categories of investors with varying sophistication is expected to bring in rich information content into the prices and efficient price discovery in the market through their trading activities. But investors enter the market with different motives such as to trade on the information that they possess, to speculate on the market information, risk sharing, to profit on the rumour or noise in the market, for the requirement of liquidity. Trade volume is the channel by which all the investor motives enter the market and further into the prices determined. Indian market in the post-reform period has witnessed entry of various types of investor categories, and the research studies on the price efficiency in the market have come out with different observations. There are studies that support the random walk hypothesis or price efficiency in Indian equity market (Gupta 1990; Singh and Kumar 2009; Mishra and Mishra 2011; Nalini 2015). At the same time, there are other studies that have reported significant dependence or inefficiency in return series from both BSE and NSE (Pant and Bishnoi 2001; Poshakwale 2002; Pandey 2003; Gupta and Basu 2007; Mehla and Goyal 2012; Garg and Varshney 2015). The market has also experienced a high level of volatility in returns, especially in the post-financial crisis of 2008.

Therefore, an investigation into the trading behaviour of investor categories and its impact on the market is essential which would shed light on the nature of return formation in Indian equity market and would benefit both the investors and regulators to carry out their trading strategies and policies more effectively to bring in transparency and efficiency into the system.

2 Brief Survey of Literature

2.1 Trade Volume, Return and Volatility

Since trade volume is the channel through which investors behaviours are reflected in the market, this sections focuses on the findings of research studies on the linkage between trade volume, returns and volatility in the market. There are a number of arguments in line with the volume return and volatility relationship in the literature. The mixture of distribution hypothesis (Epps and Epps 1976) on trade volume–return relationship pointed out that the movement of returns would be in accordance with the flow of news that is an outcome of the above-average trading activity. This hypothesis gives no space for volatility–volume relationship as they change simultaneously with the news. Information arrival hypothesis (Copeland 1976) portrays information flow in the market in sequence or in random, but it is the difference in the time of acquiring this information across investor categories that leads to correlated volume return movement in the market. Suominen (2001) proposed a theoretical model of volume return relationship wherein dependency in the price variability in the market is considered as the outcome of other traders adjustment of trading strategies with respect to private information content in the past trade volume of informed traders.

There are numerous studies that examined trade volume, return and volatility relationship empirically. Chordia and Swaminathan (2000) reported trade volume as a significant determinant of the lead lag patterns observed in stock returns. The study also found that the return of portfolios containing high trade volume led returns of portfolios comprised of low trading volume and attributed it to the slow information absorption of low volume portfolios. Mubarek and Javid (2009) observed a significant positive effect of the previous day trade volume on the current market returns and a negative relationship in the case of individual stocks. Similarly, Chandrapala (2011) observed that stocks with low trade volume changes in the past outperforming the stocks with high trade volume changed in the subsequent periods and attributed the relationship to investors' misspecification about future earnings or risk of illiquidity in the market. Yonis (2014) from their examination of Hong Kong, South Korea, Singapore, Taiwan, and USA observed a positive contemporaneous relationship between return and trade volume across these economies. The study also observed a significant positive effect of trade volume on conditional volatility in the market except in the case of South Korea. In the case of Indian market, Mahajan and Singh (2008) observed a positive contemporaneous relationship between volume, return and volatility in the market and supporting evidences of sequential arrival of information in the market and lack of simultaneous availability of the information to all traders that result in price inefficiency in the market.

2.2 Trading Behaviour of Categories of Investors

The behavioural finance literature points out that individual investor's behaviour is in line with argument of prospect theory and that the risk-taking behaviour of the person varies with uncertain outcomes in both positive and negative domains. Under uncertain situations, the decision makers resort to heuristics such as representativeness, availability and adjustment and anchoring, by assessing their similarity to judge the probability of the outcomes and to reduce the complexity. This dependence on heuristics leads to violation of Bayesian updation and to biased decision as they ignore prior probabilities and sample size in formulation of subjective probabilities (Tversky and Kahneman 1973, 1974, 1979, 1983). This behavioural traits cause inefficient investment decision making and inefficiency in price discovered in the market. Wood and Zaichkowsky (2004) in a survey-based study observed segmentation of investors which resulted in different levels of trading behaviour in the market. In the case of Indian market, Sashikala and Girish (2015) reported that factors like broker's advice, personal analysis, the current price of equity stock, analysts' recommendations play a significant role in moulding the trading behaviour of retail investors in Indian market.

Karolyi (2002), on the trading behaviour of foreign, local institutions and individual investors in Japanese equity market, observed positive feedback trading or following of momentum trading strategy by FIIs and contrarian trading strategy by the Japanese banks, financial institutions and investment trusts and companies. Richards (2005) reported FIIs following momentum strategy in emerging market economies in Asia extracting information from the emerging markets, and it results in larger level changes in the prices of such markets.

In the case of Indian market, Sehgal and Tripathi (2009) reported FIIs evincing different trading behaviours depending on the data analysed. They were found to be following positive feedback trading strategies in monthly pattern, while in the case of quarterly pattern the behaviour found to be herding at the aggregate level. Phansatan et al. (2012) examined investor-type trading behaviour in the Thai stock market. The study observed that foreign institutional investors following positive feedback trading and momentum strategies which results in superior short-term market timing but adverse security selection performance than local investors which ultimately leads to cancellation of overall net trade gains. Proprietary traders were found to be profiting from their liquidity provision role to the markets with short-term market trading gains. Individual investors were found to be following herd behaviour and gains from security selection at the expense of other investor categories which often get cancelled out with their poor market timings. Kamesaka (2013) in the analysis of investor behaviour of Japanese market post-Great East Earthquake observed institutional investors taking contrarian investment strategies and FIIs following momentum trading strategies.

From the previous sections, we learned the significant relationship between trade volume, which is an outcome of the combined behaviour of investor categories participating in the market, and return and volatility formation in the equity markets.

Since trade volume is the aggregate reflection of all the investor categories in the market, it would be informatory to identify the commonalties in the trading behaviour of all investor categories and further examine how each of these is related to economic fundamentals, irrational sentiment and equity market indices' returns based on different characteristics. This type of decomposition of aggregate trade activities in the market would help us unearth the hidden characteristics in the trade volume and each of investor categories absorption to it which ultimately affect the return formation in Indian equity market. This type of approach in analysing investor-type trading behaviour is scarcely found in the literature which is carried out in this work.

3 Data and Methodology

The study is carried out in the Indian equity market based on the data drawn from both BSE and NSE for a period spanning from 2004 to 2016. In order to examine the intrinsic characteristics of the trading behaviour of investor categories, we relied upon the net trade data of FIIs, DIIs, NRIs, client trading, proprietary trading, banks and insurance companies. Even though DIIs net trading data comprise those of banks and insurance companies, we have considered both of them in the analysis. The data are of monthly frequency spanning from April 2004 to December 2016. Principal component analysis technique is carried out to extract the common variation in the variables and indices representing statistically significant common components are constructed based on the respective loadings of the variables into it. These indices were re-examined with the variables such as money supply, index of industrial production, trade balance and an irrational sentiment index to examine their association with economic fundamentals and irrational sentiment present in the market. Irrational sentiment index we have used is the similar one after modification that is prepared by us (Suresh and George 2016). Similarly, causal relationship between these indices and BSE Sensex, NSE Nifty, BSE 500, NSE 500, BSE Large Cap, BSE Mid Cap, BSE Small Cap, NSE Mid Cap and NSE Small Cap index returns is also examined.

4 Empirical Results and Discussion

4.1 Identification of Common Characteristics Across Investor Categories

Table 1 presents the correlation coefficients of the monthly net trade position of the investor categories. The coefficients indicate the degree of linear correlation between the variables. These coefficients with their sign show the level of association and direction of movements between them. It is observed that client trading activities are positively associated with those of FIIs, banks, insurance and DIIs, while they move

Table 1 Pearsonian correlation coefficients across net trade ** of investor categories

	Clients	NRI	Proprietary	FIIs	Banks	Insurance	DIIs
Clients	1						
NRI	−0.03548	1					
Proprietary	−0.44113	0.073355	1				
FIIs	0.395847	0.082694	−0.45244	1			
Banks	0.185843	0.027038	−0.10417	0.131826	1		
Insurance	0.034694	0.051319	−0.28153	0.458646	0.06412	1	
DII s*	0.385292	−0.12543	−0.47914	0.493106	0.187874	0.489321	1

*DIIs is comprised of net trades of banks and insurance as well though they are given separate
** Net trade value indicates the z-standardized values of buy–sell difference

Table 2 Common Variations in the trading behaviour of investor categories

	Comp 1	*Comp 2*	*Comp 3*	*Comp 4*	*Comp 5*	*Comp 6*	*Comp 7*
Eigen value	2.634062	1.090827	1.020408	0.880835	0.514055	0.456751	0.357608
Variance prop.	0.378754	0.156851	0.146725	0.126656	0.073916	0.065677	0.051421
Cumul. prop.	0.378754	0.535605	0.68233	0.808986	0.882903	0.948579	1

inversely with NRI and proprietary trading activities. In the case of NRI trading, all investor categories except DIIs show a positive association with their trading activities. Proprietary trading activities were found to be in the inverse direction with those of FIIs, banks, insurance, DIIs, indicating contrarian trading by them to these categories. FIIs showed a positive association with those of all categories except proprietary trading. Banks, insurance and all DIIs showed a positive association with those of other investor categories except those of proprietary traders.

In order to extract the common variations in net trade position of the investor categories, we applied principal component analysis technique. Table 2 presents the seven unobservable components that explain the variations in the trading activities of investor categories in Indian equity market. The first row shows the eigenvalues of each component, which depicts the common patterns in the data. Variance proportion indicates the level of variation in the entire data explained by the particular component, and the cumulative proportion shows the cumulative proportion of variance explained by each component about the patterns in the system of data. Since only the first three components have the eigenvalue above one, that together explain 68% of variation in the data, we consider only those ones in the further analysis.

Table 3 shows the loadings of each investor categories into the patterns observed in the data. In the case of component 1, we observe that except NRI and bank trading activities whose loadings are significantly small all other categories contribute to it. It is dominated by the FIIs, DIIs and proprietary traders. In the case of component 2, the dominant contributors are NRIs and insurance companies followed by client

Table 3 Contribution of each of the variables** into the unobservable characteristics

Variable	*Comp 1*	*Comp 2*	*Comp 3*
CLN	0.380916	−0.39574	−0.32109
NRI	−0.0275	0.697663	−0.5627
PROP	−0.45354	0.170504	−0.04929
IFI	0.480298	0.212707	−0.01256
BANKS	0.180345	−0.16898	−0.6602
INSUR	0.37209	0.503225	0.335885
DII*	0.496776	−0.0235	0.170295

*DIIs is comprised of net trades of banks and insurance as well though they are given separate
** Net trade value indicates the z-standardized values of buy–sell difference

trading activities that is trading through intermediaries mainly individual investors, while DIIs, banks, proprietary trading activities are significantly low. Finally, in the case of the third component, banks, NRIs and insurance companies contribute more than other investors, but the former two including client trading are taking negative values in it.

The analysis reveals a pattern of intrinsic characteristic inherent in the trading behaviour of investor categories in the Indian equity market. But this does not give us clarity of what this pattern represents in the real market. Therefore, we constructed indices of each of the characteristics after eliminating the statistically insignificant variables.

4.2 *Common Characteristics of Investor Categories Trading and Economic Fundamentals*

Table 4 presents the direction and degree of association of each of the components with the macro-economic fundamental variables. The results show that none of the trading characteristics of investor categories in Indian market are associated significantly with economic fundamentals except the case of commodity prices, that is of gold and silver, which shows a negative association with first two components of the trading behaviour and money supply in the case of component 2. The table also presents the absence of association of irrational sentiment index constructed by us (Suresh and George 2016) to economic fundamentals in the Indian economy. We have already observed that although all these components explain around 68% of the common variations in trading behaviour, none are related to economic fundamental which indicates the disconnection of trading activity by investor categories with the performance of the economy.

Table 4 Linear association of trading characteristics with economic fundaments

	Comp 1	*Comp 2*	*Comp 3*	*Irr. Sentiment index*
Money supply-M3	−0.11487	−0.30049	0.118456	0.00229
Index of industrial production (G)	−0.00166	0.004812	0.10738	0.004874
International trade balance	0.126016	0.2008519	0.102092	−0.00279
Inflation rate	−0.00592	0.10646	−0.17169	0.002615
Gold price spread	−0.21347	−0.29043	0.113822	0.001059
Silver price spread	−0.22673	−0.30114	0.029721	0.001015
Exchange rate high–low difference	−0.06097	−0.01761	−0.12619	0.001699

4.3 Investor Categories Trading Behaviour and Irrational Behaviour in Indian Equity Market

Trading in Indian market is found to be not associated with movement of economy's performance. In this section, we examined their association with irrational sentiment prevailing in Indian equity market measured by irrational sentiment index constructed on the basis of various sentiment measures from the Indian equity market. It is observed from Table 5 that component 1 is highly associated with the sentiment in the market. It is clear from Table 2 that this component is heavily loaded positively by the commonality in client trading, FIIs, banks, insurance and DIIs, while negatively loaded by proprietary trading. Similarly, we learn from Table 2 that the first component explains 38% of the common variation in the market. Therefore, it can be concluded that all the investor categories in the Indian market partially brings in noise into the trading activities and contribute to the inefficiency in prices in the market.

Table 5 Irrational sentiment in the equity market and investor trading behaviour in India

	Comp 1	*Comp 2*	*Comp 3*
Irrational sentiment index	0.888603	0.047807	−0.20073

4.4 *Trading Behaviour of Investor Categories and Major Indices in Indian Market*

Table 6 presents the linear association of trading characteristics with the major indices in Indian equity market. It covers benchmark indices, broad market indices and indices based on market capitalization. It is observed that the first component which was found to be highly correlated with market sentiments is showing a relatively high negative association with all the indices returns except BSE Large Cap, while the second component does show any significant relationship with them. On the contrary, the third component shows a positive association with the index returns in the market.

One contradicting observation from the analysis in Table 6 is that the component which is significantly positively related to the irrational sentiment in the market and negatively associated with economic indicators though not significant showed a negative association with all the major indices in the market, while the third component which showed a negative relationship with irrational sentiment and a positive association with economic sentiment shows a positive relationship with most of the major indices returns in Indian equity market. FIIs, DIIs and proprietary traders (negative) are the major contributors to component 1, while banks (negative), NRIs (negative) and insurance companies contribute more than other investors in component 3.

Therefore, it can be inferred from the analysis that FIIs, DIIs and client trading activities are much associated with irrational sentiment in the market which refers to noise traders in the market but following contrarian trading strategies, while proprietary trading takes opposite position in the market by trading against these groups but indirectly increases the errors in the market in the guise of market making. Insurance companies are the group which trade in line with economic fundamentals and positively influence the movements in Indian equity market.

Table 6 Association of trading characteristics and major indices in Indian market

	Comp 1	*Comp 2*	*Comp 3*
BSE sensex	−0.59703	−0.01494	0.211978
BSE 500	−0.60864	−0.00834	0.222516
BSE mid cap	−0.61379	−0.00607	0.218079
BSE large cap	−0.06362	0.01572	0.020454
BSE small cap	−0.56966	−0.00244	0.206873
NSE Nifty	−0.60013	−0.0119	0.222243
NSE 500	−0.60847	−0.00603	0.224145
NSE mid cap	−0.62135	0.030959	0.241415
NSE small cap	−0.47502	−0.1287	0.196474

5 Conclusion

From the analysis, we have observed that the trading behaviour of investor categories is quite complex in Indian market. FIIs, DIIs and individual investors are found to be contrarian noise traders in the equity market taking position against domestic institutions, especially against insurance companies. NRI investors and banks are found to be profiting from trading against the movements of the economy.

References

Chordia, T., & Swaminathan, B. (2000). Trading volume and cross-autocorrelations in stock returns. *The Journal of Finance, 55*(2), 913–935.

Chandrapala, P. (2011). The relationship between trading volume and stock returns. *Journal of Competitiveness, 3*(3).

Economics, C. (1976). A model of asset trading under the assumption of sequential information arrival. *The Journal of Finance, 31*(4), 1149–1168.

Epps, T. W., & Epps, M. L. (1976). The stochastic dependence of security price changes and transaction volumes: Implications for the mixture-of-distributions hypothesis. *Econometrica: Journal of the Econometric Society*, 305–321.

Gupta, O. P. (1990). Stock market efficiency and random character of share price behaviour in India. *Asia Pacific Journal of Management, 7*(2), 165–174.

Gupta, R., & Basu, P. K. (2007). Weak form efficiency in Indian stock markets. *International Business & Economics Research Journal (IBER), 6*(3).

Garg, A. K., & Varshney, P. (2015). Momentum effect in Indian stock market: A sectoral study. *Global Business Review, 16*(3), 494–510.

Kahneman, D., & Tversky, A. (1979). Prospect theory: An analysis of decision under risk. *Econometrica, 47*(2), 263–292.

Kahneman, D., & Tversky, A. (1983). Choices, values, and frames. *American Psychological Association, 39*(4), 341–350.

Karolyi, G. A. (2002). Did the Asian financial crisis scare foreign investors out of Japan? *Pacific-Basin Finance Journal, 10*(4), 411–442.

Kamesaka, A. (2013). The great east Japan earthquake and investor behavior in Japan's equity markets. *Public Policy Review, 9*(1), 71–86.

Mishra, A., & Mishra, V. (2011). Is the Indian stock market efficient? Evidence from a TAR model with an autoregressive unit root. *Applied Economics Letters, 18*(5), 467–472.

Mehla, S., & Goyal, S. K. (2012). Empirical evidence on weak form of efficiency in Indian stock market. *Asia-Pacific Journal of Management Research and Innovation, 8*(1), 59–68.

Mubarik, F., & Javid, A. Y. (2009). Relationship between stock return, trading volume and volatility: Evidence from Pakistani stock market. https://papers.ssrn.com/sol3/papers.cfm?abstract_id=1536053.

Mahajan, S., & Singh, B. (2008). An empirical analysis of stock price-volume relationship in Indian stock market. *Vision, 12*(3), 1–13.

Nalini, R. (2015). Testing random walk hypothesis in Indian stock market-A study of selected stocks listed on BSE. *Vishwakarma business Review, 5*(1), 31–38.

Pant, B., & Bishnoi, T. R. (2001). Testing random walk hypothesis for Indian stock market indices. In *Research Paper Presented in UTI Capital Market Conference Proceedings* (pp. 1–15).

Poshakwale, S. (2002). The random walk hypothesis in the emerging Indian stock market. *Journal of Business Finance & Accounting, 29*(9–10), 1275–1299.

Pandey, A. (2003). Efficiency of Indian stock market. http://ssrn.com/abstract=474921 or http://dx.doi.org/10.2139/ssrn.474921.

Phansatan, S., Powell, J. G., Tanthanongsakkun, S., & Treepongkaruna, S. (2012). Investor type trading behavior and trade performance: Evidence from the Thai stock market. *Pacific-Basin Finance Journal, 20*(1), 1–23.

Richards, A. (2005). Big fish in small ponds: The trading behavior and price impact of foreign investors in Asian emerging equity markets. *Journal of Financial and quantitative Analysis, 40*(1), 1–27.

Singh, P., & Kumar, B. (2009). Variance ratio tests of the random walk hypothesis for Indian Stock Index Futures: evidence from high frequency data. *Indian Institute of Management Ahmadabad*. www.nseindia.com.

Suominen, M. (2001). Trading volume and information revelation in stock market. *Journal of Financial and Quantitative Analysis, 36*(4), 545–565.

Sashikala, P., & Girish, G. P. (2015). Factors influencing retail investor's trading behavior in Indian Equity market. *International Journal of Business and Management, 10*(11), 206.

Sehgal, S., & Tripathi, N. (2009). Investment strategies of FIIs in the Indian equity market. *Vision, 13*(1), 11–18.

Suresh, P. S., & George, S. (2016). Market sentiment dynamics and return volatility in the Indian equity market. *Indian Journal of Finance, 10*(6), 7–23.

Tversky, A., & Kahneman, D. (1973). Availability: A heuristic for judging frequency and probability. *Cognitive Psychology, 5,* 207–232.

Tversky, A., & Kahneman, D. (1974). Judgment under uncertainty: Heuristics and biases. *Science, 185* (4157), 1124–1131.

Wood, R., & Zaichkowsky, J. L. (2004). Attitudes and trading behavior of stock market investors: A segmentation approach. *The Journal of Behavioral Finance, 5*(3), 170–179.

Yonis, M. (2014). *Trading Volume and Stock Return: Empirical Evidence for Asian Tiger Economies*. http://www.diva-portal.org/smash/get/diva2:714747/FULLTEXT01.pdf.

Part VI
Corporate Finance

Ownership Classification and Technical Efficiency in Indian Manufacturing Firms: A Stochastic Frontier Approach

Sanjeev Kumar and K. S. Ranjani

Abstract The study is proposed to explore the divergence in the technical efficiencies of the group-affiliated and standalone Indian manufacturing firms using Battesse and Coelli (1992). Group-affiliated firms have been claimed to have easier access to finance by various studies in comparison with standalone firms. Standalone firms generally find difficulties in arranging financing sources, whereas group firms can access finance from the profitable group firms at a lesser cost of capital than persisting market rates. Standalone firms need to be more efficient and profitable to accumulate internal earnings to accept available positive NPV (net present value) projects. The study will be conducted using linear logarithm form of Cobb–Douglas production function, where the value added in the particular financial year will be used as the dependent variable, while independent variables will be capital stock and a number of employees working in the firm at time t. The efficiency of the firms will be captured by the non-negative term (−u) constituted in the error term of the stochastic frontier equation. The study will be conducted for the period 2010–2016 using various data sources that include prowess database from the centre for monitoring Indian economy, Reserve Bank of India and annual survey of industries. The study will help to understand the efficiency patterns of Indian manufacturing over the years and will also explore whether the situation of credit constraints will motivate firms to be more efficient than their competitors. The main motivation for the study is derived credit constraints that are faced by the firms by virtue of not belonging to a business group.

Keywords Technical efficiency · Ownership structure · Stochastic frontier analysis · India · Manufacturing firms

---

S. Kumar (✉)
National Institute of Industrial Engineering (NITIE), Mumbai, Maharashtra, India
e-mail: sanjeev.kumar.2014@nitie.ac.in

K. S. Ranjani
Department of Accounting and Finance, National Institute of Industrial Engineering (NITIE), Mumbai, Maharashtra, India
e-mail: ksranjani@nitie.ac.in

N. R. Bhanumurthy et al. (eds.), *Advances in Finance & Applied Economics*,
https://doi.org/10.1007/978-981-13-1696-8_13

1 Introduction

It is a fact that information asymmetry (between lenders and borrowers) in the capital markets causes a wedge between the cost of funds acquired externally to the internally generated by the firm. The firms under such environment can face credit constraints which persuade them to pool and escalate their internal funds for profitable investment opportunities in future. Firms in the developing economies are much more prone to these situations due to underdeveloped capital market and information asymmetry persisting. According to a survey conducted between 2013–2014 by World Bank Enterprise Surveys (WBES), 11.7% of 9281 Indian manufacturing firms reported access to finance as the fifth major obstacle to the business growth only after corruption, electricity, tax rates and practices of the formal sector (Fig. 1). The survey also highlights 71.8% purchase of fixed assets financed through internally generated funds or retained earnings of the firms. The survey clearly explains the importance of internal funds to the firms.

Indian manufacturing sector has been shown a decreased growth in recent times. Hence, it is important to understand the factors that affect the performance of the firms to help manufacturing regain consistent growth. The Indian firms face a high level of information asymmetries which impede them to access appropriate funds to finance projects. Increasing technical efficiencies of firms can help the firms to produce more internal funds to acquire more internal funds to reduce their cost of capital (Sena 2006). Business groups are particular effective in dealing with information and contract enforcement problems within the groups. When a firm needs external finance, it can obtain funds at a relatively lower cost. Therefore, it is expected that firms who have affiliation to industrial groups will face lower financial constraints than firms who are not part of an industrial group, because of the reduction in information costs for being part of the group and the access to the internal capital group. The problem of financial constraints can be dealt by increasing the efficiency of the

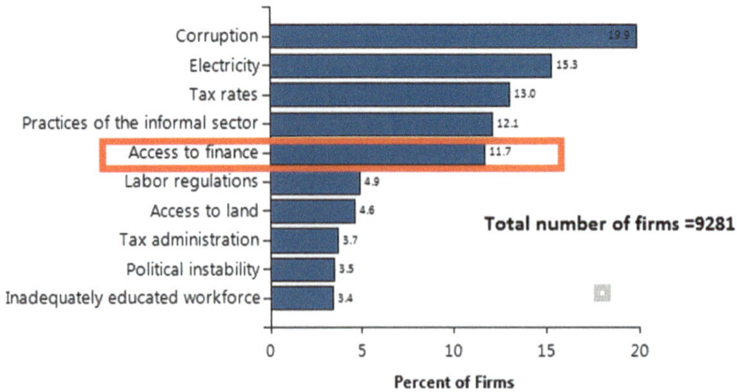

Fig. 1 Top obstacles to business growth for Indian manufacturing firms. *Source* World Bank Enterprise Surveys (2014)

firm to generate internal funds. Standalone firms are expected to have more technically efficient if they have to survive in the market due to higher cost of funds for investment opportunities. However, group-affiliated firm can have better access to internally generated funds and experience of parent group companies to be more efficient in comparison with standalone firms. Hence, the present study aims to highlight the divergence in the technical efficiencies of the firms due to ownership structure of the firms under the assumption of financial constraints. The study uses leverage, liquidity, size and age as the measures of financial constraints. The study will contribute to the body of knowledge by highlighting the divergence caused by relative importance of internal funds to the technical efficiencies of the group-affiliated and standalone firms.

2 Literature Review

To analyse the effect of financial constraints on firm investment, Fazzari et al. (1988) found a significant positive relationship between cash flow and investments of the firm. The study laid the foundation for the future studies by confirming the role of financial constraints on firm activities such as working capital management (Fazzari and Petersen 1993), exports (Greenway et al. 2007) and stock returns (Lamont et al. 2001). Financial constraints soon gained research interest in developed economies. However, there is still a dearth of studies in the developing economies with only a few studies contributing to the literature on the role of financial constraints on firm behaviour.

There are various studies which have reported the effects of financial constraints by classifying the firms according to the ownership structure of the firms. Hoshi et al. (1991) reported effects of financial constraints on the basis of group affiliation and found higher information asymmetry issues for standalone firms. Chirinko and Schaller (1995) also found credit constraints issues for the standalone firms due to unavailability of sufficient cash flows to fund present investment opportunities. Campa and Shaver (2002) classified the firms according to ownership structure and illustrated that exporting firms are more liquidity constrained than non-exporting firms. Further, Lensink et al. (2003) reported a significantly positive group affiliation effect and found that standalone firms have higher cash flow sensitivities than group affiliates. Cash flow sensitivity to investment is the most discussed measure of financial constraints in the literature (Fazzari et al. 1988).

Technical efficiency studies gained interest through the seminal study of Battesse and Coelli (1992) on Indian farms. The study calculated time-varying efficiency of 15 Indian farms in the village Aurepalle. The study used two-step approach where frontier equation and inefficiency equation are solved separately. Battesse and Coelli (1995) came up with a single-equation approach where both the equations are jointly estimated in attributing inefficiency variables in the mean term of the estimation equation. Ramaswamy (1994) calculated technical efficiencies of small-scale manufacturing firms to verify effects of size, growth and structural changes in the industries. Lundvall and Battesse (2000) calculated the technical efficiency of 235 Kenyan manufacturing firms to investigate the effects of size and age on technical efficiencies of the firms. Tybout (2000) also explored the technical efficiencies of manufacturing firms in developing countries and described the rationale for the performance of the same. Sena (2006) came up with an interesting study and analysed the role of financial constraints on the firm's technical efficiency. The study is motivated by the information asymmetry problems between lenders and borrowers that result in the higher cost of external finance to the financially constrained firms. The analysis conducted on 6498 Italian manufacturing firms reported marginal incentive for financially constrained firms to improve technical efficiency to overcome the burden of high cost of capital for assured profitability. Later Maietta et al. (2010) reported an increase in technical efficiency as a result of tightening financial constraints for Italian cooperative firms. There are few studies that address technical efficiency but neither of them is focussed on the financial constraints faced by the firms.

Indian studies such as Mitra et al. (2002) reported effects of infrastructure and industrial developments on enhancing the technical efficiency among manufacturing firms across Indian states. Further, Bhandari and Ray (2012) calculated the technical efficiencies of Indian textile industries to find out the effects of locational, proprietary and organisational characters on the performance of the firms. However, the results of these studies were not in consensus as the former study found the significant positive role of infrastructure capacities, while later denying differences in technical efficiencies due to industrial developments of Indian states. To the best of our knowledge, there is no study which highlights the effects of financial constraints on technical efficiency in the Indian context. Sena (2006) found the evidence for a relationship between financial constraints and technical efficiency, but they did not classified the firms into constrained and unconstrained firms to report clear demarcation among technical efficiencies of financially constrained or unconstrained firms. However, to the best of our knowledge, no study explores the technical efficiency of group-affiliated and standalone firms under the assumption of financial constraints. Hence, the present study classifies the firms according to ownership structure to investigate the difference in technical efficiencies due to financial constraints.

3 Empirical Estimation Framework

Technical efficiency has been calculated using the maximum likelihood estimates for the stochastic frontier production specification as suggested by Battesse and Coelli (1992) for panel data. In this model, firm effects are assumed to be distributed as a truncated normal, which allows it to vary systemically with time. Specifically, we employ time-varying efficiency model of the stochastic frontier as developed by Battese and Coelli (1995) in which the estimates can be generated through a single-equation approach with frontier and inefficiency equation. Disturbance term is composed of independent elements $v_{it}$and u_{it}. The former is assumed to be independently and identically distributed as N (0, σ_v^2). The element u_{it} is a non-negative random variable, associated with technical inefficiency in production, assumed to be independent and identically distributed with truncation (at zero) of the distribution N ($u_{it,}$, σ_u^2). The parameters can be obtained by estimating the stochastic production function using a ML technique.

$$lnY_i = lnY_i^* - u_i, \quad u_i \geq 0$$

$$\text{Where } Y_i^* = f(x_i; \beta) + v_i$$

$$\text{TE}_\text{i} = \exp(-\text{u}) = \frac{lnY_i}{Y_i^*} = \frac{lnY_i}{f(x_i;\beta)}$$

It will be convenient to write the equation collectively as

$$Y_i^* = f(x_i; \beta) + \epsilon_i$$

where ϵ_i is the composed of the random error noise term with zero mean v_i and inefficiency component u_i.

$$\epsilon_i = v_i - u_i$$

The linear logarithm production frontier specification according to Coelli et al. (2005) can be written as:

$$lnY_i = \beta_0 + \beta_1 lnk_{l,t} + \beta_2 lnl_{i,t} + v_i - u_i, \quad i = 1, 2, 3 \ldots\ldots n \; and \; t = time \; period$$

where Y_i is the value added, K is the capital stock and l is the number of employees. β_0, $\beta_1$and β_2 are the parameters to be estimated.

The inefficiency equation will be written as

$$u_{i,t} = \delta Z_{i,t}$$

We have taken liquidity, leverage, size and age of the firm as the Z variables to calculate marginal effects of inefficiency caused by these variables. The truncation in this case will be N $\left(Z_{i,t}, \sigma_u^2\right)$. Marginal effects of the inefficiency variables have been calculated to interpret the coefficients of Z variables.

4 Data and Methodology

4.1 Data

In our study, the data are extracted from CMIE (Centre for Monitoring Indian Economy) Prowess database which is India's largest database for the firm level data of the Indian companies. It constitutes the data from the annual reports, financial statements and other published reports for the Indian firms. The database has the collection of 26000 Indian firms across various sectors.

The data for eight manufacturing industries, i.e. textile, chemicals, metal and metal products, machinery, food, consumer goods, construction materials and transport equipment, have been collected to calculate the technical efficiency of the firms in manufacturing sector. There are a total of 9105 firms for which data has been collected for the period of seven years (2009–2015). Further, the data were reduced to 5696 firms after the scrutiny for missing criteria and data appropriateness. Data on labour, one of the prerequisites for the calculation of technical efficiency, are not available in the CMIE database. Hence, data on labour have been calculated by dividing compensation to employees from wages per worker collected from Annual survey of industries.

There are a total of 1193 and 4503 group and standalone firms, respectively, used in the analysis. The data were winsorized to a 99% confidence interval to eliminate extreme values from the analysis. The proxy for variables used in the analysis is highlighted in Table 1. The mean value added, number of employees and capital stock are shown in Table 2. The study uses four measures of financial constraints, i.e. age, size, leverage and liquidity.

Table 1 Proxy for variables

Variable	Proxy
Value added	Output–Input
Number of employees	Compensation to employees/wages per annum per worker
Capital stock	Perpetual inventory formula with net fixed assets as the value for the base year
Ownership classification	If a firm is associated to a particular business group, it is classified as group-affiliated firm and if not it is treated as a standalone firm
Age	Number of years since incorporation
Size	Total assets
Liquidity	(Current assets-current liabilities)/Total assets
Leverage	Debt-to-assets ratio

Table 2 Mean statistics

	Mean	Std. Err.	Mean	Std. Err.
	Group		Standalone	
Log valueadded	6.933481	0.023765	5.833743	0.012045
Log employees	7.33957	0.021948	5.696127	0.011554
Log capital stock	6.84956	0.025291	5.422349	0.011602
Leverage	0.284041	0.003304	0.347773	0.001667
Liquidity	0.177176	0.002299	0.211752	0.001372
Size	7.857015	0.023041	6.523608	0.010335
Age	39.85486	0.271629	29.44661	0.109088

4.2 Measures of Financial Constraints

4.2.1 Age

There are various studies that illustrate the importance of maturity of firms to avoid information asymmetry and funding related issues. Devereux and Schiantarelli (1990) reported that cash flows are more important to younger firms due to higher information asymmetries and higher rates of external finance. Further, Chirinko and Schaller (1995) found higher cash flow sensitivities for newer firms in comparison with older firms. Studies such as Cabral and Mata (2003) have reported that younger firms were more credit constrained than older firms. Stucki (2013) conducted a study on Swiss firms addressing the success of start-up firms found that only 12% firms were able to survive in the sample period of 1996–2006 since incorporation out of 7112 firms.

4.2.2 Size

Firm size is always found to have a significant role in defining various activities of the firms such as investments, cash flows and funding requirements. Various studies have reported higher cash flow sensitivity to investment for smaller firms (Devereux and Schiantarelli 1990; Chiriko and Schaller 1995; Almeida et al. 2004; Denis and Sibilkov 2009; Črnigoj and Verbič 2014). The studies empirically reported that constrained firms are more cash flow sensitive to investment when firms are split according to the size of the firms. However, another group studies reported counter results to above studies reporting higher cash flow sensitivities for larger firms in comparison with smaller firms (Kadapakkam et al. 1998; Cleary 1999). Further, in contrast to above group of authors Gilchrist and Himmelberg (1995) have reported similar cash flow sensitivities for smaller as well as larger firm size.

4.2.3 Leverage

Another criterion used in testing for the financial constraint is the leverage ratio which is constructed as total debts divide by total assets. It is believed that firms with high leverage may be expected to meet higher agency costs. These agency costs can arise from 'moral hazard' generated by the firms' managers by making an excessively risky investment. The reason for this risky behaviour is that with high leverage the firms may retain most of the profit from any success but lenders incur most of the losses from failure due to the limited liability nature of debt contracts. Agung (2000), using data from Indonesia, find that high leverage firms display higher investment cash flow sensitivities than low leverage firms.

4.2.4 Liquidity

The final measure of financial constraints is the liquidity ratio, which is defined as the ratio of the difference between current assets and current liabilities to the current assets. In general, liquidity ratio is a measure of financial health. Firms with a high level of liquid assets are considered less risky by creditors and lenders because the liquid assets provide an additional buffer to the creditors and lenders. A higher liquidity ratio indicates the firm is in abetter financial health, hence less likely to be financially constrained. Sena (2006) and Maietta and Sena (2010) used leverage and liquidity as the variable to measure financial constraints for the firms.

4.3 Definition of Variables

Output
Output is deflated sales adjusted for change in inventory and purchase of finished goods. It therefore needs to be subtracted from sales to arrive at the firms' manufactured output. An increase in inventory is added to sales to arrive at output and a decrease subtracted.

Value Added and Input
Value added is defined as the difference between output and inputs. The variable input is defined as the sum of material, fuel, packaging and distribution expenses. Total factor productivity (TFP) is calculated using both output and value added as the dependent variable.

Labour Employment
Labour is calculated by dividing the compensation to employees by emoluments per employee. Emoluments per employee are the all industry average emoluments per employee as given by the Central Statistical Organization (CSO). CSO is a part of the Ministry of Statistics and Planning of the Government of India.

Capital Stock

Capital stock has been constructed by using perpetual inventory formula adding current period investment to last period's capital stock net of depreciation. Capital has been depreciated at the rate of 10%. The capital stock for the base year 2009 is taken as the net fixed assets adjusted for depreciation. Investment is calculated as increase in net fixed assets less decrease in gross fixed assets.

$$k_{i,t} = (1 - \delta)k_{i,t-1} + I_{i,t}$$

where $K_{i,t}$ is the capital stock, δ is the rate of depreciation charged and $I_{i,t}$ is the investment for the current period. Also, the variables are deflated by GDP implicit price deflator at factor cost.

4.4 Methodology

We use stochastic frontier analysis single-equation approach suggested by Battesse and Coelli (1995). The single-equation approach calculates the technical efficiency in the frontier and also constitutes the inefficiency equation through providing the flexibility to assign variables contributing to inefficiency in the same equation (Belotti et al. 2012). We calculated effects of each measure of financial constraints on the technical efficiency of group-affiliated and standalone firms. The coefficients of inefficiency variables in the equation will not tell the effects of particular criteria directly. Hence, marginal effects of the inefficiency variables will be calculated to express the magnitude of variance caused due to technical efficiency of the firms. We also calculated year wise technical efficiencies for each industry through both schemes used for dividing the firms into financially constrained and unconstrained firms.

5 Findings and Discussions

The study reports higher efficiency (65%) for group-affiliated firms where efficiency calculations are not determined by explanatory variables in comparison with standalone firms (57%). However, significant higher efficiency is reported for standalone firms when leverage (36% against 82%) and liquidity (47% against 49%) are used as explanatory variables for the technical efficiency. Further, group firms have higher efficiency in case of age (65% against 46%) and size (79% against 76%) as determining variables for technical efficiency. The detailed results are highlighted in Tables 3 and 4. Further, marginal effects of each measure of financial constraint are reported in Table 5. We find that a unit increase in leverage will increase the technical efficiency of group-affiliated firms by 0.42 points whereas in case of standalone firms it is 0.24 points. This means that increase in leverage will positively influence technical efficiency both group-affiliated and standalone firms. Further, all other measures

Table 3 Group firms results

Log valueadded	Coef.	Std. Err.	Coef.	Std. Err.	Coef.	Std. Err.	Coef.	Std. Err.	Coef.	Std. Err.
Frontier										
Logemployees	0.230087***	0.010985	0.56021***	0.011829	0.553656***	0.011076	0.573223***	0.011213	0.280219***	0.011575
Log capitalstock	0.731767***	0.009784	0.347576***	0.010409	0.379189***	0.010267	0.323083***	0.009933	0.687956***	0.010083
_cons	−0.0424	0.047406	0.890086***	0.059367	0.47683***	0.05785	0.521183***	0.063582	−0.11137**	0.051765
Mean (efficiency)	0.65		0.36		0.47		0.79		0.65	
Mean (inefficiency)	0.46		1.04		0.76		0.23		0.46	
Leverage			1.152323***	0.04468						
Liquidity					0.700385***	0.075939				
Size							−0.02907***	0.010811		
Age									−0.17998***	0.016688
Sigma_u										
Leverage_u			−5.65351***	0.604373						
Liquidity_u					−10.4775***	0.585337				
Size_u							−0.30991***	0.038653		
Age_u									0.027657***	0.001173
Sigma_v										
_cons	−1.06583***	0.030278	−0.36669***	0.024195	−0.44312***	0.019991	−0.27365***	0.020086	−0.93815***	0.034115

The table highlights the results of stochastic single-equation approach specifying the mean efficiency and inefficiency for group firms. sigma_u and sigma_v highlights the variance due to explanatory variables and idiosyncratic error term. ***, **, * represents significance at 99%, 95% nad 90% confidence interval respectively

Table 4 Standalone firms results

Log valueadded	Coef.	Std. Err.	Coef.	Std. Err.	Coef.	Std. Err.	Coef.	Std. Err.	Coef.	Std. Err.
Frontier										
Logemployees	0.125272***	0.007123	0.461627***	0.00746	0.44612***	0.007072	0.4608451***	0.007179	0.209178***	0.007769
Log capitalstock	0.791261***	0.007281	0.343149***	0.007264	0.38827***	0.007353	0.3202055***	0.007145	0.749379***	0.007638
_cons	0.590947***	0.034568	1.840094***	0.037696	1.71057***	0.035425	1.680956***	0.037992	0.265818***	0.039997
Mean (efficiency)	0.57		0.82		0.49		0.76		0.46	
Mean (inefficiency)	0.63		0.20		0.73		0.26		0.85	
Leverage			−13.4491***	1.205962						
Liquidity					0.601376***	0.056403				
Size							−0.043183***	0.008856		
Age									−0.22666***	0.017221
Sigma_u										
Leverage_u			2.331071***	0.095176						
Liquidity_u					−6.58817***	0.273488				
Size_u							−0.3269681***	0.027258		
Age_u									0.042863***	0.001071
Sigma_v										
_cons	−0.58807***	0.018977	0.079034***	0.014583	0.056866***	0.011732	0.2005723***	0.011204	−0.37849***	0.023045

The table highlights the results of stochastic single-equation approach specifying the mean efficiency and inefficiency for standalone firms. Sigma_u and sigma_v highlights the variance due to explanatory variables and idiosyncratic error term

Table 5 Marginal effects

Type of firm	Leverage_u	Leverage_v	Liquidity_u	Liquidity_v	Size_u	Size_v	Age_u	Age_v
Group	0.426134	−1.18795	−2.80247	−1.29627	−0.04791	−0.01303	−0.04123	−0.03122
Standalone	0.249871	0.131664	−0.81927	−1.30427	−0.0605329	−0.0181675	−0.04224	−0.02024

The table highlights the marginal effects of explanatory variables and error tem on technical efficiency of the firms, e.g. Leverage_u highlights deviation due to leverage, whereas Leverage_v shows error term in the equation

of financial constraints shows a negative marginal decrease in technical efficiency of the firms with very little divergence in magnitude for both types of firms. The results clearly elucidates significant effects of financial constraints on standalone firms with positive coefficients for leverage and age while liquidity and size found to have negative influence on technical efficiency. However, group firms reports negative influence from leverage, liquidity and size. Further, increase in age reported to have positive effect on technical efficiency for group firms.

6 Conclusions

The study uses 5696 Indian manufacturing firms for the period of 7 years (2009–2015). The number of group-affiliated firms is 1193, while that of standalone firms is 4503. The objective of the study was to understand the influence of financial constraints on the technical efficiency according to ownership affiliation of firms. The study reports higher technical efficiency in the absence of explanatory variables for group firms. However, the results diverge when measures of financial constraints are used as explanatory variables. We found leverage and liquidity as a positive influence on financially constrained firms with higher technical efficiencies. Marginal effects for leverage suggests increase in technical efficiency for all the firms except small and high liquidity firms. The efficiency in these cases is found to be decreasing with increase in leverage. Size and age have mixed effects on the technical efficiencies of the firms. The results in conclusion highlight higher credit constraints for standalone firms in comparison with group-affiliated firms. It also highlights the divergence in the interest rates or cost of capital available to the group-affiliated and standalone firms.

References

Agung, J. (2000). Financial constraint, firms' investments and the channels of monetary policy in Indonesia. *Applied Economics, 32*(13), 1637–1646.

Almeida, H., Campello, M., & Weisbach, M. S. (2004). The cash flow sensitivity of cash. *The Journal of Finance, 59*(4), 1777–1804.

Battese, G. E., & Coelli, T. J. (1992). Frontier production functions, technical efficiency and panel data: With application to paddy farmers in India. *Journal of Productivity Analysis*, *3*(1–2), 153–169.

Battese, G. E., & Coelli, T. J. (1995). A model for technical inefficiency effects in a stochastic frontier production function for panel data. *Empirical Economics, 20*(2), 325–332.

Belotti, F., Daidone, S., Ilardi, G., & Atella, V. (2012). Stochastic frontier analysis using Stata.

Bhandari, A. K., & Ray, S. C. (2012). Technical efficiency in the Indian textiles industry: A non-parametric analysis of firm-level data. *Bulletin of Economic Research*, *64*(1), 109–124.

Cabral, L., & Mata, J. (2003). On the evolution of the firm size distribution: Facts and theory. *American Economic Review*, *93*(4), 1075–1090.

Campa, J. M., & Shaver, J. M. (2002). Exporting and capital investment: On the strategic behavior of exporters. *IESE research papers*, *469*.

Chirinko, R. S., & Schaller, H. (1995). Why does liquidity matter in investment equations? *Journal of Money, Credit and Banking*, *27*(2), 527–548.

Cleary, S. (1999). The relationship between firm investment and financial status. *The Journal of Finance*, *54*(2), 673–692.

Coelli, T. J., Rao, D. S. P., O'Donnell, C. J., & Battese, G. E. (2005). *An introduction to efficiency and productivity analysis*. Springer Science & Business Media.

Črnigoj, M., & Verbič, M. (2014). Financial constraints and corporate investments during the current financial and economic crisis: The credit crunch and investment decisions of Slovenian firms. *Economic systems, 38*(4), 502–517.

Denis, D. J., & Sibilkov, V. (2009). Financial constraints, investment, and the value of cash holdings. *The Review of Financial Studies*, *23*(1), 247–269.

Devereux, M., & Schiantarelli, F. (1990). Investment, financial factors, and cash flow: Evidence from UK panel data. In *Asymmetric information, corporate finance, and investment* (pp. 279–306). University of Chicago Press.

Fazzari, S. M., Hubbard, R. G., Petersen, B. C., Blinder, A. S., & Poterba, J. M. (1988). Financing constraints and corporate investment. *Brookings papers on economic activity, 1988*(1), 141–206.

Fazzari, S. M., & Petersen, B. C. (1993). Working capital and fixed investment: New evidence on financing constraints. *The RAND Journal of Economics*, 328–342.

Gilchrist, S., & Himmelberg, C. P. (1995). Evidence on the role of cash flow for investment. *Journal of monetary Economics, 36*(3), 541–572.

Hoshi, T., Kashyap, A., &Scharfstein, D. (1991). Corporate structure, liquidity, and investment: Evidence from Japanese industrial groups. *The Quarterly Journal of Economics*, 33–60.

Kadapakkam, P. R., Kumar, P. C., & Riddick, L. A. (1998). The impact of cash flows and firm size on investment: The international evidence. *Journal of Banking & Finance, 22*(3), 293–320.

Lamont, O., Polk, C., & Saaá-Requejo, J. (2001). Financial constraints and stock returns. *The Review of Financial Studies*, *14*(2), 529–554.

Lensink, R., Van der Molen, R., & Gangopadhyay, S. (2003). Business groups, financing constraints and investment: The case of India. *The Journal of Development Studies*, *40*(2), 93–119.

Lundvall, K., & Battese, G. E. (2000). Firm size, age and efficiency: evidence from Kenyan manufacturing firms. *The Journal of Development Studies, 36*(3), 146–163.

Maietta, O. W., & Sena, V. (2010). Financial constraints and technical efficiency: Some empirical evidence for Italian producers' cooperatives. *Annals of Public and Cooperative Economics, 81*(1), 21–38.

Mitra, A., Varoudakis, A., & Veganzones-Varoudakis, M. A. (2002). Productivity and technical efficiency in Indian states' manufacturing: The role of infrastructure. *Economic Development and Cultural Change, 50*(2), 395–426.

Ramaswamy, K. V. (1994). Small-scale manufacturing industries: Some aspects of size, growth and structure. *Economic and Political Weekly*, M13–M23.

Sena, V. (2006). The determinants of firms' performance: Can finance constraints improve technical efficiency? *European Journal of Operational Research, 172*(1), 311–325.

Stucki, T. (2013). Success of start-up firms: The role of financial constraints. *Industrial and Corporate Change*, *23*(1), 25–64.

Tybout, J. R. (2000). Manufacturing firms in developing countries: How well do they do, and why? *Journal of Economic literature, 38*(1), 11–44.

Investment Trends in Venture Capital and Private Equity in India

Poonam Dugar and Nirali Pandit

Abstract A horde of favourable events and macroeconomic conditions over a period of time have shaped the investment climate in India. Financial globalization, growth in savings and increasing risk appetite among global investors over a period of time, gave birth to a new source of corporate finance known as the venture capital and private equity. The role of VCPE investments in stimulating innovation and growth in India cannot be undermined. VCPE investments seem to have grown but whether they have impacted all industries or only a few remains to be assessed. This study makes an attempt to analyse the trends of the VCPE investments in India during the past two decades (1998–2016) and its concentration in various industries of the economy, as well well its distribution across various stages of financing. The findings of the study show the impact of various factors (both global and national level) on the growth of VCPE investments in India. It also reflects the concentration of VCPE investments in certain industries of the economy and the changing trends across stages of funding from early and seed stage to late stages of investments. The regression model reveals a significant impact of the volume of deals on the VCPE investments.

Keywords Venture capital · Private equity · Trends · Stage-wise investments

1 Introduction

Financial globalization, growth in savings and increasing risk appetite among global investors over a period of time, gave birth to a new source of corporate finance known as the venture capital and private equity (Jain and Manna 2009). Venture capital and

P. Dugar (✉)
Finance Accounting & Control Area, Amrut Mody School of Management, Ahmedabad University, Ahmedabad, India
e-mail: poonam.dugar@ahduni.edu.in

N. Pandit
Entrepreneurship Development Institute of India, Ahmedabad, India
e-mail: nirali@ediindia.org

N. R. Bhanumurthy et al. (eds.), *Advances in Finance & Applied Economics*,
https://doi.org/10.1007/978-981-13-1696-8_14

private equity (VCPE) investments have been a part of India's emerging story for more than three decades now, as there have been a horde of events that have shaped the investment climate in India.

Though VCPE financing was introduced more than three decades back, it really caught its flight after the economic reforms post 1991. Prior to 1991, India was characterised by very low levels of VCPE investment activity but post-1991 the VCPE industry experienced growth and India started becoming an attractive destination for VCPE investments worldwide.

Developing economies like India, with the beginning of twenty-first century, experienced tremendous advancement and redefining in domestic and international business activities (Deloitte Report 2012). The uniqueness of VCPE investments to support risky ventures differentiated it from other conventional sources of funding and the gradual creation of a conducive environment in the country attracted more and more VCPE investors, thereby contributing to India's growth story (Deloitte Report 2014).

Various statistics quoted, show the growth story of India as the fastest developing economy both in terms of industry growth rate and quantum of investments which facilitated the growth of VCPE investments in the country. India had the third position in terms of the quantum of investment during 2004–2008 (PWC Reports 2008) and a growth rate of 7.6% and 6.6% in 2015 and 2016, respectively, with estimates of 7.2% for 2017 as per International Monetary Fund's (IMF) 'World Economic Outlook Update' (KPMG–Private Equity Review 2016). As per Venture Economics data during the period 1990–99, India's ranking was 25 out of 64 countries, which got better in the next decade, 2000–09, when its ranking rose to 13 out of 90 countries. Specifically during 2005–2009, the trend was even more encouraging when India's ranking was 10 out of 77 countries (Deshmukh and Rajan 2011).

Thus, a close look at the trends of VCPE investments would show a clear preference for investments according to the economic climate and consumption patterns in the country. These trends have drawn the landscape for the VCPE investments in India reflecting the adaption, adoption and acceptability of this innovative asset class in the Indian business world.

This study makes an attempt to analyse the trends of the VCPE investments in India during the past two decades (1998–2016) through parameters like industry concentration and distribution across stage of investments.

2 Objective of the Study

The VCPE industry in India has been growing with great pace as discussed above and it provides a platform to study the growth trends in entirety. Previous studies in this area majorly included the evolution and the current status of the industry, multi-country studies which also included India, survey and case studies of VCPE industry practices in India. However, there is lack of empirical evidence related to the intricate analysis of the factors which have affected the growth trends of the VCPE investments along with its preference for certain industries and stages of financing.

This study is an attempt to meet the gap in research to study the trends of the VCPE investments through parameters covering Industry concentration and stage-wise shift of trends over the two-decade period (1998–2016). This would reflect all the phases including pre-growth, growth, slowdown during crisis, rise after the crisis, and recent growth stages which have not been studied in entirety.

The objectives of this study are as follows:

1. To study the investment trends of the Indian VCPE industry;
2. To find the impact of the number of deals on the value of VCPE investments;
3. To identify the concentration of VCPE investments across various industries in India;
4. To study the of trends of VCPE investments across various stages of investments.

3 Literature Review

Gompers (1994) explored the importance of venture capital financing as an important contributor in the economic growth of America and finds that increase in the flow of venture capital investments can be attributed to the various regulatory changes. The determinants affecting the demand of venture capital investments include higher GDP growth, increased R & D spending, lower capital gain tax rates, and favourable regulatory environment along with the enabling economic and political environment in the country (Gompers et al. 1998; Naqi and Hettihewa 2007; Kumari 2013; Smita and Tripathi 2015; Reddy 2015). Globalisation led to geographic distribution of venture capital sources of various countries with preference of investment given to technology industries showing a disproportionate representation in industries that have high levels of information asymmetry (Amit et al. 1998; Subhash and Nair 2004, 2006).Venture capital investments showed concentration in financial clusters, and with the growth in regional development saw a spatial shift reflecting technological and industrial clustering (Florida et al. 1993; Bowonder and Mani 2002).

In India, venture capital firms are giving more prominence to service sectors like BFSI, IT and ITES, Media and Entertainment, Healthcare and Life Sciences which are knowledge intensive which reflects uniform distribution of VCPE investments across different industries as compared to the initial skewed distribution in just technology industries. The promotion of these sectors will create a boom for the Indian economy (Kumari 2013; Srinivas 2013; Komala 2015; Reddy 2015). The growth of venture capital investments has strong correlation with the number of deals and the value of investments occurring in a country (Komala 2014).

Originally, venture capital evolved as means for early-stage financing but it also includes stage financing at various levels like development, expansion and buyout (or late stage) financing for the enterprises. There have been significant shifts in the investment trends from early- and seed-stage investments to late-stage or private equity investments (Naqi and Hettihewa 2007; Kumari 2013).

4 Data Sources and Methodology

The deal-level data for analysis has been taken from the database of Venture Intelligence, India.

The analysis is based on 6462 deals executed from April 98 to March 2016 in 3841 companies. Out of these, investment data for 5781 deals was available, totalling \$117854 mn. This might not include all of the VCPE deals during the period, since many of the deals may not have been announced, but we believe the data captures a majority of the investment that happened during the period and more importantly is representative of the industry trends.

The total VCPE investments have been analysed through YOY growth and CAGR for the entire period. Similarly, the analysis of VCPE investments across stages has been done by using percentage analysis across different sub-periods and by calculating the CAGR for each stage. Analysis of VCPE investments by industry is done for the aggregate period to check the concentration of investments and also by calculating CAGR for each industry. Empirical analysis is also done through a linear regression model to check the impact of the number of deals on the value of VCPE investments.

5 Analysis of Investment Trends of VCPE Investments in India

I. **Total VCPE Investments by Value and Number of Deals**:

The CAGR and YOY growth are calculated as follows:

$$\text{Calculation of CAGR} = (\text{ending value}/\text{beginning value})^\wedge(1/n) - 1$$

$$\text{Calculation of YOY growth} = (\text{current year's investments} - \text{previous year's investments})/\text{previous year's investments}$$

Figure 1 shows the VCPE investments in value and number of deals over the 19-year period (1998–2016). We can observe a linear growth trend both for the value of investments and the number of deals. The mountains (ups) and valleys (downs) observed on the growth graph provide a platform to study the trends in more depth by segregating it in smaller time periods. Hence, analysis of total VCPE investments and its industry penetration along with stage-wise concentration is studied by dividing

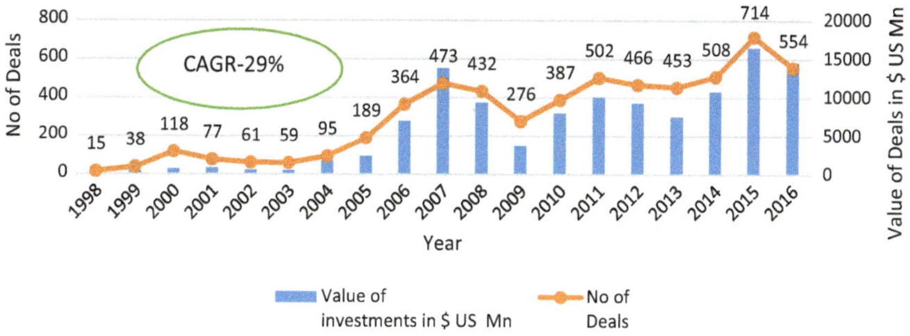

Fig. 1 VCPE investments in value and number of deals. *Source* Compiled from Table 1

them in relevant time periods in the sections given below. This will enable us to understand the various factors which have impacted the growth trends at different points of time.

6 Analysis of YOY Growth Rate for Value of VCPE Investments' Period Wise

1. **YOY Growth Rate from 1998 to 2005**

The VCPE investments have shown a remarkable growth both in terms of amount invested and the number of deals. In Fig. 2, we can observe a clear growth in the value of VCPE investments in the initial phase from 1998 to 2001 by 444% ($152–$828 mn) This was the time when Venture Capital Guidelines were formalised by SEBI for both Indian and foreign investors and world experienced an IT boom, and hence, VC Investments were attracted on new technology-based ventures. During 2001–2003, we can see a fall in YOY growth rate by 33% and further by 6% which may be attributed to the burst of Dotcom bubble in USA and its impact on other developing economies like India.

Gradually after 2004, the global VCPE firms started focusing on emerging economies like India and China. An increase in the YOY growth rate of VCPE investments to 243% from 2003 to 2004 and a further increase by 33% from 2004 to 2005 was observed. This was the time when India was regaining on its macroeconomic indicators, and many companies started growing with increasing consumption by the fast-growing middle class (Bain Report 2011).

2. **YOY Growth Rate from 2006 to 2009**

The YOY growth bar further increased substantially in 2006 and 2007 by 194% and 98%, respectively, in the value of investments where it reached to its peak of $13791 mn in 2007 as seen in Fig. 3. If we compare in absolute values, the increase in investments from $152 to $13791 mn and in number of deals from 15 to 473 was observed

Fig. 2 YOY growth rate for VCPE investments (Value) from 1998 to 2005. *Source* Compiled from Table 1

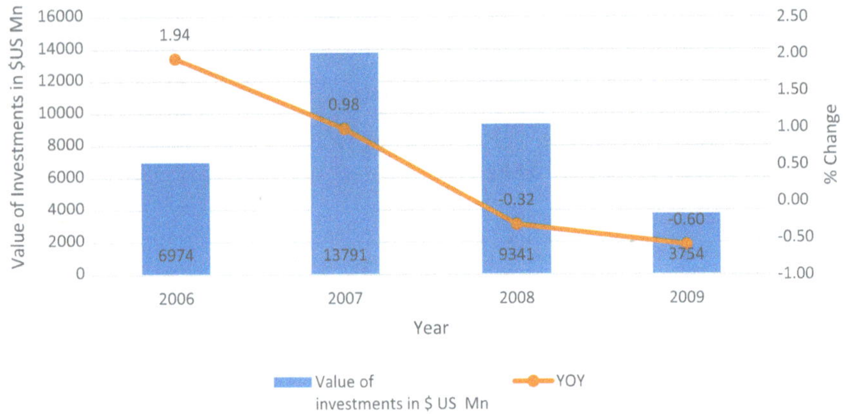

Fig. 3 YOY Growth Rate for VCPE Investments (Value) from 2006 to 2009. *Source* Compiled from Table 1

over the decade ending 2007 (Refer Table 1). Bain Report 2011 reports the inflow of capital across various industries in India like healthcare, telecom, manufacturing enterprises, technology firms, energy producers and real estate ventures during this period. As a result of this, India then moved from sixth position to the top position among the VCPE markets in Asia-Pacific region by 2007 (Bain Report 2011).

But as it is said, what goes up fast comes down fast, and the first leg of India's VCPE came to an end with the first significant drop in YOY growth rate visible in 2008 and 2009 by 32% and 60%, respectively. The whole world was affected by the impact of global financial crisis, and so was the Indian VCPE industry. Investors became risk averse, and public market valuations started falling, leading to drop in GDP to around 6% from earlier 8 to 9% (Bain Report 2011). But things started getting better towards the end of 2009, when the India markets like other emerging

Table 1 Year-wise distribution of VCPE investments in value and no. of deals

Year	Value of investments in $ US Mn	Year on year growth rate of value of investments (YOY)	No. of deals
1998	152		15
1999	402	1.64	38
2000	720	0.79	118
2001	828	0.15	77
2002	553	−0.33	61
2003	522	−0.06	59
2004	1791	2.43	95
2005	2376	0.33	189
CAGR	**48%**		44%
2006	6974	1.94	364
2007	13791	0.98	473
2008	9341	−0.32	432
2009	3754	−0.60	276
CAGR	**−19%**		−9%
2010	8007	1.13	387
2011	10042	0.25	502
2012	9279	−0.08	466
2013	7534	−0.19	453
2014	10775	0.43	508
2015	16445	0.53	714
2016	14568	−0.11	554
CAGR	**10%**		6%
Total	**117854**		5781
CAGR	**29%**		22%

Source Compiled from Venture Intelligence, India Database

economies started regaining as compared to developed economies and India's GDP started climbing again.

3. **YOY Growth Rate from 2010 to 2016**

Figure 4 reflects an increasing YOY growth rate by 113% in 2010 and 25% in 2011 showing the increased confidence of the VCPE investors in India. Post the credit meltdown, India saw some revival when, in 2010, its GDP rose to 8.7% due to increased consumer and public infrastructure spending (Bain Report 2011). In 2012 and 2013, some corrections were seen in the YOY growth rate to the extent of 8% and 19%, respectively. The decline was because of falling GDP, high inflation, low

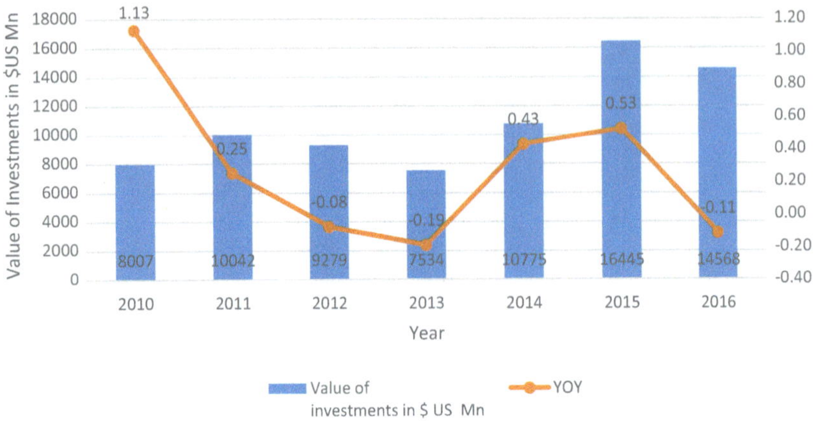

Fig. 4 YOY Growth Rate for VCPE Investments (Value) from 2010 to 2016. *Source* Compiled from Table 1

IIP, depreciating rupee, unstable interest rates, retrospective tax issues to foreign investors (Bain Report 2013 and 2014). This correction was soon rectified with a rise of YOY growth rate by 43% in 2014 with the new Government in place resulting in favourable macroeconomic situation in the country; this was also the time when FDI inflow of $29bn was the highest in last 5 years with VCPE's contribution amounting to 53% of the inflow. The new Government started working towards improving the business environment in the country making it an attractive destination for future investments (Bain Report 2015).

2015 saw an all-time high both in terms of value of VCPE investments and the number of deals being $16445mn and 714, respectively. This was a result of constructive changes in exit environment to the investors, government initiatives—such as the Start-up India programme, tax regime rationalisation and Make in India. The technology start-up and ecommerce funding boom was also responsible for the increased investments in 2015 (Bain Report 2016).

In 2016, again, we observed some minor corrections by fall in the growth rate by 11%, but still it was the second highest after 2015 during the entire period. This decline can be attributed to impact of regulatory and economic changes like the announcement of GST Act, and demonetisation in the country. Other factors affecting may be the political and economic uproar in Europe including Brexit which would have affected the foreign investors who majorly contribute to the VCPE investments in India (KPMG–Private Equity Review 2016).

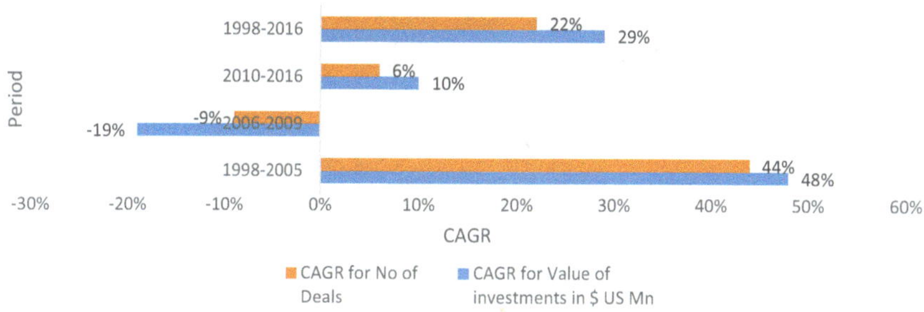

Fig. 5 CAGR of VCPE investments in value and number of deals. *Source* Compiled from Table 1

7 Analysis of CAGR for Value of VCPE Investments and Number of VCPE Deals

In Fig. 5, we then look at the CAGR of the VCPE investments over the analysed smaller periods and the entire period as well the following observations can be made:

1. 1998–2005, which reflected the first leg of growth in VCPE industry in India showed a CAGR of 48% for value of investments and 44% for number of deals.
2. In 2006 2009, with Consequences of global financial crisis the CAGR rolled down to −19% in value of investments and −9% for number of deals even after reaching a peak in 2007.
3. In 2010–2016, it showed a strong revival and recovery post-crisis where the CAGR improved to 10% in value of investments and 6% for number of deals.
4. For the entire period from 1998 to 2016, we can observe a steady growth rate over the two-decade period in spite of all the ups and downs reflecting a CAGR of 29% in value of investments and 22% for number of deals.

To summarise the above analysis, we can say that trends in the VCPE investments over the past two decades seems like a roller coaster ride which have experienced thrilling ups and downs throughout the period.

II. **Empirical Analysis of Total VCPE Investments**

After looking at the growth trends of the VCPE investments, we also empirically tested the impact of the number of deals made on the variations in the value of VCPE investments. The analysis of both, total VCPE investments and number of deals over the two-decade period 1998–2016, shows a linear growth as shown in the Fig. 6.

VCPE investments (in $US Mn) made by Venture capital firms was taken as the dependent variable, which will be regressed on the number of deals of the VCPE investment. The following hypothesis has been framed accordingly:

$\mathbf{H_0}$: The number of deals does not have a significant impact on the amount of investments made by Venture Capital firms.

From regression equation model shown in Table 2, we can see that the R-square value is quite high, which means the model explains that 93% of the variations in the

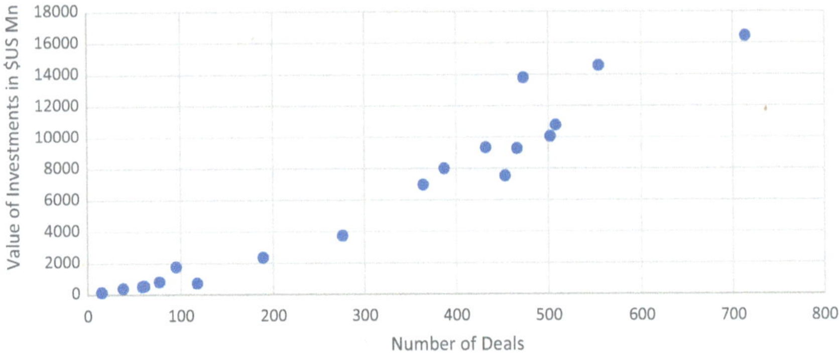

Fig. 6 VCPE investments trends across the number of VCPE deals from 1998 to 2016. *Source* Compiled from Table 1

Table 2 Dependant variable (VCPE investments) is linearly regressed on number of deals

R-square	0.9389
Coefficient of independent variable (No. of deals)	24.36
Regression equation model: Y = −1212.06 + 24.36993X P-value of coefficient (9.33E–12)	

value of VCPE investments is affected only because of the number of deals made. The coefficient of independent variable (no. of deals) is positive which means that one additional deal made by VCPE firms brings about US $ 24 Mn of fresh VCPE investments. Also, since the p-value is less than 0.01, the coefficient is statistically highly significant and so we reject the null hypothesis. Thus, we conclude that number of deals is a significant determinant of the amount of VCPE investments in India.

III. **VCPE Investments by Industry**
See Table 3.

8 Analysis of Aggregate Industry Wise VCPE Investments in Value and Number of Deals

Figures 7 and 8 show the overall distribution of VCPE investments across various industries of the economy in value and number of deals, respectively. Looking at the aggregate picture from 1998 to 2016, we can observe that IT and ITES industry occupies the largest percentage of the pie both in terms of the value of investments (28%) (US$33, 492 mn) and number of deals (39%) (2258). Industries, like Engineering (16%) (US$19, 162 mn), BFSI (14%) (US$16, 091 mn) and Manufacturing (13%) (US$14, 823 mn), also occupy a substantial portion of the share of VCPE

Table 3 Industry wise VCPE investments by value and number of deals

Industry	Value in $ US Mn	No of deals	Average investment per deal in $ US Mn	CAGR (%)
IT and ITES	33492	2258	14.83	32
Banking, financial services and insurance (BFSI)	16091	563	28.58	19
Manufacturing (MFG)	14823	765	19.37	29
Healthcare (HC)	9168	567	16.16	22
Engineering and construction (E&C)	19162	582	32.92	59
Telecom and media (T&M)	10927	254	43.02	20
Shipping and logistics (S&L)	4147	163	25.44	27
Non-financial services (NFS)	6583	407	16.17	40
Others (OT)	3460	222	15.58	16
Total	**117854**	**5781**		**29**

Source Compiled from Venture Intelligence, India Database

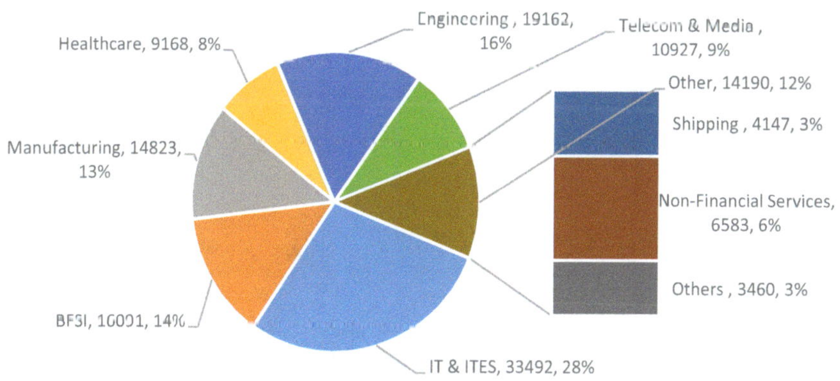

Fig. 7 Industry wise VCPE investments from 1998 to 2016. *Source* Compiled from Table 3

investments in value and 10%, 10% and 13%, respectively, in terms of the number of deals. This clearly shows the concentration of VCPE investments of almost 70% in industries like IT and ITES, BFSI, Engineering and Manufacturing.

When industries are compared on the basis of their average investment per deal as calculated in Table 3, it shows that Telecom industry tops with $43.02 mn, followed

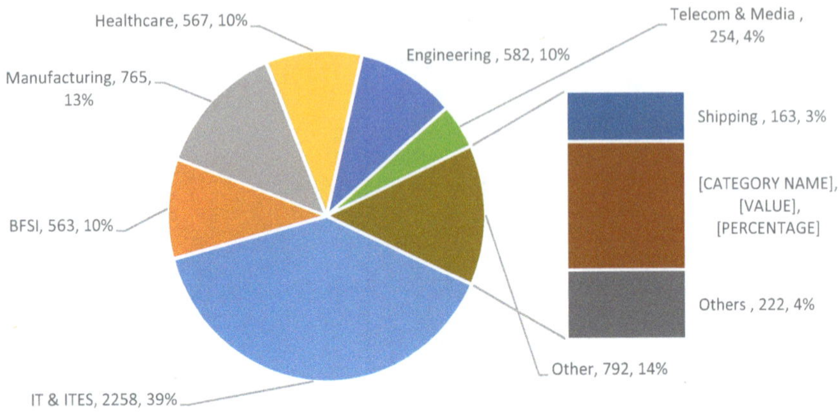

Fig. 8 Industry wise no. of deals from 1998 to 2016. *Source* Compiled from Table 3

by Engineering ($32.92 mn), BFSI ($28.58 mn) and Shipping ($25.44 mn). All the other sectors are in the range of $14 to 20 mn per deal with IT and ITES being the lowest with $14.83 mn. Thus, it can be observed that capital-intensive industries like Telecom, BFSI and Engineering would have lesser number of deals with higher values of investments per deal as compared to less capital investment industries. Similarly another probable reason could be that if, majority of the deals in an industry are in the early stage of the company the volume of investments would be lower as compared to the investments in the late stage of the company where the capital requirements would be higher.

9 Industry Growth Through VCPE Investments Measured by CAGR

The following observations were made while measuring the industry growth through CAGR as shown in Fig. 9:

1. The Engineering industry which started attracting funding only after 2004 shows a CAGR of 59% reflecting a stable growth and has emerged as a strong attractor of VCPE investments.
2. IT and ITES industry which though attracted the maximum funding has a CAGR of 32% as it saw many fluctuations with its share of contributions in attracting VCPE funding experiencing drastic changes.
3. Manufacturing industry with a CAGR of (29%) again saw many fluctuations where it started in 1998 with a percentage share of 8% towards total investments and moved towards a range of 21 to 34% up to 2011 and recently coming down to 9% again in the past few years.

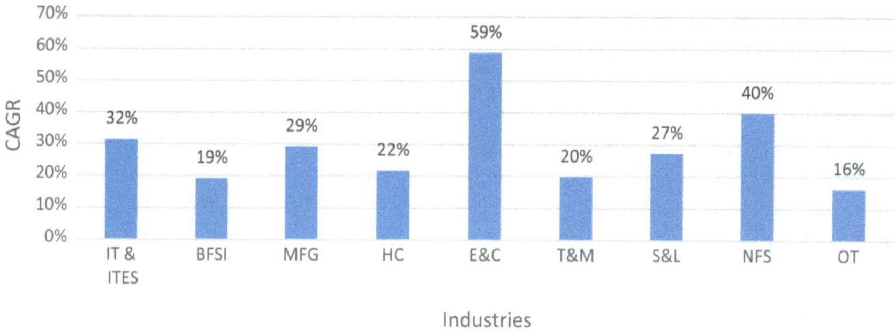

Fig. 9 Industry wise CAGR of VCPE investments (Value $US Mn) from 1998 to 2016. *Source* Compiled from Table 3

Table 4 Stages of financing

No.	Stages	Description
1	Early	Seed capital/start-up/early stage (<5 years old)
2	Growth	Expansion/growth capital (<10 years old)
3	Late	Expansion/growth capital (>10 years old)
4	Pre-IPO	Mezzanine/Pre-IPO funding
5	PIPE	Private investments in public equity
6	Buyout	Acquisition of controlling or significant stake
7	Others	Investments in special purpose vehicle (SPV)

4. BFSI (19%), Healthcare (22%) and Shipping (27%) were more or less stable throughout the years with a steady CAGR with some attractive years in the last two decades.
5. The Telecom and Media industry with a CAGR of 20% had a larger share in two digits up to 2011 which has been reduced to single digits in the past few years.

IV. **Analysis of VCPE Investments by Stage**

As per the database, the investments were classified into the following stages as shown in Table 4, based on the lifecycle of the investee firm as well as the amount of the investment

Table 5 Total VCPE investments stage wise by value and number of deals

Stages	Value in US $ Mn	No. of deals	Average investment per deal in US $ Mn
Early	6110	1948	3.14
Growth	26205	1208	21.69
Late	42556	1391	30.59
PIPE	18550	815	22.76
Pre-IPO	2264	92	24.61
Buyout	16758	226	74.15
Others	5411	101	53.57
Total	**117854**	**5781**	

Source Compiled from Venture Intelligence Database

10 Analysis of Total VCPE Investments Stage Wise by Value and Number of Deals

Table 5 shows the overall distribution of VCPE investments in value and number of deals over various stages for the period from 1998 to 2016. It also reflects the average investment per deal for all the stages of investments.

Figure 10 shows the proportion of total investments in value across various stages for the period from 1998 to 2016. In terms of the total investments in value, it is observed that late-stage investments constitute a majority share of the pie, receiving US$42556 mn (36%), more than 1/3rd of the total investments, followed by the growth stage receiving US$26205 mn (25%) share and PIPE stage receiving US$18550 mn (16%). The Pre-IPO, Buyout and Others received US$2264 mn (25), US$16758 mn (14%) and US$5411 mn (5%), respectively. The early stage accounted for only US$6110 mn (4%).

Thus, it is observed that almost 60% of the funds are invested in growth- and late-stage companies. This confirms the previous work of Deshmukh and Rajan (2011) and Mitra who observed that VCPE funds in India prefer to invest in companies in the growth and late stages with some track record of performance.

The category which is attracting substantial investment apart from growth and late stage is PIPE. This is one of the most favoured routes by foreign investors for entering Indian PE market as it allows them to tap the growth potential of already well-established public-listed enterprises with minimum risk (IVCA Report 2009).

The other two stages, i.e. Pre-IPO and Buyout, have attracted lowest investments in Indian markets so far. Pre-IPO stage funding witnessed a spurt especially in 2006 and 2007 when Indian IPO market was at its peak generating very attractive returns and there was considerable increase in PE-backed IPO exits. While Buyouts are one of the most favoured PE investments in developed markets, they are comparatively rare in India (IVCA Report 2009).

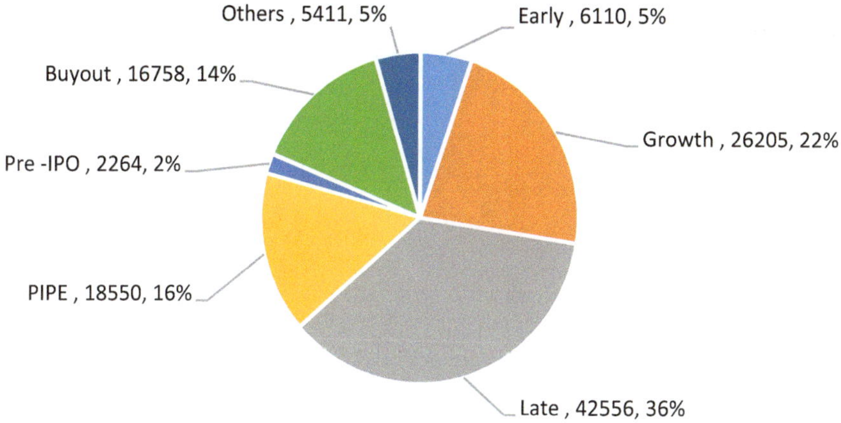

Fig. 10 Stage-wise VCPE Investments in Value (US $ Mn) from 1998 to 2016. *Source* Compiled from Table 5

Figure 11 shows the proportion of the number of deals across the various stages. It can be seen that the number of deals also follow a similar pattern of proportion across the different stages, with late, growth and PIPE having 24% (1391), 21% (1208) and 14% (815) share, respectively, and Pre-IPO, Buyout and Others having 1% (92), 4% (226) and 2%(101) shares, respectively, of the total deals. The very low level of buyout transactions concludes that Buyout activity is likely to happen in more mature markets rather than emerging economies like India (Wright et al. 1997). The only exception observed was for the early-stage investments where share by value (amount invested) is only 5% (US$6110 mn) as against share by volume (number of deals) of 34% (1948 deals), almost 1/3rd of the total deals.

11 Analysis of Seasonal Variations in the VCPE Investments Stage Wise

Table 6 below shows the VCPE investments in India across various stages in terms of percentage of total investments of the respective years over a 19-year period from 1998 to 2016.

The analysis of stage investments as shown in Table 6 is done by breaking the total period in three parts: 1998–2003, 2004–2009 and 2010–2016 which reflects interesting shifts in the concentration of VCPE investments across various stages as discussed below.

Table 6 Year-wise–stage-wise VCPE investments (Value in US $ Mn) with percentage of total annual investments' stage wise

Year	Early	%	Growth	%	Late	%	PIPE	%	Pre-IPO	%	Buyout	%	Others	%	Total
1998	15	10	101	67	19	12	14	9	4	3	0	0	0	0	152
1999	58	14	161	40	10	3	153	38	0	0	0	0	20	5	402
2000	243	34	144	20	33	5	92	13	2	0	50	7	156	22	720
2001	142	17	31	4	18	2	175	21	460	56	0	0	3	0	828
2002	102	18	107	19	175	32	116	21	0	0	53	10	0	0	553
2003	58	11	140	27	80	15	150	29	5	1	89	17	0	0	522
CAGR	31%		7%		33%		61%		5%		21%		−61%		28%
2004	70	4	190	11	241	13	661	37	27	2	596	33	7	0	1791
2005	108	5	366	15	560	24	1008	42	79	3	243	10	11	0	2376
2006	257	4	679	10	2455	35	1426	20	696	10	1229	18	232	3	6974
2007	241	2	1526	11	5128	37	3142	23	333	2	1275	9	2146	16	13791
2008	397	4	1603	17	4713	50	1513	16	78	1	343	4	694	7	9341
2009	140	4	605	16	1462	39	625	17	54	1	483	13	383	10	3754
CAGR	15%		26%		43%		−1%		15%		−4%		123%		16%
2010	309	4	2263	28	3863	48	677	8	221	3	230	3	445	6	8007
2011	512	5	3153	31	2645	26	2688	27	253	3	355	4	437	4	10042
2012	484	5	1780	19	2407	26	2395	26	4	0	1921	21	288	3	9279
2013	359	5	1682	22	2410	32	780	10	31	0	2122	28	151	2	7534
2014	446	4	3267	30	5469	51	708	7	16	0	694	6	175	2	10775
2015	1325	8	4259	26	6179	38	1413	9	0	0	3138	19	132	1	16445
2016	846	6	4150	28	4689	32	814	6	0	0	3937	27	132	1	14568
CAGR	18%		11%		3%		3%		−48%		61%		−18%		10%
Total	**6110**		**26205**		**42556**		**18550**		**2264**		**16758**		**5411**		**117854**
CAGR	**25%**		**23%**		**36%**		**26%**		**9%**		**31%**		**12%**		**29%**

Source Venture Intelligence India, Database

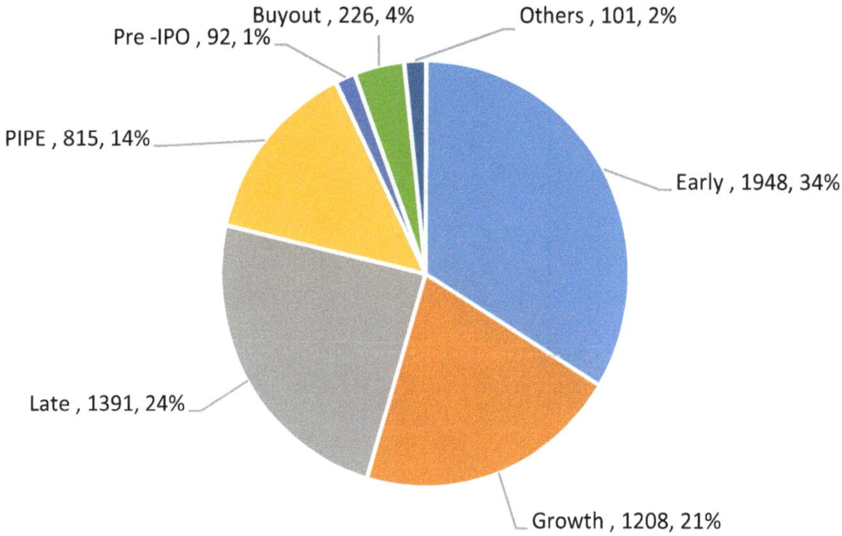

Fig. 11 Stage-wise VCPE investments in no. of deals from 1998 to 2016. *Source* Compiled from Table 5

12 From 1998 to 2003

Figure 12 shows the trends of stage-wise distribution of VCPE investments in value, and Fig. 13 shows the trends of stage-wise distribution of VCPE investments as a percentage of annual investments for the period from 1998 to 2003. It can be seen that about 50–70% of the investments were made in early- and growth-stage companies till year 2000. In the year 2001, we can observe a huge shift of the investments happening in Pre-IPO stage (56%) and PIPE (21%) probably because of the IT boom which led many companies who received early funding during 1998–2000 to reach the Pre-IPO stage and were ready for an IPO. The years 2002 and 2003 felt the impact of burst of IT bubble where funding to early- and growth-stage companies still continued though with reduced percentage (from 50 to 30%) and funding to late-stage investments along with PIPE investments started getting substantial as the investors became risk averse and started investing more in less risky, late-stage and public companies (40–50%). This was the turning point when we observed the shift of funding from early- and growth-stage companies to late-stage companies.

13 From 2004 to 2009

Figure 14 shows the trends of stage-wise distribution of VCPE investments in value, and Fig. 15 shows the trends of stage-wise distribution of VCPE investments as a

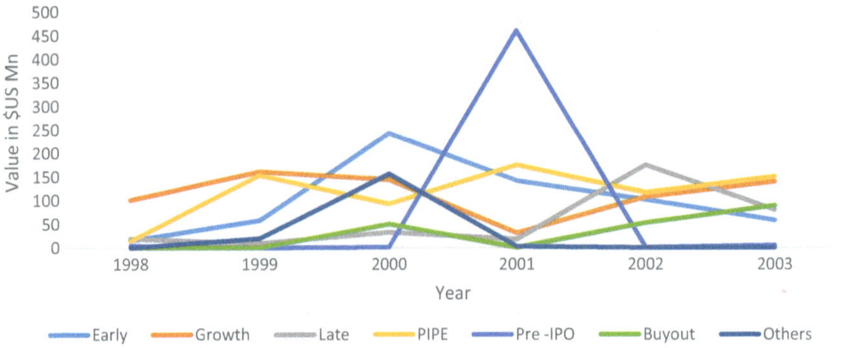

Fig. 12 Stage-wise VCPE investments (in Value US$ Mn) from 1998 to 2003. *Source* Compiled from Table 6

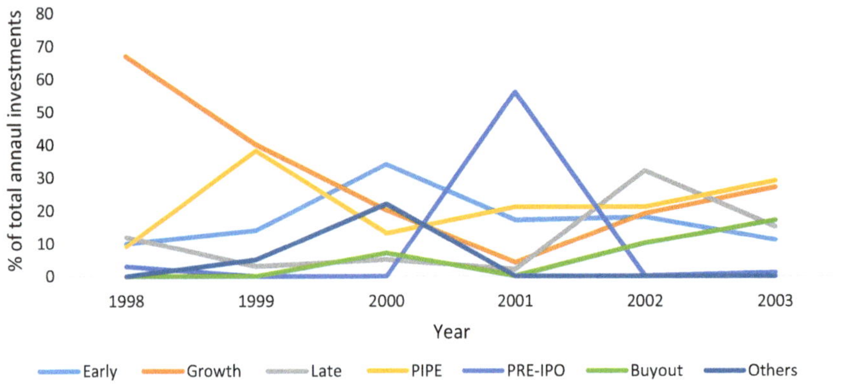

Fig. 13 Year-wise–stage-wise percentage of total annual VCPE investments from 1998 to 2003. *Source* Compiled from Table 6

percentage of annual investments for the period from 2004 to 2009. We can see that the proportion of early- and growth-stage funding has undergone substantial reduction from the range of 50 to 60% in 1998–2003 to 20–30% in 2004–2009. On the other hand, the proportion of funding in late-stage companies increased from the range of 5 to 10% in 1998–2003 to 20–50% in 2004–2009. It can also be said that late-stage investments are most preferred in the period of economic downturn with investors looking for more stable and established businesses to invest as is evident from the fact that more than 50% investments in 2008 are late-stage investments.

Similarly VCPE investments in PIPE, Pre-IPO, Buyout and Others category started getting funding consistently as compared to the earlier time period (1998–2003).

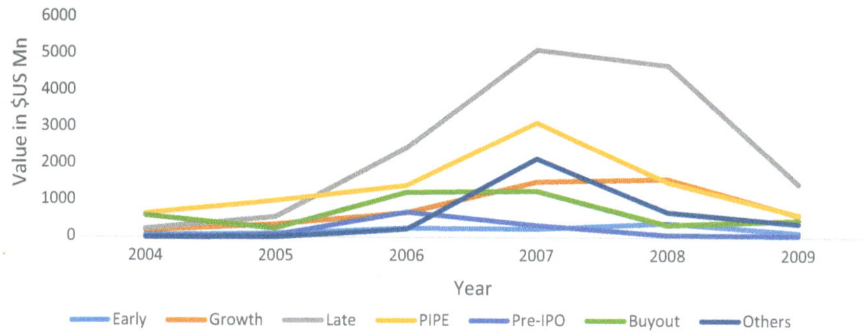

Fig. 14 Stage-wise VCPE investments (in Value US$ Mn) from 2004 to 2009. *Source* Compiled from Table 6

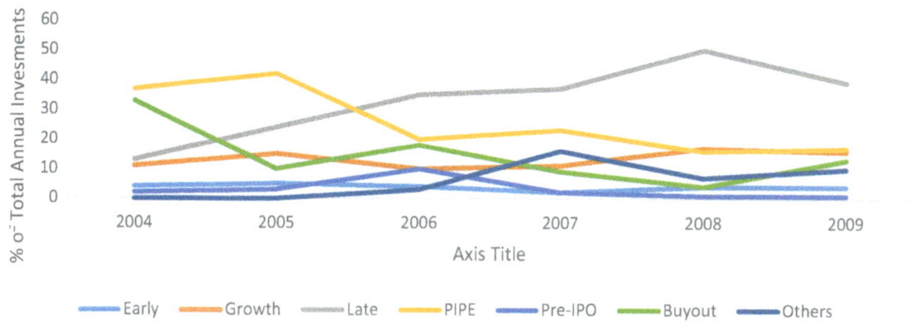

Fig. 15 Year-wise–stage-wise percentage of total annual VCPE investments from 2004 to 2009. *Source* Compiled from Table 6

14 From 2010 to 2016

Figure 16 shows the trends of stage-wise distribution of VCPE investments in value, and Fig. 17 shows the trends of stage-wise distribution of VCPE investments as a percentage of annual investments for the period from 2010 to 2016. Post the impact of global financial crisis in 2009, the macroeconomic conditions started improving in the country and therefore investors started gaining more confidence which was reflected in the increase in investments in growth stage companies (16–28%) and late-stage companies (39–48%) from 2009 to 2010. Funding in late-stage companies still continued to receive maximum attention as the curve stands above all the other stages. Early-stage funding almost remained stagnant with some revival seen in 2015 and 2016. It is desirable that there are more number of companies getting early stage of funding, since it will create a pipeline for the subsequent growth- and late-stage funding (IVCA Report 2015).

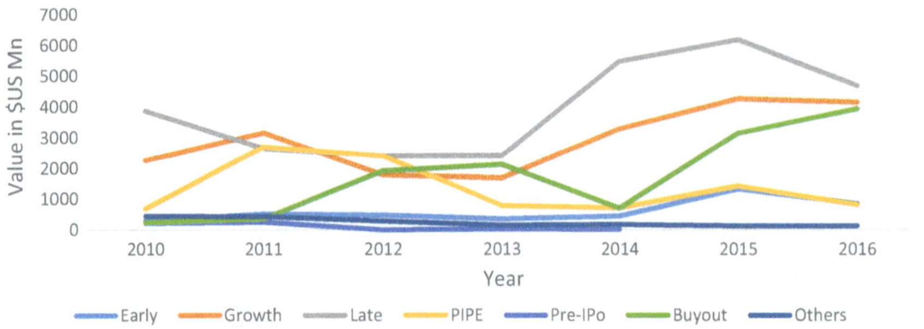

Fig. 16 Stage-wise VCPE investments (in Value US$ Mn) from 2010 to 2016. *Source* Compiled from Table 6

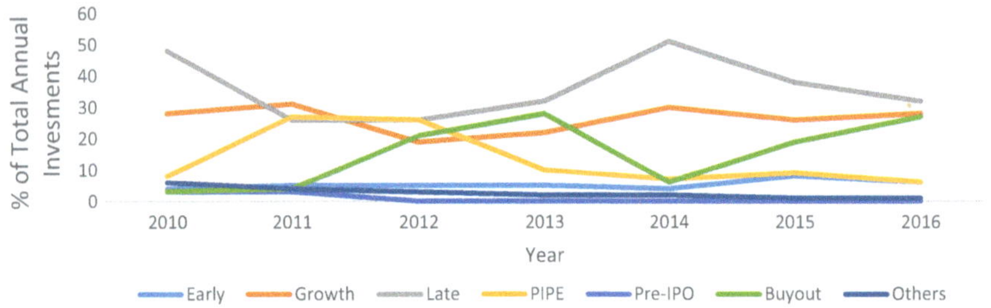

Fig. 17 Year-wise—stage-wise percentage of total annual VCPE investments from 2010 to 2016. *Source* Compiled from Table 6

15 Analysis of CAGR of VCPE Investments Stage Wise

Table 7 gives a glance of the CAGR of VCPE Investments in various stages of funding over period from 1998 to 2016 and also as divided for analysis discussed above between the sub-periods (1998–2003, 2004–2009 and 2010–2016).

The following observations are made from the Fig. 18:

1. Early-stage funding shows an overall CAGR of 25% but as discussed in the period-wise analysis above, we can see that it had a higher CAGR of 31% from 1998 to 2003 which reduced to 15% from 2004 to 2009 due to substantial decrease

Table 7 Stage-wise CAGR and Sub-period-wise CAGR of VCPE Investments (in Value US$ Mn)

Year	Early (%)	Growth (%)	Late (%)	PIPE (%)	Pre–IPO (%)	Buyout (%)	Others (%)	Total (%)
1998–2003	31	7	33	61	5	21	−61	28
2004–2009	15	26	43	−1	15	−4	123	16
2010–2016	18	11	3	3	−48	61	−18	10
1998–2016	**25**	**23**	**36**	**26**	**9**	**31**	**12**	**29**

Source Compiled from Table 6

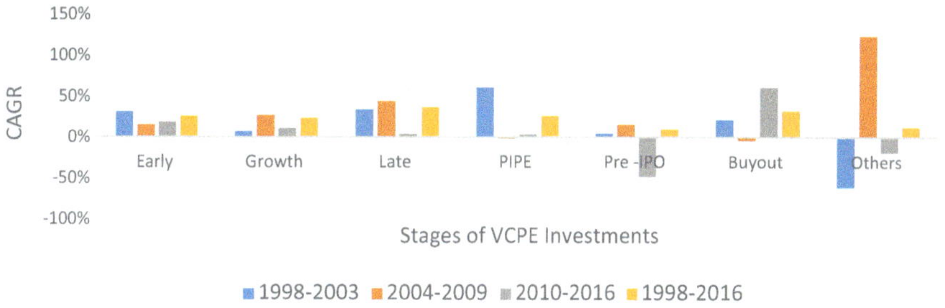

Fig. 18 Stage-wise CAGR and sub-period-wise CAGR of VCPE investments (in Value US$ Mn). *Source* Compiled from Table 6

in early-stage funding owing to the effects of Dotcom bubble and global financial crisis and investors becoming risk averse. The CAGR picked up to 18% during 2010–2016 due to favourable macroeconomic conditions in the country and various Government initiatives to encourage start-ups and early-stage funding.

2. Growth-stage funding made a slow start with a CAGR of 7% from 1998 to 2003 but increased substantially during 2004–2009 when the CAGR was 26%. This was reflected because of the shift of risk-averse investors from early-stage funding to growth-stage companies in times of unfavourable economic situations. But the CAGR further drops to 11% from 2010 to 2016 and consequently reflects an overall CAGR of 23% from 1998 to 2016.
3. Late-stage funding shows an interesting picture as it had a CAGR of 33% from 1998 to 2003 which increased to 43% during 2004–2009. This reflects that, late-stage funding was always preferred by investors though, initially, till 2001 before any crisis could affect, late-stage funding was very insignificant and increased substantially only from 2002, thereby increasing the CAGR. From 2010 to 2016, the CAGR is only 3%, though it has the highest overall CAGR of 36% which again reflects a stable growth in the late-stage funding.
4. PIPE deals funding had the highest CAGR of 61% from 1998 to 2003 though it reduced to −1% during 2004–2009 majorly because of the impact of the global financial crisis. CAGR increased to 3% during 2010–2016 representing the revival of the investors' confidence in the economy and on an average showing an overall CAGR of 26% over the 19-year period.
5. Pre-IPO funding had an increase in its CAGR from 5% (1998–2003) to 15% (2004–2009) representing enough momentum in the listed companies before the global financial crisis. This however reduced to a CAGR of −48% due to negligible Pre-IPO funding in the past five years.
6. Buyout deals funding though was not very common in India had a reasonable CAGR of 21% from 1998 to 2003 due to some large buyouts in 2000, 2002 and 2003 but later reduced to −4% during 2004–2009. It picked up significantly in the six years period with a CAGR of 61% during 2010–2016 showing the

confidence of the promoters to have received substantial returns on parting away with their controlling stakes. This stage shows an overall CAGR of 31% over the 19-year period.

16 Conclusion

Originally venture capital firms evolved in India to fill the gap in traditional financing available for funding the small enterprises based on innovation and technology and have come a long way in shaping the economic growth in the country.

The analysis of trends of VCPE investments over two-decade period (1998–2016) has witnessed significant ups and downs through the impact of various factors like global events including IT boom, Dotcom bubble, Global Financial Crisis and Brexit, macroeconomic indicators of the country like GDP growth, FDI inflow, inflation, interest rates and stock market movements, as well as the changes in the regulatory and political framework through favourable tax policies and exit environments for the investors and Government initiatives to encourage entrepreneurship.

The empirical analysis confirms that another significant factor which has impacted the variations in the VCPE investments which are the number of deals made by the venture capital firms in various industries. Bain analysis reports that every percentage point of GDP growth will need close to $30 billion of additional capital and with the current pace of financing available through other sources, VCPE investments will have to double in order to fund the country's growth. Thus, creating an enabling environment will increase the number of VCPE deals which will increase the number of VCPE investments and help the Indian business to flourish in the long term.

While analysing the inflow of VCPE investments in various industries of the economy, it was observed that VCPE investments in India have clearly shown concentration in technology-based industries like IT and ITES, BFSI, Telecom and consumer-based industries like Manufacturing and Engineering, with emerging trends reflected in the Healthcare industry also.

Similar trends are observed globally as evidenced in the literature which shows that these industries are strong attractors of VCPE investments providing scalable returns to the investors. Hence, with effective and proactive Government policies like allowance of FDI in various sectors of the economy more VCPE investments can be attracted in those sectors, thereby leading to the overall economic growth of the country.

Analysis of VCPE investments across various stages of financing show that Indian VCPE industry is dominated by Growth, Late, Buyout and PIPE deals as against Early and Seed Stage funding. Various factors have attributed to this trend of investing such as (i) lack of deals during events like Dotcom bubble, Global financial crisis and Brexit, (ii) less risk and possibility of quick returns by investing in later stages and (iii) higher costs associated with monitoring and hands on help in early-stage companies. This gap has created opportunities for angel investors and incubators to provide funding in early and seed stages of funding.

Thus, though VCPE industry in India has adapted to the growth environment which is principally led by domestic consumption it would still largely be affected by overall health of the global economy and the investment climate.

References

Amit, R., Brander, J., & Zott, C. (1998). Why do venture capital firms exist? Theory and Canadian evidence. *Journal of Business Venturing, 13*(6), 441–466.

Bowonder, B., & Mani, S. (2002). Venture capital and innovation: the Indian experience. *Financial Systems, Corporate Investment In Innovation, and Venture Capital*, 197.

Deloitte Report. (2012). *Private equity fuelling India's growth.*

Deloitte Report. (2014). *The build–up to another PE wave.*

Florida, R., & Smith, D. F. (1993). Venture capital formation, investment, and regional industrialization. *Annals of the Association of American Geographers, 83*(3), 434–451.

Gompers, P. A. (1994). The rise and fall of venture capital. *Business and Economic History*, 1–26.

Gompers, P., Lerner, J., Blair, M., & Hellmann, T. (1998). *What drives venture capital fundraising*?

http://www.livemint.com/Companies/09NBH9euHoJwfZqAe5sRnO/Private-equity-Growing-into-maturity.html.

IVCA Bain India Private Equity Report. (2009–2016).

Jain, R. K., & Manna, I. (2009). Evolution of global private equity market: lessons, implications and prospects for India. *Reserve Bank of India Occasional Papers, 30*(1), 103–162.

Komala, G. (2014, October). A paradigm shift in indian venture capital industry. *International Journal of Business and Management Research, IV*, (X), 281–86.

Komala, G., & Muninarayanappa, M. (2015). Does foreign and domestic venture capital firm differ? A comparative study in India. *International Journal of Recent Scientific Research, 6*(8), 5556–5560.

KPMG–Private Equity Review—A Review of the Indian Private Equity Sector and Developments. (2016).

Kumari, V. J. (2013). An analysis of trends of venture capital and private equity investments in India. *Indian Journal of Economics and Business, 12*(1), 73–81.

Naqi, S. A., & Hettihewa, S. (2007). Venture capital or private equity? The Asian experience. *Business Horizons, 50*(4), 335–344.

Price Water House Coopers, Global Private Equity Report. (2008).

Rajan Annamalai, T., & Deshmukh, A. (2011). Venture capital and private equity in India: an analysis of investments and exits. *Journal of Indian Business Research, 3*(1), 6–21.

Reddy, C. V. (2015). Venture capital financing by VCFs & FVCIs: A study with reference to sectoral financing in India. *JIMS8 M: The Journal of Indian Management & Strategy, 20*(3), 42–53.

Srinivas, K.T. (2013). A study on venture capitalist's funding in different sector of Karnataka. *Abhinav: International Monthly Refereed Journal of Research in Management & Technology, II*, 75–81.

Subhash, K. B. (2006). How to teach the big baby to walk: Case of the Indian venture capital industry. *Journal of Private Equity, 9*(4), Fall issue, 76–91.

Subhash, K. B., & Nair, T. G. (2004). Globalisation and Indian venture capital system. *Udyog Pragati, 28*(3), 1–14.

Tripathi, S. (2015). Trends and patterns in venture capital/private equity in India: A review. *IUP Journal of Management Research, 14*(2), 39–51.

Venture Intelligence India can be accessed at. http://www.ventureintelligence.com/.

Impact of Firms' Market Value on Capital Structure Decisions: Panel Data Evidence from Indian Manufacturing Firms

Dhananjaya Kadanda

Abstract India witnessed a significant development in stock market in the post-1990s due to series of reform measures. As a result, firms are able to raise market-based capital which helped them to reduce their dependence on institution-based finance. Consequently, market valuation of the firm has become an important variable in corporate finance decisions. However, traditional theories of capital structure fail to offer unambiguous explanation on the impact of market value on capital structure. To bridge this lacuna in capital structure literature, Baker and Wrugler (J Financ 57(1):1–32 2002) propounded market timing theory which argues that firms' time the market, that is, firms raise equity capital when market valuation is high and buy back when market valuation is lower and hence the current capital structure of the firm is the cumulative result of past attempts to time the equity market. This study attempted to understand the role of market value in influencing the capital structure decisions of the manufacturing firms in India. The study found that market value negatively influences the debt ratio both in short term and in long term, indicating the practice of market timing. Further, the study also shows that the negative impact does indeed come from changes equity issues rather than changes retained earnings or debt retirement.

Keywords Capital structure · Market valuation · Market timing

JEL Classification G3

D. Kadanda (✉)
St. Aloysius Institute of Management and Information Technology, St. Aloysius College (Autonomous), Kotekar, Mangalore 575022, Karnataka, India
e-mail: dhananjayak@isec.ac.in; dhananjayaimit@gmail.com

N. R. Bhanumurthy et al. (eds.), *Advances in Finance & Applied Economics*,
https://doi.org/10.1007/978-981-13-1696-8_15

1 Introduction

Over the last two decades stock market in India has witnessed tremendous growth due to the series of capital market reforms initiated in the early 1990s. As a result, stock market has emerged as an important alternative source of finance for corporate which helped to diffuse excessive burden on banking system (RBI 2015). Traditional theories seem to have overlooked the role of stock market in influencing firms' capital structure. For instance, in the irrelevance theory of Modigliani and Miller (1958), there is no gain from shifting between debt and equity as in efficient capital markets costs of these sources of finance do not change independently. Trade-off theory argues that the capital structure is primarily determined by the cost and benefits of debt financing; hence, temporal fluctuations in the market value of the firm should have only temporary or short-term effect on capital structure. Similarly, agency theory maintains that debt financing involves agency cost and tax benefits and optimum capital structure balances these two elements of debt financing. On the other hand, pecking order hypothesis states that information asymmetry in the capital market determines the source of finance for the firm. Firm facing least information asymmetry problem would be dependent more on external finance, and internal capital would be the major source of finance for firms facing information asymmetry. However, as argued by Demirguc-Kunt and Maksmovic (1996), optimum capital structure may not be possible in the absence of well-functioning equity market which implies that stock market is an important determinant of capital structure. However, they argue that the impact of stock market on capital structure of the firm is not unambiguous. Sudden access to well-developed stock market may result in substitution of outside equity for outside debt in the case of firms that are previously constrained to issue only outside debt resulting in decrease in firms' debt/equity ratio; substitute outside equity for inside equity in which case debt/equity ratio will not be affected; or firms may find expansion more attractive as well-functioning stock market enhances entrepreneur's ability to diversify risks and impact of this on debt/equity ratio depends on how the expansion is financed. In this connection, Baker and Wurgler (2002) expounded market timing hypothesis which argues that a firms' capital structure is the result of past market timing. Firms issue more equity when market value is high and buy back when they experience low market value. Hence, market timing theory establishes direct connection between firms' market value and its capital structure decisions. With this background, the paper attempts to empirically examine the impact of firms' market value on the capital structure decisions in Indian manufacturing firms.

The remainder of the paper is structured as follows. In Sect. 2, we briefly review the theoretical and empirical literature on capital structure decisions. In Sect. 3 we discuss composition of the capital structure of sample firms. Section 4 focuses on source of data and methodology used in the paper. Section 5 presents the results of the analysis and findings, and Sect. 6 contains conclusion.

2 Determinants of Capital Structure: Theory and Evidence

Modigliani–Miller irrelevance theorem kick started the debate on the issue of capital structure. Modigliani and Miller (1958) claimed that the value of the firm depends on the marginal productivity and cost of the capital and source of capital is irrelevant to the value of the firm which came to be known as Modigliani and Miller irrelevance theorem. According to Modigliani and Miller (1958) in a world of perfect capital market and no tax, firms' investment depends on the return on investment and cost of capital. Investment opportunity will be pursued if and only if the return on investment is equal or more than marginal cost of capital. This implies that marginal cost capital is the cutoff point for the investment and the kind of instruments used to finance the investment is irrelevant. However, unrealistic assumptions of perfect capital market, no taxes and no bankruptcy costs of debt financing of Modigliani and Miller (1958) irrelevance theorem came under severe criticisms. In response to this, Modigliani and Miller (1963) acknowledged the tax benefits involved in debt financing. They maintained that firms' value would be influenced by the benefits conferred by the debt financing through the tax deductibility of the interest payments. Due to this, firms may be motivated to rely completely on debt financing as it provides tax shield. But Miller (1977) pointed out that tax advantage conferred by debt financing would be offset by the disadvantages of personal tax, and hence irrelevance theorem would hold good even in the presence of tax. Further, Miller (1977) presumed that debt financing does not have any bankruptcy costs and, hence, riskless. Therefore, according to Modigliani and Miller (1963) there is motivation for higher leverage due to the tax advantage and absence of bankruptcy costs of debt financing. However, Baxter (1967) recognized the bankruptcy cost of debt financing. He pointed out that high leverage would increase the bankruptcy costs emanating from the probability of default. This would increase the riskiness of the earning and the consequent cost of capital to the firm. Jensen and Mackling (1976) argued that debt financing also involves agency cost. According to them, financing through debt capital will motivate shareholders (agents) to invest in risky projects. If the project generates high return, shareholders will take away most of this return, and if it fails, creditors will have to bear the cost as shareholders have limited liability.

Based on the tax benefit and bankruptcy cost of debt financing, DeAngelo and Masulis (1980) developed static trade-off theory which argues that the tax benefits offered by debt financing is offset by increased bankruptcy costs of debt financing. Trade-off theory proposes that the firm will have a target capital structure which balances between the benefits and costs associated with the debt financing. However, Hovakimian et al. (2001) expounded dynamic trade-off theory wherein they argued that the optimum target capital structure is not static. It deviates as firms' conditions change from time to time. Jalal (2007) claims that actual leverage ratio varies around the target within an acceptable range in response to the changes in the firm conditions.

On the other hand, Myers (1984) proposed pecking order theory which argues that due to the problem of information asymmetry in capital market, firms follow pecking order in their financing decisions. According to Myers and Majluf (1984) inside managers possess more information about the true value of the firm than outside managers. Because of this outside investors face adverse selection problem in their investment decisions. This may result in mispricing of the equity by the market leading to higher cost of capital. They argue that the problem of information asymmetry and resultant friction in the capital market is more in equity market as compared to debt market leading to varying cost of capital for the firm. In response to this problem, firms will follow pecking order in their financing decisions, that is, they would prefer to finance all their projects through internal capital, if possible, and if sufficient internal capital is not available, they will prefer debt capital to equity capital. Hence, equity capital is the least preferred capital in the presence of information asymmetry in the capital market. The theory clearly implies that the underdevelopment of the capital market will seriously limit the financing options available to the firms which will adversely affect corporate investment. Conversely, it argues that as capital market develops the problem information asymmetry and resulting adverse selection problem reduces and firms will be able to finance their projects from capital market.

However, none of the above theories unambiguously explains the role of market value of the firm in capital structure decisions. For instance, though modified version of trade-off theory recognizes importance of market value in capital structure decisions, it argues that market value results in only short-term deviation from target capital and these deviations quickly reverse to target capital structure (Alti 2006). On the other hand, market value reflects the growth opportunities of the firm under pecking order hypothesis. However, Myres and Majluf (1984) argues that firm with growth opportunities will not issue the equity immediately and will wait till information asymmetry reduces in order to avoid issuing at an average and unfavorable price that reflects the fact that lower-quality firms also issue. As a result, firms may have to find interim source of finance until they can issue equity. Therefore, market value may actually increase the debt capacity of the firm as adverse selection problem is less in the case of debt financing than equity. Secondly, firms may not issue equity even if they experience higher market value, if there is no need for immediate proceeds. Hence, the impact of market value on capital structure is not unambiguous under pecking order hypothesis. To address this lacuna in finance literature, Baker and Wurgler (2002) proposed market timing theory that directly links stock market and capital structure. According to them, equity market timing denotes the practice of raising equity capital at high price and repurchasing shares at low price with the objective to exploit the fluctuations in the cost of equity capital. Baker and Wurgler (2002) argue that firms are likely to issue equity rather than debt when the market value is high and tend to repurchase equity when market value is low. Hence, market timing theory argues that the current capital structure of the firm is the result of past attempts to time the market depending on the market value of the firm. The theory also implies that the financing decision is influenced by the conditions in the stock market. Baker and Wurgler (2002) documented strong negative relationship between past market valuations, measured by market-to-book value, and leverage ratio. Whereas trade-off theory argues that temporary fluctuations in market-to-book value will have temporary effects, Baker and Wurgler (2002) showed that market-to-book value will have long-term impact on the capital structure of the firm. They further demonstrated that market timing leads to permanent change in the cash balance of the firms, which indicates that firms issue equity when market value is high even if there is no need for proceeds. Therefore, according to Baker and Wurgler (2002), the natural explanation for the negative and persistent effect of market value on capital structure is market timing.

Diverse theoretical arguments ignited to extensive empirical research on the determinants of capital structure. Most of the studies focused on firm-specific determinants of capital structure such as asset tangibility, size, financial distress costs, profitability, growth rate, tax rates, non-debt tax shields, interest coverage, liquidity (Harris and Raviv 1991; Fama and French 2000; Frank and Goyal 2003, 2009; Ali Ahmed and Hisham 2009; Tong and Green 2005; Daskalakis and Psillaki 2008).

Few studies also examined the link between stock market and corporate structure. For instance, in a cross-country study, Demirguc-Kunt and Maksmovic (1996) examined the role of stock market development on debt/equity ratio at aggregate level. Using an index of stock market development consisting of stock market size, and liquidity, they found that during the initial stage of stock market development debt/equity ratio increases as both debt and equity capital increases and later equity capital substitutes debt capital resulting in lower debt/equity ratio. Following market timing theory of Baker and Wurgler (2002), few studies also examined the role market value of the firm on debt/equity ratio. For example, Chen and Zhao (2006) detected inverse relationship between market-to-book ratio and debt/equity ratio which indicates that stock market development will increase equity capital. Similarly, Rajan and Zingales (1995), Korajczk et al. (1991), Jung et al. (1996), Welch (2004) and Huang and Ritter (2009) recorded negative relationship between debt/equity ratio and market-to-book ratio which supports the predictions of market timing theory. Complement to these findings, Graham and Harvey (2001) showed that 67% of the Chief Finance Officers (CFOs) indicated that they time the market when issuing the equity. Similarly, Brav et al. (2005) report that 86% of the CFOs said that undervaluation of the stock is the major reason for stock buyback. However, Rajan and Zingales (1995) argued that higher market-to-book value may also reflect the growth opportunities of the firm in which case one may find positive relationship with debt/equity ratio. Therefore, Chen and Zhao (2006) urged that more empirical investigation is required to clearly understand the relationship between leverage and market-to-book value in corporate financing. The main focus of this study is to find out the link between market value and capital structure. The study also includes Rajan and Zingales (1995)'s asset tangibility, firm size and profitability, and Fama and French (2000)'s depreciation as control variables in the leverage regression.

Rajan and Zingales (1995) argue that higher portion of tangible assets act as collateral which minimizes the agency cost involved in debt financing. Scott (1977) and Myers (1977) contend that large amount of tangible asset may also help the firm to reduce interest cost of debt financing. Therefore, firms with higher tangible assets will have higher debt capacity and it is expected to positively influence the debt/equity ratio. Empirically, Titman and Wessels (1988), Rajan and Zingales (1995), Espinosa et al. (2012), Bhaduri (2002a,b), Khasnobis and Bhaduri (2002),

Bole and Mahakud (2004) and Mahakud (2006) documented positive relationship between asset tangibility and long-term indebtedness. On the contrary, few studies also found negative relationship between asset tangibility and debt to equity (Hall et al. 2004; Sogorb-Mira 2005). Two possible explanations may justify this result. Firstly, higher tangible assets may help in reducing information asymmetry problem in the equity market enabling the firm to raise equity capital. Secondly, the firm with large fixed assets may already have generated enough internal capital for financing new projects which reduces its dependency on external capital, particularly, debt capital. However, Berger and Udell (2005) claimed that asset structure may not be important for a firm which maintains close relationship with lenders which serves as a substitute for physical collateral.

Firm size is another important variable which is found to be influencing capital structure. It has been argued that the probability of financial distress may be less in large firm (Titman and Wessels 1988; Rajan and Zingales 1995; Bhabra et al. 2008). In this regard, Warner (1977) showed that the bankruptcy cost is the negative function of firm's size. Psillaki and Daskalakis (2009) argue that large firms will be in a position to minimize transaction cost and agency cost involved in debt financing. However, Rajan and Zingales (1995) added that relationship between leverage and size is ambiguous. They argued that there may be inverse relationship between the two as large firms may be able to raise more equity capital due to lesser information asymmetry problem. Empirically, most of the studies documented positive relationship between leverage and size (Barton et al. 1989; Rajan and Zingales 1995; Psillaki and Daskalakis 2009; Espinosa et al. 2012; Bole and Mahakud 2004; Mujumdar 2014; Mohamad 1995).

Extant literature also shows that profitability is another major determinant of capital structure. Theoretically, there are divergent views on the role of profitability in influencing leverage. According to pecking order hypothesis there is inverse relationship between profitability and leverage as profitable firms will be able generate more internal capital and hence reliance on external capital diminishes (Harris and Raviv 1991; Rajan and Zingales 1995; Booth et al. 2001). On the contrary, trade-off theory postulates opposite prediction (Jensen and Meckling 1976; Myers 1977; Harris and Raviv 1990). Debt financing offers tax advantages to the firms, and this is more so in the case of highly profitable firms which may induce these firms to go for more debt. On the other hand, creditors will be more willing to lend to a profitable firm. Empirically, several studies recorded negative relationship between leverage and profitability which is in consistent with the prediction of pecking order hypothesis (Harris and Raviv 1991; Rajan and Zingales 1995; Booth et al. 2001; Gaud et al. 2005; Ozkan 2001; Van der Wijst and Thurik 1993; Hall et al. 2004; Strebulaev 2007; Um 2001). On the other hand, Espinosa et al. (2012) found positive relationship which may support trade-off theory. Depreciation is also included in the leverage regression as another control variable. Trade-off theory highlights the tax advantages conferred by debt financing, postulated positive relationship between tax rate and leverage ratio. Alternatively, firms can also save tax through depreciation charges. In such case, depreciation acts as non-debt tax shield and hence negative relationship between depreciation and leverage may be expected (Chauhan 2015).

3 Capital Structure—Some Stylized Facts

Table 1 presents the composition of stockholders' equity. As evident from the table, reserves and funds are the major component of stockholders equity of which retained earning accounts for about 78%. This shows that internal capital continues to be the major source of finance for firms in India. High share of cumulative retained profit may also be due to stock market development and resulting capital gain for the shareholders as investors may be willing to accept lower dividends with higher capital gains. Hence, one could argue that development stock market, on the one hand, will help the firms to raise equity capital from the market; on the other hand, it would also help them build internal capital through retained earnings. This will help the firm to reduce the dependence on external finance and the risk associated with external finance, particularly, the debt finance.

Table 2 presents the composition of long-term borrowing. It is clear from the table that bank borrowing is the major source of debt for sample firms. The share of long-term borrowing from banks has steadily increased over the period of time. This shows that Indian financial system is still a bank-dominated one as far as financing the corporate sector is concerned. Secondly, the table shows that long-term capital raised through bonds and debentures accounts for only 15.9% in 2015–2016. This demonstrates that the corporate bond market in India is playing limited role in corporate financing. Clearly, there is excessive pressure on the banking sector as far as the corporate financing is concerned. As a result, there is disproportionate risk concentration in one part of the financial system. Concentration of credit and the consequent risk is a serious threat to the financial soundness of the banks with the potential to create systemic crisis, particularly, during the downturn of the business cycle. Unprecedented increase in bad loans in Indian public sector banks in the past few years is clear indication of the problem of concentration of risk.

Table 1 Composition of stockholders' equity

	2010–2011	2011–2012	2012–2013	2013–2014	2014–2015	2015–2016
	%	%	%	%	%	%
Stock holders' equity						
Paid-up equity capital	5.16	4.79	4.64	4.36	4.19	3.99
Paid-up preference capital	0.38	0.35	0.30	0.30	0.41	0.30
Capital contribution and funds by govt, others	0.00	0.21	0.19	0.17	0.16	0.15
Money received against convertible share warrants	0.13	0.08	0.09	0.03	0.03	0.02
Forfeited equity capital	0.01	0.01	0.01	0.01	0.01	0.00
Reserves and funds	94.09	94.48	94.68	95.11	95.03	95.26
Of which retained profit	76.97	75.34	77.61	79.05	78.88	78.78
Share application money and suspense account	0.23	0.08	0.10	0.03	0.19	0.07

Source Compiled from CMIE Prowess database

Table 2 Composition of long-term borrowings (in percent)

	2010–2011	2011–2012	2012–2013	2013–2014	2014–2015	2015–2016
Long-term borrowing from banks	42.67	47.36	48.17	49.17	51.39	53.92
Long-term borrowing from financial institutions	1.51	1.30	1.44	1.30	1.19	1.45
Long-term borrowings from central and state govt	2.22	1.86	1.31	0.98	1.00	1.10
Long-term borrowings syndicated across banks and inst.	0.00	0.00	0.01	0.02	0.01	0.01
Long-term debentures and bonds	15.48	14.32	14.21	12.53	14.47	15.59
Long-term foreign currency borrowings	17.46	22.86	21.98	24.42	22.70	22.30
Long-term loans from promoters, directors and shareholders	0.04	0.03	0.04	0.06	0.07	0.07
Long-term intercorporate loans	0.87	1.87	1.81	1.87	1.80	1.64
Long-term deferred credit	1.89	2.18	1.64	1.18	1.05	1.04
Long-term maturities of finance lease obligations	0.15	0.15	0.12	0.66	0.70	0.71
Long-term fixed deposits	1.17	1.08	0.93	0.76	0.35	0.19
Other long-term borrowings	1.95	1.73	1.43	1.18	1.09	1.12
Current portion of long-term borrowings	13.15	18.93	15.49	12.95	13.22	16.95
Interest accrued and due (long term) on borrowings	0.01	0.03	0.01	0.01	0.01	0.01

Source Compiled from CMIE Prowess database

Another important observation from Table 2 is that the share of foreign currency borrowing in the long-term borrowing has increased from 17.6% in 2010–2011 to 22.30% in 2015–2016. An increased foreign currency borrowing is dangerous in the event of large currency depreciation. Patnaik et al. (2016) pointed out that unhedged foreign currency borrowing is a concern in emerging market where exchange rate is not fully floating. They also observed that in an emerging market with managed floating exchange rate regime firms may choose to have unhedged foreign currency borrowing because firms expect central bank to intervene when faced with large depreciations. However, short-term foreign currency borrowing has decreased significantly from 29.31% in 2010–2011 to 13.99 in 2015–2016 as evident from Table 3. This is a welcome trend as high short-term foreign currency borrowing may put pressure on the current account, thereby widening the deficit.

Another important feature of corporate debt is the dominance of secured borrowing which has steadily increased over the period as evident from Table 4. This implies that asset-based lending approach dominates in banks and financial institutions. In this regard, Reddy (2004) questioned the practice of asset-based lending, particu-

Table 3 Composition of short-term borrowings (in percent)

	2010–2011	2011–2012	2012–2013	2013–2014	2014–2015	2015–2016
Short-term borrowing from banks	60.14	52.74	53.62	62.028	66.39	63.50
Short-term borrowing from financial institutions	0.16	0.20	0.11	0.184	0.36	0.25
Short-term borrowings from central and state govt	0.00	0.00	0.00	0.000	0.00	0.00
Short-term borrowings syndicated across banks and institutions	0.00	0.00	0.00	0.006	0.01	0.01
Short-term debentures and bonds	0.37	0.07	0.01	0.000	0.17	0.00
Short-term foreign currency borrowings	29.31	31.70	32.59	24.585	15.53	13.99
Short-term loans from promoters, directors and shareholders	0.06	0.06	0.06	0.095	0.08	0.11
Short-term intercorporate loans	2.91	3.28	2.41	1.833	2.87	3.11
Short-term deferred credit	2.37	5.74	5.63	5.533	6.40	6.83
Short-term fixed deposits	0.15	0.13	0.13	0.091	0.07	0.09
Short-term commercial papers	2.68	4.67	4.29	4.245	6.26	10.36
Other short-term borrowings	1.85	1.42	1.14	1.401	1.86	1.77
Interest accrued and due on borrowings	0.31	0.39	0.47	0.641	1.32	2.50

Source Compiled from CMIE Prowess database

larly, in an era where technology and other intangible assets are more important than material components of the firm. This is more so in the case of service sector where intangible components such as technology, software, human capital and brand are more valuable than tangible assets. One argument for collateral-based lending is that it reduces the problem of NPAs. But as argued by Reddy (2004), in microfinance, with no collaterals and high interest rates, the level of NPAs is very low.[1] Clearly, there is a need for income-based lending where the lending is based on a firm's ability to generate income rather than stock of collateral assets.

Table 5 presents the frequency of firms in terms of debt/equity ratio. About 64% of the firms are sound in terms of leverage. Around five percent of the firms are overleveraged with debt/equity ratio more than 5. Though there are few firms with high debt/equity ratio, their share in total debt is very high. For example, top twenty highly indebted firms accounted for 63.18% of the total bank borrowings of the sample firms in 2015–2016 (Table 7). This concentration of credit and the resulting concentration of NPA are major problems in India banking sector, particularly, among the public sector banks. For example, The Hindu (2016) reported that the amount

[1]For example, Bangalore-based leading microfinance institute Ujjivan Financial Services Pvt. Ltd reported gross NPA rate of just 0.28% in FY 2016–2017 as against 13.37% in public sector banks.

Table 4 Secured and unsecured borrowings

	2010–2011	2011–2012	2012–2013	2013–2014	2014–2015	2015–2016
	%	%	%	%	%	%
Secured borrowings	57.72	56.33	60.37	63.50	65.75	65.78
Unsecured borrowings	42.28	55.86	39.63	36.50	34.25	34.22
Secured long run	60.26	61.16	62.49	62.07	65.63	64.56
Secured short run	39.74	38.84	37.51	37.93	34.37	35.44
Unsecured long run	46.19	45.18	45.57	55.87	68.76	69.90
Unsecured short run	53.81	54.82	54.43	44.13	31.24	30.10

Source Compiled from CMIE Prowess database

of top twenty NPA accounts of PSBs stood at Rs. 1.54 lakh crores as of June 2016 which is about 28.52% of the total NPAs of PSBs in FY2016. State Bank of India, the largest bank in India, had NPA concentration ratio[2] of 27.36% in FY2016. RBI (2017) also found that large borrowers account for 56% of gross advances and 86.5% of GNPAs of SCBs in India. Table 6 presents the percentage distribution of firms in terms of interest coverage ratio. As evident from the table, the position has worsened over the period of time as the percentage of firms in distress has increased from about 13% in 2009–2010 to 21.10% in 2015–2016. Another 10 per of the firms have ICR in the range 0–1 which again indicates that they are very vulnerable. Further, 105 firms with negative interest coverage ratio accounted for about 30% of the total bank barrowings of the sample firms in 2015–2016. Table 7 shows the position of top twenty indebted firms which accounted for 63.18% of the total bank borrowings of the sample firms in 2015–2016. Majority of the firms reported negative profit, negative return on assets, lower current ratio, and interest cover ratio and higher debt/equity ratio which clearly points out the vulnerability of these firms. This has ramification for the banking sector in terms of rising bad debts given the fact that borrowing from the banks constitutes about 60% of the total corporate debt as shown in Tables 2 and 3. Clearly, it appears that corporate distress is one of the major reasons behind the increasing problem of bad loans in banking sector.

[2]Share of top four NPA accounts.

Table 5 Distribution of firms in terms of debt/equity ratio

Debt/equity ratio (times)	2009–2010	2010–2011	2011–2012	2012–2013	2013–2014	2014–2015	2015–2016
Equal or less than one	1035 (63)	1047 (62.77)	1036 (61.7)	1022 (60.65)	1026 (60.78)	1044 (62.62)	1051 (64.39)
More than one less or equal to 5	565 (34)	569 (34.11)	582 (34.66)	607 (36.02)	591 (35.01)	552 (33.11)	499 (30.57)
More than 5 less or equal to 10	36 (2)	28 (1.68)	33 (1.96)	36 (2.14)	47 (2.78)	43 (2.57)	38 (2.32)
More than 10	19 (1)	24 (1.44)	28 (1.66)	20 (1.19)	24 (1.42)	28 (1.67)	44 (2.69)

Source Compiled from CMIE Prowess database. Percentage in bracket

Table 6 Distribution of firms in terms of interest coverage ratio

	2009–2010	2010–2011	2011–2012	2012–2013	2013–2014	2014–2015	2015–2016
Less than 0	234 (12.97)	214 (11.73)	316 (17.27)	321 (17.64)	354 (19.50)	382 (21.50)	364 (21.10)
More than 0 less than or equal to 1	118 (6.54)	116 (6.36)	182 (9.95)	181 (9.95)	200 (11.01)	195 (10.97)	173 (10.02)
More than 1 less than or equal to 5	927 (51.38)	949 (52.05)	898 (49.09)	918 (50.46)	858 (47.27)	768 (43.24)	717 (41.56)
More than 5 less than or equal to 10	196 (10.86)	196 (10.75)	140 (7.65)	131 (7.20)	123 (6.77)	145 (8.16)	149 (8.63)
More than 10	329 (18.23)	348 (19.08)	293 (16.01)	268 (14.73)	280 (15.42)	286 (16.10)	322 (18.66)

Source Compiled from CMIE Prowess database. Percentage in bracket

4 Source of Data and Methodology

The study aims at examining the role of firm's market value on its capital structure decisions in the case of public limited manufacturing firms in India. To do this, the sample consists of firms for which the date of first trading (DFT) on BSE or NSE is available. CMIE Prowess gives the date of first trading in stock exchange and not IPO date. Therefore, the first trading date is considered instead of IPO as IPO could not be identified for all the firms. Studying firms from DFT helps us to understand the evolution of leverage from a given starting point, that is, DFT. Firms with DFT from 1995 through 2015 are included for the analysis. Data start from 1995 as stock market was largely underdeveloped prior to 1995. The data stop at March 2015 in order to get at least one year of data after DFT. The analysis is done in 3 subsamples DFT+1 year, DFT+5 year and DFT+10 year to understand both short-term and long-term impact market value on equity issues. The sample size is 605, 490 and 317 firms for DFT+1, DFT+5 and DFT+10, respectively. Sample size decreased as with the

Table 7 Top 20 indebted firms (as on March 2016)

Company name	Profit after tax (₹ crore)	Return on assets (%)	Current ratio(times)	Debt to equity ratio (times)	Interest cover (times)	Total bank borrowings (₹ crore)
Reliance Industries Ltd.	27384	6.23	0.66	0.42	10.53	67341
Bhushan Steel Ltd.	−2839.37	−5.3	0.77	9.92	−0.23	32555.68
Videocon Industries Ltd.	−55.81	−0.15	2.01	2.31	0.97	22304.06
Jaiprakash Associates Ltd.	−3239.9	−5.75	0.85	2	−0.02	21841.25
Jindal Steel & Power Ltd.	−1018.88	−2.29	0.46	2.27	0.38	18299.99
Hindalco Industries Ltd.	607.25	0.52	1.95	0.78	1.23	17644.1
Alok Industries Ltd.	−3722.8	−12.84	1.17	12.7	−1.21	16081.2
Vedanta Ltd.	5472.79	6.35	0.57	1.11	2.63	15889.84
J S W Steel Ltd.	−3529.67	−5.08	0.51	1.82	−0.68	10315.94
Electrosteel Steels Ltd.	−326.55	−2.55	0.24	23.27	0.7	9082.16
Bajaj Hindusthan Sugar Ltd.	−114.28	−0.91	1.1	3	0.86	6812.19
Bombay Rayon Fashions Ltd.	48.85	0.36	1.24	2.06	1.06	5355.27
Jyoti Structures Ltd.	−503.34	−9.04	0.94	50.46	0.09	4760.6
Century Textiles & Inds. Ltd.	−54.52	−1.1	0.61	2.63	0.77	4414.57
National Fertilizers Ltd.	197.09	1.12	1.15	1.28	1.52	4177.23
Jayaswal Neco Inds. Ltd.	−86.54	−0.86	0.74	1.96	0.89	3867.47
United Spirits Ltd.	981.16	5.22	0.91	1.5	2.47	3719.14
Kesoram Industries Ltd.	137.12	−8.8	1.1	16.81	0.07	3682.21
Piramal Enterprises Ltd.	1061.15	3.82	0.36	1.1	2.29	2870.05
Metalyst Forgings Ltd.	−270.21	−1.1	0.72	3.49	0.27	2768.95

Source Compiled from CMIE Prowess database

number of years either due to exit of the firms or due to non-availability complete data.

The study employs panel data technique for the analysis for DFT+5 and DFT+10 analysis and cross-sectional regression for DFT+1 analysis. In order to overcome the problem of heteroskedasticity and autocorrelation, heteroskedasticity and autocorrelation-corrected (robust) standard error is used. The model is specified as follows;

$$\left(\frac{D}{A}\right)_t - \left(\frac{D}{A}\right)_{t-1} = a + b\left(\frac{M}{B}\right)_{t-1} + c\left(\frac{FA}{A}\right)_{t-1} + d\left(\frac{EBITDA}{A}\right)_{t-1} + f\log(S)_{t-1} + g\left(\frac{D}{FA}\right)_{t-1} + \mu_t \quad (1)$$

Descriptions of these variables are provided in Table 8. All the dependent variables are lagged by one year as changes in leverage in response to these variables may happen in lags. This also overcomes the problem of reverse causality which may exist between dependent and independent variables.

Table 8 Description of variables

S. no	Variables	Definition	Notation in (1)
1.	Change in debt ratio	Change in ratio of total debt to total assets	$\left(\frac{D}{A}\right)_t - \left(\frac{D}{A}\right)_{t-1}$
2.	Market-to-book ratio	Market capitalization plus book assets minus book equity all divided by total assets	$\left(\frac{M}{B}\right)$
3.	Asset tangibility	Ratio of fixed assets (FA) to total assets	$\left(\frac{FA}{A}\right)$
4.	Log sales	Logarithm of sales turnover	log(S)
5.	Profitability	Ratio of operating profit to total assets	$\left(\frac{EBITDA}{A}\right)$
6	Depreciation	Ratio of total depreciation (D) to fixed assets	$\left(\frac{D}{FA}\right)$

Table 9 Results of panel data

Dependent variable: change in debt ratio	DFT+1	DFT+5	DFT+10
Market-to-book value	–0.0063 (–2.50*)	–0.00086 (–2.16**)	–01122 (–1.63***)
Asset tangibility	0.480 (2.54*)	0.0294 (0.81)	0.0877 (3.49*)
Size	–1.501 (–7.27*)	–1.6782 (3.69*)	–1.154 (3.41*)
ROA	0.126 (2.03**)	–0.1305 (–0.99)	–0.209 (–3.05*)
Depreciation	–0.1726 (–0.72)	0.0786 (0.58)	0.0786 (0.58)
F test	20.44 (0.000)	18.39 (0.000)	8.15 (0.000)

t values in parentheses. *Significant at 1%. ** Significant at 5%. *** Significant at 10%

5 Findings and Discussions

Extant literature shows that firms' capital structure is influenced by two factors, namely (a) internal factors and (b) market valuation. Variables such as firm size, asset tangibility, profitability and depreciation have been used to control the impact of internal variables on capital structure. Market-to-book ratio is used to explain the role of market valuation on capital structure. Table 9 presents the estimated results of regression (1).

As evident from the table, market-to-book ratio is found to be negatively influencing the debt ratio in all three subsamples. This indicates that firms' debt ratio decreases as market value increases, suggesting that firms prefer to issue equity when the market value is high. Our results also suggest that the impact of market valuation remains even after ten year from the date of first trading in the stock market. This indicates that market valuation has long-term impact on the capital structure. This is contrary to the predictions of trade-off theory that market value results in only short-term deviation from the optimum capital structure and quickly reverse to the target rate. Therefore, our results are consistent with the predictions of market timing theory that firms with better market value may prefer equity to borrowing, and that the market value has persistent impact on the capital structure. Alternatively, negative relationship of market value with leverage would also support the arguments of Myers (1977), Rajan and Zingales (1995) and Frank and Goyal (2009) that firm with higher growth opportunities would use more equity finance. Since market value reflects the future growth opportunities of the firm, higher market value would induce the firm to use more equity finance.

With regard to the impact of asset tangibility on borrowing of the firms, a significant positive influence of asset tangibility on debt ratio is found which indicates that higher proportion of tangible assets increases the debt capacity of the firm as lenders will be willing to lend to a firm with higher tangible assets (Rajan and Zingales 1995). Alternatively, positive influence of tangible assets also supports the proposition that higher tangible asset helps in reducing information asymmetry problem associated with debt financing which may help the firm to minimize the interest costs of the debt as argued by Scott (1977) and Myers (1977). However, firm size is found to be negatively related to debt ratio. This suggests that large firms have lower debt, indicating that they raise more equity capital to finance their operation. This may be due to the fact that in India before 1990s firms were constrained to depend more on debt capital as the stock market was largely underdeveloped. Therefore, as stock market became more efficient, firms, particularly, large firms took advantage of it and raised more equity capital from the market. Alternatively, for a large and growing firm the problem of information asymmetry reduces and hence they would be able to raise capital from the market at better terms.

Further, we found a significant and positive relationship between profitability and debt ratio in DFT+1 suggesting that profitability positively affects the debt capacity of the firm. But, in the long run (DFT+10) profitability is negatively related to the debt capacity of the firm, suggesting that as firms expand their profitability helps them to raise more equity capital. Alternatively, the negative relationship may also reflect the dependence on internal capital, which is consistent with predictions of pecking order hypothesis. However, we did not find any significant relationship between depreciation and debt ratio which suggests that tax-based explanations are not relevant in the case of our sample firms.

Results of regression (1) indicate that firm's market value negatively influences the debt ratio. However, negative relationship between market value and debt ratio may also be due to higher retained earnings or lower debt. In order to ascertain that negative relationship is actually due to changes in equity issues, we further examined relationship between fresh equity issues and market value of the firm. We study the firms in 3 subsamples DFT+1, DFT+5 and DFT+10 to understand both short-term and long-term impact market value on equity issues. Our regression model is as follows:

$$\left(\frac{e}{A}\right)_t = a + b\left(\frac{M}{B}\right)_{t-1} + c\left(\frac{FA}{A}\right)_{t-1} + d\left(\frac{EBITDA}{A}\right)_{t-1} + e\left(\frac{D}{A}\right)_{t-1} + f\log(S)_{t-1} + \mu_t \quad (2)$$

where $\left(\frac{e}{A}\right)_t$ is the ratio of fresh equity issue to total assets.

Table 10 Results of regression (2)

Dependent variable: fresh equity issues	DFT+1	DFT+5	DFT+10
Market-to-book value	0.0017 (2.77*)	0.00151 (2.14*)	7.08 (3.83*)
Asset tangibility	–0.020 (–1.26)	–0.00061 (–3.57*)	–0.00092 (–2.03**)
Size	–0.709 (–2.86*)	–0.0065 (–3.09*)	–0.00058 (–2.05**)
Profitability	0.018 (0.66)	–0.00048 (–2.30**)	0.00061 (2.92*)
Depreciation	–0.023 (–0.76)	–2.01 (–0.99)	–0.00002 (–0.07)
F test	4.18 (0.060)	9.88 (0.000)	108.39 (0.000)

t values in parentheses. *Significant at 1%. ** Significant at 5%. *** Significant at 10%

Estimated results of regression (2) are presented in Table 10. As shown in the table market value is positively and significantly related to equity issue. This shows that higher market value leads to lower debt ratio through increase in equity issues which confirms that negative impact of market value on debt ratio is indeed traced to changes in equity issues than changes in retained earnings or debt retirement.

Further, the impact of market value on equity issues is more pronounced in DFT+10 which indicates the impact of market value on capital structure is persistent as opposed to the argument of trade-off theory that market value should have only short impact on capital structure. This shows that market value of the firm leads to long-term change in firms' capital structure which is consistent with the market timing theory of Baker and Wurgler (2002).

6 Conclusion

The study attempted to examine the impact of firm's market value on capital structure and found that debt ratio is negatively influenced by market value. Further, the study showed that the negative relationship actually comes through equity issue and the impact remains even after ten years from the date of first trading in the equity market. This is consistent with the predictions of market timing theory that the market value has long-term impact on firm's capital structure. The results also suggest that better market valuation enables the firm to raise capital from equity market, thereby diffusing excessive burden of financing corporate sector on banking system.

References

Ali Ahmed, H. J., & Hisham, N. (2009). Revisiting capital structure theory: A test of pecking order and static trade-off model from Malaysian capital market. *International Research Journal of Finance and Economics, 30,* 58–65.

Alti, A. (2006). How persistent is the impact of market timing on capital structure? *The Journal of Finance, 51*(4), 1681–1710.

Baker, M., & Wurgler, J. (2002). Market timing and capital structure. *The Journal of Finance, 57*(1), 1–32.

Barton Sidney, L., Hill, N. C., & Sundaram, S. (1989). An empirical test of stakeholder theory predictions of capital structure. *Financial Management, 18*(1), 36–44.

Baxter, N. D. (1967). Leverage, the risk of ruin and the cost of capital. *Journal of Finance, 22*(3), 395–403.

Berger, A. N., & Udell, G. F. (2005, December). A more complete conceptual framework for financing of small and medium enterprises. World Bank Policy Research Working Paper 3795.

Bhabra, H. S., Liu, T., & Tirtiroglu, D. (2008). Capital structure choice in a nascent market: Evidence from listed firms in China. *Financial Management, 37*(2), 341–364.

Bhaduri, S. N. (2002a). Determinants of corporate borrowing: Some evidence from the Indian corporate sector. *Journal of Economics and Finance, 26*(2), 200–215.

Bhaduri, S. N. (2002b). Determinants of capital structure choice: A study of Indian corporate sector. *Applied Financial Economics, 12*(9), 655–665.

Bole, L. M., & Mahakud, J. (2004). Trends and determinants of capital structure in India: A panel data analysis. *Finance India, 18*(1), 37–55.

Booth, L., Aivazian, V., Demirguc-Kunt, A., & Maksimovic, V. (2001). Capital structure in developing countries. *Journal of Finance, 56,* 87–130.

Brav, A., Graham, J., Harvey, C., & Michaely, R. (2005). Payout policy in the 21st century. *Journal of Financial Economics, 77,* 483–527.

Chauhan, G. S. (2015). Capital structure in India: Implications for the development of bond markets. *Indian Journal of Economics & Business, 14*(2), 245–267.

Chen, L., & Zhao, X. (2006, June). On the relation between the market-to-book ratio, growth, opportunity, and leverage ratio.

Daskalakis, N., & Psillaki, M. (2008). Do country or firm factors explain capital structure? Evidence from SMEs in France and Greece. *Applied Financial Economics, 18,* 87–97.

DeAngelo, H., & Masulis, R. (1980). Optimal capital structure under corporate and personal taxation. *Journal of Financial Economics, 8,* 3–29.

Demirgüç-Kunt, A., & Maksimovic, V. (1996). Stock market development and financing choices of firms. *The World Bank Economic Review, 10*(2), 341–369.

Espinosa Christian, M., Carlos Maquieira, V., Vieito, J. P., & Marcelo Gonzalez, A. (2012). Capital structures in developing countries: The Latin American case. *Investigation Economica, 71*(282), 35–54.

Fama, E., & French, K. (2000). Testing trade-off and pecking order predictions about dividends and debt. *Review of Financial Studies, 15*(1), 1–33.

Frank, M. Z., & Goyal, V. K. (2003). Testing the pecking order theory of capital structure. *Journal of Financial Economics, 67,* 217–248.

Frank, M. Z., & Goyal, V. K. (2009). Capital structure decisions: Which factors are reliably important? *Financial Management, 38*(1), 1–37.

Gaud, P., Jani, E., Hoesli, M., & Bender, A. (2005). The capital structure of Swiss companies: An empirical analysis using dynamic panel data. *European Financial Management, 77*(1), 51–69.

Graham, J. R., & Harvey, C. R. (2001). The theory and practice of corporate finance: Evidence from the field. *Journal of Financial Economics, 60*(2–3), 187–243.

Hall, G., Hutchinson, P., & Michaelas, N. (2004). Determinants of the capital structure of European SMEs. *Journal of Business Finance and Accounting, 31*(5), 711–728.

Harris, M., & Raviv, A. (1990). Capital structure and the informational role of debt. *The Journal of Finance, 45*(2), 321–349.
Harris, M., & Raviv, A. (1991). The theory of capital structure. *The Journal of Finance, 46*, 297–355.
Hovakimian, A., Opler, T., & Titman, S. (2001). The debt-equity choice. *Journal of Financial and Quantitative Analysis, 36*(1), 1–24.
Huang, R., & Ritter, J. R. (2009). Testing theories of capital structure and estimating the speed of adjustment. *The Journal of Financial and Quantitative Analysis, 44*(2), 237–271.
Jalal, A. I. M. (2007). The pecking order, information asymmetry, and financial market efficiency, Doctoral Dissertation, The University of Minnesota.
Jensen, M., & Meckling, N. (1976). The theory of the firm: Managerial behavior agency cost and ownership structure. *Journal of Financial Economics, 3*, 305–360.
Jung, K., Kim, Y., & Stulz, R. (1996). Timing, investment opportunities, managerial discretion, and the security issue decision. *Journal of Financial Economics, 42*, 159–185.
Khasnobis, B. G., & Bhaduri, S. N. (2002). Determinants of capital structure in India (1990–1998): A dynamic panel data approach. *Journal of Economic Integration, 17*(4), 761–776.
Korajczyk, R., Lucas, D., & McDonald, R. (1991). The effects of information releases on the pricing and timing of equity issues. *Review of Financial Studies, 4*, 685–708.
Mahakud, J. (2006). Testing the pecking order theory of capital structure: Evidence from Indian corporate sector. *ICFAI Journal of Applied Finance, 12*(11), 16–26.
Miller Merton, H. (1977). Debt and taxes source. *The Journal of Finance, 32*(2), 261–275.
Modigliani, F., & Miller, M. (1958). The cost of capital, corporate finance and the theory of investment. *American Economic Review, 48*, 261–297.
Modigliani, F., & Miller, M. (1963). Corporate income taxes and the cost of capital. *American Economic Review, 53*, 433–443.
Mohamad, M. H. (1995). Capital structure in large Malaysian companies. *MIR: Management International Review, 35*, 119–130.
Mujumdar, R. (2014). Indebtedness in the small and midcap segments: New evidences from Indian manufacturing sector. *Management Research Review, 37*(9), 833–854.
Myers, S. C. (1977). Determinants of corporate borrowing. *Journal of Financial Economics, 9*, 147–176.
Myers, S. C. (1984). The capital structure puzzle. *The Journal of Finance, 39*(3), 575–592.
Myers, S. C., & Majluf, N. (1984). Corporate financing and investment decisions when firms have information that investors do not have. *Journal of Financial Economics, 13*(2), 187–221.
Ozkan, A. (2001). Determinants of capital structure and adjustment to long run target: Evidence from UK company panel data. *Journal of Business Finance and Accounting, 28*(1 & 2), 175–199.
Patnaik, I., Shaha, A., & Singh, N. (2016). Foreign currency borrowing by Indian firms: Towards a new policy framework. Working Paper No. 167, National Institute of Public Finance and Policy, New Delhi.
Psillaki, M., & Daskalakis, N. (2009). Are the determinants of capital structure country or firm specific? *Small Business Economics, 33*, 319–333.
Rajan, R. G., & Zingales, L. (1995). What do we know about capital structure? Some evidence from international data. *Journal of Finance, 50*(5), 1421–1459.
RBI. (2015, June). Financial Stability Report, Reserve Bank of India.
RBI. (2017, June). Financial Stability Report, No. 15. Reserve Bank of India, Mumbai.
Reddy, Y. V. (2004, March). Credit policy, systems, and culture. *Reserve Bank of India Bulletin*.
Scott, J. (1977). Bankruptcy, secured debt, and optimal capital structure. *Journal of Finance, 32*(1), 1–19.
Sogorb-Mira, F. (2005). How SME uniqueness affects capital structure: Evidence from a 1994–1998 Spanish data panel. *Small Business Economics, 25*(5), 447–457.
Strebulaev, I. A. (2007). Do tests of capital structure theory mean what they say? *The Journal of Finance, 62*(4), 1747–1787.
The Hindu. (2016, December). Details of NPA figures of public, private sector banks, December 02, 2016.

Titman, S., & Wessels, R. (1988). The determinants of capital structure choice. *Journal of Finance, 43*(1), 1–20.
Tong, G., & Green, C. J. (2005). Pecking order or trade-off hypothesis? Evidence on the capital structure of Chinese companies. *Journal of Applied Economics, 37*(19), 2179–2189.
Um, T. (2001, January). Determination of capital structure and prediction of bankruptcy in Korea Doctoral Dissertation, Faculty of the Graduate School, Cornell University.
Van der Wijst, D., & Thurik, R. (1993). Determinants of small firm debt ratios: An analysis of retail panel data. *Small Business Economics, 5,* 55–65.
Warner, J. (1977). Bankruptcy, absolute priority, and the prices of risky debt claims. *Journal of Financial Economics*, 239–76.
Welch, I. (2004). Capital structure and stock returns. *Journal of Political Economy, 112,* 106–131.

Corporate Governance and Cash Holdings: An Empirical Investigation of Indian Companies

Amitava Roy

Abstract Indian corporations were holding considerable amounts of cash and cash equivalents (CCE). Extant literature suggests that agency conflicts and financing frictions are important determinants of corporate cash holdings. This study examines the relation between cash holding and the quality of firm-level corporate governance (CG). We use 24 structural indicators of CG relating to ownership, board and boards committees, audit considerations, and leverage characteristics along with a specific set of control variables. Four different measures of corporate cash holdings and liquidity have been employed. We begin with an exploratory inquiry into the dimensions of CG using principal component analysis and then use regression to delve into the association between cash holding and CG. Our evidence suggests that the quality of firm-level CG has important implications in deciding corporate cash holdings.

Keywords Agency theory · Cash holdings · Corporate governance

JEL Classification G30 · G34

1 Introduction

Corporate cash holdings have received growing attention in recent years as blue-chip Indian companies were sitting on large cash balances. Top 500 listed companies had enough cash to double the power generation capacity of 2,00,000 mw or build over 40,000 km of six-lane highways every year (compared with the current 800 km) [1]. The figures disclosed in financial statements (as of 31 March 2013) were mind-boggling. The private sector behemoth, Reliance Industries, topped the list with ₹37,984 crores. Within the Tata Group, Tata Motors had the largest cash reserves

[1] Economic Times 20 August 2012.

A. Roy (✉)
Department of Commerce and Business Administration, St. Xavier's College (Autonomous), 30 Park Street, Kolkata 700016, India
e-mail: arsxc@sxccal.edu; arsxc@yahoo.com

N. R. Bhanumurthy et al. (eds.), *Advances in Finance & Applied Economics*,
https://doi.org/10.1007/978-981-13-1696-8_16

of ₹29,712 crores. In the IT sector, Infosys reported that its cash balance had more than doubled from ₹10,556 crores in 2010 to the current position of ₹25,950 crores. TCS, Wipro, and HCL Technologies also had cash holding between ₹10,000 crores and ₹20,000 crores. Among public sector enterprises, (hereafter, PSE) Coal India reported a balance amounting to more than ₹52,389 crores. Further, if we consider listed companies over the period of 10 years, from 2004 to 2014, cash reserves have increased by ninefold.[2]

Ammanna et al. (2011) offered compelling evidence on increased cash holdings by corporates from around the world with a data set comprising of 46 emerging and developed countries. Bates et al. (2009) reported there was an increase in cash holdings of US companies from 1980 to 2006. Further in 2011, US companies had cash amounting to $5 trillion, and this was more than for any other year since 1980.[3] Public firms in the USA as of 2011 held, on average, 20.45% of their assets in cash or cash equivalents (hereafter, CCE) (Gao et al. 2013). Similar increasing trends were reported by UK firms (Ozkan and Ozkan 2004). Country-specific studies relating to companies in Germany, Japan, and Southeast Asia have also pointed out that companies in these countries have also stuck to this trend of accumulating cash (Opler et al. 1999).

Why do companies have large stockpiles of cash?[4] In the absence of market imperfections, firms do not have transactions costs. The costs of internally generated and external funds are equal; thus, firms can readily borrow to finance investment or cover cash shortage (assuming, firms are not under financial distress). Firms do not have any incentive to accumulate cash; rather, their cash holdings tend to react passively to cash flow. In reality, financial markets are imperfect, given asymmetric information between borrowers and lenders and the literature explaining this goes back to Keynes (1936).

Firms hold cash for four reasons: transaction motive, precautionary motive (to avoid any shocks due to adverse market conditions when borrowing is expensive), tax motive (multinational companies may keep cash in foreign subsidiaries to avoid the repatriation tax on the profits earned in foreign countries), and agency motive, which is crucial for our research.

The literature asserts that managers' private benefits rise with the increase in corporate investments. Thus, reserving internally generated cash is possibly the least expensive method of maintaining sufficient amounts of capital for prospective investment. However, shareholders have agency concerns regarding managers' private benefits, especially when firms have large cash holdings, and generally will not prefer managers to accumulate excessive amounts of internal cash without robust CG mechanisms in place (Harford et al. 2008). Therefore, CG plays a pivotal role as it

---

[2]http://www.thehindubusinessline.com/portfolio/iscashreallyking/article6347166.ece © The Hindu Business Line.

[3]Why Are Corporations Holding So Much Cash? By Juan M. Sánchez and Emircan Yurdagul; The Regional Economist, January 2013.

[4]Literature reveals that the focus on corporate cash holding started with the seminal work by Baumol (1952) followed by Miller and Orr (1966).

is the main mechanism by which shareholders affect managerial discretion. CG if implemented rationally reduces agency costs thereby ensuring managers responsibly use cash. Even in the absence of agency problems, with innovative risk management techniques firms now can hedge more effectively (using derivatives), leading to lower precautionary demand. But still cash holdings have risen manifold in the last decade. This vastness of liquidity underscores the need to understand why companies accumulate cash and whether managers manage it judiciously. Also, it is pertinent to investigate whether cash accumulation results from agency problems or is a product of changes in firm characteristics and their business environment.

This study examines the role of CG in the determination of cash holdings. We examine how ownership structure, board, and audit-related attributes (used as proxies for the nature of CG) impact corporate liquidity. Further, the majority of the empirical conclusions on this subject have focused on the developed economies. Our endeavour is in the Indian context where several prominent CG issues exist (like, ownership concentration, business group affiliation, insiders dominating corporate boards, and singular leadership structure). Considering these, we propose to fill the gap in the literature by investigating how CG affects cash holdings and corporate liquidity.

We employ four different measures of corporate liquidity. The explanatory variables consist of 24 structural indicators of CG including specified control variables. Using principal component analysis (hereafter, PCA), we offer an exploratory inquiry into the dimensions of CG. We examine the causal link between cash holding and firm liquidity (the dependent variable) and CG. Using a sample of 58 listed Indian firms and considering data from 2007–08 to 2012–13, we observe that firms with stronger CG tend to reduce cash and have higher capital investments, while entrenched managers in firms with high cash reserves invest more in current assets. Companies also hold cash for financial flexibility and to take advantage of strategic opportunities as they present themselves. Parallel to this point is the fact that larger cash reserves help firms to avoid uncertainty and hedge themselves against the difficulty of accessing external funds.

The remainder of the paper is organised as follows: Sect. 2 offers a review of the theoretical determinants of cash holdings. Section 3 explains our data set followed by the variables description in Sect. 4. Section 5 presents the research design. Section 6 gives the results of our empirical analysis followed by Sect. 7 that concludes.

2 Review of the Literature

2.1 Corporate Governance and Cash Holdings

Past studies have focused on agency conflicts. Opler et al. (1999) argue that self-interested managers seek to accumulate cash, because they are risk averse and want flexibility to pursue personal goals. Myers and Rajan (1998) observed that managers have strong incentives to hold cash as it is a matter of managerial discretion, and turning excess liquidity into personal benefits is less costly to managers than transferring other assets for private benefits. Contrary to this, Jensen (1986) argued managers spend cash because even projects with negative net present value can increase managerial utility. For example, acquisitions improve managers' job security, diversify managers' human capital risks (Morck et al. 1990), and enhance executive compensation (Gao et al. 2013). Graham et al. (2005) negated the spending proposition and observed that self-interested managers may hold back certain types of spending (like, research and development) because of its adverse effect on short-term earnings. But Bates et al. (2009) offered evidence, using US firms, to show that it is inconsistent with the notion that an increase in cash holdings over time can be ascribed to agency problems.

2.2 *Corporate Governance Mechanisms*

CG mechanisms may be split into two categories, internal and external. Internal mechanisms include ownership and board structure, audit related, and debt financing. The key external mechanism is the market for corporate control, which incidentally is weak in India. It is the confluence of these internal and external mechanisms that leads to efficient CG, thereby minimising the divergent interests of the principals and agents of the firm. In this study, we concentrate on the internal CG mechanism.

2.2.1 Ownership Structure

Ownership structure of firms may be important in deciding cash holdings, and two divergent views exist. From CG perspective, ownership concentration reduces the free rider problem, reduces managerial opportunism, and leads to a reduction in agency costs of external finance since large shareholders have more incentives to effectively monitor management. To the extent that this leads to lowering of the cost of external financing, firms with higher ownership concentration would hold less cash. The alternative hypothesis suggests large shareholders could have incentives to accumulate cash to maximise funds under their control and avoid external markets' discipline and reduce managerial initiative. However, this may lead to under-diversification in these companies. Further, concentrated ownership may lead to expropriation of shareholder wealth. Within block holders, institutional investors are better in monitoring and they normally drive firms to enhance their CG practices. Among the institutional investors, domestic mutual funds play a passive role, but banks and insurance companies tend to be more active. The later also has the right to appoint nominee directors on the boards of the firms they invest in. Foreign Institutional Investors (hereafter, FII) tend to exercise their ownership rights more actively. Gugler et al. (2003) pointed out the existence of double principal agent problem in PSE. However, since PSE works in key economic sectors with strong market presence, they create attractive investment opportunities that offset the inefficiencies created by the agency problem.

2.2.2 Board Structure

Extant literature analysing the effectiveness of the board in monitoring has focused on size and composition. On the influence of board size, diverse opinion exists: the more efficient and effective decision making of a smaller board against the greater monitoring by bigger boards. Boone et al. (2006) observed that larger board's trade-offs added monitoring services with free riding and will be best when managers' opportunities to consume private benefits are high. In the Indian context, boards play a passive role as they may be friendly with management. This motivates the need to employ external directors. Boards are more independent as the proportion of their external directors increases (John and Senbet 1998). The literature on the effect of outside directors on the agency problem is contradictory. Some studies opined that external directors align with the interests of managers and shareholders while others recommend against having more external directors. But then markets reward firms for appointing external directors (Brickley et al. 1994). Studies suggest boards are becoming increasingly independent and their monitoring effectiveness has increased, thereby decreasing managerial opportunism. Anderson et al. (2004) showed the inverse relationship between board independence and the cost of debt. The literature exists on dual leadership structure, positing that agency problems are higher when the same person holds both the chairman and chief executive positions. Although duality creates strong leadership, it reduces the effectiveness of board monitoring. Board committees address specialised issues and reduce the burden on the board, although the board keeps collective responsibility for decision making. Such committees should have enough members; they should be independent and have the technical ability to ensure that they are able to discharge their mandate effectively.

2.2.3 Audit Related

The audit committee is the foundation for effective CG. It has specific responsibilities in respect of the external auditors, including agreeing on the terms of engagement, recommending its appointment and removal, and approving the fees paid for audit and consultancy. Audit committee independence is crucial as the monitoring they offer affects audit quality, auditor independence (Abbott and Parker 2000), higher disclosure quality (Karamanou and Vafeas 2005) and lowers cost of debt (Anderson et al. 2004). Agrawal and Chadha (2005) found no evidence between audit committee independence and the extent of non-audit services offered with the probability of the firm engaging in earnings restatement. Krishnan and Visvanathan (2009) showed that firms with higher-quality CG (with a financial expert on the audit committee) have lesser audit fees. Brown and Caylor (2004) offered evidence on the association between audit-related CG factors and firm performance.

2.3 *Measurement of Corporate Governance*

Larcker et al. (2007) discussed the critical issue of construct validity of CG. They argued in the absence of a well-developed theory on the multidimensional nature of CG there exists no conceptual basis for selecting relevant CG variables to be used in an empirical study. Previous studies have either used a single indicator of CG or indexes. The limitation with single factor measure is CG mechanisms are many and interaction effects are possible, but they are ignored. The use of an index helps in capturing the multiple dimensions of the firm's CG structure. Bhagat and Bolton (2008) observed that evaluating the firm's CG structure using a single variable is econometrically proper as the measurement error in computing a single variable is lower than that of an index, which needs identification of multiple attributes. Although widely used due to the lack of better alternatives, multifactor indexes may be imperfect, as index construction needs assigning weights to the identified variables, which may be arbitrary. In this study, we take a detour and use PCA and this methodological approach is consistent with earlier research (Larcker et al. 2007; Black et al. 2017).

3 Data and Sample

We use a sample of publicly traded firms listed on the Bombay Stock Exchange's S&P BSE 100 and National Stock Exchange's NSE CNX 100 as of 31 March 2013. We constructed our panel data set for this study considering the period from 2007–08 to 2012–13, i.e. 6 years. Our initial sample comprises of the set of all firms for which data are available with respect to the selected variables. This gave us a sample of 69 firms. We have excluded banks and financial firms (11 companies) because they carry cash to meet capital requirements and use different accounting policies and practices which may lead to non-uniformity in the computation of accounting ratios used as variables in this study. Further, missing firm-year observations for any variable in the model during the sample period were dropped. These criteria have provided us with a total of 58 companies belonging to 22 industry groups. We sourced data from the Annual Reports and Prowess database.[5]

[5]The Prowess database is supported by the Centre for Monitoring Indian Economy and includes information on private and listed companies. It is widely used for firm-level research on India (e.g. Bertrand et al. 2002 and Gopalan et al. 2007).

4 Variable Description

4.1 Cash Holdings

Alternative definitions of the cash ratio exist in the literature. We employ four measures of cash holding: cash to total assets, cash to net assets, net current assets to total assets, and net current assets to net assets. For our analysis, we define cash to include short term, highly liquid investments that are readily convertible into cash and are subject to insignificant risk of changes in value. We view cash as a liquid investment necessary to support the working capital needs of the company. Total assets refer to the book value of all assets as on the balance sheet date. Net assets are defined as total assets less cash. Net current assets are used as the measure of corporate liquidity. The firm's profitability is also related to its net assets.

4.2 Corporate Governance Variables

We have used several measures of CG to understand the severity of the firm's agency problems categorised into ownership, board, and audit related.

4.2.1 Ownership Structure

The corporate scenario in India is a mix of government-owned and private companies (including, family run, corporate groups, multinationals, and professionally managed standalones). High degree of ownership concentration is common. Corporate group comprises of parent and subsidiary companies that run as a single economic entity through a common source of control. Companies tend to retain their shareholding pattern over a period, thereby helping us to use data on shareholding by the various ownership groups like the promoters and institutional holding. Institutional ownership comprises of foreign and domestic institutional ownerships. Companies with group affiliation have been identified based on Prowess[6] database. We designed a business group affiliate (hereafter, BGA) dummy to check the impact of group affiliation. We have also used FII and PSE dummies.

[6]The Prowess database distinguishes between: (i) independent private domestic-owned firms not affiliated to business groups, (ii) firms affiliated with domestic business group, (iii) PSE, (iv) independent foreign firms, and (v) group affiliated foreign firms. According to CMIE, the classification of firms based on business group affiliation is based on "continuous monitoring of company announcements and a qualitative understanding of the group-wise behaviour of individual companies".

4.2.2 Board Structure

Management has a fiduciary duty to fulfil the investors' needs. We have used board size and the proportion of outside directors on the board (as a proxy for board independence). Boards consist of executive and non-executive directors. Non-executive directors have an advisory role in board meetings and deal with decision control which in turn leads to lower agency cost. A widely prevalent and recognised best practice is that a firm should have more non-executive than executive directors. Thus, we have used the proportion of non-executive directors as a variable. The decision support system of modern boards comprises of various board committees, and they play a pivotal role in management. The number of such committees constituted by the firm, and the existence of the nomination and corporate social responsibility (henceforth, CSR) committees is essential CG attributes and hence used as dummy variables. Companies with designated CSR committee are used as a proxy for the level of CSR embedded in the organisation.

4.2.3 Audit Related

Constitution of the audit committee, auditor's independence, fees for services offered are important CG mechanism. Clause 49[7] lays down rules about the composition, powers, functions, and the quorum needed at audit committee meetings. We have considered the size and the number of independent directors of the audit committee as variables. Formal meetings of the audit committee are the heart of its work. There should be as many meetings as the audit committee's role and responsibilities need, and thus, we have considered it as another variable. To decide the right audit fee, auditors assess the risk associated with the client, firm size, and its business complexity. The nature of the services offered is the determinant of the audit and non-audit fees charged by the auditor. Non-audit fees (as compared to audit fees) have risen substantially, and this has led to the notion that it may encourage the auditors to compromise on their independence. The main concerns are: first, auditors may not stand up to management because they wish to keep the added income from non-audit fees management's gift. Second, given the range of services, it may lead the auditor to identify closely with management and lose scepticism (Beattie et al. 2002). Thus, we have used audit fees scaled by total fees paid to the auditors as a measure in this study.

[7]Clause 49 of Securities Exchange Board of India (SEBI) Listing Agreement—As a major step towards codifying the CG norms, SEBI formulated Clause 49 in the Equity Listing Agreement (2000). It now serves as a standard of CG in India. It is applicable to companies which wish to get themselves listed in the stock exchanges. This clause has both mandatory and non-mandatory provisions.

4.3 Financial and Control Variables

The debt equity ratio is used as a measure of leverage and financing mix used by the firm and its financial risk. If debt is a constraint, firms will use cash reserves to reduce leverage and lower default risk resulting in a negative relation between cash holdings and leverage. Acharya et al. (2007) argued that the hedging argument is consistent with a positive relation between leverage and cash holdings. Capital expenditure is likely to be positively related to cash holdings. Riddick and Whited (2009) observed that firms hold cash to better manage adverse shocks when external financing is costly. A productivity shock that increases investment can lead firms to temporarily invest more and save less cash, which would lead to a lowering of cash balances. The pecking order theory suggests that large capital expenditure drains out cash from the firm. Further, if investments create assets that are available as collateral, it could increase debt capacity and reduce cash requirement. We use capital expenditure scaled by non-current assets (total assets less current assets) as the relevant variable. Following the literature, we control for the corporate accumulation of precautionary cash balances by employing free cash flow (defined as, profit before depreciation, interest, taxes, and amortisation scaled by total assets). The free cash flows generated by the firm may also be used as proxies for the level of agency conflict within the firm.

As a measure of firm performance, we use return on asset (hereafter, ROA). ROA is an accounting-based performance measure, and it does not suffer from any anticipation problem. However, it suffers from an inherent bias due to the historical valuation of assets. Using ROA may create problems if uniform accounting standards are not adopted. This problem does not arise in our study as India has a stable accounting regime and auditors are particularly watchful in this regard (Roy 2016). Further, in CG context, accounting measures have the potential problem of requiring a longer period to capture and reflect the effects of CG as compared to market-based measures. We include market to book value ratio (hereafter, MTBVR) as a market-based performance measure. It is a forward-looking indicator of investment opportunities and incorporates both current information and future prospects. Further, it is likely to reflect better on the overall financial health of the firm. It reflects firm valuation by using a larger universe of independent shareholders.

The literature asserts that the internal CG mechanisms are correlated with several firm characteristics. Thus, we employ the following control variables in our study. Firms that pay dividends are likely to be less risky and have greater access to capital markets; therefore, the precautionary motive for cash holdings is weaker for them. We include a dividend dummy, and it is equal to one in years in which a firm paid dividend, otherwise zero. Older firms have a longer history in the capital market, and years of successful operations enhance their goodwill and have less information asymmetry relative to their newer counterparts. Therefore, they can better reach optimal cash position and continued investments, which allowed them to survive (Faulkender 2002). Bates et al. (2009) observed that cash holdings do not increase for older and established firms that pay dividends. But firms that do not pay dividends increase their cash holdings dramatically. Larger firms reserve more cash to support its superior level and quality of operations and investment chances. Divergent view based on the trade-off theory states as large firms benefit from economies of scale and have easier access of financing with lower costs may allow them to hold lower cash. Firm size is positively related to cash holding as showed by Kalcheva and Lins (2007). Firm size also affects the composition of the board, directors' independences, the audit process, and structure of the board committees. Table 1 gives the complete list of all variables used in this study.

Table 1 List of corporate governance attributes and other variables

The table reports the 16 individual governance attributes based on data given by the sampled companies in their annual reports as per the requirements of Clause 49 and grouped by the three sub-categories: Ownership, board, and audit related along with financial and control variables

Variable		Definition
Ownership structure		
1.	PGH	Proportion of shares held by promoter group
2.	INSTH	Proportion of shares held by institutional investors
3.	BGA	Business group affiliate, dummy variable, if the firm is affiliated to any business group (*as identified by Prowess*) then one, and zero otherwise
4.	PSE	Public sector enterprise, dummy variable, if the firm is a PSE then one, and zero otherwise
5.	FII	Foreign Institutional Investment, dummy variable, if the firm has attracted FII then one, and zero otherwise
Board structure		
6.	BS	Number of directors on the board
7.	PropID	Proportion of independent directors on the board
8.	Prop_NED	Proportion of non-executive directors on the board
9.	CEODual	Dummy variable, this variable is assigned the value of zero where the CEO has the dual role of chairman of the board and CEO, and one otherwise
10.	No._BdCom	Number of board committees
11.	CSRCom	Dummy variable, this variable is assigned a value of one if the firm has a corporate social responsibility or sustainability committee, and zero otherwise
12.	NomCom	Dummy variable, this variable is assigned a value of one if the firm as a nomination committee, and zero otherwise
Audit related		
13.	AdCom_Sz	Audit committee size
14.	ID_AdCom	Number of independent directors on the audit committee
15.	AdCom_Mt	Number of meetings held by the audit committee
16.	Afee_Totfee	Audit fees scaled by total remuneration paid to auditors

(continued)

Table 1 (continued)

The table reports the 16 individual governance attributes based on data given by the sampled companies in their annual reports as per the requirements of Clause 49 and grouped by the three sub-categories: Ownership, board, and audit related along with financial and control variables

Variable		Definition
Financial and control variables		
17.	DE	Debt equity ratio
18.	CF_PBDITA/TA	Cash flow generated defined as profit before depreciation, interest, taxes, and amortisation scaled by total assets
19.	Capex/NonCA	Capital expenditure scaled by non-current asset
20.	ROA	Return on assets
21.	MTBVR	Market to book value ratio
22.	DivDum	Dummy variable, this variable is assigned a value of 1 if the company has paid dividend in a given year and 0 otherwise
23.	Ln_TA	Natural logarithm of total assets of the firm as an indicator of firm size
24.	Ln_AGE	Natural logarithm of firm age since incorporation
Cash holding ratios		
25.	CCE/TA	Cash and cash equivalents scaled by total assets
26.	CCE/NA	Cash and cash equivalents scaled by net assets
27.	NCA/TA	Net current asset scaled by total assets
28.	NCA/NA	Net current asset scaled by net assets

5 Research Design

Measurement of CG is critical to this study. The concept of CG is abstract rather than concrete and observable, hence constructing an index, and using it as a proxy for this vague concept using observable measures is inappropriate. The fit between the observable "construct" (CG index) and the underlying concept of CG is known as construct validity (Black et al. 2017). CG is "complex construct" (Larcker et al. 2007), and measuring it using a single factor or an index may not be appropriate, so we use PCA. PCA consists of finding clusters or components of related variables. Each component consists of a group of variables that correlate substantially among themselves than with other elements not belonging to that component. The variables are aggregated based on their statistical properties rather than on theoretical assumption or prior empirical evidence. Thus, unlike in index construction the weighting scheme is statistical instead of assigning equal or arbitrary weights.

In PCA, the principal components are derived by eigenvalue decomposition of the correlation matrix and the accuracy of the correlation matrix decides the validity of the principal components and this in turn decides the reliability of the conclusions. Further, Beekes et al. (2010) observed that if the variables used to follow a continuous distribution, the Pearson correlations estimated are proper for PCA. But CG variables may be discrete and Pearson's correlation coefficients tend to be underestimated for pairs of variables which include discrete data. We use PCA as it offers valuable insight into the CG structure of the firm given there is little prior theory or empirical analysis about the dimensions of CG using this tool in the Indian context (Dey 2008). We also perform regression analysis to examine the relation between CG and cash holdings.

6 Empirical Results

We begin with the univariate analysis of our data and present the key descriptive statistics followed by correlations. In Table 2, we have presented the summary statistics of all the CG and firm-specific variables. The cash and financial ratios are winsorised at the 1% level on either tail to mitigate the influence of outliers on the results. We observe, in our sampled firms, the year on year percentage growth in average cash holding ranges between 5.66 and 18.62% over the sampled period. While presenting our descriptive statistics, we have classified our sampled firms based on group affiliation. The mean value of CCE scaled by total asset is 19.9% in BGA firms and 19.3% in non-BGA firms. BGA firms have smaller boards with an average of 12 directors (14 in non-BGA) with about 54% (44% in non-BGA) independents directors. In addition, 68% of BGA (63% of non-BGA) firms have single leadership structure. The proportion of audit fees to auditor's total remuneration is higher for affiliated firms at 72% (compared to 65% in non-BGA firms). A notable observation is the absence of any skewness in the CG variables as the mean and median values are close to each other. Moving to the financial variables, the average cash flow multiple is 0.14 in BGA (0.15 in non-BGA) firms. The average debt equity is 0.49 in BGA (0.41 in non-BGA) with an average ROA of 10% (13% in non-BGA) and MTBVR of 3.9 in BGA (4.8 in non-BGA) firms, respectively. Finally, 94% of the BGA (93% in non-BGA) firms in the sample have distributed dividends to their shareholders.

Table 3 presents the correlation matrix. Correlation is a single dimension measure of the degree of association between the selected variables. We have flagged off the coefficients that are significant at the 1% and 5% levels. Among the significant correlation coefficients, some exhibit positive (or negative) relationship.

According to Hair et al. (1998), a data set must have two essential features to apply PCA. First, PCA is based on the interrelationship between the variables, and therefore, the data set must have a sufficient number of significant correlations to justify its application. Second, for determining the appropriateness of PCA we need to analyse the partial correlations among the selected attributes. Further, if factors that can explain the attributes exist, then the partial correlations values must be small. In our data set, the presence of a substantial number of significant correlations and partial correlations provides persuasive evidence for the application of factor analysis. An area of concern that remains is the high correlation values in some cases and the significant negative correlation between other variables, as this may lead to multicollinearity in our regression. Since all the variables do not have the predicted

Table 2 a. Descriptive statistics—Panel A. b Descriptive statistics—Panel B

(a)

The descriptive statistics in respect of the CG and firm-specific variables. Firms are having been classified as those having business group affiliated and non-affiliated firms

Firm classification		BGA					Non-BGA				
	Unit	Mean	Median	Max	Min	SD	Mean	Median	Max	Min	SD
CG and firm-specific variables											
1. Proportion of shares held by promoter group	%	0.491	0.50	0.804	0.253	0.16	0.548	0.551	0.9	0	0.231
2. Proportion of shares held by Institutional Investors	%	0.304	0.284	0.546	0.066	0.12	0.28	0.267	0.543	0.074	0.13
3. Board size	Persons	12	13	17	5	3.41	14	13	22	8	4.07
4. Proportion of ID on the board	%	0.54	0.52	0.8	0.35	0.1	0.44	0.44	0.66	0.17	0.11
5. Proportion of NED on the board	%	0.7	0.74	0.91	0.2	0.15	0.59	0.57	0.92	0.35	0.16
6. No. of board committees	Number	6	5	11	2	2.06	7	6	16	2	3.66

(continued)

Table 2 (continued)

(a)

The descriptive statistics in respect of the CG and firm-specific variables. Firms are having been classified as those having business group affiliated and non-affiliated firms

Firm classification		BGA					Non-BGA				
	Unit	Mean	Median	Max	Min	SD	Mean	Median	Max	Min	SD
7. Audit committee size	Persons	7	7	10	4	1.7	10	9	18	4	4.15
8. No. of audit committee meetings held	Number	6	6	12	3	1.78	6	6	10	4	1.76
9. ID on audit committee	Persons	5	5	8	3	1.36	8	7	16	3	4.19
10. Audit fee scaled by auditor's total remuneration	%	0.72	0.7	0.99	0.36	0.16	0.65	0.73	0.96	0.22	0.22
11. Debt equity ratio	Multiple	0.49	0.37	1.69	0.01	0.4	0.41	0.09	2.23	0	0.65
12. Cashflow_PBDITA scaled by total assets	Multiple	0.14	0.13	0.33	0	0.08	0.15	0.15	0.31	0	0.09
13. Firm age	Years	42	33	110	5	30	44	39	102	6	23
14. Capex/NonCA	Multiple	0.095	0.058	0.512	−0.177	0.134	0.061	0.053	0.187	0.000	0.048

(continued)

Table 2 (continued)

(a)

The descriptive statistics in respect of the CG and firm-specific variables.
Firms are classified as those having business group affiliated (total no. of firms 31) and non-affiliated firms (total no. of firms 27)

Firm classification		BGA					Non-BGA				
	Unit	Mean	Median	Max	Min	SD	Mean	Median	Max	Min	SD
15. Total assets	Rs. millions	266679	131245	2454954	17124	452089	360856	259934	1645891	39784	367218
16. ROA	%	0.1	0.07	0.3	−0.04	0.08	0.13	0.11	0.62	−0.08	0.13
17. MTBVR	Multiple	3.9	2.95	11.72	0.97	2.66	4.82	3.27	23.97	1.71	4.37

(a)

The descriptive statistics in respect of the CG and firm-specific variables.
Firms are classified as those having business group affiliated (total no. of firms 31) and non-affiliated firms (total no. of firms 27)

Firm classification		BGA					Non-BGA				
	Unit	Mean	Median	Max	Min	SD	Mean	Median	Max	Min	SD
Cash holding ratios											
18. CCE/TA	Multiple	0.199	0.149	0.954	0.019	0.185	0.193	0.151	0.532	0.036	0.126
19. CCE/NA	Multiple	0.331	0.177	2.376	0.020	0.459	0.286	0.182	1.250	0.038	0.273
20. NCA/TA	Multiple	0.577	0.592	0.995	−0.295	0.273	0.634	0.672	1.000	0.178	0.254
21. NCA/NA	Multiple	0.785	0.822	2.108	−0.371	0.46	0.835	0.778	2.039	0.212	0.43

(b)

Firm classification	BGA		Non-BGA	
Other CG and firm-specific variables	No. of firms	Proportion	No. of firms	Proportion
1. FII	29	0.94	21	0.78
2. CEO duality	21	0.68	17	0.63
3. CSR/sustainability committee	6	0.19	9	0.33
4. Nomination committee	18	0.58	5	0.19
5. Dividends declared	29	0.94	25	0.93

Table 3 Correlations matrix

	1	2	3	4	5	6	7	8	9	10	11	12	13
1. CCE/TA	1	***0.976***[a]	0.130	***0.664***[a]	−0.072	0.143	0.021	−0.046	*−0.022*	−0.077	−0.053	−0.129	0.189
		0	0.332	***0.000***	0.593	0.285	0.874	0.732	*0.870*	0.568	0.695	0.333	0.155
2. CCE/NA		1	0.130	***0.680***[a]	−0.110	0.173	0.060	−0.004	−0.062	−0.078	−0.038	−0.108	0.175
			0.331	***0.000***	0.410	0.195	0.656	0.978	0.645	0.563	0.775	0.418	0.189
3. NCA/TA			1	***0.807***[a]	−0.047	0.015	−0.109	−0.204	−0.151	***−0.347***[a]	0.081	−0.006	0.207
				0.000	0.724	0.914	0.417	0.124	0.258	***0.008***	0.547	0.966	0.119
4. NCA/NA				1	−0.082	0.087	−0.056	−0.150	−0.137	***−0.312***[b]	0.026	−0.097	0.257
					0.541	0.515	0.678	0.261	0.307	***0.017***	0.848	0.470	0.052
5. PGH					1	***−0.887***[a]	−0.146	***−0.426***[a]	***0.425***[a]	−0.106	0.063	−0.133	***−0.292***[b]
						0.000	0.274	***0.001***	***0.001***	0.428	0.639	0.318	***0.026***
6. INSTH						1	0.101	***0.473***[a]	***−0.310***[b]	0.129	−0.056	0.101	0.255
							0.453	***0.000***	***0.018***	0.335	0.677	0.450	0.053
7. BGA							1	0.228	***−0.429***[a]	−0.253	***0.412***[a]	***0.329***[b]	0.011
								0.085	***0.001***	0.055	***0.001***	***0.012***	0.932
8. FII								1	***−0.275***[b]	0.007	−0.015	0.208	0.147
									0.037	0.960	0.912	0.118	0.271
9. PSE									1	***0.344***[a]	***−0.324***[b]	***−0.381***[a]	***−0.360***[a]
										0.008	***0.013***	***0.003***	***0.006***
10. BS										1	***−0.490***[a]	−0.060	−0.084
											0.000	0.652	0.532
11. PropID											1	0.092	−0.005
												0.493	0.968
12. PropNED												1	0.244
													0.065

(continued)

Table 3 (continued)

	1	2	3	4	5	6	7	8	9	10	11	12	13
13. CEODual													1
14. No._BrdCm													
15. NomCom													
16. ID in AC													
17. AudCom_Sz													
18. AdCm_Mtng													
19. AF/TF													
20. CSR_Com													
21. DE													
22. MTBVR													
23. ROA													
24. CF													
25. Capex/ NonCA													
26. Ln_AGE													
27. LogTA													
28. DivDum													

	14	15	16	17	18	19	20	21	22	23	24	25	26	27	28
1. CCE/TA	0.085	0.081	−0.086	−0.138	−0.031	−0.052	0.082	−0.249	0.086	***0.336***[a]	0.162	**−*0.296***[b]	0.181	−0.178	0.067
	0.524	0.546	0.521	0.301	0.820	0.696	0.539	0.059	0.521	***0.010***	0.226	***0.024***	0.175	0.181	0.615
2. CCE/NA	0.116	0.089	−0.08[illegible]	−0.133	−0.016	−0.050	0.093	−0.187	0.030	0.280[b]	0.143	−0.315[b]	0.167	−0.166	0.043

(continued)

Table 3 (continued)

	14	15	16	17	18	19	20	21	22	23	24	25	26	27	28
	0.388	0.509	0.544	0.321	0.904	0.711	0.488	0.161	0.821	0.033	0.285	0.016	0.210	0.214	0.748
3. NCA/TA	−0.143	0.139	−0.038	−0.052	−0.208	0.042	−0.094	−0.106	0.054	−0.198	−0.171	***−0.646***[a]	0.198	−0.069	−0.115
	0.284	0.299	0.775	0.697	0.117	0.755	0.484	0.428	0.690	0.136	0.199	***0.000***	0.135	0.605	0.392
4. NCA/NA	0.001	0.143	−0.053	−0.092	−0.186	−0.011	−0.009	−0.187	0.049	0.030	−0.036	***−0.641***[a]	0.236	−0.136	−0.079
	0.993	0.285	0.694	0.492	0.161	0.934	0.948	0.160	0.715	0.825	0.786	***0.000***	0.075	0.310	0.556
5. PGH	0.221	−0.134	***0.330***[b]	***0.323***[b]	−0.169	−0.085	0.098	−0.005	0.053	0.041	−0.215	0.143	***−0.328***[b]	0.048	−0.141
	0.095	0.317	***0.011***	***0.013***	0.204	0.527	0.464	0.972	0.692	0.758	0.105	0.283	***0.012***	0.720	0.290
6. INSTH	−0.132	0.088	***−0.286***[b]	***−0.298***[b]	0.236	0.083	−0.072	−0.021	−0.029	0.088	0.252	−0.088	***0.366***[a]	−0.050	***0.295***[b]
	0.322	0.512	***0.029***	***0.023***	0.074	0.535	0.589	0.874	0.827	0.513	0.056	0.512	***0.005***	0.711	***0.024***
7. BGA	−0.196	0.403[a]	***−0.457***[a]	***−0.416***[a]	−0.021	0.161	−0.159	0.135	−0.131	−0.043	−0.031	0.166	−0.116	***−0.285***[b]	0.019
	0.139	0.002	***0.000***	***0.001***	0.875	0.228	0.232	0.312	0.328	0.750	0.820	0.213	0.386	***0.030***	0.889
8. FII	0.058	0.018	−0.084	−0.018	0.045	−0.043	0.008	0.088	0.081	0.151	***0.298***[b]	0.181	0.091	−0.189	***0.286***[b]
	0.663	0.896	0.532	0.896	0.739	0.750	0.953	0.512	0.546	0.257	***0.023***	0.174	0.498	0.155	***0.030***
9. PSE	***0.455***[a]	***−0.324***[b]	***0.563***[a]	***0.571***[a]	***0.281***[b]	***−0.401***[a]	***0.449***[a]	0.082	−0.149	−0.116	−0.087	−0.076	−0.008	***0.460***[a]	0.109
	0.000	***0.013***	***0.000***	***0.000***	***0.032***	***0.002***	***0.000***	0.539	0.264	0.388	0.515	0.573	0.952	***0.000***	0.416
10. BS	0.088	***−0.324***[b]	***0.401***[a]	***0.401***[a]	***0.260***[b]	−0.248	0.136	0.156	0.049	0.058	***0.310***[b]	0.195	0.146	***0.293***[b]	0.242
	0.510	***0.013***	***0.002***	***0.002***	***0.049***	0.060	0.308	0.244	0.715	0.663	***0.018***	0.142	0.274	***0.026***	0.068
11. PropID	−0.060	***0.463***[a]	−0.213	−0.188	−0.223	***0.357***[a]	−0.006	0.095	−0.078	−0.030	−0.153	−0.022	***−0.301***[b]	−0.073	−0.127
	0.653	***0.000***	0.108	0.158	0.092	***0.006***	0.964	0.478	0.560	0.823	0.251	0.871	***0.022***	0.584	0.340
12. PropNED	0.008	0.215	−0.121	−0.116	0.010	0.124	−0.076	−0.077	0.059	0.109	0.137	0.124	0.074	***−0.389***[a]	−0.017
	0.950	0.105	0.365	0.387	0.939	0.355	0.573	0.564	0.661	0.414	0.304	0.354	0.579	***0.003***	0.896
13. CEODual	0.151	0.115	−0.204	−0.220	0.070	0.092	−0.007	0.002	0.080	0.037	−0.060	−0.159	0.171	−0.183	−0.045
	0.259	0.389	0.125	0.097	0.602	0.493	0.957	0.985	0.552	0.782	0.653	0.234	0.199	0.169	0.737

(continued)

Table 3 (continued)

	14	15	16	17	18	19	20	21	22	23	24	25	26	27	28
14. No._BrdCm	1	0.082	***0.406***^{a}	***0.390***^{a}	***0.314***^{b}	**−*0.276***^{b}	***0.623***^{a}	−0.082	−0.126	0.132	−0.031	0.019	0.031	0.240	0.028
		0.540	***0.002***	***0.002***	***0.017***	***0.036***	***0.000***	0.540	0.345	0.323	0.818	0.885	0.816	0.070	0.834
15. NomCom		1	−0.229	−0.215	0.035	0.192	0.004	−0.079	−0.056	0.010	−0.084	−0.071	−0.153	−0.127	−0.058
			0.084	0.105	0.796	0.148	0.975	0.554	0.675	0.940	0.531	0.594	0.251	0.343	0.668
16. ID in AC			1	***0.961***^{a}	0.004	**−*0.337***^{a}	***0.410***^{a}	0.165	−0.017	−0.083	−0.056	−0.001	−0.044	***0.414***^{a}	−0.138
				0.000	0.979	***0.010***	***0.001***	0.214	0.901	0.538	0.674	0.993	0.740	***0.001***	0.300
17. Aud-Com_Sz				1	0.000	**−*0.340***^{a}	***0.430***^{a}	0.183	0.028	−0.118	−0.038	0.009	−0.061	***0.417***^{a}	−0.093
					0.999	***0.009***	***0.001***	0.169	0.833	0.376	0.779	0.949	0.648	***0.001***	0.486
18. AdCm_ Mtng					1	−0.174	0.230	0.047	−0.135	−0.179	−0.083	−0.028	***0.335***^{b}	***0.348***^{a}	0.158
						0.192	0.082	0.724	0.313	0.180	0.536	0.832	***0.010***	***0.007***	0.237
19. AF/TF						1	**−*0.313***^{b}	0.045	0.033	−0.020	−0.130	0.026	−0.074	−0.234	−0.191
							0.017	0.736	0.805	0.879	0.329	0.845	0.580	0.077	0.151
20. CSR_Com							1	−0.025	−0.129	−0.120	−0.095	−0.129	0.008	***0.336***^{a}	−0.150
								0.850	0.334	0.370	0.476	0.334	0.954	***0.010***	0.261
21. DE								1	**−*0.260***^{b}	**−*0.505***^{a}	**−*0.426***^{a}	0.016	0.000	0.239	−0.063
									0.049	***0.000***	***0.001***	0.903	0.999	0.071	0.638
22. MTBVR									1	***0.538***^{a}	***0.417***^{a}	0.115	0.043	**−*0.399***^{a}	0.100
										0.000	***0.001***	0.392	0.750	***0.002***	0.453
23. ROA										1	***0.634***^{a}	***0.298***^{b}	−0.065	**−*0.437***^{a}	***0.383***^{a}
											0.000	***0.023***	0.627	***0.001***	***0.003***

(continued)

Table 3 (continued)

	14	15	16	17	18	19	20	21	22	23	24	25	26	27	28
24. CF											1	0.207	0.025	−0.251	***0.301***[b]
												0.120	0.854	0.057	***0.022***
25. Capex/NonCA												1	–***0.365***[a]	−0.082	0.006
													0.005	0.543	0.964
26. Ln_AGE													1	0.081	***0.279***[b]
														0.545	***0.034***
27. LogTA														1	−0.041
															0.759
28. DivDum															1

[a]Correlation is significant at the 0.01 level (two-tailed)
[b]Correlation is significant at the 0.05 level (two-tailed)

sign in the correlation matrix and as correlation measures the effect of each variable in isolation, we have used the multivariate model.

The objective of using PCA is twofold: it helps us to understand how different variables change in relation to each other and how they are associated. This technique is useful for gaining insight into the structure of a construct like CG. Factor analysis results include Kaiser–Meyer–Olkin measure of sampling adequacy (hereafter, KMO) and Bartlett's test of sphericity. KMO helps us to understand how well the variables are predicted by the other variables and is the measure of whether the distribution of values is adequate for conducting factor analysis. Our sample yields a KMO of 0.65, which is middling, but this value should be greater than 0.5 for sampling adequacy to hold. However, for a complex construct like CG, it is difficult to set a standard and so it may be considered adequate.

Bartlett's test of sphericity is a measure of the multivariate normality of the set of distributions. In this study, the significance value is zero (<0.05) suggesting that the data does not differ significantly from multivariate normal. This also implies that the data set does not produce an identity matrix and hence is acceptable. Further, the value of the diagonal elements of the anti-image correlation matrix for all variables should be greater than or equal to 0.5 (Field 2009). Thus, variables with values below 0.5 have been excluded from our analysis. Removal of a variable affects KMO statistics, and for good analysis, these correlations are required to be small. Thereafter, we retained all factors with an eigenvalue greater than unity.

PCA converges in seven factors that retain 69.8% of the total variance in the original data. These seven factors characterise the dimensionality of our 24 individual indicators. We rotated the reduced solution using the "varimax" option, and this allowed the retained factors to be correlated, thereby enhancing the interpretability of the PCA solution. To interpret the factors, it is necessary to decide which attributes have a statistical and substantive association with each factor. We associate each factor with those variables that have a loading that exceeds 0.40 in absolute value and are different (statistically) from zero at conventional levels. Our PCA results produced an interpretable solution. A few cross-loadings existed, wherein the same indicator was associated with more than one factor. However, in the process of developing an indicator for a complex construct like CG, it is not surprising to find few unexpected results in the PCA solution.

Table 4 illustrates the variables associated with each factor. CGF#1 has six variable loadings out of which five are positive and one attribute is negative. This signifies that as the negative variable decreases in size the other five increases in size together. These six components explain 14.53% of variance. CGF#2 has four loadings of which three are positive and one negative showing that this negative variable decreases in size when the other three increase in size together. These four components explain 11.45% of variance. We interpret the other factors in an analogous way. The interpretation of these loadings has content validity as a measure of CG and the selected variables.

We compute Cronbach's α to understand the scale reliability of those dimensions that make up the factors. Cronbach's α is the most common estimate of the internal consistency of items used in a model. Cronbach's α is a measure of the correlation

Table 4 Rotated component matrix[a]

		Component						
		1	2	3	4	5	6	7
Aspect of CG		CGF#1	CGF#2	CGF#3	CGF#4	CGF#5	CGF#6	CGF#7
Panel A: total variance								
Variance retained (%)		14.529	11.445	11.310	11.095	7.310	7.086	7.067
Cumulative variance (%)		14.529	25.974	37.284	48.378	55.689	62.775	**69.841**
Panel B: factor loadings								
1.	AudCom_Size	0.856						
2.	ID in AC	0.842						
3.	CSR_Com	0.728						
4.	No._of_BrdCom	0.718					0.446	
5.	PSU	0.560				−0.406		
6.	AF to TF	−0.401						
7.	ROA		0.868					
8.	DE		−0.771					
9.	CF_PBDITA/TA		0.730					
10.	MTBVR		0.610					
11.	PropID			−0.793				
12.	NomCom			−0.728				
13.	BS			0.662				
14.	BGA			−0.465				0.453
15.	DivDum			0.420				
16.	INSTH				0.891			
17.	PGH				−0.873			
18.	FII				0.686			
19.	PropNED					0.768		
20.	CEODuality					0.651		
21.	Ln_TA	0.406	−0.452			−0.494		
22.	AudCom_Mtng						0.784	
23.	Capex/NonCA							0.816
24.	Ln_AGE							−0.489

Extraction method: Principal component analysis
Rotation method: Varimax with Kaiser normalisation
[a]Rotation converged in 20 iterations

between elements of a multipart measure that ranges from 0 to 1. The mean (median) of the alpha coefficient is 0.51 (0.65). This level of reliability is lower than the benchmarks suggested by Nunnally (1967). Despite this, we feel our measurement analysis has higher level of reliability than single indicators used to measure CG.

Our objective was to explore the association between the CG structure of the firm and cash holdings. We use four different sets of regression tests. The dependent variables are the cash holding ratios. The independent variables are CG and firm-specific variables affecting cash. Assuming a linear relationship exists between the variables, we examine whether there exists is an association. Our objective functions are

I. CCE/TA = f (ownership, board structure, audit related, financial and control variables, error)
II. CCE/NA = f (ownership, board structure, audit related, financial and control variables, error)
III. NCA/TA = f (ownership, board structure, audit related, financial and control variables, error)
IV. NCA/NA = f (ownership, board structure, audit related, financial and control variables, error)

Using the factor scores generated by PCA, we run regression. Models I and II yielded R square values of 21.4% and 17.7%, respectively. This signifies that 21.4% and 17.7% of the variability in cash holding are accounted for by the models considering the predictor variables. In both the models I and II, two factors turn out to be significant; CGF#2 is positively related, while CGF#7 is negatively related to cash holdings, respectively. Models III and IV yielded R square values of 47.3% and 45%, respectively. Model III documents a negative relationship between CG factors, CGF#6 and CGF#7, and firm liquidity. The results of model IV suggest a negative relationship between CGF#7 and firm liquidity.

The coefficients of the CG variables explain the predictions of our research problem relating CG to cash ratios. A significant negative coefficient shows that firms with stronger CG tend to reduce cash balances and have higher capital expenditures, while entrenched managers with high cash reserves spend more on current assets. A significant positive coefficient suggests that management accumulates excess cash (if it is allowed do so) and the motivation for this behaviour seems to be that the precautionary motive for holding cash is strong. Further, in emerging markets, like India, firms hold cash or own liquidity for financial flexibility compared to developed markets and it might be that such cash holding is independent of the CG structure of the firm. Firms are anticipating potentially higher growth opportunities as compared to those in advanced economies, where markets are mostly saturated. Firms resort to cash hoarding to take advantage of strategic opportunities as they present themselves. Parallel to this point is the fact that larger cash reserves help firms in avoiding uncertainty and hedge themselves against the difficulty of accessing external funds possibly because of limited collateral securities and economies of scale. It could also be that firms with weaker CG structures hold low cash reserves to mitigate the potential agency problems associated with excess cash holdings. The results are presented in Table 5.

7 Conclusion

This study examines the interaction of CG standards and firm-specific financial attributes in determining the level of cash holdings. We use 24 CG standards and firm-specific characteristics. After controlling for cash flow, leverage, capital expenditure, profitability, growth, dividend payout, age, and size, our test offers mixed

Table 5 Results of regression analysis

The results in this table examine whether the dependent variables are influenced by the CG and financial factors derived using principal component analysis. The standardised coefficients (beta) and their significance, within parentheses, are disclosed

Model	I	II	III	IV
	CCE/TA	CCE/NA	NCA/TA	NCA/NA
CGF#1	−0.016 (0.900)	−0.001 (0.992)	−0.079 (0.447)	−0.032 (0.758)
CGF#2	**0.318 (0.015)**[b]	**0.254 (0.054)**[b]	−0.045 (0.664)	0.122 (0.251)
CGF#3	−0.081 (0.521)	−0.107 (0.410)	−0.147 (0.159)	−0.174 (0.104)
CGF#4	0.055 (0.665)	0.101 (0.434)	−0.065 (0.526)	−0.004 (0.973)
CGF#5	0.003 (0.982)	0.017 (0.896)	0.070 (0.500)	0.053 (0.617)
CGF#6	0.086 (0.495)	0.088 (0.494)	**−0.210 (0.046)**[b]	−0.114 (0.282)
CGF#7	**−0.309 (0.017)**[b]	**−0.288 (0.029)**[b]	**−0.624 (0.000)**[a]	**−0.623 (0.000)**[a]
R^2	**21.4%**	**17.7%**	**47.3%**	**45%**
Constant	9.921 (0.000)	6.397 (0.000)	22.518 (0.000)	17.545 (0.000)

[a], [b] indicate that the coefficient is significant at the 1 % and 5 % levels, respectively

results on the association between CG and cash holdings. Firm with stronger CG tends to reduce cash balances and has higher capital expenditures, while entrenched managers with high cash reserves spend more on current assets. Firms also hold cash for financial flexibility and to take advantage of strategic opportunities. Also, larger cash holdings help firms to avoid uncertainty and offer hedge against the difficulty of accessing external funds. Our study contributes to the literature on CG and cash holding by using a new data set. We employ PCA which helps us reduce measurement error and develop a reliable representation. Our contribution has been the consistent estimation of the relationship between CG and cash holding and liquidity, considering the interrelationships among CG and financial variables in listed Indian companies. Our empirical findings also have implications for shareholder activism around the issue of corporate cash holdings. This research presents a platform for future research in similar context that will further confirm the interpretation of our results.

References

Abbott, L. J., Park, Y., & Parker, S. (2000). The effects of audit committee activity and independence on corporate fraud. *Managerial Finance, 26*(11), 55–68.

Acharya, V. V. & Almeida, H., & Campello, M. (2007). Is cash negative debt? A hedging perspective on corporate financial policies. *Journal of Financial Intermediation, 16*(4), 515–554. Elsevier.

Agrawal, A., & Chadha, S. (2005). Corporate governance and accounting scandals. *Journal of Law and Economics, 48*(2), 371–406.

Ammann, M., Oesch, D., & Schmid, M. M. (2011). Corporate governance and firm value: International evidence. *Journal of Empirical Finance, 18,* 36–55.

Anderson, R. C., Mansi, S., & Reeb, D. M. (2004). Board characteristics, accounting report integrity, and the cost of debt. *Journal of Accounting & Economics, 37*(3). Available at SSRN: https://ssrn.com/abstract=491883 or http://dx.doi.org/10.2139/ssrn.491883.

Bertrand, M., Mehta, P., & Mullainathan, S. (2002). Ferreting out tunnelling: An application to Indian business groups. *The Quarterly Journal of Economics, 117*(1), 121–148.

Bates, T. W., Kahle, K. M., & Stulz, R. M. (2009). Why do U.S. firms hold so much more cash than they used to? *Journal of Finance, 64*(5), 1985–2021. American Finance Association.

Baumol, W. J. (1952). The transaction demand for cash: An inventory theoretic approach; ECON 32, The Bobbs-Merrill Reprint Series in Economics. Available at: http://pages.stern.nyu.edu/~wbaumol/TheTransactionsDemandForCash.pdf.

Beattie, V., Fearnley, S., & Hines, T. (2002). The Impact of Changes to The Non-Audit Services Regime on Finance Directors, Audit Committee Chairs and Audit Partners of UK Listed Companies; Chartered Accountants' Trustees Limited. Available at: https://www.icaew.com/-/media/corporate/files/technical/research-and-academics/publications-and-projects/audit-and-assurance-publications/briefing-the-impact-of-the-changes-to-the-non-audit-services.ashx.

Beekes, W., Hong, A., & Owen, S. A. (2010). An alternative measure of corporate governance using discrete principal component analysis. Available at SSRN: https://ssrn.com/abstract=1623005 or http://dx.doi.org/10.2139/ssrn.1623005.

Bhagat, S., & Bolton, Brian. (2008). Corporate governance and firm performance. *Journal of Corporate Finance, 14*(3), 257–273.

Black, B. S., De Carvalho, A. G., Khanna, V. S., Kim, W., & Yurtoglu, B. B., Corporate Governance Indices and Construct Validity (2017). University of Michigan Law & Economics Research Paper Forthcoming; Corporate Governance: An International Review, 2017 Forthcoming; University of Michigan Law & Economics Research Paper; Northwestern Law & Econ Research Paper No. 13-05; European Corporate Governance Institute (ECGI)—Finance Working Paper No. 483/2016. Available at SSRN: https://ssrn.com/abstract=2838273.

Boone, A. L., Field, L. C., Karpoff, J. M., & Raheja, C. G. (2007). The determinants of corporate board size and composition: An empirical analysis (March 1, 2006). *Journal of Financial Economics (JFE), 85*(1). AFA 2005 Philadelphia Meetings. Available at SSRN: https://ssrn.com/abstract=605762 or http://dx.doi.org/10.2139/ssrn.605762.

Brickley, J. A., Coles, J. F., & Terry, R. L. (1994). Outside directors and the adoptions of poison pills. *Journal of Financial Economics, 35*, 371–390. Google Scholar CrossRef.

Brown, L. D., & Caylor, M. L. (2004). Corporate Governance and Firm Operating Performance, SSRN. http://papers.ssrn.com/sol3/papers.cfm?abstract_id=586423.

Dey, A. (2008). Corporate governance and agency conflicts. *Journal of Accounting Research, 46*, 1143–.

Faulkender, M. W. (2002). Cash holdings among small businesses. Available at SSRN: https://ssrn.com/abstract=305179 or http://dx.doi.org/10.2139/ssrn.305179.

Field, A. (2009). *Discovering Statistics using SPSS*, 3e (pp. 627–82). Sage.

Gao, H., Harford, J., & Li, K. (2013). Determinants of corporate cash policy: Insights from private firms. *Journal of Financial Economics (JFE)*, Forthcoming. Available at SSRN: http://dx.doi.org/10.2139/ssrn.2023999.

Gopalan, R., Nanda, V., & Seru, A. (2007). Affiliated firms and financial support: Evidence from Indian business groups. *Journal of Financial Economics, 86*(3), 759–795.

Graham, J. R., Harvey, C. R., & Rajgopal, S. (2005). The economic implications of corporate financial reporting. *Journal of Accounting and Economics*, *40*(1–3), 3–73.

Gugler, K., Mueller, D. C., & Yurtoglu, B. B. (2003). Corporate governance and the return on investment, ECGI, SSRN. Google Scholar.

Hair, J. F., Anderson, R. E., Tatham, R. L., & Black, W. C. (1998). *Multivariate data analysis* (5th ed.). Upper Saddle River, NJ: Prentice Hall.

Harford, J., Mansi, S. A., & Maxwell, W. F. (2008). Corporate governance and firm cash holdings in the US. *Journal of Financial Economics, 87,* 535–555.

Jensen, M. C. (1986). Agency costs of free cash flow, corporate finance, and takeovers. *American Economic Review, 76,* 323–329.

John, K., & Senbet, L. W. (1998). Corporate governance and board effectiveness. *Journal of Banking & Finance, 22,* 371–403.

Kalcheva, I., & Lins, K. V. (2007). International evidence on cash holdings and expected managerial agency problems. *Review of Financial Studies, 20*(4), 1087–1112.

Karamanou, I., & Vafeas, N. (2005). The association between corporate boards, audit committees, and management earnings forecasts: An empirical analysis. *Journal of Accounting Research, 43,* 453–486. Available at SSRN: https://ssrn.com/abstract=876678.

Keynes, J. M. (1936). The General Theory of Employment, Interest, and Money. Available at: http://cas2.umkc.edu/economics/people/facultypages/kregel/courses/econ645/winter2011/generaltheory.pdf.

Krishnan, G. V., & Visvanathan, G. (2009). Do auditors price audit committee's expertise? The case of accounting vs. non-accounting financial experts. *Journal of Accounting, Auditing & Finance, 24*(1), 115–144.

Larcker, D, Richardson, S., & Tuna, I. (2007). Corporate Governance, Accounting Outcomes, and Organizational Performance, SSRN.

Miller, M. H., & Orr, D. (1966). A model of the demand for money by firms. *The Quarterly Journal of Economics, 80*(3), 413–435.

Morck, R., Shleifer, A., & Vishny, R. (1990). Do managerial objectives drive bad acquisitions? *Journal of Finance, 45*(1), 31–48.

Myers, S. C., & Rajan, R. G. (1998). The paradox of liquidity. *The Quarterly Journal of Economics, 113*(3), 733–771.

Nunnally, J. (1967). *Psychometric theory*. New York: McGraw Hill.

Opler, T., Pinkowitz, L., Stulz, R. H., & Williamson, R. (1999). The determinants and implications of corporate cash holdings. *Journal of Financial Economics, 52,* 3–46.

Ozkan, A., & Ozkan, N. (2004). Corporate cash holdings: An empirical investigation of UK companies. *Journal of Banking & Finance, 28*(9), 2103–2134.

Riddick, L. A., & Whited, T. M. (2009). The corporate propensity to save, *64*(4), 1729–1766.

Roy, A. (2016, June 16). Corporate governance and firm performance: A study of Indian listed firms. *Metamorphosis: A Journal of Management Research, 15*(1), 31–46. Available at SSRN: https://ssrn.com/abstract=2796593.

Part VII
Financial Risk Management

Empirical Analysis of the Determinants of Dividend Payouts of Indian Banking Stocks Using Panel Data Econometrics

R. Venkataraman and Thilak Venkatesan

Abstract Dividend payout is the most vital decision that a company takes as it involves either satisfying shareholders today for their investments in the company or reinvestment of profits for future growth. The various theories associated with the dividend payout articulate capital structure, net profit, earnings per share and growth rate as the predictors. In this regard, the paper intends to analyse the capital structure and dividend decisions in the Indian banking sector. The study relied upon secondary data, which were extracted from the annual reports of the banks and BSE website. The selection of banks was based on data availability so as to frame the array for panel analysis and provide optimal solutions. Five banks were selected for a period of 12 years, three from private and two from public sector, respectively. Multiple regressions were used for obtaining initial variables for the study, and panel data econometrics was used to analyse the heterogeneity of cross section and time series to provide relationship among the dependent and independent variables. The return on assets and the size of the firm in terms of assets and the previous period debt/equity were observed key variables influencing the dividend payouts.

Keywords Capital structure · Dividend payout policy · Panel data model

JEL Classification G32 · G35 · C33

R. Venkataraman
Presidency College, Bangalore, India
e-mail: venkatramana.r@presidency.edu.in

T. Venkatesan (✉)
Bharathiar University, Coimbatore, India
e-mail: v.thilak@gmail.com

N. R. Bhanumurthy et al. (eds.), *Advances in Finance & Applied Economics*,
https://doi.org/10.1007/978-981-13-1696-8_17

1 Introduction

The composition of financing the assets is vital as firms strive to reduce overall cost of capital using the optimal level of debt/equity capital. The key to the financing decision is to maximize shareholder's wealth by choosing the optimal mix of debt and equity such that the earnings can be increased by the right amount of debt The basic financial decisions include investment decision, financing decision and the dividend decision. The various sources of funds comprise the preference equity, common equity, short- and long-term debt. Dividend policy of a company is used to make the decision regarding the percentage of earnings to be paid to the shareholders according to the set of guidelines formulated. A company has to analyse certain factors before framing their dividend policy and those factors are the type of industry, ownership structure, age of corporation, size of the firm, the extent of share distribution, dividend payout ratio, different shareholder's expectations, expected rate of return, leverage, future financial requirements and liquidity, business cycles, growth and Profitability, government policies, taxation policy, trend of profits, liquidity, capital market considerations, inflation, etc. In this paper, factors such as capital structure, size of the firm, return on assets, earnings per share are taken into consideration with respect to influence on dividend decisions.

2 Research Design

2.1 Statement of the Problem

There is a notable relationship between the capital structure (debt-to-equity) and the dividend payout decisions along with other factors such as earnings per share, return on assets and the size of the firm having an observable relationship with the dividend decisions according to the review of papers. But, the type of relationship between them is unanswered and varies from different type of studies conducted by the existing research. So, this paper tries to answer the observations from the various factors which influence dividend payout ratio.

2.2 Review of Literature

Faulkender et al. (2006) attempted to present an integrated theory of capital structure and dividend policy using multivariate analysis and simultaneous regression method for the financial data obtained from COMPUSTAT and stock return data from CRSP for the time period of 1981–2001 wherein they found that greater investor control can be achieved by higher dividend payouts, and moreover, dividend payout ratio is lesser when there is a better corporate governance and vice versa.

Ince and Owers (2012) developed a valuation model as an extension of Miller and Modigliani model using comparative statistics correlation and numerical analysis for the data available in S & P 1500 universe. The application of the model to 10 different US tax regimes for the time period of 1979–1990 generated various testable predictions that are consistent such as the dividend payout has no influence on the effects of leverage when the tax rates of dividend and capital gains are closer, but the payout is able to offset the value enhancing effects of leverage when the tax rate on capital gains is higher than the dividend tax rate.

Moradi et al. (2010) analysed the factors influencing the dividends such as profitability, debt ratio, beta rate, size, retained earnings rate and P/E using multiple regression method. The data for the time period of 2000–2008 of all companies listed in the Tehran Stock exchange were used for the analysis wherein they found that the dividend and profitability has a direct relationship, whereas the debt ratio, beta rate and P/E have an inverse relationship with the dividend, and moreover, company size and rate of retained earnings have no influence on the dividend policy.

Esfahani et al. (2013) examined the relationship between capital structure, corporate governance and dividend policy using regression analysis and cross-sectional design method for the data of Malaysian listed companies for the year 2009 and 2010 and found that the corporate governance has negative effect on dividend payout as predicted and that the effect of capital structure on dividend payout is also negative but not significant.

Sanvicente (2011) identified the determinants of capital structure considering the interaction of leverage, dividend payout and ownership policy decisions using three-stage least-squares method for the data obtained from the Economática® database for 91 Brazilian publicly owned firms in 2007. The results of the study were that the choice of capital structure is negatively associated with the ownership decisions and dividend payment decision is influenced by transaction cost considerations regardless of group affiliation.

Warrad et al. (2012) examined the relationship between dividend payout policy and ownership structure for industrial companies using statistical tools such as multivariate and sensitivity analysis using the data for the time period of 2005–2007 and observed a significant positive relationship of foreign ownership structure, company size, debt ratio and the dividend payout policy.

Kiprono (2012) analysed the relationship between capital structure and dividend payout ratio of companies using regression analysis for the data of 29 companies listed at the Nairobi Securities Exchange for the time period 2007–2011 and found that dividend payout ratio and capital structure has significant relationship and concluded that leverage negatively affects dividend payout ratio.

Arshad et al. (2013) investigated the potential alliance between ownership structures and dividend payout policy by examining the payout behaviour of dividends. The ownership structure of stocks was studied which comprised the information, communication and transportation sectors over the period 2007–2011. They used descriptive and correlation analysis and showed that both CEO duality have effect on firm's dividend policy, whereas the board size has no significant effect on the dividend policies of firm.

Tariq (2015) identified the joint determinants of leverage and dividend policy using multiple regression analysis for the non-financial firms in Pakistan and India for the time period 2010–2014 and found that the decision to take additional debt is influenced by the size of the firm and the liquidity of a firm jointly determines both leverage and dividend policy, whereas the profitability, asset tangibility and institutional ownership has no significant effect on leverage and dividend policy.

Sang et al. (2015) analysed the capital structure of 16 companies listed in Nairobi Securities Exchange of Kenya in the industrial and allied sector using regression analysis and concluded that the dividend payout ratio and retained earnings has weak inverse relationship whereas dividend payout ratio and leverage has strong inverse relationship.

Islam (2017) determined the relationship between the capital structure and dividend policy and attempted to develop a model for predicting dividend payout for the empirical evidence from Standard Chartered Bank Botswana using statistical analysis and found that there is a positive correlation between capital structure and dividend payment and an even stronger correlation is evident between earnings per share and dividend payment.

2.3 Research Gap

Limited research has been conducted for comparison of public and private sectors in banking industry, and therefore, this study is an attempt to measure the impact of capital structure on dividend decisions in both sectors of Indian banking industry. Further, this study uses panel data econometrics to test the relationship between debt-to-equity ratio and dividend payout ratio along with the other control variables.

Thereby, this study contributes to the literature on relationship with dividend payment policies with capital structure of the banks. It also provides insights into policy-makers that the banks should use optimum capital structure for arriving at the proper dividend payment decisions.

2.4 Scope for Further Research

The study is conducted for the companies in the Indian banking sector with respect to both public and private sector for the time period 2004–2005 to 2015–2016. The study provides scope for further research with respect to the following:

- To choose any other industry for in depth analysis of factors influencing DPR and
- To maximize the sample size in terms of cross section and time horizon for the entire banking industry.

3 Research Methodology

3.1 Objectives for the Study

1. To identify the factors affecting dividend policy and payout ratio in banking industry.
2. Explain the influencing factors and summarize the significant factors.
3. Execute panel data analysis to outline both cross-section and time series heterogeneity.
4. To devise a model of significant factors that can aid in decision making.

3.2 Research Hypothesis

The relationship between the independent and dependent variables can be tested by forming hypothesis. From the literature review, it is found that there are many other factors affecting the dividend decisions including the capital structure of the firm. So, a hypothesis was formulated as follows:

H_{01} = There is no relationship between the capital structure and dividend payout.
H_{02} = There is no relationship among the firm size, return on assets, growth, profitability and dividend payout.

3.3 Data Collection

Secondary data are from respective banks annual reports and BSE website. The financial statements and business ratios in the annual report were referred for the analysis.

Period of study—12 years from 2004–2005 to 2015–2016

Sample size—Random selection method is adopted based on the data availability. Five banks were taken (3 private sector banks and 2 public sector banks).

3.4 Panel Data Econometrics

Panel data can be represented as;

$$X_{it}, i = 1, \ldots, N\, t = 1, \ldots, T,$$

where i represents the cross-section items as x_1, x_2, x_3, … x_n. and, t representing the time period for each data point.

A general regression panel model is denoted by;

$$y_{it} = \alpha + \beta' X_{it} + u_{it},$$
$$u_{it} = \mu_i + v_{it}.$$

where $u_{it,}$ consists of both the cross-section and the time series error terms. The fixed effects model and the random effects are used to determine the appropriate structure of the variables in the study. The cross-section items in the study are the EPS, debt/equity ratio, net profit and growth rate of the firm used in determining the dividend payout ratio. The random effects are the time component of the data for 12 years stacked according to the respective bank.

An appropriate model is to be identified depending upon whether the u_{it} has correlation with at least one independent cross-section variable.

If there is no correlation between u_{it}, and independent variable, pooled OLS can yield unbiased and consistent results. If u_{it} is correlated and is fixed over time, a fixed effects model yields a consistent estimate, and if u_{it} is correlated and is changing over time, a random effects model is opted for estimation. A random effects model is a generalized least-squares model used to control for the serial correlation of u_{it} with the independent variable. A correction towards the serial correlation is the introduction of the lag of the dependent variable as a regressor.

$$y_{it} = \alpha + \beta' X_{it} + \gamma y_{it-1} + u_{it},$$

The above equation denotes the use of the lagged dependent variable widely used to correct the serial correlation as proposed by Arellano–Bond estimator (1991).

3.5 *Limitations of the Study*

There is a problem in the availability of adequate data for few time periods, i.e. the data needed were not found directly in the annual reports of the bank; instead, it was calculated by applying relevant formulas. The selection of data was based on data availability and restricted to five banks. The variables were selected based on the review of literature, and the variables were earnings per share, debt/equity ratio, net profit and growth rate of the firm.

4 Data Analysis and Interpretation

4.1 *Dependent Variable*

The dependent variable for the study is dividend payout ratio (DPR). DPR is calculated by dividing the dividend per share (DPS) to the earnings per share available to the equity shareholders (EPS).

$$\text{Dividend payout ratio} = (\text{Dividend per share}/\text{Earnings per share}) * 100$$

4.2 *Independent Variables*

The independent variables for the study is capital structure, and three other variables are earnings per share (EPS), return on assets (ROA) and size of the firm.

4.3 *Capital Structure*

Capital structure is measured based on the ratio called debt/equity ratio which is calculated by dividing the total debt of the firm to the total shareholder's equity.

$$\text{Debt/equity ratio} = (\text{Total debt/Total shareholder's equity})$$

Here the total debt includes the borrowings, deposits and other liabilities of the bank. Total shareholder's equity includes the total share capital, reserves and surplus and employee's stock options outstanding.

4.4 *Earnings Per Share*

Earnings per share is calculated by dividing the total earnings available to common shareholders to the total number of equity share holders, whereas the total earnings is obtained by deducting the preferred dividends paid from the net income.

$$\text{Earnings per share} = (\text{Total earnings/outstanding shares}) * 100$$

4.5 *Return on Assets*

Return on assets is calculated by dividing the Net income to the average of total assets, whereas the average of total assets is obtained by adding the total assets of the company for the current year to the total assets for its previous year and then by dividing the sum by two.

$$\text{Return on assets} = (\text{Net income}/\text{Average of total assets})$$

4.6 *Size of the Firm*

The size of the firm is measured by taking the natural log value of the total assets for respective years.

Table defining the variables

Variable	Definition
Dependent variable	
Dividend payout ratio	Dividend per share to earnings per share ratio
Independent variables	
Debt-to-equity ratio	Total debt to total shareholders' equity ratio
Earnings per share	Total earnings to outstanding shares ratio
Return on assets	Net income to average of total assets ratio
Size	Natural log of total assets

4.7 *Panel Data Analysis: Summary Report for Panel Data Analysis*

From the panel data analysis two models such as OLS (ordinary least-squares) and fixed effects model is used to find the level of significance between the dependent variables (dividend payout ratio) and independent variables (debt-to-equity ratio, earnings per share, return on assets and the size of the firm).

Model 1 Pooled OLS, using 60 observations. Included five cross-sectional units. Time series length = 12. Dependent variable: DPR

	Coefficient	Std. error	t-ratio	p value	
Const	11.8182	4.68519	2.5225	0.0146	**
DE	0.0896398	0.196583	0.4560	0.6502	
EPS	−0.0587564	0.0152554	−3.8515	0.0003	***
ROA	−0.00220617	1.57068	−0.0014	0.9989	
SIZE	0.184043	0.142951	1.2875	0.2034	
BANK	2.97355	0.560674	5.3035	<0.0001	***

Mean-dependent var	22.22938	S.D.-dependent var	5.854947
Sum-squared resid	1219.062	S.E. of regression	4.751339
R-squared	0.397263	Adjusted R-squared	0.341454
F(5, 54)	7.118268	P value (F)	0.000035
Log-likelihood	−175.4811	Akaike criterion	362.9622
Schwarz criterion	375.5282	Hannan–Quinn	367.8774
rho	0.293312	Durbin–Watson	1.029799

4.8 Pooled OLS (Ordinary Least-Squares) Model

The following table shows the result of panel data analysis with the pooled OLS (ordinary least-squares) model (Model 1):

An R-squared of 0.39 suggests 39% accuracy of prediction along with Durbin–Watson statistic of 1.029 signifying autocorrelation. The data must be corrected for autocorrelation. The overall model is fit which is observed by p value (F) statistic. The significant variables in prediction of DPR are EPS & Bank ID in the pooled OLS model. The results match the prior study with regards to EPS (Mand and Singh 2015). The significance of variables at 1% are denoted by "***", variables at 5% denoted by "**" and variables at 10% denoted by "*".

An R-squared of 0.61 suggests 61% accuracy of prediction along with Durbin–Watson statistic of 1.55 signifying autocorrelation. The data must be corrected for autocorrelation. The overall model is fit which is observed by p value (F) statistic. The significant variables in prediction are debt/equity ratio & ROA in the fixed effects model (Model 2).

Joint test on named regressors -
Test statistic: F(4, 51) = 4.67706
with p value = P(F(4, 51) > 4.67706) = 0.00271527

Test for differing group intercepts -
Null hypothesis: The groups have a common intercept
Test statistic: F(3, 51) = 9.49784
with p value = P(F(3, 51) > 9.49784) = 4.34326e-005

Model 2 Fixed effects using 60 observations. Included five cross-sectional units. Time series length = 12. Dependent variable: DPR

	Coefficient	Std. error	t-ratio	p value	
Const	19.7118	3.96365	4.9731	<0.0001	***
DE	0.351832	0.177833	1.9784	0.0533	*
EPS	0.00459923	0.0190098	0.2419	0.8098	
ROA	−3.92135	1.56916	−2.4990	0.0157	**
SIZE	0.215436	0.153383	1.4046	0.1662	

Mean-dependent var	22.22938	S.D.-dependent var	5.854947
Sum-squared resid	782.1033	S.E. of regression	3.916039
LSDV R-squared	0.613307	Within R-squared	0.268379
LSDV F(8, 51)	10.11095	P value (F)	2.58e−08
Log-likelihood	−162.1656	Akaike criterion	342.3312
Schwarz criterion	361.1803	Hannan–Quinn	349.7041
rho	−0.031358	Durbin–Watson	1.557258

Model 3 Random-effects (GLS), using 60 observations. Included 5 cross-sectional units. Time series length = 12. Dependent variable: DPR

	Coefficient	Std. error	t-ratio	p value	
Const	17.6487	4.83684	3.6488	0.0006	***
DE	0.253308	0.183736	1.3787	0.1735	
ROA	−3.18712	1.54204	−2.0668	0.0434	**
BANK	1.89942	1.04581	1.8162	0.0747	*

Mean-dependent var	22.22938	S.D.-dependent var	5.854947
Sum-squared resid	1901.544	S.E. of regression	5.775848
Log-likelihood	−188.8186	Akaike criterion	385.6372
Schwarz criterion	394.0146	Hannan–Quinn	388.9141

Joint test on named regressors tests whether the beta coefficients of the regressors are equal to zero. The p value being less than 5% rejects the Null, and we conclude that the coefficient are not zero and the regressors do have a impact on the predictor variable DPR.

Test for differing group intercepts was performed to check whether the banks have common intercept, and the p value (4.34326e−005) suggests that the intercept is different for different banks, and we reject pool ability of the banks (Model 3).

'Between' variance = 8.33697
'Within' variance = 15.3622
theta used for quasi-demeaning = 0.635151

Breusch–Pagan test -
Null hypothesis: Variance of the unit-specific error = 0

Asymptotic test statistic: Chi-square (1) = 15.6057
with p value = 7.80206e−005

Hausman test -
Null hypothesis: GLS estimates are consistent
Asymptotic test statistic: Chi-square (2) = 10.3526
with p value = 0.00564886

Breusch–Pagan test in the random effects model aims at concluding whether the variables can be pooled or variables exhibits random effects model (Baltagi 2008). The Null hypothesis in the test is the variance of the unit-specific error is zero, i.e. Sigma mu squared = 0, and in this case, we reject Null as the p value is 7.80206e−005; we cannot pool the data and we need to choose the random effects model.

Hausman test statistic was performed to check for concluding the model is a fixed effects model or random effects model. The Null hypothesis is that the GLS estimates are consistent, i.e. the random estimates are consistent. Since the p value is less than 5%, we conclude that we choose the fixed effects model.

Robust test for differing group intercepts -
Null hypothesis: The groups have a common intercept
Test statistic: Welch F(4, 24.6) = 3.45377
with p value = P(F(4, 24.6) > 3.45377) = 0.0225648

Robust test for differing group intercepts was performed to check whether the banks have common intercept, and the p value (0.0225648) suggests that the intercept is different for different banks, and we reject pool ability of the banks.

Distribution free Wald test for heteroskedasticity -
Null hypothesis: the units have a common error variance
Asymptotic test statistic: Chi-square (5) = 26.7903
with p value = 6.26645e−005

The observed p value suggests the data are heteroskedastic even after including the log of DPR as a regressor. The Durbin–Watson value suggests the presence of autocorrelation.

Test for normality of residual -
Null hypothesis: error is normally distributed
Test statistic: Chi-square (2) = 1.33904
with p value = 0.511955

Model 4 Fixed effects, using 55 observations. Included five cross-sectional units time series length = 11. Dependent variable: DPR robust (HAC) standard errors

	Coefficient	Std. error	t-ratio	p value	
Const	−38.8067	2.5322	−15.3253	<0.0001	***
l_ROA	−1.81419	0.242248	−7.4890	<0.0001	***
l_ROA_1	1.39557	0.316974	4.4028	<0.0001	***
l_SIZE	0.838535	0.221378	3.7878	0.0005	***
l_SIZE_1	−0.423921	0.218673	−1.9386	0.0591	*
l_DPR	19.0803	0.708347	26.9364	<0.0001	***
l_EPS_1	0.32719	0.13786	2.3733	0.0222	**
DPR_1	0.0209825	0.0185495	1.1312	0.2643	

Mean-dependent var	22.40536	S.D.-dependent var	5.472301
Sum-squared resid	13.36140	S.E. of regression	0.557432
LSDV R-squared	0.991737	Within R-squared	0.980437
Log-likelihood	−39.13013	Akaike criterion	102.2603
Schwarz criterion	126.3483	Hannan–Quinn	111.5753
rho	0.171694	Durbin–Watson	1.431830

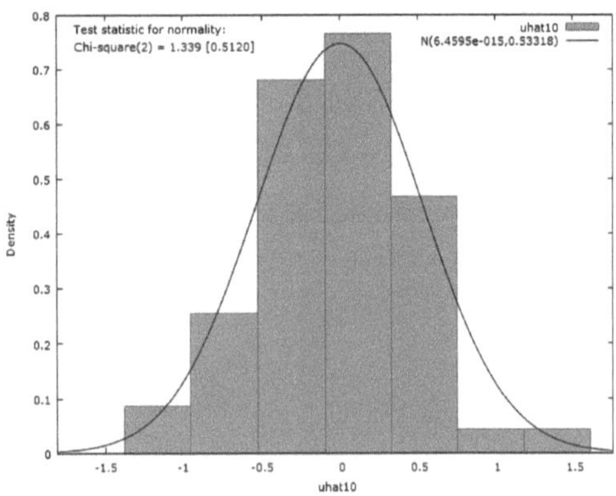

The variables are observed normal as the p value of the normality test is greater than 0.05. The observed results from Model 4, a model to condition for heteroskedasticity using the log transformation of variables, still poses the phenomenon. There is autocorrelation problem as observed by the Durbin–Watson value of 1.43. The variables are normally distributed. To conclude, Model 4 needs to be corrected for autocorrelation to have a meaningful interpretation of the regression model.

Joint test on named regressors -
Test statistic: F(15, 25) = 13.948
with p value = P(F(15, 25) > 13.948) = 1.38213e−008

Model 5 Fixed effects, using 45 observations. Included five cross-sectional units. Time series length = 9. Dependent variable: DPR

	Coefficient	Std. error	t-ratio	p value	
Const	14.9919	4.68348	3.2010	0.0037	***
DE	0.464274	0.195797	2.3712	0.0257	**
DE_1	0.00134219	0.13382	0.0100	0.9921	
DE_2	−0.182509	0.109064	−1.6734	0.1067	
ROA	−6.27541	1.61648	−3.8822	0.0007	***
ROA_1	3.1325	2.55533	1.2259	0.2317	
ROA_2	−2.57577	1.70165	−1.5137	0.1426	
EPS	0.0206519	0.017601	1.1733	0.2517	
EPS_1	−0.00224249	0.0187262	−0.1198	0.9056	
EPS_2	0.0551587	0.032551	1.6945	0.1026	
SIZE	0.529609	0.155373	3.4086	0.0022	***
SIZE_1	−0.0834286	0.161644	−0.5161	0.6103	
SIZE_2	0.176007	0.097632	1.8028	0.0835	*
DPR_1	−0.0827314	0.207762	−0.3982	0.6939	
DPR_2	0.195157	0.101087	1.9306	0.0650	*
DPR_3	−0.154084	0.074967	−2.0554	0.0504	*

Mean-dependent var	22.67700	S.D.-dependent var	5.350918
Sum-squared resid	50.70473	S.E. of regression	1.424145
LSDV R-squared	0.959752	Within R-squared	0.893263
LSDV F(19, 25)	31.37664	P value (F)	6.57e−13
Log-likelihood	−66.53776	Akaike criterion	173.0755
Schwarz criterion	209.2088	Hannan–Quinn	186.5456
rho	−0.261343	Durbin–Watson	2.381247

Test for differing group intercepts -
Null hypothesis: The groups have a common intercept
Test statistic: $F(4, 25) = 6.41636$
with p value $= P(F(4, 25) > 6.41636) = 0.00107295$

Model 5 has a Durbin–Watson statistic of 2.38 to substantiate autocorrelation and a R-squared value of 95%. The overall model is fit as observed by the p value. DPR is depended on DE, ROA, Size, Size_2, DPR_2 and DPR_2. Current size of the firm is observed more significant compared to size_2. Consistency of DPR observed with lag 2 and lag 3 are significant at 10% level.

Test for normality of residual -
Null hypothesis: error is normally distributed
Test statistic: Chi-square $(2) = 1.81039$
with p value $= 0.404463$

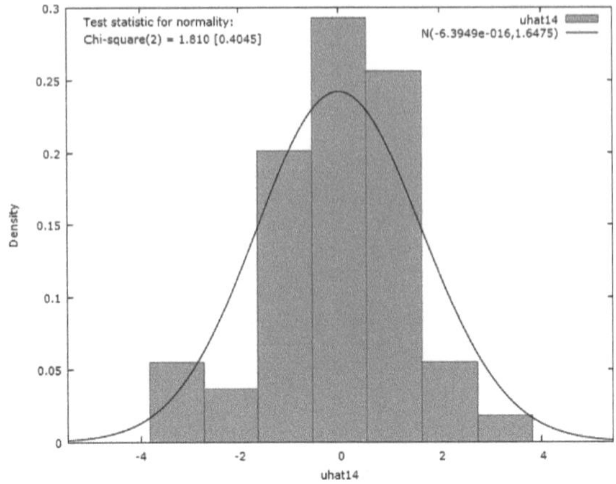

Distribution free Wald test for heteroskedasticity -
Null hypothesis: the units have a common error variance
Asymptotic test statistic: Chi-square (5) = 14.7972
with p value = 0.011265

5 Findings

From the empirical analysis using panel data econometrics, it is found that the dividend payout was influenced by debt/equity ratio of the previous period, current return on assets and size of the firm. The size of the firm is significant while observing over the past period and the current period. An increase in the asset size is a key variable in predicting DPR. Current return on assets along with the asset size proved to have a higher determination power.

6 Conclusion

This study was intended to analyse the relationship between the capital structure and dividend decisions in Indian banking sector with four main objectives. The variables taken were earnings per share, return on assets and size of the firm along with debt-to-equity ratio to know the impact on dividend payout. The study relied on secondary data which was extracted from the annual reports of the banks and the BSE website. Panel data econometrics is used to analyse the relationship among the dependent and independent variables. Gretl Software was used for the analysis of panel data econometrics. The model selection based on Hausman statistic suggested a fixed effects model, and the model so devised was observed to have normality and no autocorrelation. The model posed to have heterogeneity, and the same was observed even when the variables were log-transformed. Current return on assets along with the asset size proved to have a higher determination power.

7 Suggestions and Scope for Further Research

The study stresses upon the key variables highlighted by the literature, and only for the period from 2005–2006 to 2015–2016 for the analysis. A larger time period along with additional variables would enlighten the decision makers. The study can be focused with other sectors, at various capitalization levels to bring out deeper observations.

References

Arellano, M., & Bond, S. (1991). Some tests of specification for panel data: Monte Carlo evidence and an application to employment equations. *Review of Economic Studies*, 58 (2).

Arshad, Z., Akram, et al. (2013). Ownership structure and dividend policy. *Interdisciplinary Journal of Contemporary Research in Business, 5*(3), 378–401.

Baltagi, B. H. (2008). *Econometric analysis of panel data* (pp. 53–77). Wiley.

Esfahani, A. Z., et. al. (2013). The effect of corporate governance and capital structure on dividend payment: Evidence from Malaysia. *Recent advances in management, marketing and finance* (pp. 75–80).

Faulkender, M., et. al. (2006, March). Capital structure and dividend policy: Two sides of the same coin. *Seminar Participants at Washington University March* (Vol. 30).

Ince, U., & Owers, J. E. (2012). The interaction of corporate dividend policy and capital structure decisions under differential tax regimes. *Journal of economics and finance, 36*(1), 33–57.

Islam, A. (2017). Dividend policy and capital structure: An empirical investigation of foreign country. *Discovery, 53*(253), 67–81.

Kiprono, S. W. (2012). The relationship between dividend pay-out ratio and capital structure of companies listed at the Nairobi Securities Exchange (Doctoral dissertation, school of business; university of Nairobi).

Mand, H. S., & Singh, M. (2015). Capital Structure and Earnings per share: An empirical analysis of indian corporate sector. *International Journal of Financial Management*, *5*(3).

Moradi, M., et al. (2010). Factors affecting dividend policy: Empirical evidence of Iran. *Poslovna izvrsnost, 4*(1), 45–61.

Sang, W., et. al. (2015). The relationship between the dividend pay-out ratio and the capital structure of listed companies at Nairobi securities exchange, Kenya in the industrial and allied sector.

Sanvicente, A. Z. (2011). Capital structure decisions and the interaction with pay-out and ownership decisions: Evidence from brazil (No. wpe_264). Insper working paper, Insper Institute de Ensino e Pesquisa.

Tariq, A. (2015). The joint-determinants of leverage and dividend policy: A balanced panel study of non-financial firms of India and Pakistan. *European Scientific Journal*, *11*(10).

Warrad, L., et al. (2012). The effect of ownership structure on dividend pay-out policy: Evidence from Jordanian context. *International Journal of Economics and Finance, 4*(2), 187.

Asset Liability Management in Commercial Banks in India

Khushboo Thakker and Tanupa Chakraborty

Abstract Globalization and liberalization of the Indian economy has brought many changes in the Indian financial markets. There is an increase in the level of competition in the financial market due to deregulation of interest rate, technological and operational reforms. The Indian banking sector is facing a variety of risks such as credit risk, capital risk, market risk, interest rate risk and liquidity risk etc. The nature and magnitude of these risks have changed over time and it is very important to understand and control these risks as they directly affect the bank's efficiency and profitability. Banks have come up with new methods and techniques to measure and control these risks. Asset-Liability Management (ALM) is one such important technique which is now widely being applied in the banks. ALM is a mechanism to address the risk faced by banks due to mismatch in assets and liabilities It is a comprehensive and dynamic method for measuring, monitoring and managing the various risks of a bank. It involves identification of risk parameters, risk measurement and management and framing of risk policies and tolerance levels. This study is undertaken to understand the concept of ALM and application of ALM in Commercial Banks in India.

Keywords Risk management · Asset liability management · Commercial banks

1 Introduction

Globalization and liberalization of the Indian economy has brought many changes in the Indian financial markets. There is an increase in the level of competition in the financial market due to deregulation of interest rate, technological and operational

K. Thakker (✉)
Department of Commerce, J. D. Birla Institute, Kolkata, India
e-mail: khushboot@jdbikolkata.in

T. Chakraborty
Department of Commerce, University of Calcutta, Kolkata, India
e-mail: tanupa_cu@hotmail.com

N. R. Bhanumurthy et al. (eds.), *Advances in Finance & Applied Economics*,
https://doi.org/10.1007/978-981-13-1696-8_18

reforms. The Indian banking sector is facing a variety of risks such as credit risk, capital risk, market risk, interest rate risk and liquidity risk etc. The nature and magnitude of these risks have changed over time and it is very important to understand and control these risks as they directly affect the bank's efficiency and profitability. Banks have come up with new methods and techniques to measure and control these risks.

A bank plays an important role of intermediation by accepting deposits from the people having excess funds and providing loans and advances to those who are in need of the funds. In this process, bank faces a number of financial risks. The financial strength of the bank is measured by the way it can protect itself from the various financial risks. The primary source of funds for the bank is coming from public as deposits and majority of the deposits are short term in nature and results in shortest maturity period. On the other hand, banks usually provide loans which are long term in nature leading to longest maturity. Banks face a major risk due to the short term liquidity of deposits and long term maturity of loans. The situation of providing long term loan with short maturity funds is called as Asset liability mismatch and managing this mismatches by the bank is Asset liability management

Asset-Liability Management (ALM) is one such important technique which is now widely being applied in the banks. ALM is a mechanism to address the risk faced by banks due to mismatch in assets and liabilities It is a comprehensive and dynamic method for measuring, monitoring and managing the various risks of a bank. It involves identification of risk parameters, risk measurement and management and framing of risk policies and tolerance levels.

2 Review of Literature

Fabozzi and Konishi (1991) explained that it is important for financial institutes such as banks, leasing and insurance companies to focus on asset liability management as they face various kinds of financial risks. Asset liability management does not stop only at identification of risks, it also includes the methods and techniques to calculate and manage the risks.

Vaidyanathan (1999) discussed problems involved in asset liability management and elaborated on the different types of risk that need to be managed by the Indian banks. Previously, the banks were only concentrating on maintaining statutory liquidity norms but with a shift from administered interest rate structure to market determined rates, it has become more important for banks to use different techniques to protect themselves from interest rate risk.

Rajwade (2002) explained greater the capital intensiveness of a business, greater is the impact of interest rate changes on the bottom line. Amongst all businesses, banking is perhaps the most capital intensive since the gross value added through intermediation or the net interest income as a proportion of the capital employed is perhaps the lowest.

Charumathi (2008) explained the importance of measuring and monitoring the interest rate exposure of Indian Banks. His study focused on one bank i.e. ICICI Bank where in the interest rate risk is measured by using gap analysis technique for a period of 2005–2007. The findings revealed that the bank was exposed to interest rate risk.

Dash and Pathak (2009) developed a study to analyze the assets and liabilities of a sample of fifty-one banks operating in India for the period 2003–2008 using canonical correlation analysis. The study stated that the foreign banks and public banks actively managed their assets and liabilities management was dependent upon how well the assets were managed but the private banks were actively managing liabilities and assets management was dependent upon how well the liabilities were managed.

Kavitha (2012) presented a study on the optimal mix of asset liability management of Scheduled Commercial Banks in India. Composition of assets and liabilities affect the profitability of the banks. Ratio analysis is used to identify the optimal mix of asset and liabilities in relation to profitability on a sample of 56 banks comprising SBI and its 8 associate banks, 19 nationalized banks and 29 private banks for the period 2000–2010. The findings suggest that SBI and its associate banks are better performers as compared to private and nationalized banks.

Baser (2013) in his study evaluated the changing perspectives of the banks in identifying and facing the risks and maintaining asset quality so as to ensure profitability with the help of Asset Liability Management techniques.

Prasad and Suprabha (2014) studied the difference in Asset Liability Management of Indian banks based on the bank groups. The scheduled commercial banks in India are divided into five categories based on bank group by Reserve Bank of India as State Bank of India and its associates, Nationalized Banks, old private sector banks, new private sector banks and foreign banks. The study suggested that there is a significant difference in the gap ratio amongst the bank groups.

Balanagagurunathan et al. (2016) studied the relative importance of rate sensitive assets, rate sensitive liabilities, interest sensitivity ratio, net interest income ratio, net interest margin ratio in managing the mismatches of the selected five private sector banks in India for the time period between 2004–05 and 2013–14. The research suggested that banks to take necessary steps to reduce asset liability mismatches that would lift the banks to retain its market in public.

Objectives

- To understand the Asset Liability Management for the selected commercial banks in India
- To assess the performance of the selected commercial banks through gap analysis.

3 Research Methodology

This study is carried out for the period 2007–2016. The top ten constituent banks of BSE BANKEX (Axis Bank, Bank of Baroda, Federal Bank, HDFC Bank ICICI Bank, IndusInd Bank, Kotak Mahindra Bank, Punjab National Bank, State Bank of India and Yes Bank) were taken as a sample to be analyzed. The data for the study have been collected from Capitaline database.

This study analyses Rate Sensitivity Assets, Rate Sensitivity Liabilities, Interest Sensitivity Ratio, Net Interest Income Ratio and Net Interest Margin Ratio. Gap Analysis is also carried out to understand the impact of Asset Liability Management on the profitability of banks. Mean, standard deviation and co-efficient of variation has also been used for analyzing the data.

3.1 Rate Sensitivity Assets

Assets held by a bank that are vulnerable to changes in interest rates. This change can occur either when the asset matures or when it is repriced according to an index rate. The value of these assets is adjusted according to the rise or fall of a published rate or index. Rate sensitivity assets have been calculated by adding advances and investments (Table 1).

$$\text{Rate Sensitivity Assets} = \text{Advances} + \text{Investments}$$

The mean value of rate sensitivity assets of State Bank of India is Rs. 1178871.78 crores followed by ICICI Bank is Rs. 413069.54 crores, Punjab National Bank is Rs. 359527.53 crores and Bank of Baroda is Rs. 338961.84 crores. Thus it can be noticed that Public Sector Banks on an average have higher Risk Sensitive Assets in comparison to Private Sector Banks. During the study period, all the banks show an increasing trend in the Risk Sensitive Assets except for Bank of Baroda declining in the year 2016. ICICI Bank showed an increasing trend initially and at the later year but in the middle it was fluctuating. The co-efficient of variation of rate sensitivity assets endowed by 95.90% in YES Bank followed by 72.89 in Kotak Mahindra Bank, 66.30% in IndusInd Bank. Thus it can be observed that private sector banks are showing a rapid increase in their Risk Sensitive Assets in comparison to Public Sector banks. It clears that the rate sensitivity assets of 38.70% in Federal Bank is constant against 95.90% in YES Bank. The graphical representation of the rate sensitivity assets of various banks is given below.

Table 1 Risk sensitive assets (Rs. in crore)

	Axis Bank	Bank of Baroda	Federal Bank	HDFC Bank	ICICI Bank	IndusInd Bank	Kotak Mahindra Bank	Punjab National Bank	State Bank of India	YES Bank
2007	63773.64	118564.50	21931.76	79122.91	287123.43	16780.40	17763.05	143111.31	486485.38	9362.85
2008	93366.24	150571.39	28931.25	113375.99	337070.42	19425.01	24665.17	174413.48	606269.46	14523.98
2009	127887.12	196431.78	34510.85	157700.59	321369.15	23854.05	25706.31	218463.63	818457.13	19520.11
2010	160315.77	236217.65	40004.76	184438.21	302098.39	30952.43	33266.91	264658.90	917704.19	32403.06
2011	214399.45	299936.98	46490.91	230912.04	351051.84	39716.46	46435.62	337619.72	1052320.00	53192.48
2012	262951.64	370586.72	55158.47	292902.94	413287.71	49635.90	60633.17	415922.04	1179776.51	65745.99
2013	310703.49	449585.36	65251.29	351334.24	461643.03	67524.78	77329.07	442290.09	1396494.06	89975.60
2014	343615.20	513118.48	67553.95	423951.35	515724.47	79955.79	78512.18	494243.63	1608628.31	96583.32
2015	413425.86	550384.86	71853.81	517136.78	545651.26	98367.54	96294.72	532420.21	1781785.13	118778.31
2016	460779.92	504220.67	80307.64	628479.74	595675.74	124173.64	169599.70	571132.33	1940797.66	249622.41
Mean	245121.83	338961.84	51199.47	297935.48	413069.54	55038.60	63020.59	359527.53	1178871.78	74970.81
SD	136198.91	160567.91	19812.90	181060.52	110568.45	36488.07	45933.26	153999.60	494130.15	71894.16
CV (%)	55.56	47.37	38.70	60.77	26.77	66.30	72.89	42.83	41.92	95.90

Source Capitaline database

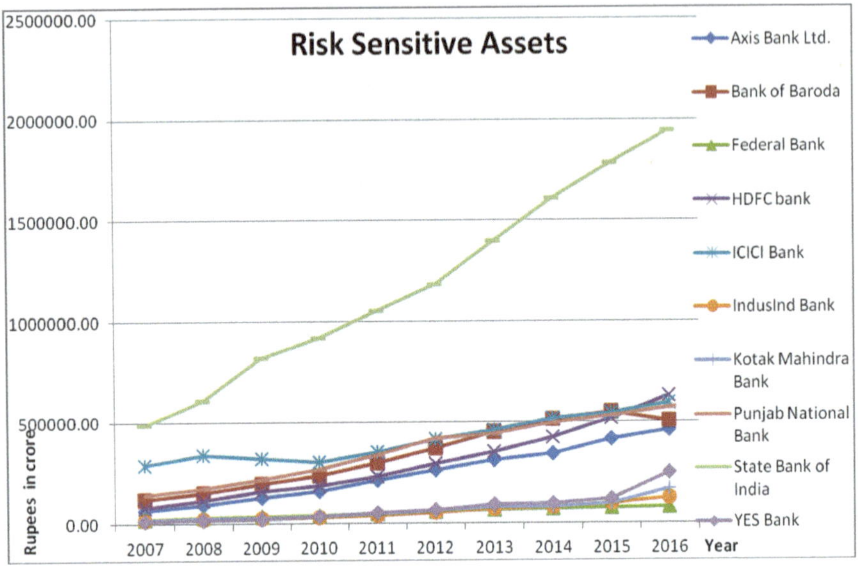

3.2 *Rate Sensitivity Liabilities*

The short-term deposit held by a bank pays a variable rate of interest to the customer. Interest sensitive liabilities include money market certificates, savings accounts and the super now account. The rate sensitivity liabilities have been calculated by adding deposits and borrowing (Table 2).

$$\text{Rate Sensitivity Liabilities} = \text{Deposits} + \text{Borrowings}$$

The mean value of rate sensitivity liabilities of State Bank of India is Rs. 1170808.77 crores followed by ICICI Bank is Rs. 398529.14 crores, Bank of Baroda is Rs. 383714.02 crore and Punjab National Bank is Rs. 365725.77 crores. Thus, it can be seen that Risk Sensitive Liabilities are high for public sector banks in comparison to private sector banks. During the study period, all the selected banks showed an increasing trend in Risk Sensitive Liabilities except for Bank of Baroda had a fluctuating trend. ICICI bank also showed an increasing trend except for a fall in the year 2010. The co-efficient of variation of rate sensitivity liabilities endowed by 75.37% in Kotak Mahindra Bank, followed by 73.00% in YES Bank, 62.36% in IndusInd Bank. It clears that the rate sensitivity liabilities of Federal Bank as 40.10%, State Bank of India as 42.41% and Punjab National Bank as 44.39% is constant. The other selected banks' rate sensitivity liabilities are moderate during the study period. The graphical representation of the rate sensitivity liabilities is given below.

Table 2 Risk sensitive liabilities (Rs. in crore)

	Axis Bank	Bank of Baroda	Federal Bank	HDFC Bank	ICICI Bank	IndusInd Bank	Kotak Mahindra Bank	Punjab National Bank	State Bank of India	YES Bank
2007	63981.18	126053.54	22824.45	71113.33	281766.22	17461.55	16099.84	141808.53	475224.42	9087.71
2008	93250.26	155961.18	27175.31	105363.51	310079.48	20132.85	21542.90	171903.78	589131.35	14259.37
2009	132893.98	198033.04	33417.12	151975.22	311503.26	24927.21	22378.01	222220.16	826131.06	19871.10
2010	158469.77	254394.35	37604.71	180320.13	296280.16	31644.46	30026.98	268592.17	907127.85	31547.65
2011	215505.68	327747.30	44903.14	222980.47	335156.39	39890.79	40984.92	344488.41	1053501.76	52629.84
2012	254175.97	408444.14	53178.15	270552.96	395664.86	51043.55	55132.04	416852.74	1170652.94	63308.20
2013	296564.69	500460.57	62801.85	329253.57	437955.11	63576.28	71439.39	431180.98	1371922.33	87877.74
2014	331235.50	605707.77	65419.24	406776.46	486672.71	75264.25	71967.91	499431.16	1577539.38	95506.31
2015	402200.21	652823.77	73133.23	496009.19	533980.06	94752.42	87010.02	547973.42	1781943.55	117396.25
2016	457193.94	607509.57	81348.28	599442.66	596233.10	115156.21	159618.36	612806.37	1954913.09	143378.51
Mean	240547.12	383714.02	50180.55	283378.75	398529.14	53384.96	57620.04	365725.77	1170808.77	63486.27
SD	131841.88	199615.75	20120.10	173489.05	110688.30	33292.95	43430.72	162352.23	496483.11	46346.55
CV (%)	54.81	52.02	40.10	61.22	27.77	62.36	75.37	44.39	42.41	73.00

Source Capitaline database

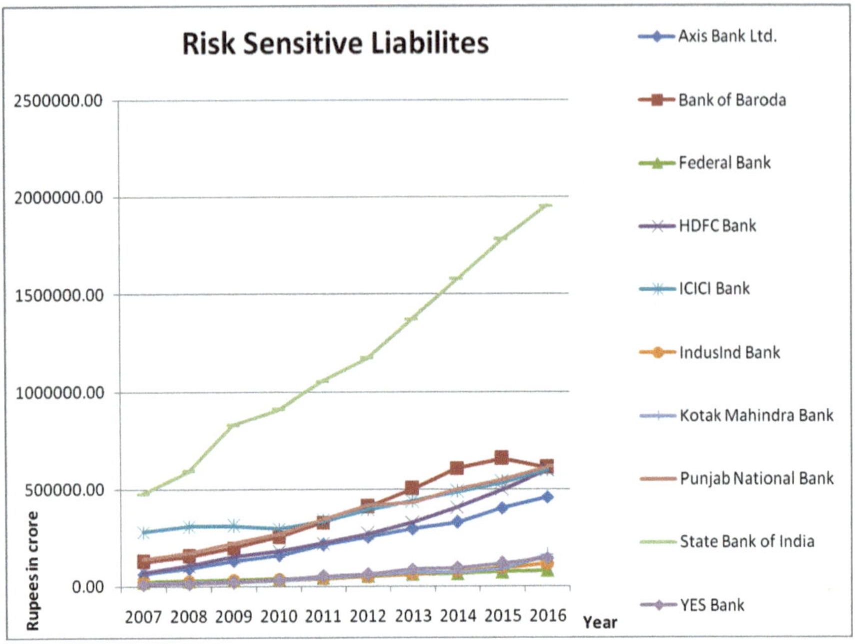

3.3 *Interest Sensitivity Ratio*

A measure of how much the price of a fixed-income asset will fluctuate as a result of changes in the interest rate environment. Securities that are more sensitive will have greater price fluctuations than those with less sensitivity. Normally this type of sensitivity must be taken into account when selecting a bond or other fixed-income instrument that the investor may sell in the secondary market. The interest sensitivity ratio is calculated by division of Rate Sensitive Assets by Rate Sensitive Liabilities (Table 3).

$$\text{Interest Sensitivity Ratio} = \text{Rate Sensitivity Assets}/\text{Rate Sensitivity Liabilities}$$

The mean value of interest sensitivity ratio of Kotak Mahindra Bank is 1.108 times followed by Yes Bank is 1.090 times and HDFC Bank is 1.057 times. The co-efficient of variation of interest sensitivity ratio endowed by 21.055% in YES Bank followed by 5.923% in Bank of Baroda, 4.764% in IndusInd Bank. It clears that the interest sensitivity ratio of State Bank of India as 1.323% which is moderate. The graphical representation of the interest sensitivity ratio is given below.

Table 3 Interest sensitivity ratio (in times)

	Axis Bank	Bank of Baroda	Federal Bank	HDFC Bank	ICICI Bank	IndusInd Bank	Kotak Mahindra Bank	Punjab National Bank	State Bank of India	YES Bank
2007	0.997	0.941	0.961	1.113	1.019	0.961	1.103	1.009	1.024	1.030
2008	1.001	0.965	1.065	1.076	1.087	0.965	1.145	1.015	1.029	1.019
2009	0.962	0.992	1.033	1.038	1.032	0.957	1.149	0.983	0.991	0.982
2010	1.012	0.929	1.064	1.023	1.020	0.978	1.108	0.985	1.012	1.027
2011	0.995	0.915	1.035	1.036	1.047	0.996	1.133	0.980	0.999	1.011
2012	1.035	0.907	1.037	1.083	1.045	0.972	1.100	1.000	1.008	1.039
2013	1.048	0.898	1.039	1.067	1.054	1.062	1.082	1.026	1.018	1.024
2014	1.037	0.847	1.033	1.042	1.060	1.062	1.091	0.990	1.020	1.011
2015	1.028	0.843	0.983	1.043	1.022	1.038	1.107	0.972	1.000	1.012
2016	1.008	0.830	0.987	1.048	0.999	1.078	1.063	0.932	0.993	1.741
Mean	1.012	0.907	1.024	1.057	1.038	1.007	1.108	0.989	1.009	1.090
SD	0.025	0.054	0.035	0.027	0.025	0.048	0.027	0.026	0.013	0.229
CV (%)	2.509	5.923	3.411	2.584	2.440	4.764	2.472	2.658	1.323	21.055

Source Capitaline database

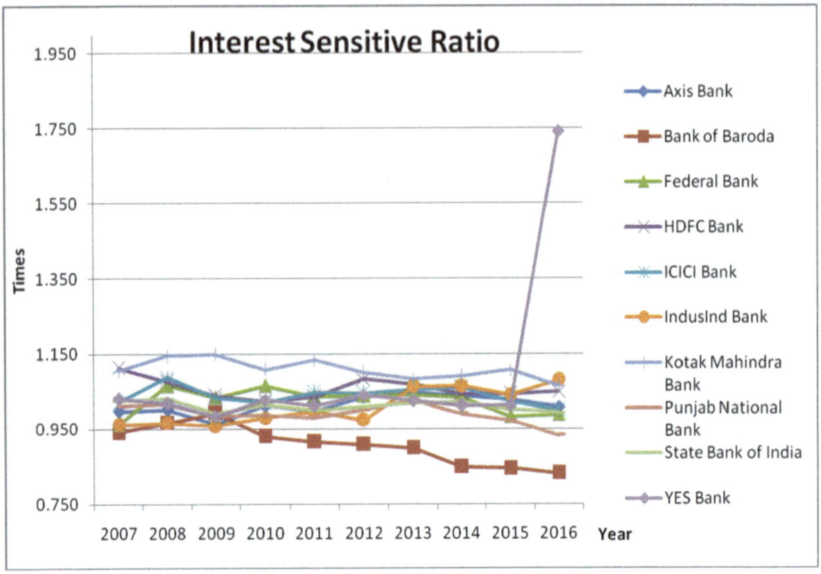

3.4 *Net Interest Income*

The difference between revenues generated by interest-bearing assets and the interest-burdened liabilities are referred as Net Interest Income. For banks, the assets typically include commercial and personal loans, mortgages, construction loans and investment securities. The net interest income is calculated by subtracting Interest expended from Interest earned (Table 4).

$$\text{Net Interest Income} = \text{Interest Earned} - \text{Interest Expenditure}$$

The mean value of Net Interest Income of State Bank of India is Rs. 38099.09 crores followed by HDFC Bank is Rs. 13221.26 crores and ICICI Bank is Rs. 11977.88 crores. During the study period, all the selected banks are showing an increasing trend except for ICICI Bank which showed a slight decline in 2010 in Net Interest Income and Punjab National Bank's Net Interest Income declined in the year 2016. The co-efficient of variation of Net Interest Income endowed by 80.01% in IndusInd Bank followed by 74.00% in YES Bank and 64.12% in Axis Bank. It clears that the Net Interest Income of Federal Bank, Punjab National Bank and State Bank of India shows less volatility. The graphical representation of the net interest income is given below.

Table 4 Net interest income (Rs. in crore)

NII	Axis Bank	Bank of Baroda	Federal Bank	HDFC Bank	ICICI Bank	IndusInd Bank	Kotak Mahindra Bank	Punjab National Bank	State Bank of India	YES Bank
2007	1468.34	3577.53	716.50	3468.48	5637.09	271.40	619.86	5514.57	–	–
2008	2585.36	3911.81	868.02	5227.89	7304.1	300.80	1225.80	5534.16	17021.23	330.57
2009	3686.21	5123.41	1315.46	7421.16	8366.61	459.03	1518.54	7030.86	20873.14	509.30
2010	5004.49	5939.48	1410.84	8386.42	8114.36	886.41	1858.14	8478.07	23671.44	787.95
2011	6562.99	8802.25	1746.58	10543.13	9016.9	1376.50	2097.57	11807.34	32526.40	1246.93
2012	8017.75	10317.01	1953.40	12884.61	10734.15	1704.24	2512.49	13414.44	43291.08	1615.64
2013	9666.26	11315.26	1974.66	15811.12	13866.42	2232.86	3205.67	14849	44329.30	2218.79
2014	11951.64	11965.35	2228.61	18482.63	16475.56	2890.71	3720.05	16145.97	49282.16	2716.26
2015	14224.14	13187.24	2380.41	22395.66	19039.61	3420.27	4223.74	16555.57	55015.24	3487.84
2016	16832.97	12739.85	2504.24	27591.52	21224.04	4516.57	6900.37	15311.78	56881.82	4566.72
Mean	8000.02	8687.92	1709.87	13221.26	11977.88	1805.88	2788.22	11464.18	38099.09	1942.22
SD	5129.23	3744.04	616.53	7805.81	5369.54	1444.81	1831.40	4436.69	15041.62	1437.26
CV (%)	64.12	43.09	36.06	59.04	44.83	80.01	65.68	38.70	39.48	74.00

Source Capitaline database

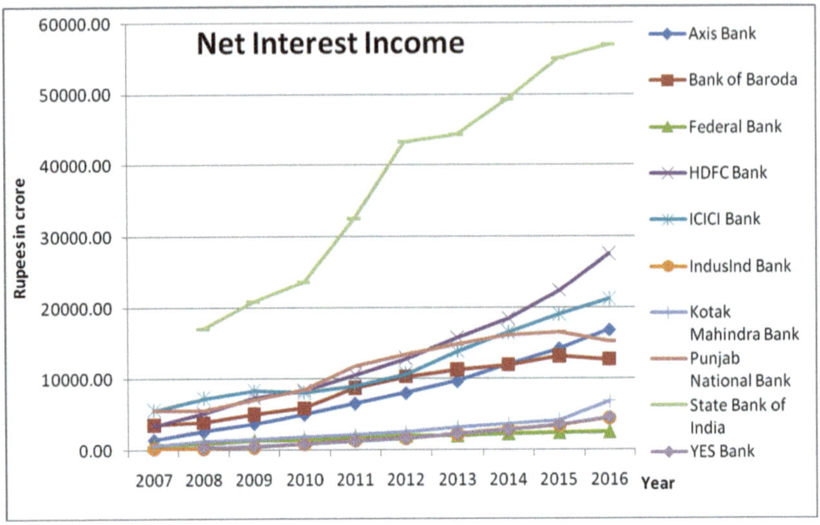

3.5 *Net Interest by Total Funds Ratio*

Net interest is a measure of the difference between the interest income generated by banks or other financial institutions and the amount of interest paid out to their lenders (for example, deposits), relative to the amount of their (interest-earning) assets. It is similar to the gross margin (or gross profit margin) of non-financial companies. It is usually expressed as a percentage of what the financial institution earns on loans in a time period and other assets minus the interest paid on borrowed funds divided by the Total Funds in that time period. The net interest by Total Funds ratio is calculated as follows (Table 5):

$$\text{Net Interest Margin Ratio} = \text{Net Interest Income}/\text{Total Funds}$$

The mean value of net interest by total funds ratio of Kotak Mahindra Bank is 4.68 times followed by HDFC Bank is 4.29 times and Federal Bank is 3.23 times. The co-efficient of variation of net interest by total funds ratio accounted by 32.68% in IndusInd Bank followed by 18.13% in ICICI Bank and 14.44% in Bank of Baroda. All the selected banks under study show a fluctuating trend except for ICICI Bank which has increased every year. The co-efficient of variation of HDFC indicates that the Net Interest by total fund ratio had been less consistent during the study period. The graphical representation of the net interest by total funds ratio is given below.

Table 5 Net interest income by total funds (in times)

	Axis Bank	Bank of Baroda	Federal Bank	HDFC Bank	ICICI Bank	IndusInd Bank	Kotak Mahindra Bank	Punjab National Bank	State Bank of India	YES Bank
2007	2.39	2.79	3.13	4.21	1.89	1.41	4.12	3.59	–	–
2008	2.83	2.42	3.01	4.66	1.96	1.37	5.08	3.08	2.64	2.35
2009	2.86	2.52	3.68	4.69	2.14	1.82	5.33	3.17	2.47	2.55
2010	3.05	2.35	3.41	4.13	2.18	2.83	5.62	3.14	2.34	2.66
2011	3.10	2.77	3.66	4.22	2.34	3.41	4.75	3.51	2.85	2.61
2012	3.03	2.57	3.48	4.19	2.40	3.31	4.31	3.22	3.38	2.44
2013	3.09	2.28	2.99	4.28	2.70	3.42	4.29	3.18	3.05	2.57
2014	3.30	1.99	3.05	4.14	2.91	3.61	4.34	3.14	2.93	2.61
2015	3.37	1.92	3.01	4.14	3.06	3.45	4.36	2.87	2.86	2.85
2016	3.41	1.84	2.87	4.25	3.10	3.59	4.62	2.42	2.64	3.03
Mean	3.04	2.35	3.23	4.29	2.47	2.82	4.68	3.13	2.80	2.63
SD	0.30	0.34	0.30	0.21	0.45	0.92	0.50	0.32	0.31	0.20
CV (%)	9.91	14.44	9.28	4.85	18.13	32.68	10.79	10.33	11.27	7.78

Source Capitaline database

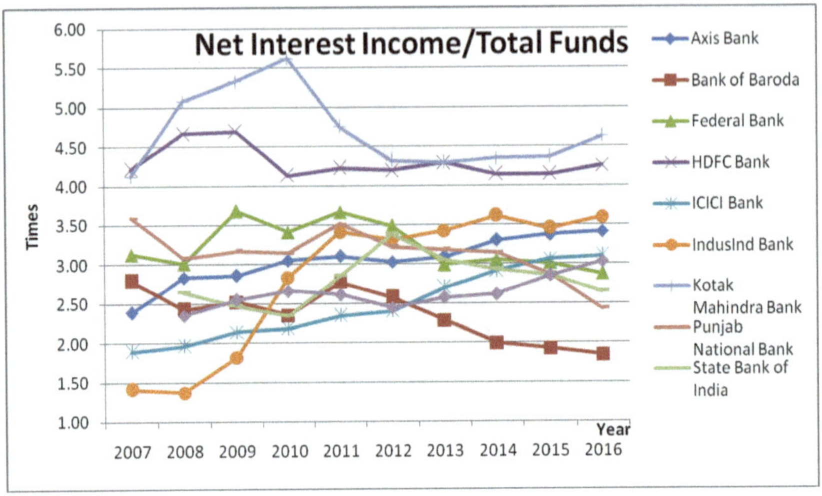

3.6 *Gap Analysis*

Gap analysis is a method that conveys the difference between rate sensitive assets and rate sensitive liabilities over a period of time (Table 6).

$$\text{Gap Analysis} = \text{Rate Sensitivity Assets} - \text{Rate Sensitivity Liabilities}$$

From the above table, we can observe that HDFC Bank and YES Bank have a positive Gap throughout the period of study followed by ICICI Bank, Federal Bank and Axis Bank. Bank of Baroda has a negative Gap throughout the period of study. All banks except for Bank of Baroda and Punjab National Bank have a negative mean as shown in the table above. Axis Bank has a negative gap almost in all the years from 2007 till 2011, thereafter it has a positive gap for all the years covered in the study. Federal Bank has a negative gap only in the year 2007, 2015 and 2016. ICICI Bank has a negative gap only in the year 2016. IndusInd Bank has a negative gap till 2012, thereafter it is positive. Punjab National Bank has a negative gap in almost all the years except 2007, 2008, 2012 and 2013. State Bank of India has a positive gap except for the year 2009, 2011, 2015 and 2016. While considering the co-efficient of variation, Kotak Mahindra Bank has a less volatile gap and YES Bank has a more volatile gap. The graphical representation of the gap analysis is given below.

Table 6 GAP analysis (in crore)

GAP	Axis Bank	Bank of Baroda	Federal Bank	HDFC Bank	ICICI Bank	IndusInd Bank	Kotak Mahindra Bank	Punjab National Bank	State Bank of India	YES Bank
2007	−207.54	−7494.04	−892.69	8009.58	5357.21	−681.15	1663.21	1302.78	11260.96	275.14
2008	115.98	−5389.79	1755.94	8012.48	26990.94	−707.84	3122.27	2509.70	17138.11	264.61
2009	−5006.86	−1601.26	1093.73	5725.37	9865.89	−1073.16	3328.30	−3756.53	−7673.93	−350.99
2010	1846.00	−18176.70	2400.05	4113.08	5818.23	−692.03	3239.93	−3933.27	10576.34	855.41
2011	−1106.23	−27810.32	1587.77	7931.57	15895.45	−174.33	5450.70	−6868.69	−1181.76	562.64
2012	8775.67	−37857.42	1980.32	22349.98	17622.85	−1407.65	5501.13	69.30	9123.57	2437.79
2013	14138.80	−50875.21	2449.44	22080.67	23687.92	3948.50	5889.68	11109.11	24571.73	2097.86
2014	12379.70	−92589.29	2134.71	17174.89	29051.76	4691.54	6544.27	−5187.53	31088.93	1077.01
2015	11225.65	−102438.91	−1279.42	21127.59	11671.20	3615.12	9284.70	−15553.21	−158.42	1382.06
2016	3585.98	−103288.90	−1040.64	29037.08	−557.36	9017.43	9981.34	−41674.04	−14115.43	106243.90
Mean	4574.71	−44752.18	1018.92	14556.73	14540.41	1653.64	5400.55	−6198.24	8063.01	11484.54
SD	6578.80	40716.60	1497.18	8778.76	9882.89	3484.03	2702.90	14257.67	14123.85	33305.91
CV (%)	143.81	−90.98	146.94	60.31	67.97	210.69	50.05	−230.03	175.17	290.01

Source Capitaline database

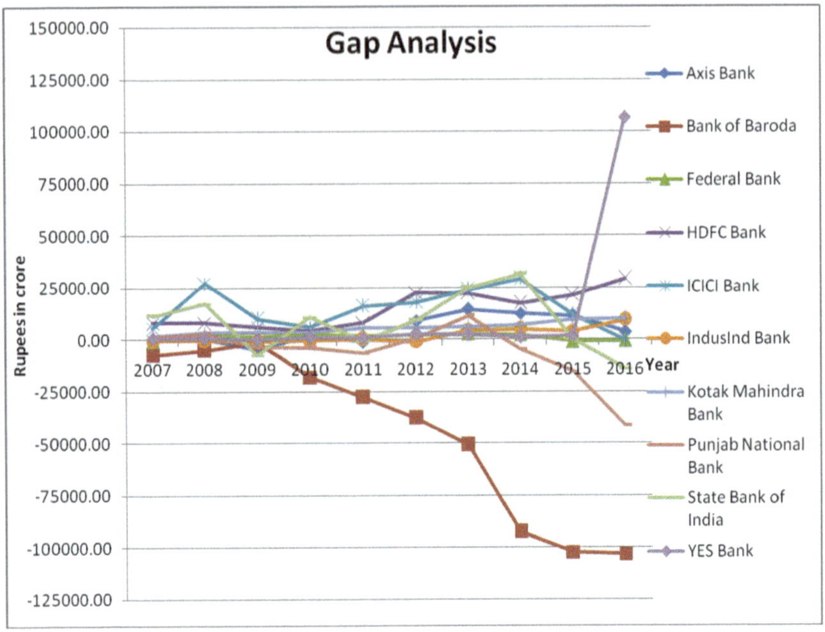

4 Findings and Analysis of the Study

- The Rate Sensitive assets are showing an increasing trend in general for all the selected banks in the study period. Mean value of rate sensitive assets are high in public sector banks as compared to private sector banks. It is observed that there is a very high covariance for private sector banks such as YES Bank (95.9), Kotak Mahindra Bank (72.89), IndusInd Bank (66.30) and HDFC Bank (60.77) in comparison to Public Sector banks like Bank of Baroda (47.37), State Bank of India (41.92) and Punjab National Bank (42.83).
- It is noticed that trend from the rate sensitivity liabilities is also rising for almost all the banks under study. Mean value of rate sensitive assets are high in public sector banks as compared to private sector banks. It is observed that there is a very high covariance for private sector banks such as YES Bank (73), Kotak Mahindra Bank (75.37), IndusInd Bank (62.36) and HDFC Bank (61.22) in comparison to Public Sector banks like Bank of Baroda (52.07), State Bank of India (42.41) and Punjab National Bank (44.39).
- It is observed from the interest sensitive ratio that the mean value are recorded as high in private sector banks such as Kotak Mahindra Bank (1.108), YES Bank (1.090), ICICI Bank (1.038) and Federal Bank (1.024) as compared to Public sector banks. The co-efficient of variation indicates that the interest sensitivity ratio is highly volatile in YES Bank and Bank of Baroda and high volatile in ICICI Bank.

- It could be noticed from the net interest income that the mean value recorded as high in Public sector banks such as State Bank of Indian and Punjab National Bank in comparison to private sector banks. IndusInd Bank and YES Bank have a high volatility in net interest income.
- It is observed from the analysis of Net Interest Income by Total Funds Ratio that the mean value recorded as high in private sector banks such as Kotak Mahindra Bank and Federal Bank and it is lowest in Bank of Baroda. The co-efficient of variation indicates that the Net Interest Income by Total Funds Ratio is less consistent in HDFC Bank and highly volatile in IndusInd Bank and ICICI Bank.
- It is found from the GAP analysis that the mean values of all the banks except Bank of Baroda and Punjab National Bank are positive. While considering the co-efficient of variation, Kotak Mahindra Bank has less volatile and YES Bank has more volatile GAP during the study period.

5 Conclusion

The growth rate of private sector banks such as YES Bank and Kotak Mahindra Bank is very high, where as ICICI Bank has maintained its normal position without much fluctuations in any of the elements. All banks except bank of Baroda and Punjab National Bank show a positive gap. The performance of Bank of Baroda for the year 2016 shows a decline in most of the variables considered in the study which needs further investigation.

The banks should try to integrate liquidity management as a part of banks asset liability management. The bank's asset and liability management policy should clearly define the role of liquid assets along with setting clear targets and limits.. The banks should reduce the ALM gap by increasing the deposits from the public. All the selected banks should focus more on reducing the mismatches because it creates risks for the banks and it should be addressed immediately.

6 Limitations of the Study

The present study has a few demerits also because the study data was selective in nature. Only loans & advances and investments were taken as Risk Sensitive Assets and deposits and borrowings as Risk Sensitive Liabilities. All other assets, liabilities and off balance sheet items were not included in the study. The study considers only the total Risk Sensitive Assets and Liabilities at the end of the year of only selected private and public sector banks constituting the BSE SENSEX.

7 Future Research Possibilities

Further studies can be carried out by applying improved methods for better management of bank's maturity gap by dividing the Risk Sensitive Assets and Liabilities into different time periods based on its maturity during the year.

References

Balanagagurunathan, K., Selvaraj, M., & Sathyakala, S. (2016). Impact of asset liability management for the growth of selected private sector banks in India. *International Journal of Economic Research, 13*(1), 2016.

Baser, N. (2013). Asset-liability management in the Indian commercial banks. *Asian Journal of Research in Banking and Finance, 3*(10), 28–40.

Charumathi, B. (2008). Asset liability management in Indian banking industry—With special reference to interest rate risk management in ICICI Bank. In *Proceedings of the World Congress on Engineering 2008*, Vol. II, 2–4 July, 2008, London, U.K.

Dash, M., & Pathak, R. (2009). Canonical correlation analysis of asset-liability management of Indian banks. *Social Science & Research Network.* Retrieved June, 2009 from http://ssrn.com/abstract=1412739.

Fabozzi, F. J., & Konishi, A. (1991). *Asset liability management*. India: S. Chand & Company Ltd.

Kavitha, N. (2012). An assessment—Asset and liability management of scheduled commercial banks. *International Journal of Marketing and Technology*, 2(4).

Prasad, K., & Suprabha, K.R. (2014). Anomalies in maturity gap: evidence from scheduled commercial banks in India. *Procedia Economics and Finance*, 11, 423–430 (2014). www.sciencedirect.com.

Rajwade, A.V. (2002). Issues in asset liability management. *Economic and Political Weekly*, 37(5). http://www.jstor.org/stable/4411679.

Vaidyanathan, R. (1999). Asset-liability management: Issues and trends in Indian context. *ASCI Journal of Management*, 29(1), 39–48. http://www.iimb.ernet.in/~vaidya/Asset-liability.pdf.

FSC
www.fsc.org
MIX
Papier | Fördert
gute Waldnutzung
FSC® C083411

Kolibri 360 GmbH
Ferdinand-Jühlke-Straße 7
99095 Erfurt, Deutschland
produktsicherheit@kolibri360.de